# No One Home

# NO ONE HOME

*Brazilian Selves Remade in Japan*

Daniel Touro Linger

Stanford University Press
Stanford, California

Stanford University Press
Stanford, California
©2001 by the Board of Trustees of the
Leland Stanford Junior University
Printed in the United States of America

Library of Congress Cataloging-in-Publication Data

Linger, Daniel Touro
  No one home : Brazilians selves remade in Japan / Daniel Touro
Linger.
        p.    cm.
  Includes bibliographical references and index.
  ISBN 0-8047-3910-2 (alk. paper) —
  ISBN 0-8047-4182-4 (pbk. : alk. paper)
    1. Brazilians—Japan.   2. Brazilians—Ethnic identity.   3. Japan—
Ethnic relations.   I. Title.

DS825.B6 L56      2001
952'.004698—dc21                              2001020026


This book is printed on acid-free, archival-quality paper.

Original printing 2001
Last figure below indicates year of this printing:
10   09   08   07   06   05

Typeset in 10/12.5 Sabon

—But do you know what a nation means? says John Wyse.
—Yes, says Bloom.
—What is it? says John Wyse.
—A nation? says Bloom. A nation is the same people living in the
    same place.
—By God, then, says Ned, laughing, if that's so I'm a nation for I'm
    living in the same place for the past five years.
  So of course everyone had a laugh at Bloom and says he, trying
    to muck out of it:
—Or also living in different places.
—That covers my case, says Joe.
—What is your nation, if I may ask, says the citizen.
—Ireland, says Bloom. I was born here. Ireland.

Joyce, Ulysses (1990 [1934]:331)

# Acknowledgments

My debts are many. I cannot thank everyone who contributed to this study; I beg forgiveness of those whose names I do not mention. My chief debt is to the people, identified herein only by pseudonyms, whose words give this book its substance.

For assistance in Aichi I am grateful to the staff of the Toyota International Association (in particular, Dr. Bui Chi Trung, Mr. Takao Kishi, and Ms. Marie Matsuoka), the faculty and students of Homi Middle School (especially Mr. Takefumi Takenaka and the unforgettable members of the Kokusai class), Norma Anraku, Marcos Sawada, Tie Ikeda, Margarida Murai, Mayumi Sawada, Volker Stanzel, and Suely Jashiki. The Japan Foundation funded my research and gave me welcome practical advice. The University of California, Santa Cruz, provided helpful seed and supplementary grants. Professor Peter Knecht of Nanzan University generously offered his counsel and support.

For friendship and miscellaneous kindnesses received in Japan, I thank Isabel Gomes Enomura and Jogi Enomura, Lara and Rogério Paiva, Flávia and João Carlos Bespalhok, Roberto Abe, Keiichi Nagase, Rosa Shimoji, the Higa family, the Kamiōsako family, and the Tsujimoto family. Yuko Hamada assisted with research and translations. Steve Parish, F. G. Bailey, Linda-Anne Rebhun, Jeff Lesser, Chieko Koyama, UCSC students in two classes, and an anonymous reviewer for Stanford University Press read the manuscript in its entirety and offered important commentary. For their critiques of various chapters I thank Don Brenneis, Nancy Chen, Dorothy Holland, Jean Lave, Takie Sugiyama Lebra, Joshua Roth, Carolyn Martin Shaw, Claudia Strauss, and Karen Yamashita. I valued, but could not take, all suggestions, and can only hope my choices have been sensible.

Laurie Wigham drafted the excellent maps. Muriel Bell, John Feneron, and Martin Hanft provided editorial counsel at Stanford University Press.

Finally, thanks to Eli for his forbearance and adventurous spirit and to Lynn (Maria) for finding humor and beauty in so many unpromising situations.

# Contents

Preface      xiii

Note on Terminology and Names      xviii

### Part One: Orientations

1. Global, Local, Personal      3
2. The Blue Hemisphere      19

### Part Two: Scenes

3. Postmodern Times      45
4. Middle-School Days      57
5. Eating Brazil      74

### Part Three: Persons

WORKERS

6. Eduardo Mori: "One day I'm going home"      95
7. Elena Queiroz de Assis Takeda: "I defeated them all"      115
8. Bernardo Kinjoh: "All the doors would open"      131

STUDENTS

9. Miriam Moreira: "I lived there, I was born there, I grew up there!"      153
10. Catarina Noriko Iemura: "If it was up to me, I'd never leave Japan"      169
11. Elisa Aoshima: "To be Brazilian is to be clever"      191

INTERMEDIARIES

12. Rosa Kitagawa: "Send me a blond wig!"     209

13. Eriko Miyagi: "Even I don't know how I feel"     227

14. Naomi Mizutake: "The eighth wonder of the world"     247

*Part Four: The Nation in the Mind*

15. National Banners     275

16. Human Warmth     290

17. Discontinuities     304

Glossary     317

References     321

Index     335

*Photographs follow pages 38, 70, and 86*

# Maps

1. Japan     xx
2. Brazil     xxi
3. Aichi Prefecture     29
4. Homi area     34
5. Homi Danchi and environs     35

# Preface

Ethnicity provides rich material for cultivating perspectives and personalities, but when fetishized it fosters exclusivity, self-absorption, and hostility. The century just drawn to a melancholy close capitalized such dangers, adding grotesque euphemisms to our vocabulary: final solution, co-prosperity sphere, pacification, ethnic cleansing.

My Japanese-Brazilian friends in Toyota City are wise in these matters. For them, ethnicity is not a life-or-death issue. Identity matters—but it is not cast in stone. They are generous with others, and with themselves. I thank them for engaging me across conventional barriers of blood and nationality, and for teaching me important lessons by word and example.

I asked them personal questions about who they were and how they had changed. They cobbled memories into narratives. They tried to give form to fragments of experience scattered through space and time. They recounted partings and meetings, recalled sounds and sensations, regretted lost opportunities and wrong turns. Their stories were crystallizations of nostalgia, celebration, and pain; additionally, they were experiments in self-making.

I recognize this kind of work: I do it myself. My stay in Japan changed me. I became more attentive to my own entanglements with other places and other times, and above all with people who were absent. Or was it I who was absent? For "home" has become an ever more elusive concept for me. Like Eduardo Mori, I sometimes wish I could return; but unlike him, I doubt I ever will.

On a rainy February morning in 1973 the *Brazil-Maru*, an aging and unpretentious but immaculate passenger ship, sailed through the Golden Gate out toward the Farallones and beyond, as Tony Bennett crooned "I Left My Heart in San Francisco" over the loudspeakers. San

Francisco was the midpoint of its voyage, which had originated in South America and would terminate in Tokyo Bay. The passengers were mostly Latin Americans of Japanese descent. The combination seemed incongruous. I had not known such people existed, but the boat was full of them, conversing in Portuguese and Spanish.

One evening Captain Kawashima[1] told me softly, as we gazed into the turbulence, that this was the ship's last Pacific crossing. Henceforth she would run only among the islands of Japan. She was going home, for good. There was sadness in his voice.

Ignorant of the ship's remarkable history, I did not fully grasp his sentiment. Only recently have I discovered that my prosaic *Brazil-Maru* had been Japan's first great postwar emigrant vessel. In two decades of transoceanic service she carried tens of thousands of Japanese settlers to Peru, Argentina, and Brazil. After her retirement she became a museum ship, docked in Mie prefecture. Mie is not far from Toyota City, where I did anthropological fieldwork in the mid-1990s. I kept thinking of visiting the *Brazil-Maru*, but before I could do so she set sail once again. It was a graveyard run to China. By the time I left Japan in the summer of 1996, the *Brazil-Maru* was being disassembled, reduced to a pile of anonymous junk.

The 1973 trip from San Francisco via Honolulu took seventeen days, the last stretch through rough winter seas. On the worst days we were barred from the deck as gray waves washed over the bow. I passed the mornings with Marta, a young woman from Buenos Aires who had volunteered to teach me the rudiments of the Japanese language. Upon our arrival in Yokohama, Marta, who had spent more than a month on board ship, vanished. I stayed in Japan over a year, but I never met another Latin American.

In July 1994, having eventually become an anthropologist with some knowledge of Brazil, I returned to Japan to do preliminary research on Brazilian migrants of Japanese descent. Once, out of nostalgia and curiosity, I paid a visit to the site of the beat-up Kyoto *geshuku*, or lodging-house, I had lived in twenty years earlier. The wooden fence was gone, revealing a weedy lot strewn with rocks and parked cars. To one side, like an ancient lookout, stood a reeling, two-story vestige of the original

[1]In this preface, I use the real names of Captain Kawashima, Marta, and Mrs. Tamura.

tenement. Its windows were dusty, opaque. It was dark inside and ne-
glected outside, time having stripped the faded green paint from the
wood. The building looked abandoned. My small room, which had ad-
joined the decrepit relic, was gone.

I pressed the buzzer at the beauty parlor next door. During a 1974
visit, when the cherry trees were blooming, my mother had had her hair
done there. The beauticians had marveled that she wanted her waves
straightened. Afterward they brought over a beautifully wrapped present: shampoo.

An old woman answered, and I asked about Mrs. Tamura. An American woman and I had occupied the room adjacent to hers. We brewed
coffee every morning and drank it with Mrs. Tamura. Widowed by the
Pacific War, she was then in her sixties. She lived with her mother, a
pleasant person who was hard of hearing and stooped with age. They
survived on a pittance, a pension and the few yen Mrs. Tamura made
giving kimono lessons to young women.

Down the hall was the kitchen, shared by the dozen or so residents.
There was a mini-refrigerator, always full to bursting; a black-crusted
gas burner; and a cement basin for washing dishes. The wet dishes at-
tracted slugs. Flat stones led through the yard to a toilet and sink, beside
which stood Mrs. Tamura's washing machine, her only substantial pos-
session. You could not bathe in the geshuku unless, as some of the foreigners did in the summer, you hosed down in the garden with cold water. Otherwise, everyone went to the *sentō*, the public bath, around the
corner. The steamy sentō was especially inviting during that winter,
when fuel was rationed in the wake of a Middle-Eastern war. With cold
1973 fading into cold 1974, Mrs. Tamura's liter of kerosene did double
duty: she roasted *mochi*, the gummy rice cakes eaten at New Year's, for
us on top of her room heater.

Mrs. Tamura was a communist, which was one reason why our mutual landlady, Mrs. Koyama, despised her. During the heyday of Japan's
student unrest, leftist militants had occupied Mrs. Koyama's geshuku
and draped it with red flags. Mrs. Tamura had sympathized with the
students. Mrs. Koyama was trying to evict—or drive out—Mrs. Tamura and her mother. She took them to court. She subjected them to foreign neighbors. She made surveillance and harassment forays at odd
hours. She swept up glass, dirt, and debris, depositing the mess on Mrs.
Tamura's threshold or dumping it into her washing machine.

When my friend and I moved into the tenement, Mrs. Koyama demanded that we have no contact with Mrs. Tamura or her mother. Desperate for a place to live, we reluctantly signed a bizarre agreement. But how could we spurn neighbors who showed us kindness and good will? Mrs. Koyama never forgave the treason. She once accused me of being a hippie and a communist—in short, a consummately evil person.

One evening during my mother's visit, Mrs. Tamura, a dignified woman who dressed in sober kimonos, brought over a plate of sushi rolls. Suddenly Mrs. Koyama's piercing voice sounded in the dark: "I saw her go into your room," she cried accusingly in English. Mrs. Tamura moved quickly and soundlessly into the low closet where we kept the futons, huddling out of sight until Mrs. Koyama, listening intently outside the closed door, left. My mother was aghast; the experience countered the impression of gentle cordiality left by the beauticians.

During my final days in Kyoto, I had to abandon the geshuku. The police were coming by with subpoenas. I suspected that Mrs. Koyama had informed them of my illegal employment. Nevertheless I returned, warily, on my very last morning, to drink coffee with Mrs. Tamura. I took my shoes inside in case the landlady should appear. That April breakfast was the last I saw of the geshuku or Japan for more than two decades. Alas, it was also the last I was to see of Mrs. Tamura.

The old woman at the beauty parlor was surprised to meet someone who had lived at the geshuku. She did not remember me or my mother, but my visit seemed to transport her back in time. She said many things I did not understand, but I learned that Mrs. Tamura's mother had died. Mrs. Tamura herself had become very ill and was now living in Osaka, she did not know where. I thanked her and mentioned that my mother still remembered the kindness of the women who had done her hair. She bowed.

I walked out into the sun. It was noon. The air radiated a uniform brilliance, reducing everything to two dimensions. I took a picture of the ruin. Otherwise there was nothing to photograph. The sentō was gone; the streetcars that used to rattle down Imadegawa-dōri were gone; the Nagasaki restaurant was gone. The people were gone. There were only shreds of memories, and bright haze. Everything, everyone, was somewhere, or sometime, else, displaced.

As I write, it is over four years since I left Toyota City. The life I led there seems impossibly far away. Friends have moved; children have gone from school to factory, or from Toyota apartments to the homes of relatives in São Paulo; and my mother, after some years of poor health, has died.

Like many displaced Brazilians, I passed an anxious stay in Japan, worried that some catastrophe would occur at home before I could return. Like many displaced Brazilians, I found the telephone untrustworthy, tenuous, and frightening. My stay in Toyota, badly timed, will be forever colored by regret. As I was about to breathe a sigh of relief at finishing my job in Japan, I received a dreaded phone call. I flew home the next day, arriving as my mother lay critically ill in a hospital bed on the eve of a desperate operation. This book is dedicated to her.

*Santa Cruz*
*November 2000*

# Note on Terminology
# and Names

Anthropological prose typically suggests that societies and cultures are holistic, bounded milieux (e.g., "Brazil," "Japanese culture"). It likewise suggests that people are overwhelmingly cultural or social products ("Japanese-Brazilians"). Such notions are incorrect, but language is approximate and evocative, not precise and constitutive. In writing this book I often found ethnic and national terminology a practical shorthand—one cannot endlessly explain, repeated disclaimers are tedious, and neologisms have a high cost. Characterizing people as "Brazilians" simply points to one (and perhaps not a very important) aspect of their identities, just as describing a cultural practice as "Brazilian" simply means that it is widely employed by "Brazilians." I urge the reader to resist the inference that people live within bounded cultures, or that cultures produce them, or that they are exemplars of social categories. My reservations about such claims will, I trust, become obvious.

Ultimately, this is not a study of "Japanese-Brazilians," "Brazilian culture," or "Japanese culture." It is about men and women, girls and boys, who engage the categories to which they are assigned and the circumstances that befall them. In other words, their lives, which are not cultural artifacts and are not reducible to a set of social coordinates, are the chief topic of this book.

With respect to names, I use people's real names only when I am confident that my portrayal is in no way hurtful or prejudicial. To those I formally interviewed I promised anonymity, though not everyone cared about that. *Personal names appearing in the acknowledgments and photo captions are real names. All others are pseudonyms unless otherwise noted.* I have likewise assigned fictitious names to almost all companies.

Names of Japanese are customarily written surname first. But Brazilians with Japanese names write them surname last. Adhering to national conventions, usually a desirable way to treat name order, would in this case unfortunately mandate differing treatment of Japanese and Japanese-Brazilian names, causing confusion to readers unfamiliar with Japanese names. With some misgivings, for the sake of consistency I write all names in this book in the Brazilian style, given name followed by surname.

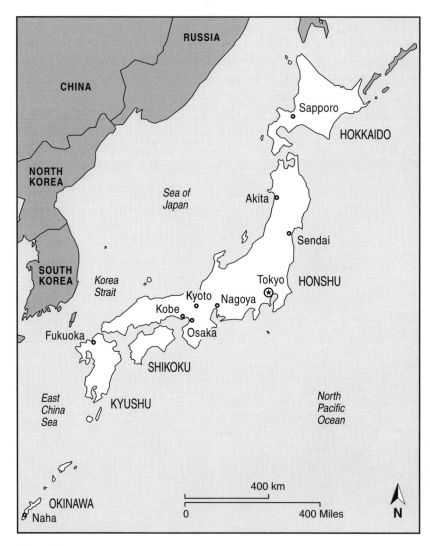

Map 1. Japan

Map 2. Brazil

# PART ONE

# Orientations

CHAPTER I

# Global, Local, Personal

## *Sayonara, Brasil*

The millennium ended early in Brazil. Composed in 1979, Chico Buarque's song *"Bye Bye, Brasil"* catches a historical cusp.[1] A truck driver is calling his sweetheart from a curbside telephone, an orange hood stuck on a pole somewhere in Amazonia. He's been away a long time, crisscrossing the endless highways of equatorial Brazil. The tokens are falling fast, and there's a *japonês*—a Japanese-Brazilian man—in line behind him.[2]

The driver's words come out in a tangle. He tells of the torrid heat, his broken fan, pollution in the sea, an Indian chief, a plane overhead, diseases he contracted, a looming rainstorm. Fugitive sensations mix with vignettes of the road, reminiscences of home, musings about the future, and confessions of loneliness. "I saw a Brazil on TV," he remarks, enigmatically. Time seems fractured; the present slips away before it can be grasped. He's not quite there, not quite anywhere.

The last token drops. *"Bye bye, Brasil,"* he says. "Tell them everything's okay. I want to come home, you can believe it. . . . I suddenly missed you," he explains to his lover at the last minute, adding, "I'd sure like to lay eyes on a crab. The sun," he concludes, "won't ever set again."

End of song; connection severed.

What Brazil was, it is not; what it is, who knows, except that it is careening into the future—some future—with barely a look back. The song's jumble of longings, projects, and startling images sizzle under a blazing sky. "That watercolor has changed," the driver observes. The incongruous comment, slid into his tale of the road, alludes to another

[1]Buarque's lyrics are set to music by Roberto Menescal. The song is the theme for Carlos Diegues's marvelous film of the same name.

[2]Foreign words are italicized the first time they appear; consult the glossary for meanings. See the glossary also for conventions adopted for the romanization of Japanese words.

song, Ary Barroso's famous paean of the 1930s, *"Aquarela do Brasil"* ("Watercolor of Brazil"), a gauzy reverie of palm trees, dancing *mulatos*, swaying hammocks, and moonlight. That watercolor was a languorous, sentimental portrait of a "Brazilian Brazil." But Brazil is no longer Brazilian: *Bye bye.*

Today, at the millennium's chronological end, it's already time to update Buarque's slice of postmodern life. My sequel, an ethnographic sketch, is a composite drawn from my recent fieldwork in Japan.

It's finally the Japanese-Brazilian's turn. He enters a glass booth. The phone displays instructions on a tiny screen. The man, a factory worker, inserts a prepaid card. He's not in Amazonia, but somewhere even more remote—Toyota, Oizumi, Hamamatsu, Gifu, or Yokohama. It's the Land of the Rising Sun, but winter gloom presses down. The credits melt away. How are you all, how's Jorginho? What does the doctor say? It's snowing like crazy, it's beautiful. I said, I might be moving to Sendai, it's up north somewhere. I burned my hand but it's better now. What I wouldn't give for a summer day. . . . Did you get the photos? Has it been that long? No more earthquakes, no more poison gas. It was far away anyhow, everything here is calm. Too calm. *(The phone is beeping.)* I miss you, hugs and kisses, kisses to Mom and Dad and Grandma and Bete, tell them everything's OK, give Jorginho a big hug, I'll be home by next Christmas—

Sayonara, Brasil. Down to zero: the card, emptied of its magnetic contents, slides out.[3] Ideographs parade across the screen, and a tiny cartoon figure, a woman, bows.

He wants to go home, believe it. But even if the Amazonian truck driver made it back to his sweetheart and family, he didn't stay there long. You can bet he's still on the road. As for the Japanese-Brazilian—time will tell.

### No one home

Sometimes the call travels the other way. That is not always a good thing. Consider this account from one of Japan's Brazilian newspapers.

I have just returned late from the factory after another hard day of work. The telephone rings and from the other end of the line I hear the unmistakable voice of my doctor brother there in Brazil. I think it's strange to get a phone call at

[3]Average length of a telephone call from Japan to Brazil in 1994: 8.68 minutes (International Press 1996 [January 28], data from the Japanese Ministry of Communications).

that hour, especially since just a few days ago I got a letter from him. So I conclude that something serious happened to my aged parents.

He tries to disguise it by asking me if I'm well, but the tone of his voice doesn't fool me. I ask him curtly and straight out:

"Who was it, Mom or Dad?"

The response seems to take centuries to arrive when in reality it took just a few seconds:

"It was our dear mother."

I fall silent. My brother tells me that five days ago our mother fell to the ground and went into a coma. That she died in the hospital of a stroke a few hours before this call.

That's when I feel the sad drama of the hundreds, or maybe the thousands, of migrant workers who came to Japan and lost their loved ones in Brazil. I want to be there at the burial of the woman who bore me and gave me life, but the distance that separates us is too great: 22,000 kilometers! (Tokairin 1995)

Even in the age of telephones and jet planes, halfway round the planet is too far. Through some law of transcontinental relativity, words go haywire between there and here: they delay, even at the speed of light, and then they collide and fall in fragments. Conversations are rushed, out of sync. Lives too fail to mesh. There can be no embrace at the moment it counts. Separation across vast distance produces feelings not just of absence but also of vulnerability. You are aware of not being there, of not being able to be there should you need to be.

Can one feel truly at home in such a divided, arrhythmic state? Among the multitudes of Brazilians now living in Japan, some no doubt do. But not those I met during the fourteen months I spent in central Honshu in the mid-1990s.[4] The Brazilians I knew were, and felt, displaced. They were living in Toyota or Nagoya and working in Fujioka or Kariya. They came from Moji das Cruzes, Belém do Pará, Tucuravi, Paraguaçu Paulista, Ji-Paraná, Ribeirão Preto, França, Rio de Janeiro, Cansação, Tremembé. They would be going back *talvez no ano que vem*—maybe next year—an incantation that came to remind me of the Passover vow: "Next year in Jerusalem!" For they were not at home where they were and not quite sure they would finally be at home once they returned—if and when they did. And they wondered if they were now someone other than who they had been in Maringá or Minas Gerais, and who they might be becoming.

[4]I did field research in Japan during July and August of 1994, and from July 1995 to July 1996. Most of that time I lived in Toyota City, near Nagoya. I also made short visits to Toyohashi, Hamamatsu, Tokyo, Ota-Oizumi, Okinawa, and other locales where Brazilians have settled.

## Alô, Toyota

All transnational migrants, distant from familiar people and surroundings, confront new, unfriendly conditions that raise questions of identity. But the situation of most Brazilians in Japan has a twist, for they are *nikkei* Brazilians, themselves of Japanese descent, the children or grandchildren or great-grandchildren of Japanese migrants to Brazil. In Brazilian nikkeis, Japanese "blood" coexists, often uneasily, with Brazilian "culture." How my Brazilian friends worked through this identity scramble while away from home is the topic of this book.

The locale is Toyota City, a suburb of Nagoya, in eastern Aichi prefecture. Nearly 200,000 Brazilians now reside in Japan, about 30,000 of them in Aichi-*ken* and 3,000 in Toyota City.[5] Toyota City, a center of auto manufacturing, is the headquarters of Toyota Motors, for which it is named. Countless auto-parts factories, suppliers (and suppliers of suppliers) for Toyota and other major Japanese firms offer unskilled jobs to foreign workers, mainly Brazilians.

Our family—Lynn Simons ("Maria," to Brazilians and Japanese), our teenage son Eli, and I—lived for almost a year, from August 1995 to July 1996, in Building 109 of Homi Danchi, a public apartment complex in northwest Toyota not far from the Nagoya city line. The *danchi* houses about 8,000 people, roughly 1,600, or 20 percent, of whom are Brazilians.[6] Homi, as the foreigners familiarly call it, has probably the greatest concentration of Brazilians in any neighborhood in the country. Homi is where Brazilian workers go when they leave the factory, and where Brazilian children return after school. Homi is where Brazilians receive and send telephone signals that connect them with mothers and sons half a world away. The Brazilians I knew neither loved nor hated Homi. They accepted it as a tolerable, decent, inexpensive, temporary place to live. Homi was not home, but it was, in the limbo of Japan, the closest thing to it.

It was our surrogate home, too, during the year we spent away. Homi was my chief listening post in Japan; some of what I heard I present here.

[5]Mid-1990s estimates. As of December 1994, there were 27,600 Brazilians in the prefecture, with 2,887 in Toyota City (source: Aichi Prefecture). More Brazilians live in Aichi than in any other prefecture.

[6]My estimates rest on figures the Toyota International Association (TIA) obtained from Kōdan (the Housing and Urban Development Corporation) and the Aichi prefectural government.

## Turning outward

This is a propitious moment for ethnography. It is a good time to turn outward, to attend to what others have to say.

These days it can seem that the incredible shrinking planet has shriveled to the size of the academy. Astonishing spectacles—the debacle of socialism, renewed balkanization, a recrudescence of religious fervor, Depressionlike misery amidst sustained general affluence—have inspired profound reflection among those of us who deal in social phenomena. Many of the grand predictions of grand theory now sound rather quaint. The state did not wither away; capitalism, for all its contradictions, did not immolate itself; the modern world did not stay disenchanted, if ever it was; and the century's devastating wars led not to imperial collapse but to a reincarnation of Rome. Surveying the ruins of majestic, world-shaking theories, we analyze and reanalyze the shocking mess, and then analyze our analyses.

The result has been a brilliant burst of critical writing. Anthropologists are keenly aware of the limitations of our practice and the artifices of our prose. This critical episode, not the first or the last, has had immense value.

But too great an indulgence in critical scrutiny has a cost. In redirecting attention to our own activities, and the activities of people like us, such criticism turns us away from those who live outside our own circles. It attains a dynamic of its own, accelerating into ever-higher orbits, with the result that most people outside the academy, and many within, consign it to outer space.

Meanwhile, the world spins on. People are everywhere pursuing their own projects, oblivious to arcane debates in professional journals. If anthropologists are not to sink into deserved irrelevance, it behooves us, duly chastened by past overreaching, to take notice of them as best we can. That, in my understanding, is the point of our difficult discipline. It is why I have chosen to write an "extroverted ethnography" (Parish 1996:x) that strains to hear others' voices.

## Getting specific

This book examines identity-making by nine Brazilians residing in or near Toyota City. In its sustained focus on personal experience, it departs from most of the recent literature on globalization and postmodernity. That literature, currently a thriving academic industry, emphasizes the mass migrations and media bombardment that purportedly distinguish the speedy, nervous contemporary world—variously described as "postmodern" or "late-capitalist" or "fin-de-siècle"—from its historical predecessors.[7] Here I address "microcosmic" aspects of transnationalism. The scare quotes point to a paradox: those microcosms turn out to be very big indeed.

Sometimes it is said that the confused postmodern global condition has produced a fragmented postmodern subjectivity characterized by a detached mood and identity bricolage. That is an intriguing but dubious claim.[8] The situation I describe, viewed from afar, is a product of restless, late-twentieth-century capitalist corporate enterprise, planetary in scope (Harvey 1989). But magnification reveals an amazing array of complex, coherent, intense subjective worlds forged in the immediacies of daily lives.

It is tempting now, as it was to pioneering urban theorists at the dizzying turn of the past century, to describe current social changes in sweeping and dramatic terms, and to link them to new mentalities. But what happened to that theory should give us pause. Perhaps the most provocative essay ever written on urban experience is Georg Simmel's "The Metropolis and Mental Life" (1964 [1902–3]). Simmel was interested in psychological adaptations. He argued that the city's commercial ambience and its assault on the senses and the emotions fostered an urbane, sophisticated, blasé, matter-of-fact attitude. Further, the city encouraged antipathy toward others, feelings of isolation amidst the crowd, and cravings for individualistic expression.

[7]Recent anthropological works emphasize global political economy (Basch et al. 1994), "imagined communities" within a changing global order (Gupta 1992), tensions between cultural homogenization and heterogenization (Appadurai 1990), memory and exile among refugee groups (Malkki 1995), transnational cultural flows (Hannerz 1992, 1996), and reconceptions of the relation between "culture" and "space" (Gupta and Ferguson 1992). Edited volumes include Schiller et al. (1992), the articles collected in *Cultural Anthropology* (1992), and Holland and Lave (in press). For recent reviews of this wide-ranging literature, consult Kearney (1995) and Waters (1995). Their surveys cover works on world-systems, postcolonialism, postmodernism, migration, media, tourism, borders, deterritorialization, cultural flows, networks, diasporas, and global communities. Though some studies (e.g., Ong 1992, 1993; Rouse 1992) make use of interview material to identify strategies of migration and ethnic identification, a more robust portrayal of sense of self—the intrapersonal side of identity—is not a prime ethnographic goal.

[8]See Strauss (1997) for a critique of Jameson's (1991) notion that late-capitalist consumerism, media saturation, and transnational organization of production produce "postmodern fragmented subjects."

These ideas echoed through the work of the sociologists of the Chicago School, notably Robert Park (1969 [1916]) and Louis Wirth (1938), who likewise saw anomie and emotional distancing as psychological correlates of urban life. Simmel's essay is acute and innovative, but taken as an ethnographic generalization, it fails. Whatever relevance his observations may have had for the inhabitants of a large, dense, heterogeneous, early-twentieth-century American-style metropolis (Wirth 1938), ethnographers and historians discovered that cities, and city-dwellers, are not all cut from the same urban cloth. There are, for example, preindustrial cities (Bascom 1955; Sjoberg 1955; Smith 1960); archaic, enchanted cities (Levy 1990; Parish 1994); and cities that open to divine realms (Eck 1985). Such cities are unlike those of contemporary Euroamerica, and their inhabitants do not resemble the mythical Chicagoan.

But modern and postmodern cities are themselves surprising. In São Luís, the Brazilian state capital I worked in during the 1980s and early 1990s, *bairros* were often cohesive, local tradition was vibrant, and though the streets were hardly peaceful, hostility took on personalized, emotionally complex, culturally structured forms (Linger 1992). And residents of a giant futuristic world city such as Tokyo typically live in tranquil, intimate neighborhoods dense with shared meanings and close personal relations (Bestor 1989).

As cities differ, so do transnational situations. A "condition," be it urban or postmodern, does not determine environmental immediacies or mentalities. Certainly, revolutions in transportation, communication, and the economy have produced what Ulf Hannerz (1996) terms a "global ecumene," a state of "long-distance interconnectedness" (p. 17). But, as Hannerz cautions (ibid.:90): "[T]he nation and its culture are not being replaced by any single 'transnational culture.'" He emphasizes diverse innovations and creolizations. And to be sure, transnational links in Toyota City have given rise to intricate, unfolding subjective patterns rather than a vertiginous postmodern swirl. Toyota is not a global anyplace, and Brazilian lives there are not generic transnational phenomena.

## Seeing double

In Toyota City's factories, in the apartments and public spaces of Homi Danchi, in the neighborhood schools, in Brazilian restaurants, transnationalism comes to earth. One of my objectives is to highlight

Toyota's *transnational scenes*, local face-to-face environments spawned by the global events that have brought Brazilians to eastern Aichi prefecture.

But I am mainly concerned with the people who inhabit those scenes. Inevitably they come face to face with themselves. The results are puzzling. Why does Catarina Iemura, a Brazilian student at Homi Middle School, long to be Japanese, whereas her colleague Miriam Moreira now feels more Brazilian than ever? Why does the translator Eriko Miyagi, born in Japan and a Japanese citizen, conclude that she is irrevocably Brazilian? Why does the factory worker Bernardo Kinjoh come to see himself as both ethnic and cosmopolitan? My answers are at once psychological and psychographic, poised in the gap between theory and cases. Psychology posits overarching explanations for human behavior, but a life, in its infinite complexity and contingency, is irreducible. The modest theory I develop does not try to account for lives, but to account for their profusion. Singularities blossom just beyond its domain.

I encourage the reader to cultivate a double vision. At one resolution, this book is an account of the workings of reflective consciousness, which I take to be a universal, but variably actualized, human capacity. At another, finer resolution, these are accounts of people's lives, each a unique product of a person's engagement with circumstance. Reflective consciousness is the wild card that introduces unpredictability and creativity into life paths.

Unruly by design, the argument refuses to subordinate lives to theory. I think that contemporary anthropologists overvalue theory. They tend to disparage nontheoretical accounts as "mere description," a symptom of primitive professional thought. I do not share that view. Theory is unavoidable, for it abstracts. We need its categories, explanations, and predictive guidelines because the world is too complex to grasp whole. But that does not mean that we should mistake theory for the world, or cease our efforts to reach beyond it. If we do not cultivate sensitivity to the event, the moment, the person, can others ever be present in our accounts of them?

In short, too much theory tends to automate persons and animate abstractions. It turns people into the fodder of History or specimens of Science. Here I seek to reanimate persons. I am trying to recover a sense of each person's singularity and irreducibility, a corrective to our more usual categorizing frame of mind.

I have tried to fashion a restrained theory that can accommodate—I would not say "explain"—the human diversity I saw. To comment sensitively on the human world, we must first of all recognize everyone's capacity to astonish us. That is not a new insight in American anthropology, but it is one deserving renewed attention.

## Everyone is Two Crows

In 1917, Edward Sapir asked, "Do we need a superorganic?" He viewed concepts such as "culture" as "fantasied universes of self-contained meaning" (Sapir 1949 [1939]:580–81), analytical abstractions that, when carelessly employed, mystify the tangible realities of human lives.

For Sapir, people are complicated and diverse. He made the point tellingly in a reflection (1949 [1938]) on J. O. Dorsey's account of Omaha customs (1884). Dorsey details equivocations and disagreements, referring often to his informant Two Crows, a chief and medicine man. Over and over we read that Two Crows "never heard this" or "doubts whether this was a genuine tradition" or "said it might be true" or "does not know all the particulars."

Sapir summarized the dilemma: "Apparently Two Crows, a perfectly good and authoritative Indian, could presume to rule out of court the very existence of a custom or attitude or belief vouched for by some other Indian, equally good and authoritative" (1949 [1938]:570). For Sapir, the standoff was a plain fact, not a sign of someone's deviance: "We shall have to admit that Two Crows is never wrong" (ibid.:572). Neither, by implication, are La Flèche, Gahige, Big Elk, or Yellow Smoke, Dorsey's other quarreling informants. Everyone, like Two Crows, is always right.

If everyone is always right, diverse (even contradictory) understandings are the very stuff of culture.[9] Fine-grained studies of personal meanings will serve us better than normative interpretations of public symbols or gross characterizations of epochal mentalities. Accordingly, this book features people, not macroenvironments; minds, not signs; reflexive and creative responses, not discursive or media constructions. To say it plainly: I focus on human beings, for to reduce them to epiphenomena of language, culture, discourse, or Zeitgeist would be, in my view, to erase them—as Sapir once pointedly observed, to "commit personal suicide" (1949 [1939]:580–81).

---

[9]Examples of such "distributive" approaches to culture include Wallace (1961), Schwartz (1978), and Sperber (1996).

Personal suicide—"the studied down-playing" of the "active and reflective individual"—is a trademark of contemporary social theory (Finnegan 1998:176; see also Baert 1998). But as several authors have recently argued (Cohen 1994; Cohen and Rapport 1995; Field 1993; Parish 1996; Rapport 1997; Sökefeld 1999), it is time for us to reinstate people into our accounts of culture and society. Such a move brings with it mind-boggling complexities and uncertainties. But that is the price of bringing theory to life.

## Redressing the balance

People are not free to do as they please, and we are right to highlight the circumstances in which they must find a way to live. But—the obvious point is crucial—neither are they dead matter. As Marx and Engels recognized, in publishing their polemical *Communist Manifesto* (1972 [1848]), even dialectical materialism required a subjective engine. The historical inevitability born of the logic of relations of production needed convinced actors, believers that history was on their side, to propel it.[10] "WORKERS OF THE WORLD, UNITE!" Marx and Engels were exhorting Two Crows, in his guise of reflective proletarian.

Hence I regard this book as a contribution to a rich anthropological literature, partially eclipsed (but never superseded) in recent years, that recognizes both extrapersonal and intrapersonal dimensions of culture.[11] That literature, once at the very center of American anthropology and associated with the lineage Boas, Mead, Sapir, and Benedict, currently travels under the rubric "psychological anthropology." The adjective is unfortunate, for it suggests that to be concerned with personal subjectivity makes one a disciplinary straddler or narrow specialist. I would argue the reverse: an adequate account of meaning, the central concern of cultural anthropology, *requires* serious attention to personal experience and consciousness.

Although interpretive and discursive theorists within anthropology have argued that we should treat meaning as contained in or constructed by representations, that strategy, underwritten by misleading commonsense beliefs about communication, is both dubious and

[10]This embryonic revisionist insight became, in the works of Gramsci (1971) and others, a centerpiece of later Marxist theory, which, correctly I think, emphasized the key role of consciousness in revolutionary praxis.

[11]See Sperber (1996) and Strauss and Quinn (1997) for extended discussions of the distinction between extrapersonal and intrapersonal domains.

theoretically limiting (Langacker 1987, 1991; Linger 1994; Reddy 1979; Strauss and Quinn 1997). Extrapersonal communications, or "public representations" (Sperber 1996), are differentially appropriated into the intrapersonal realms of consciousness and experience. The point is not that the extrapersonal and intrapersonal are mutually exclusive domains, a claim no responsible anthropologist of any stripe would make. It is rather that they are *different, linked, domains.*

I address that linkage directly in the final chapters of this book. Elsewhere I deal mainly with intrapersonal aspects of transnationalism. The existing literature is, as I noted, overwhelmingly extrapersonal in orientation, dealing with the global political economy, the formation of migrant networks, the circulation of public representations, and so on. That literature tends to treat subjectivities as "subject positions" (Gupta 1992:73), spaces carved out by competing and intersecting discourses, rather than as the personal appropriations, negations, or transformations of those discourses. Extrapersonal approaches are indispensable, but they are, as some who write about them recognize (Hannerz 1992), incomplete and therefore potentially misleading. This book, concerned with public narratives of identity but focused more closely on diverse *senses of self*, is a step in redressing the balance.[12]

### Reflective consciousness

One's sense of self is usually implicit—that is, nonconscious—but can become an object of reflection.[13] Anthropology needs to emphasize people's capacity to objectify, reflect upon, rework, and transcend concepts and categories sedimented out of an experiential stream.

Interactions on the shop floor, in the classroom, and among compatriots in leisure settings amplify Brazilians' feelings of displacement. Often such interactions are deeply disorienting and disturbing, as when a laborer is ignored by coworkers or a student is misrecognized by

---

[12]I take "sense of self" from the title of a recent book edited by Nancy Rosenberger (1992). See especially the articles by Rosenberger, Lebra, and Bachnik. Another excellent ethnography of senses of self in Japan is Plath (1980).

[13]I follow Strauss's and Quinn's distinction between "implicit" and "unconscious" thoughts, feelings, and motives. "Implicit" refers "to psychological contents . . . that are normally out of awareness but face no resistance in coming to consciousness. Those we distinguish from 'unconscious' ideas, feelings, and motives, which are repressed" (1997:259). "Nonconscious" is my term for "implicit."

classmates. Other moments—an afternoon whiled away in a Brazilian restaurant, or an evening spent drinking with friends—may arouse nostalgia for home and familiar modes of sociability. In these instances, one's heightened sense of dislocation arouses reflective consciousness, which then can turn inward, reassessing and reformulating the most intimate, sensitive, and paradoxical of all phenomenal objects, the self. How people objectify and respond to such feelings varies, leaving an observer admiring and perplexed. Reflective consciousness is an awkward phenomenon, too rowdy for us to welcome wholeheartedly into the sedate club of theory. We can lock it out, but I am afraid it will keep banging at the door, demanding entry.

Eduardo Mori, Elisa Aoshima, Naomi Mizutake, and others I knew were perfectly good and authoritative Japanese-Brazilians, and, like Two Crows, they were never wrong. They transformed identities according to their own circumstances and proclivities. Their sometimes anguished, sometimes funny, often unpredictable and ironic feats of self-reflection and self-fashioning demonstrate the limits of cultural and historical dominion. Some say "the subject" has become all fractured surface, the victim of a media-wracked postmodern global village; others have declared it dead (or never-alive), a figment of history and discourse. Eduardo Mori denies this through his presence. If that is a problem for our theories, so be it.

## Person-centered ethnography

The core of this book is a set of exchanges in which people tried to explain to me what they were thinking and how they felt about their lives and about themselves. Such conversations exemplify the practice of person-centered ethnography, direct engagement with others in order to explore states of mind (LeVine 1982; Levy 1973, 1994; Hollan 1997). The conversations were complementary rather than symmetrical, for as ethnographer I tried to listen as closely as possible to what my interviewees, if I may impolitely and somewhat inaccurately call them that, were saying. I believe they wanted to make themselves understood.

Practitioners of person-centered ethnography sometimes think of themselves as uncovering personal worlds of meaning. One criticism has been that this assumption is false, that there is no stable there there. The objection is only partially valid (Strauss and Quinn 1997). People do have certain enduring concepts and sentiments, and they often do express them to sympathetic listeners. But it is true that the ethnographic objects—thoughts and feelings—do not sit frozen like a Victorian countenance before a primitive camera. An ethnographic exchange unfolds in time; it is a process, not a photograph, with give and take between the conversational partners (Collins 1998).

And in speaking we also speak to ourselves, seeking to clarify our own ideas and to sharpen our own internal debates, by moving from objectification to reflection to reobjectification, in a continuing relay between thought and verbalization. At times, I think those I interviewed spoke their hearts, for I tried to create an environment in which that might be possible. At other times, I think they did not know their hearts. They spoke tentatively to themselves, or used me as a sounding board. Because in many ways I do not know myself, I am sure I did the same.

Often our exchanges moved toward closure or equilibrium, toward fragile mutual recognition, small epiphanies, or understanding, but occasionally they veered into contradiction and conjecture. Perhaps it is more accurate then to characterize the conversations as occasions for experiment, providing those I interviewed with opportunities to think through and find more satisfactory ways of formulating their experiences.[14] They provided the same opportunity for me, and one way I have to verbalize the insights I reaped is to write this ethnography.

That the ethnographic object might move under observation makes it harder to pin down, but ultimately, I believe, confirms the main thesis of this book. I hope to show that self concepts do not sit still, and more precisely, that reflective consciousness continually reworks them. If an ethnographic interview awakens reflective consciousness, it can hardly fail to operate in other, more challenging situations—for example, when a Brazilian worker enters a Japanese factory, or when a Brazilian child enters a Japanese school. My interviewees bring to the interviews the very faculties they exhibit in the stories they tell about themselves. The interviews have an iconic quality. Aliveness in the interview testifies strongly to the reflective consciousness brought to bear on the more insistent events of everyday life.

Accordingly, rather than paraphrasing interviewees' comments or stitching them into monologues, I have opted to reproduce portions of field conversations, inviting readers to join the unfolding exchange and draw their own inferences. The presentation reveals something of the way I did ethnographic fieldwork and provides a check on my conclu-

---

[14]Of course, people constantly engage in conversational practice of this kind—not just when talking with ethnographers.

sions. But more important, it conveys vividly and with immediacy the presence of others. In the past, ethnographies tended to smother people in culture and society. Today, our ethnographies tend to bury others in discursive constructions, the babble of signs, historical currents, or the author's own persona.

Of course, any ethnography grows from an author's participation in others' lives and has, for good and ill, a personal provenance. I cannot, and would not wish to, erase my presence from this ethnography. But it is not autobiography. Nor do I claim it is "reflexive," a word freighted with overtones of self-knowledge and confession. One should not put undue weight on authors' self-presentations—we never tell all, nor, as Freud insisted and Bateson persuasively seconded (1972 [1968]), can we in principle fully know ourselves. I do try to provide some personal context for my work, and I converse with my informants. I am here to the degree I need to be here to say what I want to say about them.

Some of my intellectual limitations are obvious. Though I have a fair acquaintance with Japan, I am not a specialist in Japanese studies. The literature on Brazilians in Japan, most of it recent or in press, continues to grow. I do not have direct access to all that literature, some of which is in Japanese, a language I do not read. Most current studies in English—for example, Koyama (1998); Oka (1994); Roth (1999); Sellek (1997); Tsuda (1998, 1999a, 1999b); and Yamanaka (1996, 1997)—draw substantially on Japanese-language literature, and focus on nikkeis as a new minority group within Japan.[15] I admire that important work, but I cannot hope, and do not seek, to tread on the same ground.

But perhaps I am able to contribute in ways that others cannot. I approached nikkeis from the Brazilian side, as an ethnographer fluent in Portuguese and reasonably knowledgeable about Brazil.[16] I managed to connect with many, to gain respect as a sympathetic person accompanying them in their sojourn abroad. My Brazilian friends could usually count on me to get jokes, to understand allusions, to see what was bugging them and what they were driving at. I think that many trusted my professional abilities and thought, rightly, that I was on their side—that

[15]But see Fox (1998) for a discussion of non-nikkei Brazilian migrants, whom recent studies usually overlook.

[16]My direct knowledge of Brazil is based on extensive fieldwork in the state of Maranhão and travel within Brazil, including visits to the hometowns of some of my interviewees. I have not however done significant fieldwork in Brazil with Japanese-Brazilians. For a fine overview of Japanese immigrant life in Brazil see Lesser (1999).

I could and would represent their points of view to Japanese people privately and in public forums.

Although everyone knew that I was a U.S. citizen with an agenda of my own, I often felt that my relation with Brazilian friends was conspiratorial, in the good sense. That is why, I believe, our conversations brought to light experiences and feelings invisible in, and complementary to, studies conducted "from the Japanese side." But that is a claim best judged by the reader.

## From transnationalism to self-making

Before we go further, a brief guide may be helpful. The book has four major sections. The next chapter closes Part One ("Orientations"). It presents a historical overview of the relationship between Japan and Brazil, and then brings the current transnational link under progressive magnification. I shift from a global perspective to close-ups of Toyota City, Homi Danchi, and finally a specific interactional setting, Homi Danchi's impromptu Brazilian *praça*. At Homi Praça, the transnational becomes interpersonal.

Such transnational sites of interaction are the foci of Part Two ("Scenes"). The chapters examine important face-to-face environments developing in the wake of Brazilian migration to the Toyota area. These include, in addition to Homi Praça, the shop floor in factories employing Brazilians (Chapter 3), the international classroom at Homi Middle School (Chapter 4), and a local "Brazilian restaurant" specializing in ethnic foods and products (Chapter 5).

Transnational scenes, where Brazilians spend most of their waking hours and where they rub shoulders with each other and with Japanese, engender ideas and feelings about human relations, nationality, and identity. In particular, one's sense of self—the experiential, or intrapersonal, aspect of identity—becomes an intermittent object of conscious reflection. In Part Three ("Persons"), the core of the book, the transnational and interactional become subjective. These chapters highlight transnational experience and reflection upon it, reproducing portions of conversations I held with Brazilian factory workers (Chapters 6–8), middle-school students (Chapters 9–11), and cultural brokers in factories and schools (Chapters 12–14).

Part Four ("The Nation in the Mind") presents an expansive discussion of the interviewees' national and ethnic self-experience. One striking consistency is that although almost all the nikkeis feel both Japanese and Brazilian, there is an asymmetry. Over time, "Brazilianness" tends to intensify and "Japaneseness" tends to weaken.[17] In Chapters 15 and 16, I suggest that discomfort with personal encounters in Japan draws most nikkeis, despite their Japanese descent, to Brazilian national narratives. Those narratives emphasize interethnic intimacy rather than racial purity. Brazilian "warmth" comes to overshadow Japanese "blood" as a compelling idiom of personal linkage and national sentiment.

Nevertheless, I argue in Chapter 17, national narratives do not determine any particular person's identity. People personalize, rather than absorb, such narratives, transforming them into dense, changing, distinctive components of selves. A responsible account of subjectivity therefore demands attention to the complex interplay of biography, consciousness, and public representations.

[17]Other researchers have found the same skew. See for example Yamanaka (1996), Koyama (1998), Kawamura (1999), Roth (1999), and Tsuda (1999b).

CHAPTER 2

# The Blue Hemisphere

## The globe of the imagination

The word "transnational" encourages us to imagine a world sliced into tinted patches, across whose boundaries flow economic transactions, media communications, and human beings. But the globe of the imagination has an orientation. The manufacturers of my own table-top globe placed a trademark and analemma in the Pacific Ocean, having determined that there geography could be sacrificed to corporate advertising and obscure reference materials. Similarly, in the Mercator projections used as backdrops to network news broadcasts, the United States often lies at the far left, suggesting that the world stretches from San Francisco to New York to Europe and then across the Asian land mass to Yokohama. In both cases the Pacific Ocean is geographically implicated but treated as an immense void.

Unless we have transoceanic personal ties, professional interests, or specialized knowledge, the Pacific is the dark side of the earth, banished from view as a featureless azure expanse where few live, where human contacts thin out, where sheer distance warps and weakens communication, and at whose shores the world ends and begins. But suppose we risk a novel perspective on the planet. Rotate the globe carefully, positioning Japan and Brazil at the extremes of a hemisphere occupied almost wholly by ocean. Japan, in the northwest, curves toward the concealed Asian mainland, and Brazil, in the southeast, reaches toward the hidden continents of Europe and Africa. This blue Pacific hemisphere, bracketed by distant countries that face away from each other, does not seem like a natural geographical or human unit. In recent years academics have begun talking about the Pacific Rim, attempting to describe, or perhaps invent, a region. But the very phrase suggests gaping discontinuity: one stops at, or falls off, a rim. The Pacific still has little of the conceptual coherence of the familiar, cozy Atlantic world. No one would call the Pacific "the pond," as Britons sometimes refer to the Atlantic.

This sense of the vastness and incoherence of the blue hemisphere is shared by most who live on its margins. Referring to enormous physical and cultural distance, Brazilians sometimes say that if you dig a hole deep enough, right through the center of the earth, you will come up in Japan. Japanese have no comparable saying about Brazil, which hardly registers in the Japanese imagination. My Japanese acquaintances described Brazil as a remote outpost of the Third World: hot, jungly, dark, and impoverished, not readily distinguishable from other countries of the unfortunate South. It is, many recalled, a wilderness into which some Japanese long ago disappeared. Aside from fans of the J League, the professional Japanese soccer association that has a few star Brazilian players, and excepting devotees of bossa nova and those who regularly deal with Brazilian migrants, the Japanese I knew took little or no notice of Brazil.

## Crossing the void

Surprisingly, the immense chasm between Japan and Brazil has often been, and continues to be, spanned. Complementary economic interests of the two countries first brought Japanese immigrants to Brazil. Even before Brazil's 1888 abolition, plantation owners had been pressing for the substitution of "white" for "black" labor—for the importation of Europeans, presumed to be skilled, hard-working, and racially superior to Afro-Brazilians. But the European immigrants, who came in large numbers, proved to be insufficiently submissive to bad working conditions and delayed payment of wages. The planters became disillusioned with those whom they viewed as anarchists, agitators, and malcontents.

By the time the Japanese special immigration envoy Sho Nemoto arrived in Brazil in 1894, promoting Japanese immigrants as the "whites of Asia"—hard-working, docile, and adaptable—Brazilian coffee barons and the Brazilian government were prepared to listen. The Meiji government, for its part, was eager to jettison citizens it could not employ or feed. Rural Japan was overpopulated; moreover, the establishment of Japanese colonies abroad, in Manchuria, Brazil, or elsewhere, promised an overseas food supply for the homeland. The goals of the two governments meshed. Their implementation—diplomatic and bureaucratic measures, the burnishing of each country's image in the other, negotiations over subsidies and concessions, and recruitment—took some time, but in 1908 the *Kasato-Maru*, after nearly two months at sea, discharged the first 781 Japanese immigrants into the unimaginable place that was the port of Santos.[1]

In the following decades, up until the outbreak of World War II, nearly 200,000 Japanese crowded boats bound for Brazil.[2] Those immigrants (*isseis*) worked as field hands on coffee and cotton plantations. Nearly all stayed on and made lives in Brazil, as the home islands receded into memory and hopes of return faded.[3] Most settled in the state of São Paulo, not far from where they had landed, clustering in famous centers of Japanese Brazil such as Bastos, Moji das Cruzes, Suzano, and the bairro Liberdade in the great city itself. Some went to live in remote *colônias*, agricultural communities noted for their productivity, their ethnic homogeneity, and their cooperative innovations.[4] Others moved on to the cities of Maringá and Londrina in neighboring Paraná. Still others ranged further afield, into the central plains and up into Amazonia.[5]

Eventually many isseis managed to buy farms or to establish small businesses. Their children (*nisseis*) and grandchildren (*sanseis*), Brazilian citizens by birth, mostly grew up speaking Portuguese, eating rice mixed with beans and manioc flour, and rubbing elbows with those of

[1]This summary account is taken from Lesser (1999:Chapter 4). The Tokugawa Shogunate (1603–1867) forbade emigration from Japan. Japan's first international migrants went to Hawaii in 1885, after the Meiji Restoration. Most came from Kyushu and southwestern Honshu, areas afflicted by rural poverty. The direction of Japanese emigration to the New World thereafter depended largely on American policies. Latin America, and Brazil in particular, became a destination after the so-called Gentlemen's Agreement between Japan and the United States in 1907 limited Japanese entry to this country.

[2]The exclusionary immigration act of 1924 terminated Japanese immigration to the United States, diverting another huge wave of migrants to Brazil. For a brief introduction to the history of Japanese emigration, see Yamanaka (1996, 1997); Lesser (1999) provides a fuller account. From 1908, with the arrival of the *Kasato-Maru*, through 1942, 188,986 Japanese entered Brazil, the vast majority arriving after 1924. After World War II, immigration tapered off, totaling 53,849 in the postwar period (Folha de São Paulo 1995; data provided by the Japanese Consulate General in São Paulo).

[3]Many were women, owing to the Brazilian insistence, based on considerations of labor stability, that Japanese be admitted only in family units. In the period 1908–45, 41 percent of Japanese immigrants were female (Yamanaka 1996:91, citing CCEYH 1991:86; see also Yamanaka 1997).

[4]See Yamashita (1992) for a vivid fictional portrayal of a colônia in a remote corner of the state of São Paulo.

[5]Major historical and ethnographic sources on Japanese-Brazilians in Brazil include Comissão de Elaboração da História (1992), Saito and Maeyama (1973), Saito (1980), and Lesser (1999). Folha de São Paulo (1995) provides a useful journalistic summary.

different colors and cultures, even as they linguistically distinguished themselves (*japoneses*) from those whom they called *brasileiros*, or *gaijin* (strangers). Those from the second and third generations graduated from Brazilian high schools and often attended prestigious universities, entered the professions, and married "Brazilians," raising *mestiço* children.[6] At one and a half million, the country's current nikkei (Japanese-descent) population is the largest in the world.[7] Though not everyone has prospered, by the usual standards—education, income, job status—Brazilian nikkeis as a group have done relatively well.[8]

Brazil, however, has not. Though better off than it was during the great wave of Japanese immigration, Brazil remains a nation of unrealized promise, afflicted with a troubled polity and a precarious economy that make even the middle class feel insecure. In the meantime, of course, Japan pursued a disastrous war and achieved a spectacular recovery, becoming an industrial power of the first rank (Allinson 1997).

By the mid-to-late 1980s, these divergent trends together produced a sea-change in Japanese ethnic affairs. Japan's prewar surplus of unskilled rural labor was a distant memory. Japanese capitalism now suffered from a deficit of unskilled industrial labor, as young Japanese, having grown up in relative comfort, began to shun the so-called 3-K (or 3-D) factory jobs (*kitanai, kitsui, kiken*—dirty, difficult, dangerous). Japanese employers, especially the second- and third-tier companies that supplied the big manufacturers, were in a bind. Having exhausted the supply of migrant labor from the less affluent Japanese provinces, they began hiring undocumented workers from Pakistan, Iran, Bangladesh, and elsewhere in Asia.[9]

[6]Reported rates of *mestiçagem* are, among nisseis, 6 percent; among sanseis, 42 percent; and among *yonseis* (fourth-generation descendants), 61 percent (Bernardes 1995a, citing data from a 1988 study by the Centro de Estudos Nipo-Brasileiros). Many Brazilian families in Homi Danchi, as elsewhere in Japan, are ethnically mixed.

[7]Folha de São Paulo 1995:Especial 1. Brazilian nikkeis now extend over five generations.

[8]Bernardes (1995b). According to a 1995 Datafolha survey cited by Bernardes, 80 percent of nikkei families residing in the city of São Paulo had incomes of ten minimum salaries or more. (The legally established monthly minimum salary in Brazil is approximately $100.) Bernardes notes that a 1994 survey by the Fundação Sistema Estadual de Análise de Dados (Seade) found that only 30 percent of all families in metropolitan São Paulo had salaries that high. Similarly, 53 percent of nikkei adults had university educations, versus 9 percent of all residents.

[9]Much of the following account of the legal shift comes from Yamanaka (1996). See also Oka (1994) and Kawamura (1999).

The influx of foreigners who looked different and followed different customs made many Japanese uneasy. But fortuitous events halfway around the world made another option thinkable.

Economic troubles plagued Brazil throughout the 1980s. Rocketing prices and stagnating performance led some Brazilian nikkeis, such as Eduardo Mori (Chapter 6), to try their luck in Japan. Most of the pioneering migrants had Japanese or dual citizenship; others were spouses of those who held Japanese passports, or nikkeis who entered Japan with tourist visas and overstayed them. Brazilian nikkei organizations began to lobby the Japanese government to offer overseas Japanese special entry considerations (Yamanaka 1996:72–77).

Pressured from several directions, the Japanese Ministry of Foreign Affairs hit upon what seemed like a brilliant solution. The reasoning, described in the ruling Liberal Democratic Party's monthly magazine, was elegant, if naive:

Admitting Nikkeijin legally will greatly help to ameliorate the present acute labor shortage. People who oppose the admission of the unskilled are afraid of racial discrimination against foreigners. Indeed, if Japan admitted many Asians with different cultures and customs than those of Japanese, Japan's homogeneous ethnic composition could collapse. However, if Nikkeijin were admitted, this would not be a problem.... Nikkeijin, as relatives of the Japanese, would be able to assimilate into Japanese society regardless of nationality and language (ibid.:76, quoting Nojima 1989:98–99).

The new law took effect on June 1, 1990. At a stroke, it criminalized the employment of undocumented workers and legalized the residence in Japan, with no restrictions on gainful activities, of nisseis, sanseis, and their spouses and minor children.[10] The law promised a flexible, low-cost, culturally tractable and racially correct labor force to do the industrial dirty work disdained by Japanese citizens.

The Brazilian economy sank to a nadir in 1990, when incoming Brazilian president Fernando Collor de Melo implemented a new policy. The so-called Plano Collor, initiated when the president assumed office in March, administered a violent shock through a package of drastic measures. Middle-class Brazilians especially resented Collor's move to block bank accounts, a prohibition that left many small businesses in jeopardy and rendered significant personal expenditures difficult or im-

[10]Nisseis are generally awarded three-year visas, and sanseis, spouses, and dependent children one-year visas, all renewable. Immigration officials have some flexibility in determining the length of visas.

possible. The prolonged economic malaise, now aggravated by gross governmental mismanagement, induced hundreds of thousands of Brazilians—not just nikkeis—to leave the country.[11] But unlike most Brazilian émigrés, nikkeis now had the attractive option of legal immigration to a First World country, and they left Brazil in disproportionately high numbers.[12]

Time after time I met nikkeis, such as Bernardo Kinjoh (Chapter 8), who still spoke bitterly of Collor. Moreover, ultimately the Plano Collor failed to achieve its objectives: inflation resumed with a vengeance, and continued tinkering in the years since, under other presidents, has failed to produce a convincing general turnaround in the economy. Salaries in Brazil, even in its most economically developed regions and even for highly skilled positions, remain low, and future employment and business prospects are uncertain.

No wonder, then, that Japanese wages have proved a powerful attraction for those wishing to save money for a new house, a child's education, family needs, or a small shop or factory in Brazil.[13] And despite Japan's astronomical prices, a worker's income, judiciously spent, permits a reasonable standard of living. Moreover, Japan offers migrants a modicum of security. The Japanese social welfare system provides decent medical and dental care at reduced rates.[14] The move to Japan,

---

[11]The Brazilian Foreign Ministry estimates that 1.5 million Brazilians now live in other nations: 610,000 in the United States, 325,000 in Paraguay, and 170,000 in Japan, the third-largest Brazilian diaspora (Klintowitz 1996). See Margolis (1994) for an informative ethnography of Brazilians living in New York.

[12]A Datafolha survey conducted in August 1995 revealed that 28 percent of nikkei residents of the city of São Paulo had already traveled to Japan at least once (Folha de São Paulo 1995:Especial 10).

[13]Remittances to Brazil from dekasseguis were estimated at $2 billion annually in the mid-1990s, or about $13,000 per person (International Press 1995 [July 30]:4-A, citing the Asahi Shinbun).

[14]Some Brazilians would dispute my assessment of Japanese health care as "decent." Firms that employ Brazilians are often unwilling to enroll them in *shakai hoken*, the company-subsidized social security system (which includes medical insurance); most workers must therefore foot their insurance bills themselves. Moreover, Brazilians have trouble communicating with Japanese doctors and dentists, and typically find the treatment they receive overly impersonal. Some complain of outright discrimination against foreigners. Finally, mental health care is woefully inadequate, consisting of a few telephone lines attended by lay volunteers and occasional one-day informal consultation marathons by Brazilian psychologists. There are clear, and serious, problems in the delivery of health care to Brazilians. Nevertheless, the access of working people (especially foreign workers) to acceptable health care seems better in Japan than in either Brazil or the United States.

where the streets are safe at all hours,[15] offers an escape from the climate of fear in Brazilian cities, where both crime and punishment are out of control.

There are also less material inducements. Rather than consuming international sophistication at a distance, through imported movies, music, and clothing, one can now become—almost—a bona fide First World cosmopolitan. And finally, the journey has, for many, intensely personal dimensions.

Most Brazilian nikkeis hail from southern Brazil, home to an impressive array of immigrant ethnic groups and to the multihued descendants of Africans, Europeans, and indigenous Brazilians who inhabit all regions of the country. Many nikkeis feel a deep affinity with multiracial, multicultural Brazil and also a sentimental attachment to insistently Japanese Japan, having grown up in families that emphasized the distinctness and even superiority of Japanese culture and blood.[16] Until recently, however, it was rare for a Brazilian nikkei to have set foot in Japan. One learned and reaffirmed Japaneseness through family and community assertions of identity, occasional consumption of traditional foods and celebration of traditional festivals, rudimentary Japanese language classes, and the complementary recognition of difference, sometimes with overtones of prejudice, by "brasileiros." Nikkeis often receive Japanese first or middle names at birth as a badge of community membership. From parents and grandparents they also hear stories of the Japanese migration to South America, variants of an ethnohistory of suffering and redemption.

Nikkeis who travel to Japan are adding confusing new chapters to that ethnohistory. Academics write of their "reverse immigration" (Oka 1994) or "return migration" (Koyama 1998; Yamanaka 1996), suggesting a diasporic homecoming. But where is the point of reference, the "home"? Whether a Brazilian nikkei is part of a Japanese or Brazil-

[15]Or seemed so during my stay in Toyota. But for Brazilians, the situation may be changing. On October 6, 1997, a group of twenty Japanese youths assaulted Brazilians at random in the city of Komaki, near Nagoya. They stabbed and viciously beat Herculano Reiko Lukosevicius, age fourteen; Herculano died three days later (Otake 1998).

[16]According to a Datafolha poll of nikkeis residing in the city of São Paulo, 59 percent state that "Japanese" (i.e., nikkeis) are prejudiced against "Brazilians," whereas only 35 percent think that "Brazilians" are prejudiced against "Japanese" (Folha de São Paulo 1995:Especial 11). The same poll shows that 67 percent of São Paulo nikkeis say they prefer Brazil to Japan, versus 22 percent who say they prefer Japan to Brazil.

ian diaspora is a matter of perspective, which varies by location, by person, and sometimes even from one moment to the next.[17] Perhaps one could call Brazilian nikkeis a *dual diaspora*. In a dual diaspora, people shuttle between two "homelands." Ties to each country wax and wane in intensity and vary from person to person.[18]

But such technical terms as "return migration" or "dual diaspora" fail to do justice to nikkei migrants' dynamic encounter with the home of their ancestors. A Japan hitherto an inner landscape, an anachronistic shadowland assimilated uncertainly into the self, suddenly materializes. That tangible Japan provokes the complex reworkings of identity featured in this book.

## In the new old world

The isseis' arduous transworld odyssey has become, for their descendants, a boring twenty-four-hour glide in the reverse direction, punctuated by a disagreeable layover in a cramped waiting room at LAX. Nikkeis who enter Japan to work call themselves *dekasseguis*, migrant laborers, just as their forebears entered Brazil as *dekasegi* in the early decades of the century. The Japanese word, absorbed into Portuguese, has been re-exported to Japan, now with a strange inflection: its travels could be a metaphor for the movement of people.

Dekasseguis labor mainly in 3-K factory jobs that pay them many times what they can earn in most white-collar occupations in Brazil. They scatter throughout Japan, though Brazilians now have a marked presence in certain towns. These include Toyota (Kawamura 1999; Linger 1996), Toyohashi (Yamanaka 1997), Nagoya (Fox 1998), and other locations in Aichi prefecture; Hamamatsu, in Shizuoka prefecture (Cornelius 1998; Kitagawa 1993, cited in Tsuda 1999a; Roth 1999); and

[17]For an outstanding discussion of the usefulness of "diaspora" as an analytic category, see Clifford (1994). Clifford argues that diaspora experience is historically specific: "Whose experience, exactly, is being theorized?" he asks. This is the right question—but (like almost all current writers) Clifford does not push his insistence on specificity of experience into the realm of the personal. For a nuanced ethnographic study that explores complexities of diaspora experience in "Black Liverpool," see Brown (1998), though the focus is on categories of persons rather than individuals.

[18]Dual diaspora differs from the "positive transnationalism" that Clifford (1994:321) assigns to Jews and those who inhabit the Black Atlantic (Gilroy 1993). Positive transnationalism features "overlapping networks of communication, travel, trade, and kinship [that] connect the several communities of a transnational 'people'" (Clifford 1994:321–22).

the Ota-Oizumi region of Gunma prefecture, where the proportion of Brazilians is nudging 10 percent (Kawamura 1999; Tsuda 1998). In 1995, Brazilian residents of Japan numbered close to 200,000, and many more have made the round trip through Japanese workplaces back to their homes in Brazil.[19] Often this transnational migrant circuit (Rouse 1991) becomes a circle. With Japanese savings exhausted and Brazilian prospects discouraging, or afflicted by the so-called returnee's syndrome (*síndrome de regresso*) and unable to readapt to Brazil, former dekasseguis again board airplanes headed for Tokyo and Nagoya.[20] Over the years some go back and forth repeatedly, engaging in "yo-yo migration" (Margolis 1994:263–67), a slow-motion, long-distance commute.

Brazilians in Japan shuttle in company vans between clockwork factories and narrow apartments. They fill out documents they cannot read and obey instructions they cannot understand. All but a few descend into a state of illiteracy or, at best, semiliteracy, learning to recognize just enough ideographs to navigate their daily routines.[21] In any case, there is little time or energy available for language study. Dekasseguis typically work six days a week, sometimes ten or twelve hours a day, with virtually no paid vacations. When not at work, people make the rounds of the supermarket, the department store, the Circle K, the Japanese pinball (*pachinko*) parlor, the video shop, the Brazilian restaurant. They catch up on sleep. On a free day one might travel to Tokyo Disneyland with the children, or to the next prefecture to visit a brother or sister.

Brazil remains distant, but the telephone provides an intermittent link with family and friends. The Portuguese-language weeklies carry

[19]The Japanese Ministry of Justice, Department of Immigration, reports 168,662 Brazilians resident in Japan as of June 1995 (International Press 1995 [December 17]:1-C, citing the Japanese Ministry of Justice). This figure does not include approximately 20,000 Brazilians of dual nationality (Klintowitz 1996:28). The change in the law also attracted other South American nikkeis and their families, mainly Peruvians, though their numbers are far lower (36,111 in June 1995, a fifth of the Brazilian total).

[20]A Brazilian doctoral researcher, Eunice Akemi Ishikawa Koga, interviewed fifty-four former dekasseguis in Brazil. She observed that "Brazilians . . . end up returning to Brazil without any know-how whatsoever" (International Press 1995 [September 17:5-A]). They typically buy a house or car, but rarely invest in a successful remunerative activity.

[21]Japan uses four scripts, three phonetic (*hiragana, katakana,* and *rōmaji*) and one ideographic (*kanji,* or Chinese characters). These are combined when writing, though kanji are the most important elements of written Japanese. Few Brazilian nikkeis I know have competence in kanji, sometimes humorously described as *pés de frango* chicken feet.

Brazilian news, and Brazilian shops rent copies of recently aired soap operas, talk shows, and TV tabloids. Thus dekasseguis can, after a fashion, participate in everyday Brazilian life. But the electronic prostheses come to seem increasingly artificial as time melts away in the exhausting routine of the workplace and in the numbing isolation of the company-run dormitory or the public housing project.

The dekasseguis' Japan—opaque, rich, demanding, aloof—bears little resemblance to a father's or grandmother's faded prewar recollection. It assigns Brazilian nikkeis to a controlled, stigmatized margin. Japanese descent is the price of admission to the country, but hardly, for South Americans, a source of distinction. Japanese typically expect and accept cultural incompetence from a white North American or European, but Latin American nikkeis receive criticism for minor lapses in behavior and language. Cultural and linguistic imperfections brand them defective Japanese, and as Brazilians they lack the redeeming First-World origins and fluency in English of Japanese-Americans or Japanese-Canadians. Japanese acquaintances occasionally charge them with having abandoned the country and having failed to participate in its postwar reconstruction. And whereas many Japanese accord North American and European civilizations attention and a certain respect, if not necessarily admiration, most seem to imagine Brazil as a blur of jungles and slums, and Brazilianness as at best a mystery, at worst a sad Third-World affliction.

In the collision with this shockingly new old world, nikkei selves made in Brazil get remade in Japan. Nikkeis' "Japaneseness," formerly a taken-for-granted cornerstone of self, comes into question, as does its meaning. Nikkeis do not all respond the same way to their encounters with Japan, but often they seem jarred into reflecting at length upon who they are, reformulating themselves continually as the months in Japanese limbo stretch into years.

Such reflections arise from immediate experience. The remainder of this chapter takes us from the disembodied global perspective to the microenvironments in which the transnational manifests itself in human interaction and perception.

## Toyota City

Varig, Brazil's national airline, runs direct weekly flights from Rio and São Paulo across the blue hemisphere to Nagoya, Toyota City's giant neighbor. Nagoya Airport, orderly, busy, and nondescript, offers an

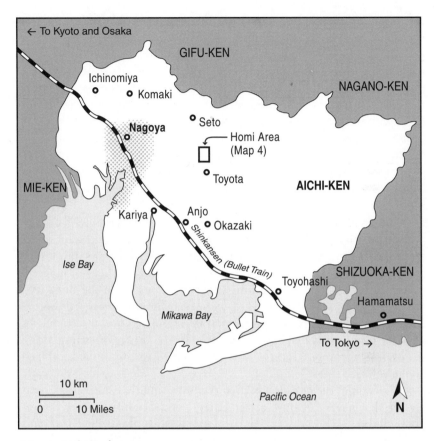

Map 3. Aichi Prefecture

apt introduction to the city, a manufacturing center and seaport of over two million people. Regarded by outsiders as bland and stolid, Nagoya is undeniably energetic.

Today's business is Nagoya's chief concern, but one can read history in its architecture. There is an impressive castle crowned by golden dolphins. It was built in the seventeenth century by the warlord Ieyasu, a native of the area. Ieyasu, founder of the Tokugawa Shogunate, wanted to anchor his regional defense and consolidate his control of Honshu. During World War II, bombs destroyed Ieyasu's fortress and leveled much of the city. The castle was reconstructed in 1959, but the traditional wooden neighborhoods are gone forever.

New and garish, Nagoya's city center buzzes with activity. Cranes rise high into the air, moving steel and cement. People crowd the department stores; dart into coffee shops and bars; queue at KFC, McDonald's, Mister Donut; roam the bookstores and fluorescent-lit pachinko parlors. With mechanical regularity the city's subways disgorge crowds into underground malls. The chief commercial and entertainment district is called Sakae. Old women in kimonos, socialites dressed to the nines, ragged street people, uniformed students, workers in hardhats, orange-haired dropouts, and gray-suited businessmen in stiff white shirts all cross paths on clean, brightly lit sidewalks.[22] Sakae is intensely urban and remarkably safe, a wondrous combination for those who inhabit countries where "city" and "danger" are synonymous.

Nagoya is the metropolis of Aichi prefecture, a province with a large population and a vigorous economy powered by auto and auto-parts manufacturing. Though an industrial giant, Nagoya is no satanic mill town. Most of its factories are modest, unassuming edifices of indeterminate color, tucked away among other buildings or, in the outskirts, among rice fields. There is poverty here—cardboard cubicles of homeless persons arrayed beneath the freeway, cramped Buraku settlements near the port, grimy neighborhoods close by the tracks or strung along waterways acrid with industrial waste—but privation too is scattered and subdued.

At its edges, the city slowly dissolves into suburbs and then a countryside that never becomes convincingly rural. Aichi's scenery is monotonous but not unpleasant. The province is calm, mundane. Most land is devoted to some economic pursuit, but there is a feeling of space. One is aware of the sky, and there are occasional vistas of rolling forest and distant mountains.

The Aichi Loop Railway, or Aikan,[23] traces a sinuous arc through eastern Aichi prefecture, a region known as Mikawa. The slow, old-fashioned Aikan trains pass through Homi station, a kilometer's downhill walk from the danchi. On a January day drenched in chill, angular sunlight, I boarded a train bound for central Toyota and eventually the castle town of Okazaki, forty-five minutes to the south.

From the window of the car I recorded the passing scenery: a succes-

[22]Dropouts are called *furyō*, inferior or broken goods. This word is learned early on by Brazilian workers and schoolchildren, though with different meanings. *Furyōhin* are defective pieces on the production line; furyō are young idlers and delinquents.
[23]Aikan is the familiar term for this railway line, the Aichi Kanjō Tetsudō.

sion of factories, paddies, houses, gardens, streams, warehouses, cemeteries, shrines, power plants, restaurants, junkyards, orchards, bowling alleys, greenhouses, pachinko parlors. Excepting Okazaki, a picturesque minor tourist destination that was Ieyasu's birthplace, the workaday settlements seemed interchangeable, displaying little of the fabled charm of traditional Japan. The towns were barely distinguishable from their environs. Neither rural nor urban, or perhaps both at once, this is a region in which the same elements recombine endlessly in different proportions and densities.

Toyota City, with over 300,000 inhabitants, is one of Mikawa's largest settlements, but it too seems semirural. On another winter afternoon I followed the Aikan line on foot within Toyota's city limits, heading south from downtown, away from Homi Danchi. The day was raw and windy, the sky smeared with low clouds. It was not quite cold enough to snow. The cement posts of the elevated railway track threaded among fields dotted with russet stubble. The cars running beside the rail line were white, cream, silver, black. Desultory shops, restaurants, and vending machines lined the road, with tire, cement, and auto-parts plants scattered in the foreground and electric pylons marching into the distance. Dark hills rose and fell along the northern and eastern horizons; to the south and west the land slid into Nagoya's coastal plain. The whole scene was bleached, leaden, and spare, a modern landscape awash in shades of gray. After an hour or so, I stopped in a coffee shop to warm up. The pop music was an incongruous burst of mid-century American color: "Surf City," "Wipeout," "Red Roses for a Blue Lady." I am sure no one there knew that Santa Cruz, my hometown of sorts, was Surf City. Sipping coffee, I shared a secret with Jan & Dean and watched men flip through newspapers and salacious comic books. I took the train back toward the center of town, accompanied by uniformed students and women with shopping bags.

Railway lines intersect in downtown Toyota, a nucleus of the Mikawa region. Near the junction is an efflorescence of department stores, tiny bars, beer gardens, convenience stores, specialized shops, and coffee houses: the standard commercial mélange of urban Japan. Toyota's City Hall and the Toyota International Association, frequent destinations for foreign residents, are a short walk from this central business district.

Homi Danchi sits a few miles northeast of downtown Toyota, about halfway to the Nagoya line. By train it takes ten minutes to reach Homi from Toyota station, but often I preferred the tranquil two-hour walk.

At first you navigate through tidy, quiet back streets lined with new buildings. Gradually you enter a crazy quilt of rice fields and small plots of onions, cabbages, eggplants, and Japanese radishes. In much of Toyota, for much of the year, the smell of organic fertilizer hangs in the air. You pass mostly single-family houses—two-story wooden structures with tile roofs—and here and there a condominium (*manshon*), a workers' hostel (*ryō*), or a public apartment complex. Some dwellings show cracked, faded wood askew and patched with corrugated plastic sheeting.

Little noise escapes these houses. But gentle sounds obtrude: the sibilance of a washing machine, the notes of a piano, the rustle of a broom. Sometimes you spot a housewife hanging up clothes, or a man polishing a car, or an old woman stooped in the fields. Gardens feature sculpted trees and dramatic rocks. Bamboo grows on hilltops, feathering Shinto shrines and Buddhist temples. Schools, rectangular blocks with dirt playgrounds, dot the countryside.

Rice is everywhere in Toyota. Its agricultural cycle marks the passing of the seasons. The newly flooded paddies turn mirrorlike in spring, then lush and emerald as the warm summer rains arrive. Later the fields dry out; the plants bend from the weight of the grains; and then suddenly it is all gone. Smoke from burning rice debris curls into the crisp air, and once again the land lies bare, its winter drabness relieved only on the rare occasions when snow falls.

The long walk through the fields brings you to Homi station, at the foot of a long incline. There are always Brazilians making the climb on foot or bicycle, past the police post, the Chinese noodle house, the coffee shops, convenience stores, and more rice paddies. Others ride past in cars or company vans, and still others ascend in the red-and-white Meitetsu Company buses that serve the danchi. Passing a huge irrigation pond, you weave your way home through the forest of white cement that crowns the hill.

## Homi Danchi

Homi Danchi is bounded by fields below and encircled on three sides by a middle-class suburban neighborhood of new houses with plexiglass carports. Dozens of apartment blocks ranging in height from five to twelve stories stand within an oval loop road inclined and elongated on its north-south axis. It takes about half an hour to circumambulate the danchi. The buildings are narrow, so that each apartment has both a southern and northern exposure. This orientation allows residents to dry laundry and air bedding on the south-facing balconies, facilitates cross-ventilation during the sweltering summer, and admits sunlight during the cold, damp winter.

The complex is split roughly in half, with apartments rented through the prefecture (known collectively as the *Ken-ei Jūtaku*) to the south and east and those leased from Kōdan, the government-funded Housing and Urban Development Corporation, to the north and west. The Ken-ei apartments, available only to families with limited incomes, are older, less spacious, darker, and cheaper than the Kōdan units, but the differences are modest. Interspersed among the apartment buildings are sandy playgrounds for children and outdoor smoking or rest areas for adults. There are trees and bushes, and though the landscaping is not elaborate, the grounds are well maintained. Most of the inhabitants have cars, parked in numbered spaces in convenient lots. The apartments are cramped, the buildings are boxy and monotonous, and living density is high, but the complex is safe and usually quiet. Aside from some graffiti and minor vandalism in the larger buildings, there is no hint of slovenliness or decay.

Walkways converge on a shopping and business area anchored by a two-story commercial center. Each floor of the center opens onto a paved square. The squares are interconnected by a stairway and ramp. The center's upper floor houses a branch of Nagoya Bank, a general store, a laundry, beauty salon, barber, noodle restaurant, and coffee shop. Across the upper square is high-rise Building 142, where the Kōdan office, community rooms, and a post office are located. The busier lower square adjoins the overpriced but much-patronized Meitetsu supermarket, the only major food store for miles.[24] Facing the market across the square, at the base of high-rise Building 141, are an electronics shop, the Little Gulliver toy store, another coffee shop, and a sushi restaurant. Further down, below the Meitetsu, is a parking lot accessible by the major east-west street cutting through the danchi.

Around the loop road, outside the danchi, are public playing fields

[24]The supermarket makes little effort to cater to Brazilian tastes. The Meitetsu Company monopolizes both food and bus transportation at Homi Danchi. It also owns the train line, an extension of the Nagoya subway, that has a stop two miles away at Jōsui station.

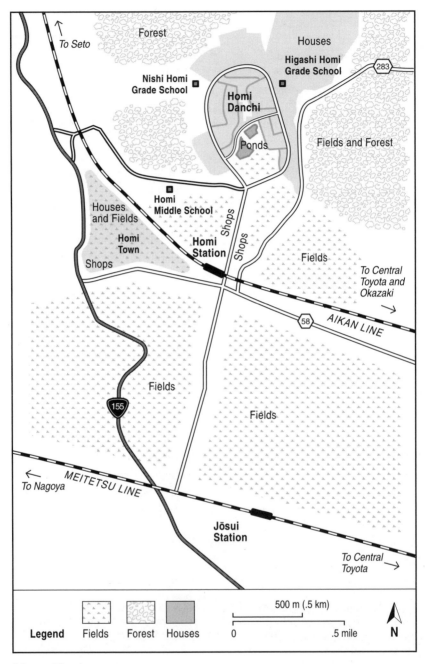

Map 4. Homi area

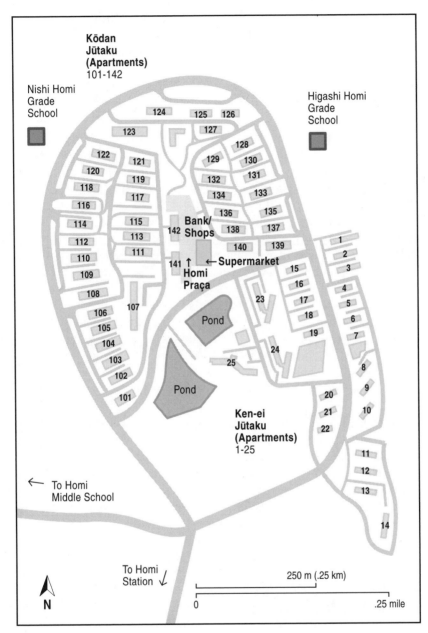

Kōdan
Jūtaku
(Apartments)
101-142

Nishi Homi
Grade
School

Higashi Homi
Grade
School

124   125   126

123   127

128

122   121   129   130

120   119   132   131

118   117   134   133

116   136   135

114   115   **Bank/** 138   137

142 **Shops**

113   140   139

112   111

110   141 ↑ ←**Supermarket**

109   **Homi**
  **Praça**

108   107

1
2
3
4
5
6
7

15
16
17
18
19

23

106
105
104
103
102
101

Pond

Pond

24

25

8
9
10

20
21   10
22

**Ken-ei**
**Jūtaku**
**(Apartments)**
**1-25**

11
12
13

14

← To Homi
Middle School

To Homi
Station ↓

250 m (.25 km)

0        .25 mile

**N**

Map 5. Homi Danchi and environs

suitable for baseball or soccer; shops selling food and drink, appliances, and (in winter) kerosene; beauty salons; a kindergarten; a day-care center; and two grade schools, Nishi Homi (West Homi) and Higashi Homi (East Homi). A short distance away, accessible by sidewalk or footpath, is Homi Chūgakkō, the public junior-high school.

Days at Homi are quiet. In the early morning, company vans collect Japanese and Brazilian workers at established rendezvous points. White-collar Japanese commuters with briefcases, mostly men, leave by car or catch a Meitetsu bus. Youngsters with backpacks, neatly dressed and groomed, climb overpasses on their way to the grade schools; weary teenagers, the boys in black military uniforms and the girls in blue-and-white sailor dresses, troop off to Homi Chū. By 9:00 the morning bustle subsides, and a torpor settles over the place. In the playgrounds women converse softly with one another as their small children dig in the sand. Gardeners prune trees, painters spruce up buildings. As the afternoon wears on, the danchi's rhythm gradually accelerates. After school, children use the square by the supermarket for playing ball, roller-skating, bike-riding, or just running around. Around 5:00, activity picks up further as people rush to the Meitetsu to make last-minute dinner purchases. Airy baguettes vanish from the shelves, snapped up by Brazilians returning from work. Then things gradually quiet down once again, and night settles over Homi, transforming it into a huge, slowly dimming constellation of electric lights.

On workdays there are only telltale signs of a Brazilian presence at Homi Danchi. Notices in Portuguese are the most obvious evidence. Those posted on Building 141, made official with seals, warn against playing loud music or otherwise creating disturbances after 10:00 at night. The bulletin boards announce job openings, items for sale, and services.

"MOVES TO BRAZIL. Why leave behind everything you've acquired in Japan? That refrigerator, the newest-model TV and VCR, that fantastic stereo, the latest-generation computer, the fax machine, the cordless phone . . . in short, everything that you can't replace in Brazil. WE OFFER SECURITY, QUALITY, AND ECONOMY IN TRANSPORTING YOUR BELONGINGS TO BRAZIL."

"URGENT: We are hiring men and women, and nikkei couples without children, with preference for nisseis and those who speak Japanese, 18–35 years old, for the Nagoya and Gifu regions."

"We have work for women: In Miyoshi, in a factory making fish cake. Normal wage: ¥800 [$8.00] per hour.[25] Overtime: ¥1100 per hour. We have a bus to take workers to the factory and back."

"TABLE OF PRICES: Renewal of visa (filling out form) ¥7,000. Renewal of passport ¥10,000. Birth or marriage certificate ¥7,000. Accompaniment to Immigration Office ¥10,000."

"DORA'S APPAREL. The best new offerings in intimate feminine attire."

"BRAZIL NATURAL FOODS. Now with sales of air tickets. Lease of telephone lines, ¥800 per month."

"CHILD CARE, PREFERABLY UP TO ONE YEAR OLD. Call Dona Rosa anytime."

In the evenings and on weekends, Homi's Brazilian population emerges. Until about 6:00 P.M. on weekdays, one of the community rooms in Building 142 is used for *juku*, private after-school school for Japanese students preparing for high-school entrance exams. Then this dreary space metamorphoses into a lively shop called, in an unaccountable mixture of English and Iberian, The Amigos, specializing in South American products. Removing their shoes at the entrance, the patrons, Brazilians and a few Peruvians, buy canned black bean stew (*feijoada*), manioc flour (*farinha*), lasagna, tropical fruit juices, underwear, magazines, and Andean foods such as Inka Kola and quinoa. On an upper floor of the same building, Seu Teodoro has converted a room of his apartment into a video store that carries slick TV *novelas* and action and comedy films subtitled in Portuguese. Teodoro's is the largest of three or four such operations at Homi, some of which offer home delivery.

Vehicles peddling Brazilian products regularly visit Homi. They range from small local vans to itinerant general stores. One April evening I conversed with the driver of an enormous truck belonging to the Plaspa Meat company, a chain serving Brazilians throughout Japan. Cleber, a non-nikkei Bahian married to a nikkei woman, had parked at the base of the Meitetsu parking lot. He circulates through Gifu, Aichi, and Shizuoka prefectures. Speaking with him, I thought of Lauro, a nissei acquaintance whose father used to peddle sticky rice and seaweed to

[25]For most of the period 1994–96, the exchange rate fluctuated around ¥100 to the dollar, give or take 10 percent. Using that conversion rate yields a convenient rough estimate of prices and wages in official dollar equivalents, though the purchasing power of ¥100 in Japan is considerably less than that of $1 in the United States (or its equivalent at the time, one *real*, in Brazil). On the other hand, yen saved in Japan go a long way in Brazil.

Japanese scattered through the backwoods of Brazil. The Plaspa truck carries sandals, palm hearts, comic books, spices, and, as the name suggests, huge quantities of beef, pork, and chicken.

On another evening, as I was strolling through the parking lot below our apartment, I happened on a group of young men, Brazilians still in factory uniforms, sitting around a garbage bin, drinking, smoking, and cracking jokes. Conveniently, just across the loop road were *hanbaiki*, vending machines selling beer and cigarettes.

Upon reflection, I realized that this was a natural gathering spot. Brazilians laughingly described the *gomi*, walled concrete garbage dumps that dotted the perimeter of the danchi, as *shopping vinte e quatro horas* (twenty-four-hour shopping centers) or, in a play on the supermarket's name, the "Gomitetsu." Aside from mundane household waste, the dumps held valuable discards—furniture, pots and pans, kerosene heaters, fans, televisions, VCRs, even refrigerators and washing machines. (One evening Eli, our teenage son, alertly spotted what became our own washer, a Toshiba in excellent condition.) As a Brazilian man once commented to me, appraising the mound in front of him, "At least here the prices are reasonable." Because the small Homi apartments have little storage space, new acquisitions push old articles outside. Japanese residents rarely scavenged from these piles, but we foreigners kept an eye on them, often trading up by exchanging a formerly reclaimed item for a better or more stylish one. It was like mining; you lived for the lucky strike. The trash heaps were marginal spaces comfortably frequented by marginal people.

Marginal social spaces are not, however, confined to Homi's physical margins. At night the heart of the danchi becomes a Brazilian rendezvous. There is a large breezeway on the upper square, cut through Building 142, furnished with some ratty benches and a soda machine. A refreshing wind tunnel on sweltering summer nights and a popular haunt for Brazilian teenagers, the breezeway is decorated with Portuguese-language graffiti, some of it obscene, and a hand-lettered sign reading *Favor de não urinar aqui embaixo* ("Please do not urinate down here"). More interesting is the lower square by the supermarket, which many Japanese consider something of a trouble spot. This area, which Brazilians refer to simply as *a praça*, the plaza, is a prime example of what I call a transnational scene—a place where transnational forces of economy, history, and cultural difference manifest themselves in social interaction and thereby enter the realm of experience.

*Top*: Kōdan apartment buildings, Homi Danchi.

*Bottom left*: Downtown Toyota City, from the Toyota Meitetsu train station.

*Bottom right*: Jogi Enomura (factory worker) and Isabel Gomes Enomura (English teacher), in our apartment, Homi Danchi.

*Top left*: Isabel Gomes Enomura and her son Key, in their apartment, Homi Danchi (photo by Jogi Enomura).

*Top right*: Brazilian girl, in "country" garb at a São João gathering in Kariya, Japan, 1996. São João is a traditional Brazilian summer festival celebrated with special treats, dances, and bonfires.

*Bottom left*: Lara Paiva and Rogério Paiva (factory workers), in a Homi Danchi hallway.

*Bottom right*: Brothers, Key (left) and Jin Enomura (grade-school students), spring snapshot (photo by Jogi Enomura).

## *Homi Praça*

Several paces from the entrance to the Meitetsu, facing the row of hanbaiki banked against the store's outer wall, is a rectangular cement planter, about three feet high, surrounded by a narrow ledge and holding some straggly bushes. Brazilians have transformed the planter into what some refer to jokingly as the *Bar do Zé*, Joe's Bar, the focal point of this displaced version of a Brazilian praça. The vending machines offer beer, coffee, and cigarettes, commodities associated with relaxation; the planter offers a place, albeit uncomfortable, to hang out; and the spot is a crossroads where one might run into acquaintances. It invites Brazilians, especially (but not exclusively) men and especially (but not only) when the weather is good, to have a beer with friends, or just to shoot the breeze. From dusk, when people get home from work, until the late evening, Brazilians frequent this spot, drinking, telling stories, joking, and laughing.

Japanese never join these groups, giving them a wide berth and moving quickly past, without stopping. A praça is not a significant cultural object for Japanese, who usually prefer to meet in enclosed, intimate places. And the manner of the Brazilians—effusive, playful, at times raucous—seems strange, even threatening, to many. Most Japanese in the Mikawa region are unused to such exuberance, accompanied by bodily touching, horseplay, guffaws, and loud talk in a thoroughly unfamiliar language. A local Japanese woman once confided uneasily to Maria, my wife: "When I go to the Meitetsu supermarket, I wonder what country I'm in."

One of the delights of this praça is that it is improvised. A busy open space conducive to happenstance encounters, it feels like a Brazilian praça although it was not designed to be anything of the sort. Once I asked a Brazilian friend, one of the Homi pioneers, what the praça had been like in the past. Originally, he told me, there had been several benches, intended as places for people to rest. But Brazilian men began to occupy the benches in the evenings and after soccer games on weekends. The Brazilians often perched on the backs of the benches, parking their feet on the seats. Sometimes they took off their shirts or lay directly on the ground as they talked. The scene was too much for the Meitetsu Company, which had the benches removed—to no effect. Deprived of benches, the Brazilians simply began to congregate at the planter, a few steps away.

The situation at the praça is rife with elements of parody, aside from the substitution of planter for benches. In Brazil, one might buy food or drink at a *quitanda*, a neighborhood mom-and-pop store, on a corner of the square. Local residents tend to frequent the same quitanda and to develop first-name relationships with the owners. Here in Japan, in a praça that is not a praça, one deals with a quitanda that is not a quitanda. One buys from humming machines rather than human neighbors. This substitution introduces an ironic element: the machines are more comprehensible, more familiar, than the locals, about whom you know little, with whom you cannot converse, who do not frequent the square, and who may resent your own presence there. In contrast, the machines, which can simultaneously dispense hot and cold drinks, and can change ¥10,000 ($100) bills, are comprehensible, tolerant, and cross-culturally adept.

There is, in short, something carnivalesque about Homi Praça. During Carnival in Brazil, the poor appropriate the city center from the rich; the formal praças of the commercial and bureaucratic zones become playgrounds of the dispossessed. In Japan, Brazilians appropriate a key commercial space from Japanese, turning it into a humble open-air, after-hours bar and club, a place of impromptu celebration. There is good-natured Brazilian rebelliousness at work in Homi Praça, a subversive spontaneity. Homi Praça is, among other things, a joke on the Japan that confines Brazilians within dirty factories and tiny apartments, communicates with them in a mystifying language, and enforces norms of behavior that are not their own.

But this is Japan, and the temperate nightly Carnival has an early curfew. Residents of Building 141, which overlooks the Meitetsu supermarket, often complain about the noise and the litter, occasionally adding to it by yelling and pitching objects onto the low-key revelers. Compliant, most of the Brazilians leave early, relinquishing the area to a few older men who, bathed in the whitish glow of the vending machines, continue to converse softly in Portuguese until 10:00 P.M. or so, when they too go home. After this the danchi falls quiet, except when *bōsōzoku*, groups of young Japanese motorcyclists, gun their engines as they race around the circle in the hours after midnight. Late one night Eli saw bōsōzoku invade the space by the supermarket to break open the hanbaiki and flee with money, beer, and cigarettes.

In Homi Praça, the transnational becomes manifest in Brazilians' actions of drinking together, conversing in their native language, complaining of work, joking about misadventures, appropriating a public space, ridiculing themselves, and annoying others. Such transnational scenes, the topic of Part Two, are, I suggest, arenas in which identities are implicitly affirmed, parodied, and appraised in social interaction, becoming available for critique and transformation.

# Scenes

# CHAPTER 3

# Postmodern Times

## Carlitos in Japan

The Depression-era silent film *Modern Times* (1936) opens with a clock face, the second hand sweeping round as the hour moves toward 6:00 A.M. A herd of sheep dissolve into men jostling one another as they funnel into the Electro Steel factory. The whistle blows. The boss, spying on the workers from his electronic watchtower, orders a speedup. We see Charlie Chaplin, a wrench in each fist, frantically tightening nuts on gizmos that fly past on a conveyor belt. Even when he steps away from the line, his hands keep twitching. At one point he becomes literally trapped in the gears of the plant's enormous machines. A salesman convinces the boss to try out the Bellows Automatic Feeder, a time-saving device. The feeder, attached around the neck and equipped with mechanical utensils, frees up the hands, refueling workers without interrupting their tasks. The efficiency experts hitch up Chaplin, the inevitable guinea pig, for a test demonstration, but the machine goes berserk, dumping soup down his neck and assaulting him with a spinning corn cob.

Soon thereafter Chaplin himself has a nervous breakdown. Men in white coats cart him off to a mental hospital, initiating a series of misadventures with authorities of all kinds. Chaplin meets a waif, Paulette Goddard, who is as star-crossed and sweet-tempered as he is. Kindred spirits living in a shack, they fantasize about sharing a bungalow with a garden and lacy curtains. But all their efforts to gain a modicum of security come to naught. At the film's end, hounded by police and having lost everything, Chaplin and Goddard cling to one another. They trade words and gestures of desperate encouragement. We last see them hand in hand, brave grins pasted on their faces, as they strike out down a deserted highway to the strains of "Smile."

Sixty years later, in Japan, the Depression seems like a bad dream that someone else had a long time ago. We are in postmodern times, smooth, subtle, and quietly efficient. Manual workers in Toyota City's auto-parts factories commute from the Third World by jet. The migrants receive First-World wages, nutritious food in the company cafeteria, and adequate, if unavoidably cramped, housing. They can buy cars, video cameras, cellular telephones, and official NBA jackets. Their children attend well-equipped, well-run public schools. These days, advanced Japanese capitalism is administered discreetly and with a certain decorum: the production line will not move too fast; the lunch hour, though unpaid, will not be abolished; and the workers will not be pushed to the brink. The crudeness of Electro Steel's piggish boss and the Bellows Automatic Feeder belong to an earlier era.

Almost. For in some ways these streamlined, softened, comfortably mystified postmodern times are not so different after all. I do not know how many of the Brazilian factory workers I knew in Toyota City may have seen *Modern Times*, but I am confident that the film would have struck a responsive chord in them. In the Fordist Electro Steel plant they would have recognized their own routinized procedures and hierarchical regimes. They would have identified with Chaplin's befuddlement and yearnings for a freer life in which spontaneous, satisfying personal relationships might take precedence over the factory's single-stranded, rationalized command structure.

Chaplin, known in Brazil as Carlitos (Charlie), is in fact a transnational adoptee, a folk figure who has spun free of his films to occupy a prominent place in Brazilian popular culture. "God is Brazilian," goes a deceptively simple popular saying; so, and in a similarly complex manner, is Chaplin, whom one encounters in Brazilian posters, figurines, song lyrics, and even Spiritist websites. The tramp's warm-heartedness, subversion of authority, eternally down-and-out condition, hatred of regimentation, and hope against all odds resonate with attitudes and values widespread among Brazilians—including Brazilian factory workers in Japan.

In a manner of speaking, Brazilian workers play the part of Carlitos on Japanese production lines, struggling to meet their quotas of mystery objects[1] under the eye of invisible overseers, the managers of a complex politico-economic system designed to make of them a reliable, flexible, and ultimately (if need be) dispensable source of unskilled labor. Like Carlitos, the Brazilian workers often have grand but unrealistic dreams. Like Carlitos, some of them suffer mental disturbances.[2] Like Carlitos,

---

[1] I was surprised how often people could not tell me exactly what they made, or how it fit into the final product (usually an automobile).

[2] Many Brazilians at Homi Danchi, especially but not only women, complained of

many feel a gut-level antipathy for the work they do and the rule-bound, mechanical lives they must lead. But most Brazilian workers, however much they would like to ditch their jobs and, like Carlitos, hit the road, find it difficult to do so. The postmodern Japanese factory—stinking, dirty, and numbing—is for them an unlikely honey trap.

The shop-floor viewpoint of *Modern Times* brings us face to face with 1930s American corporate capitalism. The movie concretizes "capitalism" in Chaplin's dealings with others and in the thoughts and emotions rendered visible by his expressive body and countenance. Though our own empathy is cushioned by the film's humor and twisted by its satire, Chaplin helps us understand what it is like to be sped up, castigated by bosses, berated by colleagues, prodded by police, and experimented on by efficiency experts.

*Modern Times* ironically bills itself, shortly after the opening credits, as "a story of industry, of individual enterprise—humanity crusading in pursuit of happiness." But "industry," "enterprise," and "humanity" are not characters in the film. Rather, *Modern Times* delivers its critical message by displaying, in tactile images, the peregrinations of a proletarian misfit. Similarly, though without humorous or satiric intent, in Part Two I try to bring an abstraction down to earth. I hope to convey a sense of how Brazilians in the Toyota area live 1990s "transnationalism" in factories, schools, and leisure sites.

### Transnational scenes

Person-centered ethnographers specialize in close-ups. They try to translate sociocultural abstractions into languages of experience, a

---

"stress." They had problems of nervousness, difficulty in sleeping, and social withdrawal. Brazilian newspapers in Japan carry constant reports on nervous ailments and related issues. Brazilians (mostly men) commonly vanish in Japan. One newspaper took to publishing photos sent by relatives seeking to locate "disappeared" persons. Suicides of Brazilians, again mostly men, also receive prominent treatment in the Brazilian press. Suicides are blamed on overwork, financial problems, marital conflicts, and the so-called "returnee's syndrome" (síndrome de regresso). It is said that victims of this syndrome, people who have shuttled between Brazil and Japan and have been unable to readapt to life in Brazil, become increasingly alienated and desperate (see, for example, Ozaki 1996 and Sakae 1996). Parlato (1996:7-A) quotes a Brazilian psychiatrist, Décio Nakagawa: "Suicide is the last stage of the [returnee's] syndrome." Judging by the symptoms cited—irritability, loss of concentration, self-destructive tendencies, anxiety, and listlessness—the "returnee's syndrome" is a variety of depression. For a journalistic discussion of depression among dekasseguis, see Mitsugui (1995).

term fraught with ambiguities but one that usefully draws attention to the materiality, immediacy, and aliveness of human subjectivity.

The justification for an experience-oriented ethnographic enterprise is twofold: that individual human lives and human subjectivities are worthy of sustained, sympathetic attempts at understanding; and that the experience and making of human lives cannot be inferred directly from sociological abstractions. The first point needs no further comment; one concurs or not, and the matter ends there. Granted the first proposition, however, the second is contentious. It insists that an adequate account of human lives requires a displacement of perspective. So long as we objectify human lives as epiphenomena of "society," "culture," "history," or "discourse," we will inevitably miss the thing we are trying to describe. Human experience has an irreducibly first-person quality; we need to *subjectify* rather than *objectify*.[3] Grasping what it is like to be another human may be easier than inferring what it is like to be a bat (Nagel 1974), but the problem is no different in principle. Without direct access to the consciousness of another sentient being, the feat demands an imaginative projection of oneself into the mind and body of another. Imaginative projection, a move toward the first person, in turn has a precondition: the translation of sociological abstractions into some semblance of the terms in which the world is encountered by those we wish to understand.

Such translation is exceedingly difficult but necessary. "Transnationalism" is a term that social scientists have invented to refer to flows and exchanges across national boundaries. Its compass is global. But "transnationalism" is inadequate to the task of describing what it is like to be a Brazilian migrant in Japan. A migrant does not encounter "transnationalism" in her daily life, nor is "transnationalism" an element of her experience. Below I suggest some of the ways that this grand sociological abstraction manifests itself to the senses and to the minds of those who live it, coaxing the reader into an attempt at imaginative projection.

Part Two considers, from the medium range of the interactional, the question: How do large-scale global changes present themselves to Brazilians who have traveled to Japan? The chapters describe a range of

---

[3]The ontological status of consciousness has been a long-standing issue in the philosophy of mind. See Güzeldere (1997) for a guide to the debates. The volume edited by Block, Flanagan, and Güzeldere (1997) collects important representative articles on a range of positions.

*transnational scenes*, significant interactional environments encountered or created by migrants. I use the word "scene" to convey a sense of setting, a place where, loosely speaking, people play out the dramas of daily life. But I do not mean to push the dramatic metaphor too far. The dramas are not always scripted precisely, and even when they are, the actors do not always follow the script.

I want also to emphasize that a scene is not "out there," but simultaneously "out there" and "in here." It is a perspectivally differentiated interactional setting (cf. Appadurai 1990). Your experience of and participation in the factory depend on whether you are Japanese or Brazilian, a Japanese-Brazilian or an Italian-Brazilian, a man or a woman, Clarice or Julieta.

Note also that the modifier "transnational" here is not synonymous with "cross-cultural" or "multicultural." That is, "transnational scene" refers to a *manifestation* of transnational flows, not necessarily to a situation in which contact takes place between persons of differing nationalities. In thus qualifying the meaning of "transnational," I am trying to avoid the implication that transnationalism viewed up close is homologous with transnationalism seen from afar. From a global perspective, transnational movement means crossing international borders. But having crossed those lines on a map, people often live transnational situations in subtle, hidden ways. A transnational scene is, in sum, one of the significant perspectival interactional correlates, occurring across or within ethnic groups, of a specific global migration. Some transnational scenes bring Brazilians and Japanese together in structured interactions—the public school is a good example—whereas others, such as Brazilian restaurants, are the nearly exclusive preserve of Brazilians.

For the Brazilian residents of Toyota City, the most important, involving transnational scenes are undoubtedly the shop floor (for adults) and the public school classroom (for children). Work and school, the topics of this and the next chapter, absorb huge amounts of time, energy, and attention. Their domination of daily life enhances the significance of transnational scenes associated with leisure, such as the Brazilian restaurant discussed in Chapter 5.

Transnational scenes are conducive to critical reflection. For example, the monotony, routineness, and bare-bones sociality of factory work generates for some Brazilians feelings of loss or diminution of self. Those feelings become objects of acute reflection at other moments. Attempts to recuperate the self may lead, as we shall see, to the discovery of a Brazilianness heretofore invisible. Hence a transnational scene can spur critical reflections on self and identity, a connection I explore at greater length in later chapters.

So let us begin at the factory, the cardinal destination of the transnational human flow from Brazil to Japan.

## *Working in the stink*

In Japan, Brazilians' jobs run the gamut of unskilled and semiskilled positions. Brazilians make auto bumpers, instant noodles, airbags, tofu, electronic devices, friction disks, hard candies, car seats, sewer pipes. They labor as caddies, maids, butchers, hostesses, construction workers. They work in gas stations, pachinko parlors, and love hotels. They care for invalids and wash the bodies of the dead. A few practice more skilled industrial occupations—welder, lathe operator—and a very few work in petty commerce or in white-collar professions as, say, teachers or translators.

Most adult Brazilians in Toyota City, men and women alike, are employed by brokers known as *empreiteiras* to work unskilled manufacturing jobs, typically in auto-parts plants.[4] Shifts usually run nine hours (including an unremunerated hour for a meal at the plant), but most people are eager to work *zangyō*, overtime, because it customarily pays an additional 25 percent over the usual hourly wages (in 1994–96) of about $8 to $9 for women and $12 to $13 for men.[5] It is common there-

---

[4]Empreiteiras, known as *hakengaisha* in Japanese, operate in a legally gray area. The empreiteira is the Brazilian's official employer—not the factory in which that Brazilian works. The arrangement provides flexibility for the manufacturer in the management of its labor force, and frees the manufacturer from concerns over employees' housing, health, and documentation. In short, the empreiteira's contractor can easily add or shed low-cost unskilled laborers, who need not be treated as permanent employees with attendant rights to benefits and employment security. At best, an empreiteira practices benign paternalism; at worst, crude exploitation. Although many empreiteiras are scrupulously honest, cases of abuse seem common. The most frequent are the illegal retention of passports, failure to provide social insurance, underpayment of wages, overcharges for services, and accident- and disability-related disputes. Most, but not all, Brazilian factory workers are employed by empreiteiras. A few, especially veterans of the Japanese scene or dual nationals, manage to arrange direct employment with factories, which usually means higher wages, better jobs, and more respectful treatment.

[5]Despite a Japanese law mandating equal pay, men and women are almost never paid equally, employers customarily claiming (often contrary to fact) that men's work is more arduous.

fore for people to spend ten or more hours a day, sometimes six days a week, doing arduous manual labor. Men must often work the day shift (*hirukin*) one week and night shift (*yakin*) the next, a pattern known as *kōtai* (switching) that many find disorienting and unpleasant. Work is the central fact of life for most Brazilians in Japan, a devourer of time and an overwhelming concern, as even a casual visitor will immediately discover.

Brazilian factory workers described their jobs to me in minute detail. They wanted to evoke in talk the smells, sights, sounds, and sensations of the factory. They wanted me to feel what it was like to do what they did. Indeed, the physical demands, irritations, and dangers of work seemed almost obsessive preoccupations.

I propose to enter the factory through the words of Eduardo Mori, whom we get to know better in Chapter 6. Eduardo's parents went to Brazil from Hokkaido, Japan's northernmost island, during the peak period of Japanese immigration in the 1930s. The youngest of nine siblings, Eduardo was born in 1965 in the central Brazilian state of Goiás. He briefly studied economics in college. Just before coming to Japan he was working in Brasília, the country's capital, as a computer operator for a state-run telecommunications company, earning about $100 per month.

Eduardo describes himself as one of the nikkei "pioneers": he arrived on a tourist visa two months before the 1990 change in the immigration law. He arranged his trip through a "travel agency" in Brasília that was recruiting nikkeis for Japanese empreiteiras. The agency provided an air ticket in return for Eduardo's agreement to pay several times the normal fare over the first three months in Japan, during which time he could not change employers. The empreiteira held his passport as a guarantee.[6]

Since coming to Japan, Eduardo has worked in auto-parts manufacturing, in jobs contracted through a broker. Such jobs customarily pay $2,500 to $3,000 or more per month, depending on overtime. Eduardo's longest stint was at Aichi Industries, which makes bumpers, polyurethane seat cushions, and airbags. He also worked at Tōsei Machine, as did Bernardo Kinjoh (Chapter 7).

---

[6]The Brazilian became in effect an indentured laborer. Parallels with the system that brought Japanese workers to São Paulo coffee fields (see pp. 284–85) are obvious. Although better information and connections now make it easier for Brazilians to arrange Japanese employment, many still use the system that Eduardo describes.

I visited Aichi Industries, a subsidiary of the giant Meiji Tire and Rubber Company, in April 1996. Aichi Industries sends its products to several Japanese car-makers. The firm began hiring Brazilians in 1991, bringing 40 directly from Brazil; later it also began contracting them through empreiteiras. The number doubled to 80 by 1993 (out of about 350 plant employees) and has stayed constant since then. About half are women, most of whom sew airbags. A manager informed me that Aichi Industries employed Brazilians for two main reasons: it was hard to find willing Japanese, and Brazilians were "hungry" (he used the English word) and worked hard. But he complained that few knew much Japanese, or "even English," and that they readily left the plant to take jobs elsewhere.[7]

My guide, a (Japanese) section chief, first showed me the line that produced blue foam car cushions. An acrid odor permeated the building, but it was clean, decently lit, and marked with bilingual safety signs in Portuguese and Japanese. The process, explained the guide, was exactly like making *takoyaki*. Takoyaki are dumplings made of octopus bits, ginger, and wheat batter, steamed in an iron mold. Indeed, Brazilian men were opening molds, pulling out the still-floppy seats, and placing them on a conveyor belt. The pace was steady, demanding constant attention. Further on, women inspected the seats, trimmed excess foam, and repaired defects. We followed green safety lanes to another building. Here bumpers, made elsewhere in the plant, were cleaned, hosed with air, and primed by robots. They then moved into a room where workers wearing respirators were spray-painting them white. The room was thick with paint; the floor, a metal grate, was sticky and the air heavy with fumes.

Eduardo's career at Aichi Industries started out badly. His job interview brought him face to face with a disparaging department chief [*buchō*]. "Right away," said Eduardo, "I didn't like him, because he told me that the job they were going to put me in, even an idiot could do." He almost walked out. They sent him to make car cushions. He described the takoyaki process:

> First you take out the foam, you toss it onto a belt that goes to another section, where they clip the [irregular] edges. The [empty] mold goes [along a conveyor belt] to a person who throws a yellow

[7] I heard similar complaints repeatedly when talking with factory supervisors in the Toyota area.

liquid into it. It's like butter: it doesn't [let the foam] stick. Then it goes through a cooling tunnel, where water is splashed over it. [Then someone] dries it off. Then two people put in wires and iron pieces [the skeleton of the car seat], and it goes to the robot, which fills it. And then it goes to the oven, where it cooks.

The worst job is pulling out the foam after it has cooked. That is where we pick up the conversation:[8]

Eduardo: Because it's really hot, [people] use two, three pairs of gloves. There have been incidents of Brazilians losing all their fingernails, it can cook your fingernails and tear [them] off.

Daniel: What exactly are you doing with your hands?

Eduardo: You have to pull out the foam. It's a mold, like a cake, except you have to stick your hand inside the foam, along the sides, and pull it out. But all the metal you put in there [comes out too]. So it's really heavy. The smell is very strong. It's a chemical they use in the foam. You were supposed to use a mask, but you couldn't possibly work with a mask there.

Daniel: Because of . . .

Eduardo: The heat. The mask made it hard to breathe, so we'd take it off. After a while you'd get used to the smell, but the heat was still very great. In summer it was worse. Sometimes they'd use fans, but with the [intense] heat here, the more they blew the hotter it got. So then they decided to put in air conditioning.

Daniel: How long did you work [in that section]?

Eduardo: Three years. Then they put me in another section, a cleaner one. I say cleaner, less grease, but the section was even worse because it was painting. The hairs of your nose would get all white, the mask couldn't keep it out.

Daniel: I went in without a mask, quickly, just to see, a minute or two, but I could smell paint for days.

[8]For the purposes of this book, literal transcripts would be unnecessarily lengthy and distracting. I have edited the transcripts with an eye to preserving meaningful exchanges, eliminating redundancies, and giving a sense of the conversational dynamics. Ungrammatical punctuation and wording are intended to capture the flavor of speech. Ellipses indicate pauses and hesitations. English glosses, clarifications, and, occasionally, original foreign terms are bracketed. Where there are significant shifts in the conversational flow due to changes in topic or intervening discussions, I separate passages with a line break. I use paragraphs to indicate slight topical shifts, sometimes the result of an omitted exchange.

Eduardo: Right. You're always turning and messing around, so sometimes there's a leak and the smell enters. The paint sticks in your eyelashes, people turn white. You get used to it *(amused)*; sometimes it looks pretty *(both laugh)*. But it's hard, because at every break you go to the bathroom and wash your eyes, you use a lot of eye drops, because they dry out a lot. Did you see the grate [below the painting level]?

Daniel: Yes.

Eduardo: Down below is water. The ventilation goes from top to bottom, so that dust won't rise up onto the bumper. That's why they have that grate there. So the paint falls into the water. But it gets thick and turns into a paste. Every month we remove that grate and do *sōji* [cleanup] down below, but it really stinks.

Daniel: Does the paint also stick in your hair?

Eduardo: No, because of the ventilation, but it sticks in your nose because you *(sniffs)* breathe. Did you notice that the mask has a filter?

Daniel: Yes.

Eduardo: The safest thing is to change it every two hours, except that the company started trying to save money, so you use that filter all day. Sometimes *(covering mouth and nose)* you get so you can't . . .

Daniel: You can't breathe?

Eduardo: Right, the air gets very heavy.

Daniel: How long did you work there [painting]?

Eduardo: Not long. Around six months. When I started painting, I couldn't sleep right. I had breathing problems.

Eduardo was laid off from Aichi Industries in December 1993, moving to Tōsei Machine. There were so many Tōsei workers at Homi Danchi that the empreiteira's bus made three regular stops on the danchi's loop road.

Tōsei Machine, founded shortly after World War II and headquartered in Aichi prefecture, has over a dozen plants worldwide, manufacturing everything from toilet seats to air conditioners to mechanical heart pumps. But its main business is automobile parts. The Tōsei plant in Kariya, near Toyota City, which specializes in brake and transmission components, employs many Latin American workers contracted through an empreiteira I will call Ueyama.[9]

[9]I tried to arrange a visit to the plant, but was instead shuffled off to the empreiteira. At the empreiteira's office I met with a vice president and a Brazilian nissei translator. About half an hour into our conversation, the cautious manager asked that

Ueyama exists only to funnel employees to Tōsei, which it has been doing since its founding in the mid-1980s. With the change in the immigration law, Ueyama began contracting foreign workers as well as Japanese. As of 1996, about 80 percent of those foreigners were Brazilians and the rest Peruvians. Almost all were men. Ueyama supplied about eighty Latin Americans to Tōsei, and fifty Japanese, many of whom were farmers from the southern island of Kyushu.[10] Ueyama does not advertise, operating instead by word of mouth. After being interviewed, prospective employees visit the work site. If they agree to take the job, and if they meet Ueyama's minimal requirements—willingness to sign a six-month contract—they are hired.

Reputedly, Tōsei is a place where anyone can get a job. One Brazilian worker described it to me as "the paradise of the Peruvians." Certainly the firm accepts more Peruvians, whom Japanese managers consider to be inferior workers, than most other companies in the Toyota area. But many foreigners dislike the repetitive tasks and poor working conditions at Tōsei. The worst aspect of the job, everyone agrees, is the bad environment. Brazilians call it "working in the *kusai*," in the stink. The air is filled with threads of fiberglass and other noxious materials. "When a ray of sunlight entered [the factory]," one worker told me, "everything would shine purple." That worker, like Eduardo, quit because he feared contracting lung cancer. Few last as long there as did Eduardo, who made disc brake pads.

Eduardo: You place the compacted material [in the press], close it, and in ten or fifteen seconds the press opens automatically. A smell of ammonia hits you in the face, and a lot of heat. Then you take the piece and place it in another tray. The problem there is the smell. . . . Anyone who comes there for the first time is [also] terrified because they can see a very white dust in the air.

The worst press I worked on is [really] two presses. You have to step up onto a platform, stick your hand in, and put the [material] inside. Then you have to step down, because there's another press down below. There are six [pieces] on top and six below. This gives you knee problems.

The heat there is terrible. When you take out the pieces on top, the

I not use the empreiteira's name, or that of the manufacturing company, in any publication dealing with this meeting. As usual, I refer to them by pseudonyms.

[10]Like the South Americans, these Japanese workers are known as dekasegi, migrant laborers.

heat hits you right in the face. And when you take pieces out of the bottom, you've got to be careful not to burn your hand. You go up, close [the press], go to the other one, over and over.

Daniel: All day, the same thing.

Eduardo: All day.

Daniel: So there was also a danger of burning yourself?

Eduardo: There was a Japanese man who lost this finger here, while I was working there. There was also a Brazilian who worked in the other section. His section made a kind of ring, and if the ring didn't fit exactly in place, the press wouldn't close. If the ring moves out of place, you have to take a small piece of metal and push it. Except that it was quitting time, the whistle had already sounded, and, because he was in a hurry, he decided to—

Daniel: He put his hand in.

Eduardo: He put his hand in, I think it crushed these two fingers like this.

Daniel: Have you had problems with burns or—

Eduardo: Ah, several. At Aichi Industries, too, they have those really hot [molds that pass by on the line]. During the night shift, you get very tired, and sometimes you have to burn yourself to wake yourself up. There's no other way, you rest your hand [on a mold].

Daniel: Did you use a mask there at Tōsei?

Eduardo: You had to use two masks. When I first started working there, I had eye irritation, a breathing problem, for a month or so.

Daniel: I heard that some people don't use [masks].

Eduardo: They don't use them because sometimes they don't like them, but anywhere there's dust or liquid, you're supposed to. When I worked at Aichi Industries, I couldn't stand using a mask, I couldn't breathe. But with these brake pads, that was the time that the World Health Organization declared that asbestos is carcinogenic. That's when I decided to leave [that job].

Since early 1995, Eduardo has worked at a factory making components for car suspensions and auto air conditioners. He now works at a computerized lathe, turning metal disks of a composition unknown to him. The lathes are enclosed; they eject no fragments, nor is there powder in the air. He does not need to use gloves or a mask. This is by far the cleanest and least dangerous job he has held in Japan.

CHAPTER 4

# Middle-School Days

## Up in the morning and off to school

Work and school routines govern activity at Homi Danchi. Those routines have much in common. As in most places, but perhaps more self-consciously in Japan (Kawamura 1999), school is an extended rehearsal for local forms of work. It is a place where children gradually learn how not to play.

Eli, our teenage son, who prefers to sleep in, greeted the clear, breezy September morning with little enthusiasm. Annoyed at the hour and apprehensive about his first day at Homi Chūgakkō, he grumbled as he put on his new summer uniform: a short-sleeve powder-blue shirt, black polyester pants, white socks, and white sneakers with no markings.

Homi Chū, as everyone called the local middle school, regulated more than clothing. When we enrolled Eli during the 1995 summer recess,[1] we were told that he could not commute by bicycle—a privilege restricted to students living at least two kilometers away—and that he would have to walk to and from school without detours, following a prescribed itinerary along city streets. We had discovered a trail that led around a pond and through the woods, but students were prohibited from using this shortcut, which we dubbed the Forbidden Path. So Eli and I trudged together along the approved route from the danchi to the school, twenty minutes distant, eyed surreptitiously by girls in white-and-navy sailor suits and boys dressed exactly like him. Everyone carried the mandatory, indestructible vinyl backpack, color-coded to indicate the child's year of study and inscribed with the Homi Chū insignia.[2]

We followed the students into the school yard. They entered the building, placed their shoes in cubbyholes, put on school slippers, also

[1]The Japanese school year runs from April through March. The six-week summer vacation is the longest break.

[2]For examples of detailed regulations governing student dress and comportment in a Japanese middle school, see White (1994) and Kawamura (1999).

color-coded by year of study, and headed to their homerooms. Eli and I removed our shoes and padded to the office, where we were seated in a reception room with two teenage girls.

By the way the girls carried themselves I guessed they were Brazilians, so I greeted them in Portuguese. Miriam and Tamara Moreira (Chapter 9) had moved to Homi Danchi two weeks earlier from Nagoya. The sisters were wearing the gray uniforms of their former school, and hoped they would not be forced to buy new ones.[3] Miriam was a *sannensei*, a third-year student, and would be graduating from ninth grade in March, when the academic year ended.[4] The younger, Tamara, was a *ninensei*, like Eli in her second year. Making conversation, I confessed to them that my Japanese was poor. They said, in the indulgent tone of voice I had reluctantly come to expect, "Just like our dad." Adults were to be pitied for their slowness; they just couldn't help it.

Their parents had come to Japan in 1992, leaving the sisters in Brazil in the care of relatives. That time had been lonely. Now, after more than a year in Nagoya, Miriam and Tamara could speak some Japanese. When I asked how they liked Japan, they exchanged glances and said, "Sort of." Both hoped this school would be more comfortable than the last, where they had been the only foreigners. Here at Homi Chū, there were a lot of Brazilians.

The girls talked of the beaches in their hometown of Guarujá, where the sand was fine, bathers went into the water, and families and friends grilled enormous quantities of meat. Not like Japan, they said: here the sand was coarse, people stayed on the shore, and they barbecued vegetables, if you could believe that.

Twenty minutes later the assigned homeroom teachers joined us. I uneasily consigned Eli to one of them; she, just as uneasily perhaps, led him away. As I left the school, I heard shrieks coming from the upper floors; later I discovered that it was the normal bedlam of the interval between class periods. That evening Eli told us that his first day at Homi Chū had been the strangest of his life.

[3]The cost of school uniforms (summer, winter, and physical education outfits) totals several hundred dollars.

[4]Japanese must attend six years of primary school (*shōgakkō*) and three years of middle school (*chūgakkō*). High school (*kōkō*) is not mandatory, but since the mid-1970s enrollment in high school has exceeded 95 percent. See Inagaki (1986) for a history and overview of the Japanese educational system; Rohlen (1983) focuses on high schools.

### Middle-school dramas

Eli eventually got used to middle school, but for me it grew increasingly unfamiliar, as I began to understand it better. Homi Chū became a major part of my life in Japan. I had not intended to work with teenagers, but events conspired to draw me into the school. The Japanese government would not permit me to work part-time in a factory: my "cultural visa" status ruled that out.[5] Homi Danchi itself offered limited possibilities for weekday ethnography, for hardly any Brazilians were at home after 8:00 in the morning. In late September 1995, I petitioned Mr. Yasuaki Kagasawa,[6] Homi Chū's principal, to observe classes. I continued visiting the school twice weekly until I left Japan in July 1996.

Since we ourselves had a teenager at Homi Chū, Maria and I quickly discovered that the school dominated children's lives, peppered the family with requests and demands, and dispatched teachers to the house on scheduled consultations. Often Eli would leave home, sleepy-eyed, before 7:00 in the morning, for before-school baseball, not returning until almost 7:00 at night, exhausted from after-school baseball. There were classes until noon on alternate Saturdays, and school-related events occurred all through the vacations. School had its version of zangyō, overtime: to Eli, at least, it felt like that. Hence school activities gobbled up most of each student's waking hours, leaving little time for free recreation.

Whether one considers this arrangement good or bad, it certainly contrasted strongly with my own school experience. Working among teenagers, I sometimes drifted into memories of adolescence. Chuck Berry's song "School Days" ran through my head, cast in a new light. Berry's teenager is "studying hard, hoping to pass," and "working [his] fingers right down to the bone," in his relentless march through classes populated with irritating colleagues and demanding teachers. Berry could almost be talking about a Japanese school. But "soon as three o'clock rolls around," Berry's alter ego jumps up and runs into the street and around the bend, to the "juke joint." The song climaxes with the

[5]Given my nerve-racking departure from Kyoto two decades earlier, described in the preface, I was not inclined to press my luck by working unofficially.

[6]His real name. Names of Japanese are customarily written surname first. Brazilians with Japanese names write them surname last. For the sake of consistency, I write all names in this book in the Brazilian style, given name followed by surname.

teenager dropping a coin into the slot of a jukebox, which erupts in liberating rock-and-roll.

In contrast, the students at Homi Chū do not leave school at the afternoon chimes, for club activities (*bukatsu*) are obligatory. And after bukatsu they must go straight home, following the approved walking route. In any case, carrying money to school is not allowed: were there a juke joint in Homi, there would be no coin to drop in any slots. Even the convenience store is out of bounds. Teachers occasionally monitor the nearby Circle K to make sure that students have not stopped there, and they sometimes lie in wait at the exit of the Forbidden Path, lecturing those who take the shortcut through the trees.

Thus school days at Homi Chū are hardly carefree. But this is not only because they are hedged with rules. Middle-school days are consequential for the years that follow. One of the most popular television shows during my stay in Japan was *Sannen B Gumi, Kinpachi-Sensei*, which recounted the trials and tribulations of a class of third-year middle-school students from homeroom B, led by a wise, benevolent teacher, Kinpachi-sensei. The episodes were coordinated with the actual calendar, so that when the program ended in March 1996, the fictional students graduated along with real students all over Japan. Emotions in Kinpachi-sensei's third-year B class were intense. He never had a moment's peace, even at home: his phone or doorbell was likely to sound at any moment, bringing news of a student's personal crisis calling for his intervention. The students were either bubbling with excitement over romances and achievements or plunged into misery over rejections, family troubles, and the pressures of school.

Gradually it became clear to me why the show was set in the third year of middle school. Adolescence in Japan does not have the same "blackboard jungle" qualities or associations that it does in the United States, but, as Merry White demonstrates (1994), it is nevertheless an intense time of change and self-discovery. Japanese teenagers immerse themselves in friendships; experiment with sexuality; imagine themselves as adults; and gain skill, sometimes painfully, in the presentation of self. All that is material enough for a melodrama. But the third year of Japanese middle school stirs the pot further with multiple and fateful transitions that have no close parallels in the United States or Brazil.

Upon entering middle school a child faces mounting educational and behavioral demands that contrast strongly with the indulgence shown in Japanese primary schools. The school's aim is straightforward: to get its graduates into the best possible high schools. Admission exams, taken toward the end of the third year, scatter students to different schools—academic and vocational, some good and some not—and ultimately therefore into different life tracks.

In the last moments of the last episode of the TV series, after the test results are in, graduation is over, and the students are about to go their own ways, Kinpachi-sensei lines them up in the hallway.[7] He gives a signal for them to race. The students take off, sobbing; they disappear from view. The camera moves in on Kinpachi-sensei, now standing alone and waving, tears in his own eyes. "Sayonara, everyone," he murmurs. The scene is maudlin, but effective. He has shepherded them to the starting line; life's preliminaries are over. The end of middle school is the start of the competition; the students are now on their own.

Students in their third year feel external pressure from parents, teachers, and classmates, and internal pressure from their own ambitions and needs for self-esteem. The third year is, by reputation, one of stress and unhappiness. But the third year is also a social hothouse. Companions from early childhood have passed together through grade school and junior high. The Sannen B class students, like their counterparts in the real world, live a bittersweet last moment of camaraderie, working through their private dramas with the help of one another in social settings—the classroom and relational networks associated with it—that are about to dissolve forever.

Of course, incoming Brazilian students understand nothing of all this: the dramas lived by the Japanese students are not theirs, and are hardly even imaginable. Language severely impairs contacts between Brazilian and Japanese students, but life histories and circumstances constitute a more profound barrier. The Brazilians inhabit a parallel world. Kinpachi-sensei himself might have trouble resolving their crises; the Japanese teachers at Homi Chū, though they gamely tried, were forced to improvise, often unsuccessfully, in situations for which they had no script. Those who operate the Japanese educational system find it difficult to locate the Brazilians within it, for the system is designed, from the beginning, to prepare students for examinations that few Brazilians will ever take and for careers that few of them will follow in a country that few of them will make their permanent home. Add to that linguistic and cultural differences, and you have a recipe for massive miscommunication.

Homi Chū is geared into a sociocultural matrix that at present has

[7]Aired March 28, 1996.

no clear place for the Brazilian students. The messages circulated within the school were intended for Japanese students headed for Japanese high schools, Japanese universities, and Japanese companies. Those messages evoked other meanings for Brazilians, often producing confusion, annoyance, sadness, and alienation.

## Messages

Notwithstanding its recent vintage, Homi Chū's use of space promotes values described a half-century ago in Ruth Benedict's controversial classic *The Chrysanthemum and the Sword* (1946). These include emphases on self-discipline, respect-based hierarchies, ascribed statuses, "everything in its place," and group affiliation and cooperation. Of course, such values no longer reinforce militaristic nationalism, as in Benedict's time; they now serve other, mainly economic and familial, purposes. Moreover, they are not universally appreciated. Homi Chū's faculty differ in perspectives and politics, and students do not always comply with explicit and implicit directives. But despite such anomalies I was struck by certain insistent, redundant messages encoded in the school's spatial and ritual practices.

Homi Chū looks like schools all over Japan. It offers a clean, orderly, unpretentious, well-equipped environment for learning, but one that does not privilege comfort. The facilities embody, and school activities reflect, a public commitment to education and an implicit claim that study prospers in a certain absence of physical ease. Japanese educational philosophy affirms that learning is a joint product of opportunity, discipline, and effort. Learning depends above all on focus and determination (White 1994:22–23). One of the first exhortations Brazilian newcomers hear, from both teachers and Japanese students, and one that they sometimes come to resent, is *Ganbatte!*—"Keep trying!" Homi Chū's official motto is "Will power, patience, courage" (Homi Chūgakkō 1995:4).

The school's architecture reveals much about its educational philosophy and social hierarchy, which are continually reinforced through a range of everyday practices and special rituals. The grounds are groomed, there is no graffiti, and the condition of the physical plant is good. A row of out-buildings stands along the northern perimeter of the campus. These include a small greenhouse, used in botanical instruction; the *jūdōkan*, a hall for practicing martial arts; and the enormous gym, with a stage and basketball courts, flanked by a large but unheated outdoor swimming pool.

Students enter the classroom building via the south-side playground, a level dirt expanse used as a track, soccer field, or baseball diamond. They pass first through banks of *kutsubako*, wooden shoe compartments used when changing between outdoor sneakers and school slippers. There are umbrella stands here but no coat racks: students are not permitted to wear jackets to school, even on frosty January days. This rule is especially rough on the girls, whose winter uniform, a lightweight, long-sleeved blouse and knee-length skirt, is flimsier than the boys' military-style black tunic and trousers. Defying the rules, Brazilian girls sometimes wear extra layers of clothing beneath their uniforms. Many of the Brazilian girls resent what they see as the school's unequal treatment of boys and girls and chafe at gender distinctions made with respect to authority, tasks, treatment by teachers, and curriculum.

The classroom building is functional and bland: a long, rectangular beige structure running east and west. Exhibits of calligraphy and arrangements of freshly cut flowers greet those who pass through the north-side visitors' entrance into the immaculate vestibule, which also displays polished trophies and historical photos of the school. In the main hallway is a gleaming aquarium with neon tetras. The building's four stories are virtually identical. Classrooms and halls are painted off-white and brown, with green floors. There is little color anywhere. If not quite stark, the effect is certainly institutional. Each hallway, lined with panels of windows to the north and classrooms (or administrative spaces) to the south, runs east and west. Every classroom thus has a southern exposure overlooking the playground. The orientation permits classrooms to catch sunlight in the winter, providing an illusion of warmth. The school has no central heating, and the kerosene room heaters, broken out only in December, emit acrid fumes. Even with the heaters operating, on cold days one's breath forms clouds.

In most classrooms desks stand in rows. To the rear are cubicles where students keep books and other materials. In front are the blackboard, teacher's desk, and a video monitor suspended to one side. Opaque glass windows shield students' eyes from the corridor. Students rarely leave their homeroom; teachers come to the class. This practice is one of many ways in which a sense of homeroom solidarity is reinforced. At lunchtime, students push desks together, spreading the makeshift tables with cloths and eating simple, often lukewarm food trucked to Homi Chū from a central kitchen elsewhere in Toyota City. The students themselves prepare the tables, dish out the food, and clean up afterward. Students do leave the homeroom for certain subjects—for example, music, art, science, and physical education—but they do so collectively.

There are girls' and boys' restrooms, side by side, at the midpoint of each floor. Red bathroom slippers lie in rows just inside the entranceways. A fire extinguisher is attached to the wall near the restrooms. In the corridors are metal racks draped with the cloths used in sōji, the daily noontime cleanup period when students scrub and neaten their classrooms. Students also perform yard duties such as removing litter, burning trash, and weeding.

Homi Chū's spatial organization reflects and cultivates pervasive hierarchical relations between teachers and students, and among students themselves, binding them all into a differentiated, complementary unity. Homerooms are organized by floor, according to year. The top floor, the fourth, with the longest climb, is for *ichinensei*, first-year students; the third floor, for ninensei; the second, for sannensei. The ground floor is assigned to administrators and teachers. Hierarchy, here encoded spatially, is a dominant feature of life at Homi Chū, as in secondary schools throughout Japan (White 1994:chapter 4). Of course, the school's discourse aims to cultivate, against other tendencies, what its creators view as appropriate sentiments. It does so through representations and performances of status distinctions between groups, on the one hand, and of status equality within groups, on the other.

On our son's baseball club, for example, seniority was paramount.[8] Baseball, played exclusively by boys, is a prestigious activity at Homi Chū, with the air of a formal Japanese discipline.[9] Unlike some clubs with relatively relaxed regimens, the baseball team practices long hours before and after classes, year-round. When it snows, the players use orange balls. The *senpai-kōhai* (senior-junior) relationship, a prominent feature of Japanese social arrangements in general (Nakane 1970) and of school club activities in particular (White 1994:94–96), strongly gov-

[8]First- and second-year students at Homi Chū must join either a sports or cultural club. Among the sports are baseball, basketball, table tennis, and *kendō*; cultural activities include art, ceramics, band, and tea ceremony. Third-year students, preparing for the all-important high-school entrance exams, are exempt from club participation.

[9]Homi Chū is not unique: baseball has high status in Japanese secondary schools generally. The annual summer high-school baseball tournament may be the most avidly followed national sports event of the year. Baseball in Japan has undergone a thorough cultural transformation. Note that the gender-exclusiveness of baseball reinforces distinctions that privilege males.

erns player interactions. Younger students address older students as "senpai." Kōhai are to show senpai respect, and to do what senpai tell them. In the infrequent games—for training occupies infinitely more time than competition—senpai play ahead of kōhai, regardless of who is more skillful. First-year students have to chase down stray balls, carry water, and clean up after the older students. The cry *Ichinen!*—"First-year student!"—always brings a seventh-grader on the run.

In 1990, when not a single foreign student attended Homi Chū, I imagine that, aside from a conservative leaning, it differed little from other Japanese public middle schools. But today Homi Chū is extraordinary. In the ground-floor hallway, beside the neon tetras, is a large hand-drawn map of the Americas. Surrounding it are photos of Homi Chū's foreign-born students, clustered by place of origin. The Brazilians, now accounting for approximately 5 percent of the school's enrollment, are further grouped by home state. In September 1995, thirty-three of Homi Chū's thirty-six foreign-born students were Brazilians, most from the state of São Paulo.[10]

Topping this unusual photo display is a striking poster, a red-and-white, green-and-yellow composite flag announcing the school's transnational status. Scattered through the halls are other signs of a Brazilian presence. The specialized classrooms bear bilingual wooden plaques, in Japanese and Portuguese, as do the infirmary, the staff room, and the public address room. On the stairwell landings are bulletin boards devoted to students' work. Occasionally displayed are postcards of Brazil, pictures cut from Brazilian magazines, or information on Brazilian geography, customs, or language. At the far east end of the fourth floor, perhaps the most socially marginal location in the entire school, is the *Kokusai Kyōshitsu*, literally "international classroom," where foreign students receive special instruction. The Kokusai, as the Brazilians called it, is where I spent almost all my time during my frequent visits to Homi Chū.

## Brazilian students at Homi Chū

The school offered a fascinating opportunity to explore what, unaccountably, anthropologists often neglect: the worlds of young people. That Homi Chū had as many Brazilian students as any other junior high

---

[10]Source: Homi Chūgakkō. The other foreigners included one Peruvian and two Americans (Eli and a nikkei girl born in the United States who had grown up in Peru).

in Japan—or more, the number fluctuating between the mid thirties and the low forties during 1995–96—made it yet more attractive, given the objectives of my research.[11] Moreover, all the Brazilian students lived at Homi Danchi, which meant that I often saw them after school and got to know some of their families. Toward the end of the school year in early 1996, I interviewed several of the students whom I knew best; some of those conversations appear in Part Three. I focused on third-year students, the fifteen-year-olds who were about to graduate. I thought that their reflections at this critical juncture of their lives would be especially valuable. My unexpected detour into the school was, in the end, a stroke of luck.

The Kokusai was the crossroads of Brazilian student life at Homi Chū. Depending on their knowledge of Japanese, foreign students spent varying amounts of time in the Kokusai. The hours diminished as their Japanese improved, but most were there at least several hours of the school day, working mainly on Japanese vocabulary, reading, and writing.

In time, I came to appreciate what a challenge to Japanese school values the Kokusai represented. Japanese middle-school students normally pass the school day with members of their homeroom; moreover, many nonacademic school activities—sports competitions, cultural festivals, class trips, and so on—are designed to reinforce age-set boundaries as well as homeroom solidarity. To separate out students from the homeroom and send them elsewhere for part or most of the day endangers both, for the Kokusai mixes students from various homerooms and years. In addition, the establishment of a supplementary curriculum for

[11]The numbers change constantly, as students leave and arrive. On September 1, 1995, in all of Japan, there were 3,350 middle-school students who purportedly needed special instruction in Japanese. These foreign-born students were spread over 1,237 public middle schools. About a third (31.7 percent), or 1,062 students, were native speakers of Portuguese (and hence, with few exceptions, Brazilians). More than half the schools had only one foreign-born student needing language assistance; 97 percent had ten or fewer (source: Ministry of Education). These statistics confirm Homi Chū's status as one of the most multinational schools in all of Japan. A telephone inquiry to the Japanese Ministry of Education revealed that on September 1, 1995, Homi Chū ranked fourth in Japan in the number of foreign students needing language assistance. Only one of the three higher-ranked schools, Kaisei Middle School in Hamamatsu, is located in an area with many Brazilians. The figure offered by the Ministry for Homi Chū (twenty) was far lower than the number I know to be correct. According to the Ministry, the criteria used by schools to determine "students needing language assistance" are inexact.

foreigners violates the ethic of equal treatment (of same-status students) professed in Japanese schools. Finally, a classroom like the Kokusai threatens to, and does in fact, create a novel, non-homeroom-based solidarity, organized in this case primarily around ethnicity.

Not surprisingly, Japanese students sometimes resented the Kokusai class and envied what they saw more generally as lenient and special treatment given to Brazilian students. For example, a female Japanese student we knew complained that the Brazilian girls got away with growing their hair long and not tying it back, a violation of regulations. And when Eli and a Brazilian friend one day tinted their hair with a suggestion of orange, the teachers kept silent—though a Japanese student would not have escaped censure. I guessed that the teachers did not want to confront the foreign students over small issues, fearing that absenteeism, already a chronic problem among the foreigners, might worsen, or that the rebellion might take more serious forms (as it did on occasion). Moreover, communicating with Brazilian parents was always difficult: there was the language barrier, and the parents often considered the school's rules petty, hesitating to devote the short time they spent with their children to admonitions. Though the teachers I knew generally tried hard to make the Brazilians' schooling worthwhile, I heard it said, on good authority, that a few of the teachers at Homi Chū opposed the Kokusai's continued existence.

The Kokusai was, then, an anomaly within the Japanese school. But the alternative—keeping the Brazilian children in the usual classes all day—was problematic. The Japanese language is difficult for a nonnative speaker, and bilingual education is nonexistent in academic subjects. If foreign students do not receive special language instruction they will be lost and likely to quit school.

A Brazilian student encounters much greater linguistic difficulties in Japan than in the United States, where one need not learn two new alphabets plus ideograms. Moreover, for all its huge challenges, English has much grammar and vocabulary in common with Romance languages. Japan, however, shares little with any European language. Japanese has adopted some words from those languages, but the cognates— a small percentage of the lexicon—come almost entirely from English, and their sounding in Japanese is a corruption of the English pronunciation. Even loan words, then, are usually incomprehensible to a Brazilian student.[12]

[12]Portuguese was not easy for me, but I could progress and eventually make my-

Despite the extra language classes provided in the Kokusai, most Brazilian students complained that they were mystified and bored in their literature, science, math, and history classes. They could not follow the teacher and could not understand the textbooks. Exams were administered in Japanese, which few Brazilian students could read or write with any degree of skill. They became accustomed to scoring at or near the bottom of the class, as did our own son. And like most Brazilian parents, Maria and I did not have the heart to push Eli to do better, knowing what he was up against.

But Eli would be returning to his own country in a year, and it did not matter so much. For the Brazilian children, poor performance in school had serious consequences. Most had little prospect of passing Japanese high-school entrance exams, and no chance whatsoever of getting into one of the prestigious high schools in Aichi prefecture. As for a future college career . . . one need only consider that the admission of a Brazilian into a Japanese undergraduate program is so rare that it merits long and celebratory feature articles in Japan's Portuguese-language weeklies (Ozaki 1995; Shintaku and Nakamura 1996). Hence except for the one or two each year who get into a technical or second-rate high school, Homi Chū's graduating Brazilian students either continue their schooling in Brazil, which often means separation from their parents, or head straight to the Japanese factory floor.

The Kokusai was not the educational salvation of Brazilian students. But in the more relaxed atmosphere of the Kokusai classroom those students were able to exercise a degree of autonomy within the middle school. They found ways to subvert the school's authority, however mildly, and to create a more congenial social atmosphere. In short, they were able to make this space their own and find a home of sorts within the school.

## The Kokusai classroom

Homi Chū faced an unusual multicultural situation for which there were, in Japan, few precedents or guidelines. The school's teachers and

---

self more or less at home in the language. But trying to learn even spoken Japanese—much less reading and writing—was a discouraging experience. Without a much greater commitment of time and energy than I could realistically afford, it would be impossible for me to gain a sophisticated command of Japanese. I would have to be content with a fractured version of the language suitable only for practical purposes, restricted domains, or small talk.

administrators had to invent ways of dealing with Latin Americans who could say little in Japanese, could read and write less, had difficulties in adapting to the regime of the Japanese school, were unlikely to get into high schools, and formed a critical mass in the student body. Mostly the staff were trying to integrate the Brazilians into the educational system with a minimum of disruption, force-feeding them the Japanese language and hoping against hope that they would conform to the school's general expectations and that a few might be able to continue their education. Some of the teachers—I would single out Mr. Takefumi Takenaka,[13] who supervised the Kokusai classroom during the period I was there—were highly sympathetic to the plight of the foreign students, taking a pragmatic, tolerant attitude that encouraged experimental approaches to their education and softened their otherwise harsh school experience.

Twice a week for nine months I walked to school via the Forbidden Path, usually in midmorning. Tardy students eyed me curiously as they rushed by. I arrived during the break between classes, weaving up the stairs through clumps of raucous teenagers. These recess periods at first astonished me. During class the school was so quiet you could hear a pin drop, but when the break came, students would spill into the hallways and onto the stairs. They would tear through the corridors, yelling and laughing. Boys put each other in headlocks; girls talked excitedly in groups. The teachers abandoned the field, retreating downstairs to their lounge to gulp tea and puff cigarettes.

I never ceased to be a curiosity to the Japanese students. Getting to the fourth floor was like running a benign gantlet of giggles, salutes, and good-natured cries of "Hello!" and "What is your name?" Relieved, I would eventually reach the hallway outside the Kokusai classroom, where there were always Brazilians hanging out. Then the chimes would sound, the Kokusai teachers would arrive on the run, we would go in, and the stragglers, out of breath, would slide through the door just as it closed.

The Kokusai is unlike any other classroom in the school. It has four tables, each seating up to eight students. Although gender segregation and diffidence between the sexes are outstanding features of life at Homi Chū, in the Kokusai boys and girls mix with greater ease. The wall decorations are unusually colorful and plentiful. Large, bright posters, appropriate to a primary school, show *hiragana* and *katakana* sylla-

---

[13]His real name.

baries. There are flags of Brazil; a picture of Brazil's 1994 World Cup champion soccer team; Brazilian tourism brochures; and photos of all the foreign students, identified by name. Some of the Brazilian boys periodically deface these photos with magic markers, adding mustaches, goatees, prison stripes, or sunglasses, which the teachers then erase. Posted on the walls are the latest announcement of school events and a copy of the most recent *Jornal do Kokusai Kyōshitsu* ("International Classroom Newsletter"), both in Portuguese. Attached to the curtain, the door, the blackboard, and other items are bilingual labels in Portuguese and in Japanese syllabary. Along one wall stands a rack draped with a motley assortment of Portuguese-language reading materials: astrological magazines, old newspapers, and dog-eared guides to Japanese life published by KDD, a Japanese long-distance company. Shelves hold bilingual dictionaries and preschool reading games. The Kokusai schedule, indicating which students come which hours, flanks the blackboard, as does an utterly unavailing diagrammed exhortation to sit up straight.

My "observation" in the Kokusai class immediately mutated into a volunteer job. I began, oddly, as a Japanese-language instructor for newly arrived foreign students. My Japanese was good enough to get them through the introductory language manual, but within a couple of months my charges would leave me in the dust. Nevertheless, I continued to see those students in the Kokusai class and around the danchi, and I established close relations with some of them. Eventually, I came to teach a class in Portuguese covering topics in Brazilian social studies.[14] I also befriended the two outstanding bilingual teachers, Rosa Kitagawa (Chapter 12) and Naomi Mizutake (Chapter 14), who visited the Kokusai periodically to assist the foreign students. I worked under the general supervision of Mr. Takenaka, the head teacher of the Kokusai class. All in all, I was therefore able to learn a great deal about the students' lives both at school and at home.

[14]It was obvious that the students' difficulty with Japanese was raising tremendous obstacles to their education. They were learning little math, science, or history, and their knowledge of Brazil and the Portuguese language was eroding rapidly. So Maria and I proposed, at the beginning of the school year in April 1996, to offer Kokusai classes in Portuguese for the Brazilians. Maria, who teaches high-school dropouts in Watsonville, California, offered to tutor the Brazilian students in math, and I would do so in Brazilian social studies. The school accepted this proposal, and for the last three months in Toyota we offered such classes, bringing me back together with some of the students to whom I had taught Japanese months earlier.

*Top*:  Kokusai students, with Mr. Takenaka and Dan Linger (photographer unknown).

*Left*:  Visitors' entrance, Homi Middle School.

*Overleaf*:  Homi Middle School, official third-year homeroom photo (including four foreign students), 1996 (photographer unknown).

### An empty place inside you

Two of the students I got to know well were Miriam and Tamara Moreira, the girls who entered Homi Chū together with Eli. They had transferred to Homi from Nagoya. Miriam and Tamara were glad to escape to a school that was accustomed to Brazilian students. For them, Homi Chū was comfortable, despite their longing for closer friendships.

Tamara: It felt a lot different here, because the Japanese are different.
Daniel: How so?
Miriam: They give you more attention. They're more accustomed to foreigners, they know that foreigners are *zenzen wakaranai* [clueless; "they don't understand anything at all"], and they try to help. ... The girls take you by the arm, "You speak *nihongo* [Japanese], how wonderful." So you start to talk, exchanging ideas.
Tamara: When Catarina[15] arrived, [the Japanese girls] made faces at us, they turned away from us. I thought, Why are they acting like this? I asked [one of the girls]. She said that the girls in her class didn't like Catarina. She said, "It's because Catarina makes friends so quickly and we don't." I thought, It's their problem, not Catarina's. Catarina makes friends because she's a Brazilian. So I said, "But you mean you're not going to talk with her on account of that?" I couldn't believe it. I said, "I don't understand, there's no reason for you—"
Daniel: But I don't get it. [Catarina] had problems with the Japanese girls just because she was making friends—
Tamara: Right.
Miriam: And also because there was a time when she brought chewing gum [to school], and she dropped it, and the girls—
Tamara: She said it wasn't hers, but it was, and the girls *saw* that she had dropped it, and then . . . they called her a liar, only she hadn't known [the rules]. But now, *later*, when they found out she was going back to Brazil, the Japanese girls started to get friendly with her. "You're going back to Brazil, we're going to miss you," I don't know what all.
Miriam: Because it's always like that, in the beginning they always reject you.
Daniel: But this didn't happen to you?

[15]Catarina Iemura (Chapter 10).

Miriam: Here at Homi, no, because right when we arrived we introduced ourselves in Japanese, so they saw, "They know how to speak
Japanese." They came up and started to talk, it was great. I felt a big
difference, Brazilians are really doing well here.

Daniel: Do you also get along well with the Brazilians here?

Miriam: Yes, better with the Brazilians, because you can have a friendship with the Japanese but not that really intimate friendship. . . .
Look, their way of thinking is different, their vision is different. It
seems like they're a friend, they are a sort of friend, but . . . I don't
know how to explain it exactly, but . . . you're just coexisting with
them. I've been here just six months, and they're kind of friends,
they've started to talk to me all the time, they've started to laugh
with me. But to converse, to exchange ideas, it's no good.

Miriam and Tamara are lucky: they have each other for companions, and they have managed to achieve "coexistence" with their Japanese colleagues. Once in a while, a Brazilian student actually flourishes
at school, as did Elisa Aoshima (Chapter 11). But Brazilian teenagers
are more likely to feel at odds with the school, frustrated at home, and
socially isolated. Amália Nakajima, on the eve of her return to São
Paulo, reflects on her year at Homi Chū.

I'm sort of used to [Japan] . . . a little bit used to the school, to the
teachers, even though *(laughs softly)* sometimes I'm sort of . . . sick
of the school, going to school every day. I understand almost everything, but to speak, I don't, sometimes I talk a little with one of the
girls.

The year I've spent here in Japan, it seems that you . . . you get
more and more tired, you feel . . . a desire to talk with someone, you
talk, but it's different. You want to have someone close to you, because they practically don't talk, they're very cold.[16] It's like you're

[16]Of course, Amália's view is heavily skewed. White's discussion of teenage
friendships in Japan is instructive (1994:chapter 6). Referring to *shinyū*, best friends,
White writes: "With a shinyū, you are fully your private self, sharing your best and
worst" (ibid.:145). Both boys and girls typically spend long hours talking with
shinyū, who provide a counterpoint to the more stylized and constrained relationships within groups or between senpai and kōhai. But language barriers and differences in immediate concerns (among other factors) inhibit the establishment of
shinyū relations between Brazilians and Japanese, leaving the impression among
many Brazilian teenagers that their Japanese colleagues are fundamentally untalkative and restrained.

lost, there's no one close to you, you spend a year without talking to anyone. . . . I get home, I do my homework, and then . . . by then it's late, time to sleep. My mother gets home but there's hardly time to talk about anything, and the next day I go to school early. . . . The other day they gave us a paper [to take home], saying that parents should talk more with their children. It's like there's an empty space inside you, you want to talk with someone because they [the Japanese students] don't converse. I think that spending . . . three years studying in a school here in Japan . . . I think that would be very hard, I think I . . . maybe I could do it, but . . . *(voice falls and becomes inaudible)*.

Yesterday I was sitting in the classroom, I think I was daydreaming, and suddenly a Japanese girl there whispered in my ear, "Amaria [Japanese pronunciation of her name], it seems like you were . . . drifting away, to another [place]" *(laughs softly)*.

# CHAPTER 5

# Eating Brazil

## *Killing Japan*

"Never," writes Johan Huizinga (1950:192) of nineteenth-century Europe, "had an age taken itself with more portentous seriousness." In his groundbreaking *Homo Ludens*, Huizinga observes that the expansion of bureaucratic and economic routine pushed playful pursuits to the margins of social activity. Earlier, the ludic and the sacred, fused into an extraordinary whole, had been central concerns of human groups.[1] But the Industrial Revolution jolted society into its "indicative mood" (Turner 1987:76), privileging the rational and devaluing subjunctive states of mind such as desire, playfulness, and fantasy.

If capitalist regimes tended to disenchant the world, they nevertheless spawned their own subjunctive forms. Those caged in the utilitarian world of work and production (or school and education) reconstituted play in splinters of "leisure," "break time," "Sunday," and "recreation." Homi teenagers who enjoyed tramping through the woods or frequenting the Circle K did so after shedding school uniforms. Diminished and reconfigured in the shadow of work, play was born again as a pleasurable contrast to material pursuits. Work and play were codefined but antithetical, like matter and antimatter.

If modernity split time into work and play, it split selves accordingly. At work, one had to conform to standardized requirements; at play, one was permitted to indulge idiosyncratic fantasies, tastes, and pleasures. Chaplin was a problem for Electro Steel, and Electro Steel for Chaplin: there was no place for a clown in the factory.

In these postmodern times, playful self-affirmation acquires a national twist. In the Japanese manufacturing plant, Japanese citizens hold positions of authority and make the rules. The economic regime is a national regime. Thus for many transnational migrants, play offers not

This chapter is a version of Linger (1997).

[1]This is still true in areas not yet thrust into Weber's iron cage. See for example Levy (1990) and Parish (1994).

only an escape from time-and-motion discipline, but also a chance to assert national difference. Leisure space, like work space, becomes nationalized space.

Think back to the impromptu praça carved out by Brazilians in the center of Homi Danchi. Hanging out in Homi Praça is a way to "kill time" (*matar tempo*). For Brazilian workers, time is money, a commodity exchanged for a wage. To kill time is to cease being a worker, to live without regard to the Electro Steel whistle, the efficiency experts, and the paycheck. Brazilians have a ready-made cultural antidote to "portentous seriousness": Carnival. Homi Praça, a carnivalesque space, draws its recreational forms and modes of sociability from a Brazilian blueprint.

Homi Praça is not, however, simply a Brazilian play space relocated to Japan. To be sure, Homi Praça resembles a Brazilian praça in ethnic composition and dominant activities. But its context is radically different. The Brazilians who gather in the praça are playing *in Japan*. Homi Praça occupies the center of a Japanese housing complex; its Brazilian denizens work long hours in Japanese factories and move in a world that most of them consider to be both temporary and foreign. The meaning of Homi Praça is as dislocated as those who inhabit it, for they are "killing Japan" along with the measured time of the assembly line.

In Brazil, there are praças, but not *Brazilian* praças like the one at Homi Danchi. Similarly, in Brazil there are restaurants, but not that indispensable play space of any sizable Brazilian community in Japan, a "Brazilian restaurant." This chapter examines Restaurante 51, a transnational leisure scene in the center of Nagoya, Japan. Of the many Brazilian restaurants in Aichi prefecture, 51 is perhaps the most popular, drawing from both the big city and its environs. People come to 51 not just to eat, as they might in Brazil, but to eat Brazil—to engage in the self-conscious reaffirmation and reformulation of their identities as displaced Brazilians.

### A rose is not always a rose

Every credible theory of meaning—structural, interpretive, cognitive, psychoanalytic—emphasizes that significance depends upon context. Gregory Bateson (1972 [1955]) explains the contingency of symbols in terms of cognitive "frames." Let me offer an example. A wild rose evokes a certain meaning; the same rose, cut and placed in a vase on the dining-room table, evokes another. Framed by what we think of as "nature," the rose may elicit ideas of harmony, spontaneous beauty, the wonder and integrity of the nonhuman world. Framed by the interior of a house, the rose's dissonant color, form, and origins stand out as deliberate accents in a humanly designed habitat. Our attention is drawn to the interplay of wildness and domesticity rather than the seamlessness of flower, vegetation, earth, and sky. Figured against a new ground, the rose communicates something else.

Here I compare Dona Lica's, a "restaurant in Brazil," with 51, a "Brazilian restaurant" in Nagoya.[2] Both serve types of food widely consumed and appreciated by Brazilians. Like 51, Dona Lica's is a leisure rendezvous. But symbolically speaking, the two establishments are distinct. Consequently, I shall argue, they propose different forms of Brazilian identity.

The earliest studies of migration distinguished between what we might call *identities-in-place* and *identities displaced*. Clyde Mitchell's classic ethnography (1956) of Bisa migrants to Luanshya, a mining town in the Zambian Copperbelt, emphasized that the contrastive identity Bisa-in-town, intentionally cultivated in a milieu of ethnic diversity, diverged fundamentally from the traditional Bisa identity formed in the monoethnic countryside. Bisa-in-town and Bisa-in-the-countryside were both authentically Bisa, but they were differently Bisa.

The central argument, restated and elaborated in countless works (for example, Barth 1969; Eriksen 1993; Hannerz 1992; Leach 1977 [1954]; Oliven 1992), is that identities are situational. The same autodesignation—"Bisa"—is no guarantee that the meaning of "Bisa" is stable, for the content of "Bisa" identity depends, among other things, on the context in which it is lived. Nor, then, should we expect "Brazilian" identity to have the same value in Brazil and in a foreign land. That is, a "Brazilian in Brazil" likely has a different sense of self from a "Brazilian overseas," and that different self is likely fashioned using communicative forms unknown at home.

Restaurants are key sites of identity-making and identity confirmation. By definition they are places of commensality, and commensality tends to map people into groups—family, caste, gender, class, age set, community of believers. Eating together reinforces sentiments of sameness, even distinction, as people share a table and incorporate common substances into the body. Moreover, foods themselves are powerfully

[2]The restaurant's real name is 51. I have also used the real names of Dona Lica and Flávia Bespalhok. I made about two dozen visits to 51 in 1994–96.

evocative. They can signify well-being or sickness, security or danger; they conjure up times, places, whole scenes from the past, or, perhaps, visions of the future. Finally, eating in a restaurant is a practice requiring knowledge of a cultural script. That is, jointly with others one produces a culturally specific social event. Hence a restaurant provides important symbolic resources for building an identity.

The subdued diffusion of Brazilianness at Dona Lica's "restaurant in Brazil" contrasts sharply with the conspicuous propagation of Brazilianness at Restaurante 51, a "Brazilian restaurant." If Dona Lica's restaurant-in-place quietly reinforces a Brazilian identity-in-place, the displaced Restaurante 51 forthrightly cultivates a displaced Brazilian identity.

## Dona Lica's: a "restaurant in Brazil"

During our 1991 stay in São Luís do Maranhão, a city in northeastern Brazil, my family and I used to eat at Dona Lica's, a no-name cafe a few steps from our house in the bairro Madre Deus.[3] Dona Lica's occupied a placid intersection animated only by neighborhood residents going about their daily chores, a passing peddler or cart, the occasional procession heading to the nearby cemetery, or a rare car jolting up from the bayside highway.

You could miss Dona Lica's if you weren't paying attention. The nondescript building was like most in the bairro: plaster walls, tile roof, wood-shuttered windows, of indeterminate age. Inside the cramped, sultry dining room were two or three wooden tables, languidly circled by flies. Out-of-date calendars served as decor. A TV was always blaring from a shelf. The menu, which bore a variable relationship to the actual offerings, was painted on the wall. A huge rubber tree arched overhead, partially shading a narrow cement patio; we often ate outside, seeking relief from the heat. But this was, after all, São Luís, latitude three degrees south: at midday the city's air went still, and even in the shadows the rays of the equatorial sun glanced up from the broken cobbles. Later on, after work, men drifted in, gathering on this same patio. Bottles of Cerma beer, each arriving, frigid, in a white Styrofoam case,

[3]At the time, occupied as I was with research on politics and violence, Dona Lica's was of no particular ethnographic interest to me. I have recollections of it, agreeably tinged with the wistfulness that Brazilians call *saudade*, rather than detailed field notes.

slowly amassed on the tables, as stars began to show through the tree's heavy leaves. Conversation and laughter flowed as easily as the evening breeze off the water.

The cafe was a family operation. Dona Lica herself cooked the meals—usually fried fish, chicken, or beef, with rice, beans, farinha, noodles, and slices of fresh tomato, cucumber, and onion. Her food was hearty, plentiful, and unaffected, made with straightforward ingredients and unusual care. Dona Lica's cheerful children wiped tables and served the patrons, most of whom lived or worked in the neighborhood. Few came from elsewhere to eat here, for the cafe was not chic and did not serve the regional delicacies featured in the famously "typical" *maranhense* restaurants. Dona Lica's did not appear in tourist brochures, nor was it an underground sensation. It was exceptional only within its unpretentious genre of neighborhood diner.

Eating at Dona Lica's was something like eating at home. She and her children treated us well. We exchanged jokes and small talk. They knew our names, and we knew theirs. For me, the anthropologist, eating there fed the welcome illusion that, camouflaged by the cafe, I had melted into the background. I think that eating and drinking at Dona Lica's had a comparable, if less conscious, effect on the local residents, who thereby reaffirmed, with no ado whatsoever, their sense of secure connection to the neighborhood and to the Brazilian universe extending infinitely around it.

Dona Lica's cafe blended effortlessly and naturally into Madre Deus, and Madre Deus rested comfortably in a series of conceptually nested social units: city, state, region, nation. Dona Lica's was implicitly *são-luisense*, *maranhense*, *nordestino*, brasileiro. It is hard to picture Dona Lica's outside its modest bairro. Dona Lica's offered the senses of familiarity and ease that only the local can provide. Having a place at Dona Lica's, one felt one had a place in the world.

Restaurante 51 is half a world away from Dona Lica's, in Nagoya, Japan. It is a combination of snack bar (*lanchonete*), barbecue pit (*churrascaria*), and Brazilian-products shop. Although the cooks at 51 serve up food familiar to Brazilians, 51 bears little resemblance to Dona Lica's, where restaurant is of a piece with setting and Brazilianness is unmarked. Unlike Dona Lica's, 51 is a place of conscious, and paradoxical, connection. It invites expatriate Brazilians to feel at home, offering a multistranded symbolic link to Brazil. But if 51 *were* home, it would not be so overtly, incongruously Brazilian. Framed by a Japanese city, 51 simultaneously accentuates Brazilianness and alienness. In contrast to the matter-of-fact Brazilian identity inadvertently fostered at Dona Lica's, a complex, explicit, dislocated Brazilian identity is thrown into relief at Restaurante 51.

### 51: a "Brazilian restaurant" in Japan

As we have seen, in Japan, Brazilians' workdays are long and their holidays few. Most Brazilians, including nikkeis, speak only halting, limited Japanese, and many find Japanese food and forms of recreation strange or unexciting. Their frustration finds expression in the persistent complaint that "there's nothing to do around here," or, "In terms of leisure, Japan is backward." Brazilian restaurants are therefore important centers of recreation for dekasseguis.

Among Nagoya's many Brazilian restaurants, 51 is perhaps the best known. Its lively neighborhood, called Osu, is an earthy zone of Japanese *shitamachi* (downtown, or popular city) culture. Osu lies just south of Sakae, Nagoya's chief entertainment and commercial district, on the other side of a highway overpass. The shops in Osu—smaller, more specialized, less formal than Sakae's great department stores—display their wares along the sidewalk, announcing their discount prices with hand-lettered signs. At the orange-trimmed Osu Kannon Temple, probably the most visited Buddhist temple in Nagoya, people light incense, deliver short prayers, and feed the pigeons. Then they head into the adjacent arcade to shop.

This arcade, like the temple an Osu landmark, is home to 51, which rubs elbows with noodle shops, takoyaki stalls, sake bars, pinball parlors, dry-goods stores, hair-cutting salons, electronics dealers, and vendors of used American clothing. Many Japanese slow with curiosity when passing the Brazilian restaurant, but few have the courage or inclination to take a seat alongside the foreigners.

Above the tables of the ground-floor snack bar, a Brazilian flag and the logo of Cachaça 51, a notorious brand of inexpensive sugar-cane liquor, adorn the restaurant's bright green-and-yellow plastic sign. The jumble of words in roman script means as little to Japanese passers-by as does the surrounding forest of ideographs to the Brazilians. This disheveled sidewalk cafe is a distinct anomaly. Nagoya has few open-air eateries, and no other that features *guaraná* (a soft drink made from seeds of an Amazonian berry), palm-heart pastries, and desserts made of coconut, tropical fruits, and tapioca.

Up a narrow stairway is the restaurant proper, a temperature-controlled room decorated with Brazilian travel posters and furnished with sturdy tables and high-backed chairs. Just around the corner is 51's boutique, selling Brazilian-made sandals, CDs, greeting cards, perfumes, cosmetics, trinkets, and apparel. Many dekasseguis think Japanese clothes disguise, rather than flatter, body lines. Next door, under separate management, is a food shop that stocks packaged, frozen, and canned goods, imported mainly from Brazil but also from southeast Asia and Peru.

But the center of activity at 51 is the snack bar. Freezing in winter, torrid in summer, it nevertheless attracts a clientele year-round. A counter faces the foot traffic of the mall. Behind it are shelves that hold reading materials and videos of Brazilian TV programs.[4] Bilingual dictionaries and road atlases of Japan are also for sale, but the most popular publications are the Portuguese-language expatriate weeklies: *Jornal Tudo Bem, Folha Mundial, Nova Visão*, and the *International Press*, which also publishes a Spanish (but, despite the name, no English) edition. A refrigerator containing Brazilian sausage, cheap Australian beef, and carbonated beverages runs across a back wall.

In front of the counter, rickety wooden tables ringed by rickety metal stools spill into the arcade walkway. The arrangement, tacky but congenial, is unique to the mall. Ashtrays and squeeze bottles of condiments top the plastic tablecloths. Alongside the tables a rack bulges with advertising propaganda from Brazilian banks and Japanese long-distance phone companies, big businesses competing for dekassegui money. One of these companies, the giant KDD, has mounted an international pay phone on the opposite wall, near the grease-encrusted chicken rotisserie.

Standing at the counter, Flávia Bespalhok, a Brazilian from Londrina, Paraná, dispenses snacks, drinks, raw meat, videos, newspapers, sympathy, and advice. Bracketing the cash register sit a thermos of sweetened coffee and a murky aquarium with bubbling water and gloomy goldfish. To one side, savory pastries desiccate under heat lamps. Below them, a misty case displays chilled sweets made with egg whites, chocolate, and coconut. Available drinks include Brazilian beer, guaraná, and of course, Cachaça 51.

Inelegant and haphazard, 51 is cozy and inviting, an arresting contrast to the ultra-shiny, ultra-hygienic Japanese noodle-and-dumpling

---

[4]In early 1996, 51 moved its videos and reading materials to the boutique during a fit of remodeling.

place across the arcade. Around 51's tables gather mostly Brazilians, with a sprinkling of other Latin Americans, Japanese, and sundry gaijin. On weekends, chickens turn and crisp in the roaster; at Christmas, when the weather turns frigid and tinsel dangles above the counter, tiny, expensive turkeys take their place. People come and go. A carefully coiffed *senhora* buys a bottle of cachaça. A young man on a bicycle returns four videos and takes four more. Customers sit down with a newspaper or an Antártica beer. They talk about work, ask about mutual acquaintances, complain about the weather, reminisce about Brazil. "Whatever happened to Lucinha?" A musician recalls that years ago the Varig crews used to smuggle in beef jerky (*carne-seca*). But nowadays you could be in Brazil; the newsmagazine *Veja* arrives before the cover date. Peruvians drink Inka Kola and buy charcoal. An Indian man silently nurses a beer. A Japanese couple warily inspect the cases and opt for a *rocambole de chocolate*, a rolled sweet. An Australian missionary rails about "Clinton's plan to stick a computer chip inside everybody's head." I ask the man next to me: "Do you like Japan?" He shrugs. "I wouldn't say I like it. I've adapted to it."

There are regulars. Kawada, a nikkei, and his wife, Neusa, a brasileira, both in their fifties, work at a nearby love hotel, a popular trysting place. Kawada was a metalworker in São Paulo, but here they told him he was too old for the factory. Neusa describes their job as secure and not too heavy. The two work together. They can change a room in five minutes—the faster the better, because the hotel makes more money with a quick turnover. They get no vacations except for New Year's Day (an unpaid holiday) and one day per week. Every Friday, their assigned day off, they eat lunch at 51.

Takashi, a Japanese traffic worker, comes often. He snacks, exchanges Japanese lessons for Portuguese, struggles through Brazilian magazines, and dreams of the tropics and a Brazilian girlfriend. Makiko, another Japanese, works as a cook in a primary school. She likes *caipirinhas*, made from cachaça, sugar, and lime, and has learned to mix them. Sadao, a nikkei in his forties from Minas Gerais, comes almost every day, downing draft beers in slow succession. An accountant in Brazil, here he is a solderer. One day he announces he is moving to Osaka. He has taken a job in a sewer-pipe factory there; his brasileira wife and two children will finally join him, ending his four years of solitude in Japan. We hoist our glasses and wish him well.

### The view from the counter

Perhaps the best way for me to convey the atmosphere of 51 is through the eyes of Flávia, the woman who presided amiably over the lunch counter during the mid-1990s. She and I talked after work one cold evening in January 1996. Flávia is a professional journalist; her reporter's sensibility is evident in her descriptions of persons and events.

Our clientele is Brazilian, I'd say between 90 and 95 percent. People come not only from Nagoya [but also from] Toyota, Gifu, Hamamatsu. There are two types of Brazilians. There are those who buy their magazine or newspaper, buy their snack, and leave. I know them, joke around with them, and talk to them, but they just buy and go away. Now, there are also those who come every week and stay hours and hours sitting there, talking, making friends.

We've got three or four groups [*turmas*] that come every weekend, to drink, talk, and hang around for hours. There's a group of six or so, who we call the *Turma do Barulho* [the Raise-the-Roof Gang], you can imagine why. They live in different places, they meet here. They're all men. In the beginning each had a Filipina girlfriend. They used to come to the [upstairs] restaurant, in a group of fifteen, sixteen. These days they hang out more in the snack bar. The last time they were here six people drank three cases of beer.

There was a guy who used to bring his guitar, he sings badly, out of tune, just between us *(laughs)*, and every weekend [he and some others] used to come and play music. So it turned into a real Brazilian bar. The Japanese would stop and look, it was really great. I'd improvise *chacoalhos* [shakers]. I'd ask for [dry] beans or rice and [an empty] can of guaraná, and then seal it and give it to them. One of them brought a *surdo* [a drum] once, and so they'd make a band and sing sambas.

It's funny how the Japanese let themselves go [at 51]. Because it's a very Brazilian atmosphere. They start to talk loudly, like the Brazilians. Several have told me, "This is really good, next Sunday we're coming back," and the next Sunday, there they were again.

There are [other] customers who come every weekend. There's a chubby man who comes every week, he buys all four [expatriate] papers, and then he goes up to the restaurant, he eats, he comes down, buys meat, buys [a roasted] chicken, and sits down. He starts to read the paper and chitchat. And so he's already made two or three friends. I think he doesn't even read. It's more like an excuse.

Sadao comes almost every day. He doesn't have anywhere [else] to go. It's always the same thing: first he asks for a draft, then a 51, and he buys a newspaper. He starts to read the paper, but he's not much for talking. Then he drinks five or six drafts. And afterwards he buys another magazine and reads. Sometimes he buys two or three magazines and says to me: "Would you hold these for me? I'll be back tomorrow. It's just that if I keep them on the table, I'll read them today, and tomorrow I won't have anything to read." I hold them for him.

Some customers come just for videotapes. There's one guy, Alberto, his rental record is eight pages long, he rents three, four videos a day. He says this is the only diversion he has here in Japan. He doesn't read or speak Japanese. He works in a pachinko parlor. He almost never eats or drinks anything. He doesn't buy newspapers, he's a video client. And meat too, he buys a lot of meat. Alberto rents the *Fantástico*, *Jornal Nacional*, *Aqui Agora*, *Domingão do Faustão*, the Sílvio Santos show. . . .[5] He never rents sports, and not even novelas [soap operas]. I've told him, "You have to go out, you and your wife." He says, "Go out where, we don't speak Japanese, we've been really discriminated against." I don't know if he's a nissei or sansei, but he's got a Japanese face. He says, "They make fun of us when we can't speak." So they don't leave the house, and the only recreation they have is to watch videos. They watch a lot of videos.

A lot of people have a need to converse, you wouldn't believe it. People come up to me and say they have no contact with Brazilians, or they work in a place where there are few Brazilians. One time there was a person who really made an impression on me. He never came back, I don't know why. He went up to eat dinner, it was already late, about 9:20, we close at ten, but he ate quickly and he came down. He stood there, looking at magazines, and then he came up to me. "I'm suffering a lot because I don't have anyone to talk to." I said, "Listen, come here anytime, there are always a lot of Brazilians." But he was really depressed. . . .

In the beginning, I worked about three months [upstairs] in the restaurant. Now, in the restaurant it's hard to make friends, you're always eating at separate tables. There was a little guy. I called him

[5]These are widely viewed news and variety shows.

Xororó, since he looked a lot like [a Brazilian country singer by that name]. He piled his plate high, and he started to eat, very fast, he was the only one in the restaurant, and then he stopped eating, it seemed like he was feeling sick from eating his food so fast, but he only wanted to talk with me. And he never stopped. And you could see that he needed to talk. He told his whole story, from the time he arrived in Japan, how much he earned, everything. Telling about his job, that he worked by a furnace, that it was very dangerous, that it was very hot. He came back several times. The last time he came he had injured his eye and had almost been blinded. It was his last day of work, it spurted, I don't know what he was working with. . . . It was something that burned at a very high temperature and he was near the furnace, it spurted, except that he managed to close his eye, but it was very ugly here *(gesturing around the eye)*, he was wearing dark glasses. This was before Christmas in 1994. He was going to spend Christmas [in Brazil] with his girlfriend. He never came back.

I spent a month in Brazil in April of last year. [When I returned to 51] everyone came up to me, asking the same thing: "How is it there? Is it OK to go back?" So I'd say, "Listen, my advice is, this is not the time to go back." Many people here say they're going once and for all, never to return. And in three, four months . . . they're back again. I give them advice. People say, "I'm not going to get a re-entry visa, huh-uh, because I don't want to come back here." I say, "Look, it doesn't cost anything for you to go there [to the Immigration Office], you'll spend just an hour, you'll pay ¥3000, you don't know what's going to happen, what you're going to find in Brazil." And a lot of people to whom I've given this advice *(laughs)*, afterwards needed the visa and returned.

People [come to 51] who don't [yet] understand the money. People who've just arrived, who are still looking for work. Because we're Brazilians, and the restaurant is Brazilian, they [come] looking for help. There was the case of a man who had just arrived two weeks earlier. When he came here it wasn't the job they'd promised him, the work conditions were really awful and he wanted to leave. But because he was leaving they were going to assess a fine, and they threatened to keep his passport. He told me the story, and said, "What should I do, Miss? Where should I go?" So I said, "Look, go to the consulate, go to the Association of Nikkeis" [an office that counsels nikkeis with work-related problems]. He came back the next day and said, "I'm not even going to try to collect the money [they owe me]. But I'm going to get my passport." He must have got it, because he never came back.

I remember a guy who came [to 51], he'd wrecked the [empreiteira's] car. . . . Two of his friends were in the car, they were in the hospital, and the empreiteira was threatening to fire him. He didn't know what to do. Once when the [Brazilian] consul came to the restaurant, right after they opened the consulate [in Nagoya], I had him make a map for me, showing how to get to the consulate, I asked for all the information, telephone number and everything, and I posted it. So I gave this to [the guy who had wrecked the car] and said, "Either they will solve the problem there or send you somewhere else."

Another thing that struck me here is the world of the women of the night. For example, during the week, most of our clients are these women. Most of them are hostesses [in night clubs]. But I know of some who are prostitutes. According to what they say, some were deluxe prostitutes in São Paulo who came here and want to keep on being so.

There's a group of women, they work in a hospital. They're older women of fifty or sixty, except that they don't sit down. They buy chicken, on Saturdays. [Sometimes] whole families [come]. Not just mother, father, and child but mother father son uncle aunt brother-in-law . . . The musicians of the [Clube Nova] Urbana [also come].[6] Every six months, [the club] changes its group of musicians. This group that's here now, two of them come, to rent videos. One told me it's the only recreation they have here in Japan.

And Takashi comes two or three times a week. He serves as a guide for those Japanese [who don't know the food], and he always asks me things. Sometimes he fixes on a headline from the newspaper, he says, "This right here I understand, but this I don't understand." So I try to explain to him. And he tries to learn Portuguese. He buys newspapers, he buys magazines, and he buys comic books, and rents videos, but he only rents cartoons, because he says the other things he can't understand. And Xuxa's program—he's a Xuxa fanatic.[7] When I said that Xuxa was coming to Tokyo, he went crazy. "But, she's coming to Nagoya?" I said, "No, only to Tokyo. Are you

---

[6]The Nova Urbana (real name) is a Brazilian nightclub in Nagoya's Sakae district. It employs Brazilian bands on a rotating basis and has its own samba school.

[7]Xuxa, the star of a long-running children's program on Brazilian television, presents herself as an icy blond bombshell.

going there?" He said, "I'm going to try." He's a . . . *fan* of Xuxa.
Any magazine that has Xuxa on the cover, he buys. And there are
two [Japanese] men, rather old, one already has been to Brazil, he
stayed five years in the *sertão* [the arid Northeast backlands], and
the other works in the immigration office. They're learning Portuguese, so every week they buy newspapers.

Takashi frequents a lot of Brazilian restaurants. He goes to another shop where the guaraná is really cheap. One day he just asked
for two *coxinhas* [a savory snack]. I said, "And the guaraná?" "Today I've already had five." *(Laughs.)* He drank five guaranás, can
you believe it. He wants a Brazilian girlfriend, his dream is to live in
Brazil. He wants to go to Carnival too, he adores samba, he plays in
the samba school of the [Clube Nova] Urbana.

There was a [Japanese] boy. He only bought coxinhas, he loved
coxinhas. He had a fascination for Brazil on account of soccer. He
started to learn Portuguese, he learned how to make coxinhas, he
was working here with us. Later he finished [high school] and had to
find a steady job. His mother arranged a job in a *rāmen* [Chinese-
style noodle soup] place. Then he stopped working with us. He was
washing dishes. One day he stopped by in a suit and I didn't know
where he was working. I said, "Ah, today you look handsome, you've
got a date with some girl, right?" He said, "No, this is how I [have
to] work, I hate it."

Most customers know me by name, because I'm always here.
They have me as a friend and a point of reference. So they come up
like this, "Listen, I'm leaving, many thanks for the treatment you've
given me." A man last week, he was always here, [told me,] "I'm
leaving, thanks for the attention, thanks for the kindness." I said,
"Good luck to you, I hope you never have to return." He said,
"That's what I want, God willing I'll never return, I'm leaving for
good." They come up calling you by name. It's not a relationship of
I'm from the restaurant and you're my customer, no, it's a relationship of friendship.

But my boss doesn't like this. He wants me to say to everyone who
comes up, "*Irasshaimase!*" [a formal Japanese welcome]. But I've
been around a long time, I'm the most veteran employee. So there
are people to whom I don't say, "Irasshaimase," I say, "Hi, everything OK? How are you doing?" [*Oi, tudo bom? Como é que vai?*] A
Brazilian never wants to be treated like a Japanese. "Hey, hey, hey,
I'm a Brazilian, what's this." *(Laughs.)*

*Top*: Restaurante 51: the arcade snack bar.

*Right*: Advertising flyer, Restaurante 51: "Feel right at home: Coming to this house, it's just like you were in Brazil!" (photo by Tarmo Hannula).

*Top*: Field research at 51 on a winter day (photo by Keiichi Nagase).

*Left*: Flávia Bespalhok presiding over the counter at Restaurante 51, Nagoya.

## *Anybody home?*

Brazilians in Japan often feel isolated. Most obviously, they are separated from loved ones in Brazil by an enormous distance. Although the telephone provides a slender thread of contact, it is expensive and unidimensional. The occasional sound of a voice substitutes inadequately for what had been a constant, full physical presence. Even within Japan, many Brazilians have only fleeting and unsatisfactory contact with others. Workers spend long hours in silent labor amidst a din of machinery, snatching bits of conversation with colleagues on the way to the factory, during the break, at lunch. Dealings with superiors are limited and usually one-way. Friends and family members often work different shifts, or are too exhausted to converse much when they finally get home. The crushing work routine therefore discourages the cultivation of deep and extensive social ties and can even subvert existing bonds of blood and affection.

One might think that outside the workplace the city would offer a good deal of casual human contact, but that is not necessarily the case for Brazilians. Japanese men often gather in closed settings, in small bars and clubs, behind opaque sliding doors. To a Brazilian, such places can seem uninviting, even forbidding. At Homi Danchi, and in neighborhoods elsewhere, Japanese women meet at playgrounds while supervising their children, or sometimes join one another for daytime outings. Most Brazilian women work during the day, and in any case few know enough Japanese to converse readily. Because they cannot understand what others are saying, Brazilian women do not usually participate in local organizations such as the P.T.A., another activity popular among Japanese women. Indeed, the simplest exchange of pleasantries between a Brazilian and a Japanese can be awkward, owing to linguistic confusion, social clumsiness, or outright incomprehension.

Moreover, the bustle of urban Japan can be deceptive. As Simmel once wrote, "One nowhere feels as lonely and lost as in the metropolitan crowd," for "the bodily proximity and narrowness of space makes the mental distance only the more visible" (1950 [1902–3]). His observation holds with added force for Brazilians in Japanese cities. Brazilian city-dwellers have contradictory attitudes. They have grown up cautious and street-smart, with good reason, but they nevertheless value spontaneity among strangers and a certain serendipity in human affairs. Japanese street life, though busy, tends to be peaceful and routine. It appeals to Brazilians' desire for public safety but frustrates their desire for agreeable novelty and informal dealings that soften urban anonymity. Public space in Japan can be intensely private.[8] The reticence that permits one to maintain a haven of desired solitude in packed public places reads as coldness to many Brazilians, just as many Japanese, witnessing effusive gestures and raucous word play among Brazilians, read loudness and extravagance into Brazilian presentations of self.

Brazilians complain that when Japanese do engage them in conversation, they show little curiosity about Brazil and offer only standard greetings and banal questions. Differences in interaction style and etiquette, about which I will have much to say later, feed this Brazilian irritation. Japanese courtesy discourages direct personal inquiries, unless one knows the other well; Brazilians take personal inquiries as evidence of interest and desire for approximation. What may be respect from a Japanese perspective feels like rejection to a Brazilian.

These culturally based misperceptions tend to drive the two groups apart. Brazilian frustrations give rise to a romantic celebration of, and longing for, *calor humano*, human warmth, a quality supposedly lacking in Japanese. Stereotypes of Brazilians as "warm" and Japanese as "cold" obviously discourage Brazilian attempts at contact. And for Japanese, apprehensions that Brazilians are erratic, boisterous, or threatening make avoidance seem prudent.

But Brazilian perceptions may be accurate in one important respect: most Japanese do not seem eager to include Brazilians among their foreign acquaintances. The Japanese who drop in at 51 are unusual. Brazilians feel that Japanese view them as second-class foreigners (after North Americans, especially Caucasians, and Europeans), and it is hard to argue the point. The gaijin hierarchy evidences itself in the Japanese fetishization of certain "American" consumer goods and cultural icons (McDonald's hamburgers, the Carpenters, James Dean), in the common lack of knowledge about countries outside the industrialized North, and in the calibration of demeanor according to a foreigner's national status.

My own experience as a first-class gaijin has been instructive. Though Japanese have complex and not always positive attitudes toward Americans, everyone knows something about the United States. Moreover, Americans, simply by virtue of their nationality, are viewed

[8]A nikkei friend once advised me, in all seriousness, to kill time on the train by observing the variety of noses, since there was no hope of a conversation or amusing event.

as people to be reckoned with. Sometimes they receive embarrassingly deferential treatment. In contrast, Brazilians, who come from a faraway tropical land, rarely speak fluent English (the "international language"), and usually do manual labor in Japan, command little attention or respect.

In some ways, as I pointed out in Chapter 2, the situation can be even worse for nikkei Brazilians, who are treated as second-class Japanese as well as second-class gaijin. As a light-skinned North American, I receive inordinate praise for my ability to speak rudimentary Japanese; nikkeis are frequently censured for minor linguistic imperfections.[9] The discrimination can be so intimidating as to cause some, such as Alberto and his wife, to retreat into a world of their own.[10] Hence work conditions, discrepancies in interaction styles, and the differential treatment of foreigners all exacerbate many Brazilians' feelings of distance and alienation.

Even leisure activities do not necessarily lead to meaningful connections with others. For one thing, dekasseguis have little spare time. Furthermore, unfamiliarity with Japanese language and culture discourages many Brazilians from participating in the gregarious pursuits widely enjoyed by Japanese—conversing in intimate pubs, soaking in hot springs, participating in seasonal excursions, or taking up traditional handicrafts, for example. One can, of course, frequent the ubiquitous pinball parlors and coffee shops, which are cheap and readily accessible to foreigners, but these are places where people rub shoulders without speaking to one another. Shopping, a major pastime, is another activity involving minimal communication.

Finally, in Japan abstract links with the outside world—through print, film, electronic media—are severed. Brazilians become instantly illiterate. Even those who speak Japanese fairly well have trouble understanding television, and most programs are, by Brazilian standards, visually dull, slow-moving, and uninvolving. Going to movies, in Japanese or in English with Japanese subtitles, seems pointless. Thus Brazil-

[9]Alternatively, on occasion I have heard a Japanese effusively praise a nikkei for speaking "just like a Japanese." Such comments may be subtly patronizing: in honoring the recipient they implicitly point to defective origins.

[10]As Tsuda (1999b) rightly points out, Brazilians sometimes perceive discrimination where none exists. But Tsuda (1998, 1999b) also notes that prejudice against nikkeis is widespread. The interviews here demonstrate that such prejudice often leaks into interaction in subtle ways readily perceived by Brazilians, though it may not take the form of gross discriminatory behavior.

ians are culturally and linguistically marginalized even from mass entertainment and the mass media.

In short, dekasseguis commonly find themselves trapped in an exhausting routine, far from home, with few opportunities for enjoyable distraction or social engagement. As an acquaintance once told me, "Japan is a place to work. Period." Brazilians sometimes describe themselves as aliens from outer space, as Martians. In going halfway round the planet, many feel as though they left it entirely.[11]

Under these circumstances, a Brazilian restaurant such as 51 projects a green-and-yellow beacon of welcome. It offers reassuring food and drink—a bit of mother and home—in its cakes and puddings, pastries and skewered meats, stewed beans and gritty farinha, cachaça and guaraná. Above all, 51 feeds a hunger for familiar communication, serving up a feast of appetizing, easily digestible words and images. At 51, language circulates without hesitation. Idealized Brazilian-style social interaction—casual, fluid, without adornment—is 51's most compelling attraction. The customers expect an informal greeting; they use first names, without an honorific *san*; strangers treat each other with intimacy, asking personal questions, making sly jokes, and sometimes divulging confidences. Literate once more, dekasseguis reconnect with Brazil and with the world. The expatriate newspapers report the latest Rio kidnappings, government scandals, society gossip, São Paulo apartment prices, dollar exchange rate. Familiar cartoon characters, childhood friends, have crossed the Pacific in comic books. Through the videos one can tap the Brazilian airwaves; copies of television programs arrive in Japan within days of their airing in Brazil. Settle back with *Fantástico*, a popular variety show, on Sunday night: it's as if you were in Maringá, Belém, or Liberdade watching with millions of others in the TV-Globo village.[12]

The sale of trademark Brazilian products reinforces the connection: Zoomp jeans, Senzala coffee, Sonho de Valsa bonbons, Flamengo soccer pennants, Mamonas CDs, perfumes made from Amazonian flowers . . . In a single outing to 51 you can feed, clothe, scent, and surround yourself with goods that speak eloquently and forcefully of Brazil.

[11]As always, generalizations violate some people's experience. Some Brazilians in Japan learn to speak the language well, adapt readily, find Japanese life satisfying, and have no desire ever to return to Brazil. Similarly, some Japanese do take a strong interest in Brazil and Brazilians. Japanese are, of course, hardly unique among First-Worlders in their general ignorance of and lack of interest in countries of the South, and Brazilians are often surprisingly uninformed about Japan.

[12]TV-Globo is Brazil's biggest network and the fourth largest in the world.

The very name 51 is a brilliant choice. Instantly recognizable to a Brazilian, antithetical to the world of work and serious pursuits, "51" is a concise code for the common people and the neighborhood; for evenings at the corner bar; for nights filled with confessions, complaints, belly laughs, and nonsense; for the sound of samba at dawn; for the dangers, uncertainties, and pleasures of the Brazilian streets. And what could be more meaningless to a Japanese than these two digits? From its name to its food and drink to its social ambience, Restaurante 51 presents itself as an open secret, inviting those who know and mystifying those who don't. It has the air of a slightly malicious joke—a wry Brazilian jest—perpetrated on the Osu arcade, on the country itself, which so often bewilders Brazilians with forbidding ideographs, complicated etiquette, unidentifiable foods, and unfathomable rules.

A Brazilian place in an alien environment, 51 revels in its Brazilianness, thereby delivering a paradoxical message—that one is not in Brazil, for Brazil itself is never so overtly, intensely Brazilian. Dona Lica's uses no cunning name, no green-and-yellow sign, no posters of Sugarloaf. It peddles no soccer jerseys, no perfume, no raw meat, no newspapers, no videotapes. The Southern Cross hangs in the sky above Dona Lica's, not in the plastic replica of a flag suspended in a wintry arcade. Dona Lica's is down-deep Brazilian, Brazilian somewhere below the threshold of awareness.

In contrast, 51's displaced Brazilians consume displaced food and displaced goods. Mitchell's study of Copperbelt ethnicity (1956) once again comes to mind. The Brazilians who frequent 51 resemble the Bisa-in-town, not the Bisa-in-the-countryside. The Bisa men of Luanshya created a dance, which they called the *kalela* dance. The kalela dance was a novel urban cultural form, performed on Sunday afternoons before a tribally mixed audience, that celebrated an insistent Bisa identity within a multiethnic universe. The dancers, immaculately groomed laborers smartly attired in European dress, moved in a circle, singing the praises of their own group and lampooning others. For Bisa-in-the-countryside, the kalela dance, whose symbolic language was formulated in an ethnically fractured mining town, would have lacked sense. In short, tribal identity was not an issue, or was a very different sort of issue, in the rural areas.

There are suggestive parallels between such earlier urban migrations and current transnational movements. Colonial Luanshya elicited a shift in Bisa identity, which Bisa workers rebuilt at the new urban ethnic frontiers through innovations in expressive culture. Similarly, Brazilian workers in industrial Japan, having ventured far from home in more ways than one, find themselves entangled in transnational social relations that bring their Brazilianness to the skin. In seeking to cope with and grasp this unsettling condition, they gravitate to Brazilian restaurants.

There are restaurants in Brazil, but no Brazilian restaurants. The latter constitute a Brazilian response to life in Japan. There is ethnic pride, trumpeted through colors, banners, and language; there is a hint of the carnivalesque in 51's disorder, frayed edges, and air of artful complicity; there is something of a jeer in its assertive difference; there is much *saudade*, longing, everywhere at 51. If 51 is a place of relaxed Brazilian-style encounter, it is also a place of intense yearning, of desire to touch what is absent. Isolation and loneliness are as integral to 51 as are connection and sociability. Alberto, the renter of videos; Kawada and Neusa, the love-hotel couple; the anonymous depressed man who never returned; Xororó, the metal worker who couldn't stop talking; Sadao and the women of the night—these and others gravitate to 51's green-and-yellow sign, seeking a link to others perhaps like themselves.

At 51, aliens meet and attempt to convince each other that they are at home. But their very meeting here, at this lusophone rendezvous in a shitamachi mall close by the Osu Kannon temple, simultaneously confirms that they are not. When all is said and done, commensality at 51 celebrates, with considerable spirit and undertones of melancholy, the state of displacement that has become the enduring condition of so many Brazilians at the century's end.

# PART THREE

# Persons

*Workers/ Students/ Intermediaries*

# CHAPTER 6

# Eduardo Mori

## *"One day I'm going home"*

### *Eduardo Mori is not in this book*

The first problem is to hear what Eduardo Mori, or Elena Takeda, or Elisa Aoshima has to say. This is difficult, uncomfortable, and perhaps intimidating, even for anthropologists, who are trained to pay attention.

Specificity, by definition, subverts generalization, and generalization is the stuff of conventional social science. Theories turn specificities into examples. Of course, generalizing is perfectly normal and, to a point, useful. But because it is so normal, so expected, and so extravagantly rewarded in our profession, we might ask what we lose by pursuing theory so ardently.

Theory obscures the uniqueness and unpredictability of persons and events.[1] Person-centered ethnography, when it is not simply illustrative, has, like the variety of fiction advocated by James Baldwin, a paradoxical, sober, potentially liberating indeterminacy. In a scathing attack on the formulaic "protest novel," Baldwin writes:

[A human being] is not, after all, merely a member of Society or a Group or a deplorable conundrum to be explained by Science. He is—and how old-fashioned the words sound!—something more than that, something resolutely indefinable, unpredictable. In overlooking, denying, evading his complexity—which is nothing more than the disquieting complexity of ourselves—we are diminished and we perish; only within this web of ambiguity, paradox, this hunger, danger, darkness, can we find at once ourselves and the power that will free us from ourselves. It is this power of revelation which is the business of the novelist, this journey toward a

---

This chapter is a modified version of Linger (in press).

[1] Any approach that absorbs persons and events into discourse, culture, and social relations has no more chance of illuminating a human life than a grammar and lexicon have of illuminating a particular utterance. To address the specificities of action in the world, anthropology, like linguistics, must turn to pragmatics. And the more radical our pragmatics, the more we confront uncertainty.

more vast reality which must take precedence over all other claims. What is today parroted as his Responsibility—which seems to mean that he must make formal declaration that he is involved in, and affected by, the lives of other people and to say something improving about this somewhat self-evident fact—is, when he believes in it, his corruption and our loss; moreover, it is rooted in, interlocked with and intensifies this same mechanization (1990 [1955]:15–16).

On a more personal note, Baldwin, a black man and a gay man all too aware of the repressive effects of normalizing discourses, describes the "disquieting complexity" of identity-making:

We take our shape, it is true, within and against that cage of reality bequeathed us at our birth; and yet it is precisely through our dependence on this reality that we are most endlessly betrayed. Society is held together by our need; we bind it together with legend, myth, coercion, fearing that without it we will be hurled into that void, within which, like the earth before the Word was spoken, the foundations of society are hidden. From this void—ourselves—it is the function of society to protect us; but it is only this void, our unknown selves, demanding, forever, a new act of creation, which can save us—"from the evil that is in the world." With the same motion, at the same time, it is this toward which we endlessly struggle, and from which, endlessly, we struggle to escape (ibid.:20–21).

Like Baldwin, I am unwilling to reduce human realities to fantasies of exhaustive explanation or to wishful, but likewise mechanistic, polemics. The novel offers an alternative; person-centered ethnography does too. Both novels and ethnographies can be crude, clumsy, pinched, self-serving, self-defeating. Never can they, in good faith, guarantee liberation, and when they pretend to do so, perhaps they imprison us still further. Yet certain ethnographies, like certain novels, can refrain from reducing us to types by recognizing the complex particularities of our struggles in a world we did not create.

That is the kind of ethnography I am trying to write. To be sure, my own presentation of Eduardo Mori, as a Brazilian, as a nikkei, as a thirty-year-old man, and so on, is a retreat into generalization. If I am to speak, I have no choice but to use words that miss the mark. When mistaken for persons and events, generalizations turn us away from the world. But we can also take them into the world, alert to their insufficiencies and ready for surprises. I urge the reader to resist the exemplification of Eduardo, to struggle to hear his voice through the muffling of my prose. I intend my presentation of him as a springboard for the imagination, not a description of a specimen.

## *Living at the crossroads*

Eduardo Mori remembers working as a bank teller in Brasília. Enormous queues formed in front of him. A coworker advised him to lower his head and just deal with the person at the window. But he could not escape the nightmarish sensation that the lines kept growing, no matter how fast he worked. He felt besieged and trapped. One day he closed the window and walked away from the job. He worries now that he may not know when he has reached his limit—that he may simply get used to life in Japan.

On Eduardo's living-room wall is a painting of whitewashed houses, an indigo sea, windmills. It might be Crete, or Mykonos. Eduardo's great dream is to travel to Greece, to a perfect island in the blue Aegean.

I met Eduardo through a notice I had posted around Homi Danchi. Beneath a schematic map of the world, I introduced myself and my family, stating that I intended to write a book about nikkeis and thanking in advance anyone who might consent to talk with me. This was for me an unprecedented field technique, born of desperation. The problem was that moving into Homi was like moving into a cemetery. Brazilians lived there, but they were phantoms. On weekdays, and even Saturdays, everybody was working. On Sundays people shopped, or went on an excursion, or slept, or lounged around their apartments. In São Luís ten years earlier, I couldn't stop meeting people. At Homi, in August 1995, I was anxious to meet anyone at all.

Eduardo, a thirty-year-old nissei, and Elene, his twenty-seven-year-old non-nikkei wife, were, like the others who called in response to my little ad, curious and bored. Boredom was my ace-in-the-hole in Japan—people were desperate for novelty in their lives, so why not novelty in the form of Americans who had lived in northeastern Brazil? We first met a couple of days later, at our apartment. Eduardo and Elene brought a bottle of German Riesling. She was vivacious, talkative; he, quiet and reflective. They were amiable people, pleasant and witty. A week later Maria and I went to their place, where Elene had prepared some Brazilian pastries and we traded more stories and jokes.

Eduardo, whom we met briefly in Chapter 3, arrived at Homi Danchi on April 18, 1990. Like many Brazilians, he remembers the exact date. The empreiteira, Daiichi Kōgyō, placed him in an apartment with three other men, a couple, and a child: seven people squeezed into three bedrooms. Later Daiichi transferred him from building to building, three times. Use of the apartment's common spaces, kitchen and bath, was always a matter for negotiation. The housemates quarreled over cooking, cleaning, bathing, entertaining, and washing clothes. Because people worked different shifts, coming and going at all hours, noise was also an issue.

The same year that Eduardo migrated to Japan, Elene traveled to Rome to work as a nanny. Though the Roman family was, she says, neurotic, she loved the year she spent in Italy: the country was beautiful, the people were charming and stylish, the food was marvelous. I could read the subtext: Italy was completely different from, and better than, Japan. Eduardo and Elene married in Brazil in 1991, and she followed him back to Toyota. But from the start she hated it. They lived in one of the empreiteira's Kōdan apartments, which they shared with a procession of Brazilians, couples and single men. Living with single men was bad, said Elene, because they would make passes at her; living with couples was worse, because the wife inevitably got jealous. At first she did not work. But for Elene, who had grown up in a large house in the dynamic city of Rio de Janeiro, rattling around a tiny Homi flat was intolerable.

Elene despised Japanese food, which she thought unappetizing and insubstantial. One day her roommate was boiling *daikon* (Japanese radish) in the kitchen. Elene detests the smell of daikon and berated the woman for not respecting her roommates. On another occasion a Japanese acquaintance served her a sliced fish that was still moving; she almost threw up. Ironically, eating was her main form of recreation during this period, and the cooking demonstrations were the only television shows she could follow.

At first Elene understood no Japanese. Going out was risky, because she could not ask directions. Anyway, there was nowhere to go, and no one to go with. Eduardo was working kōtai, with a lot of overtime. When he worked days, he would get home late, take a bath, and fall asleep in a chair. When he worked nights, he slept by day and then vanished. Homi Danchi was dead, and a night on the town in Nagoya was prohibitively expensive. They both loved movies, but a ticket cost $20. When they did go out, usually they drove the short distance into central Toyota. Elene recalls her pathetic excitement at the spectacle of people in the streets and signs of varied colors and sizes.

When Elene finally went into the factory, the older Japanese women in her section practiced a kind of *ijime* (bullying), passing on extra work to her but otherwise treating her as if she didn't exist. The Brazilian women also seemed distant. Nikkeis from the countryside, they talked of farming and they sprinkled in Japanese words, which left her befuddled.

Home was as bad. One housemate, a man, always stank up the bathroom. Once Elene and Eduardo had to pour two large bottles of Coca Cola down the toilet to unplug it. Her job, cutting material with a large shears, made her hand sore; factory life was wearing on her; the apartment was a disaster. In treating a medical problem, the doctors gave her a drug that made her horribly nervous; then they gave her another to calm her down. The combination of uppers and downers didn't work right. At the factory, she blew up at a Japanese coworker who had the habit of driving a forklift within inches of people. She screamed in his face and shook him; he didn't respond at all. Depressed and at the end of her tether, she returned alone to her family in Brazil.

Several months later, in the fall of 1994, Elene rejoined Eduardo in Japan, determined to look on the bright side. Fed up with the tensions of living with strangers, Eduardo and Elene rented a Kōdan apartment themselves. When I first met them a year later, she was making airbags. She tolerated but did not like the job. The work was tiring, because she was on her feet all day. And it was mentally stressful: one mistake in an airbag could have disastrous results. Moreover, the bosses were always yelling. Once a foreman shouted at a young worker, and then slapped him across the cheek. Just as in the schools, Elene observed. She knew a Brazilian woman whose life oscillated between house and factory. The woman never went anywhere or spent anything. Obsessed with saving money, she began to develop strange mannerisms. She suffered a breakdown and had to return to Brazil.

Although Elene felt better now about Japan, and wanted to learn the language and *ikebana*, the art of flower arranging, she was still bored and annoyed. She complained that Japanese people averted their gaze when talking to her; her father had always taught her to look people in the eye. Elene despised the mechanical life she found in Japan, and found people's fixation on work and money disturbing. At one birthday party, she forbade factory talk, to no avail.

In September 1995, Elene quit her airbag job. She became a hostess in a Brazilian restaurant and night club in Nagoya. The weather turned cold; Eduardo's workdays grew to twelve hours as the factory rushed to meet its annual quota. Eduardo and Elene hardly crossed paths anymore. By the year's end, Elene had moved to Nagoya and the two had separated.

Because Elene was now living in the city, we saw her rarely. Eduardo remained a close friend, but his work schedule was heavy and he withdrew somewhat following the blow of his separation. In early 1996 he bought a computer, joined an Internet service, and started studying English on his own. He began to muse about working in Australia. He could never, he insisted, settle permanently in Japan.

Eduardo was in limbo—but in truth he had been there for some time. He had settled in at a crossroads, unsatisfied where he was and unsure where to move. Eduardo sees many sides of things, and many sides of himself. Since I have the same tendencies, I recognize in him part of myself, the swarm of conflicting impulses and ideas that is sometimes liberating and sometimes paralyzing. It was easy for me to talk with him. I would characterize our conversations as explorations in uncertainty.

## Hierarchy and belonging in the factory

For Eduardo Mori, interactions at work brought a host of conflicts to the surface. The factory is a transnational space: the acrid odor of polyurethane foam is the stink of the lower ranks to which Brazilian workers are consigned. Their vivid descriptions of factory life signal pride in their powers of endurance and deliver a critique of the ethnic hierarchy. Occasionally, however, superiors invited Brazilians into more exclusive, ethnically Japanese, circles. The cues were subtle, and triggered conflicting emotions, for such invitations tended to redraw lines of identification and solidarity. Below, Eduardo describes a series of incidents that reflect both the reinforcement and the redrawing of hierarchical boundaries.

Daniel: Do you feel at ease [among Japanese coworkers]?

Eduardo: I'm not at ease, because . . . I'm a foreigner. They're really nationalists. Sometimes at lunch they talk among themselves, and you just sit there, paying attention because they might want to say something to you. But they're kind of withdrawn. And that contributes to the great barrier, the great distance.

Daniel: Even knowing the language well—

Eduardo: Right. Let's say there are three technicians, and you're a trainee, they'll never discuss an adjustment in a machine with you. They'll never ask your opinion about where to put that machine. So you stay at the margin.

Daniel: Has this happened to you? Can you tell me about an incident like this?

Eduardo: OK. [Once at Aichi Industries] the line stopped. I told [the leader], and he went over there, looked, and went over to mess with the computer. Just in front [of where I was working] there's a tunnel, and you could see through an opening what was going on inside. I noticed that one of the carts [the car-seat molds] had turned over. Everyone was looking for the defect in the computer, and I went over trying to tell them that it wasn't the computer, it was the line. They didn't pay any attention.

So I had to speak with a Japanese man who worked next to me. I grabbed him and showed him, and then, fine, he, as a Japanese, went to tell the group chief, the group chief told [the section chief], there's always that hierarchy.

Daniel: But you were doing the same job as the Japanese—

Eduardo: The same job.

Daniel: And even doing the same work, you as a foreigner—

Eduardo: As a foreigner, I feel like a negative point. I mean, you can't give your opinion. This distance, I can't accept it. This barrier is very great. It's very hard to communicate. Sometimes you know about something electronic, they simply don't ask you. There's a lot of ignorance, like once when they asked me if there are bananas in Brazil. Just from that question I figured out that they knew nothing whatsoever about Brazil *(amused)*. There are bananas everywhere.

Daniel: Yes, they're the most common [tropical fruit].

Eduardo: The most common. I just stood there, what could I say.

Daniel: But maybe it was just an attempt, don't you think, to start a conversation—

Eduardo: It's obvious, but don't ask whether there are bananas in Brazil, maybe if he'd asked if there were Indians I might be able to respond. After all, there aren't Indians everywhere. But bananas *(laughs)* . . .

Daniel: What do you think is the problem in getting into a group here—

Eduardo: It's very great.

Daniel: But because . . .

Eduardo: Well, first of all . . . being a foreigner. Foreigners are different, even with this Japanese face I have. Right away they say you're a *gaijin*. And that takes away all the opportunities you have. I can only manage to get into certain places. I can go to the movies, I can go to a *sunakku* [a "snack bar"—that is, an intimate night club], I can go to the theater, I can go to a baseball game, or a sumo match, sure, those are places anyone can go to. But let's say . . . the golf group, which only a few people can get into . . . Right? I can only go to a certain point. I can only pass through the easiest doors. So there is that barrier.

Eduardo: I was working at [Aichi Industries]. There's a part of the job where the cart has to go through a cleaning process. They called me and said, "You've got to operate a big machine, you've got to pick up this cart with a crane, you've got to suspend it with the crane and carry it to this chamber, close [the chamber], and push a series of buttons." It was all easy for me, I understood how to use the computer, how to use that crane. I was there talking confidentially with the Japanese, and they were saying, "This is the time for him to learn something new." So I started to manipulate the machine, when two [newly arrived Peruvian nikkeis] came up, who were supposed to help clean those carts. I said to them, "Look, this is how the job has to be done, you work the machine like this. You've got to pick it up, open the chamber, put it inside, and close it." Except at that exact moment a section chief was passing by. . . . And a Japanese, when he wants to be discreet, says things quickly while he's walking past. He passed behind me and said, "It's not up to you to teach this to them," and went on. So at that moment there was a closed group. I can't teach you how to work that machine. This has happened to me four or five times. He's on top, and I'm here on the bottom. And those who have just arrived are down here *(indicates even further below with his hands)*. The instant they taught me I went up a notch.

Daniel: So it was a way of saying, we've included you in a privileged group—

Eduardo: Right.

Daniel:—and you can't just include other people, as you wish—

Eduardo: Right.

Daniel:—in this group, that you have to respect the borders of the group that you belong to now.

Eduardo: Right.

Daniel: He spoke so the Peruvians couldn't hear, right?

Eduardo: Right. I felt . . . very strange. I thought, It really isn't a good time for me to teach them. I couldn't tell [the Peruvians] exactly what the section chief had said to me. [But] they must have noticed [something].

The factory excludes, includes, orders, discriminates. It operates on principles of authority, seniority, gender, and nationality. Despite company talk of cooperation and consultation across vertical lines, my Brazilian friends complained that, as Eduardo's stories suggest, the factory had a clear and rigid hierarchy of authority, with designated ranks as in a military service. Hence the company president (*shachō*) outranks the department chief (*buchō*) outranks the section manager (*kachō*) outranks the group leader (*hanchō*) outranks the line worker. Within ranks, those with more seniority (*senpai*) command respect and, to some degree, obedience from those with less (*kōhai*).

The authority hierarchy has an ethnic dimension: Japanese nationals give orders, whereas Brazilians and Peruvians do not. Since their employers are usually empreiteiras rather than the manufacturing companies themselves, most Latin American workers also lack the substantial benefits and safeguards enjoyed by regular Japanese workers. Gender discrimination is evident. Some jobs are not open to women, and women receive lower pay than men for comparable work. Brazilian women sometimes complain of harassment on the job from Japanese men, in the form of suggestive comments or touching. And it may be that nikkeis are favored over their non-nikkei compatriots. Certainly some non-nikkeis think so, though no factory manager ever admitted this to me. On the other hand, several did tell me that they favored Brazilians over Peruvians, a preference that might arise from the somewhat greater cultural distance and racial diversity among the latter.[2]

Eduardo, a Japanese-speaking nikkei Brazilian male with considerable experience in Japan, enjoys only one disadvantage: his Brazilian nationality. That, as he is perfectly aware, is the biggest impediment of all. But from time to time he "goes up a notch," gaining limited admission into circles usually reserved for Japanese. With a comment, sotto voce and in Japanese, his Japanese superiors remind him that he has entered a circle closed to the Peruvian newcomers. Eduardo feels "strange"; he is being forced to take sides here. He feels conscripted into an unwelcome position, torn between gratitude to the Japanese bosses, who have indicated their trust in him, and a sense that he has betrayed the Peruvians. His pragmatic decision to exclude the Peruvians has, for him, a whiff of collaboration with a hierarchical system of which he disapproves.

[2]Immigration to Peru began in the 1890s, a decade before the first Japanese went to Brazil.

Because ethnicity maps onto factory hierarchy, conflicts such as those described by Eduardo touch his ethnic identity. Eduardo's nikkei Brazilian status automatically places him at a disadvantage vis-à-vis the Japanese bosses, and at an advantage vis-à-vis the Peruvian workers. But there is play at the boundaries of those ascribed identities. When Eduardo's superiors ignore his diagnosis of the problem in the line, he runs into the "great barrier" erected against foreigners. The situation foregrounds his Brazilianness. When he learns to operate the computer for cleaning the carts, and his superiors confidentially insist that he withhold this knowledge from the others, he moves closer to an exclusively Japanese domain.

Eduardo is not, of course, a passive participant in such encounters. They spur him to grapple with their meanings, including their implications for who he is. Eduardo's ethnic career has followed a convoluted path, the product of his conscious, reflective participation in transnational scenes such as the Japanese shop floor.

### The identity path of Eduardo Mori

I described my conversations with Eduardo as explorations in uncertainty. Nowhere was this more true than in our discussions of identity issues. The combination of Japanese descent, Brazilian culture, and Japanese residence is for Eduardo a recipe for identity quandaries. Eduardo's move from Brazil to Japan has an ironic counterpart in his tentative, fitful passage from Japanese to Brazilian. The latter trajectory is what I term his identity path—his sequence of identifications with various national and ethnic categories. I believe Eduardo's identity path could have followed a different course and that its future direction is uncertain. Such unpredictability is a sign not of his postmodern insubstantiality but of his gravitas. In our own discussions Eduardo used his playful, nostalgic, and painful reflections to think about who he had been, who he was, and who he might become.

The following interview excerpts highlight four moments in his life when Eduardo seemed to consolidate a different identity. The consolidations are tentative: at all points, Eduardo's identities are at least somewhat blurred. They also vary in duration and degree of emotional commitment. Strung together, the four moments constitute what I am calling an identity path.

## *Moment 1 (before 1990): Japanese in Brazil*

Eduardo: When I got here, the first thing I saw was that Japanese culture had been very much influenced by the West, it had already been transformed, transfigured. I was shocked by this. If my parents came to Japan, they would be very surprised at the difference.

Daniel: Could you talk a little more about [your parents'] image of Japan?

Eduardo: It's a photograph. Once you've found the place, you take the photograph. And whatever's registered in the photograph will last for a long time. That was the image that my parents brought, only it was in a time when Japan was Japan. Traditional Japan, without mixture, without living alongside, maybe practically without contact [with] foreigners. There was a time when posters were distributed in Japan, with a glorious map of South America, and standing before this map was a young woman pointing her finger precisely at South America. And then there was a great movement in which many boats went to Brazil, carrying immigrants to a better life, who knows. My father went alone to Brazil, practically just out of curiosity. And when he arrived, getting off at the port of Santos, he began working in the [cotton] fields.

You had to pull out the cotton early in the morning. Since it was still covered in dew, [the fieldworkers] would be soaked from the waist down, and their hands became callused because you had to break the husk and pull out the cotton.

And soon afterward came his parents. Then came my aunts, my father's sisters, and so began an orderly life, it was Japan carried to Brazil, the Japanese colony within Brazil. Some things from that time still remain today, precisely from that [ancient] tradition. I learned that Japan had been abundant in rice, but lacked other foods, vegetables, fruits, which were very expensive. [There was also] the cultural image, that was the pride of Japan, the seriousness, honesty, the duty, the obligations, and it was always this that I received. It's a beautiful image that I projected, really, all of this I still, always venerated.

My upbringing was rigid, and my father always lamented that he hadn't given us a more comfortable life, because during this whole time we worked a lot. It was a tradition, since I was small, if a family is made up of nine brothers and sisters, all nine would have to work. Later on, with respect to school, my mother was more rigid than my father, studying was a duty, an obligation. Without the understanding that was in school, you could never have a better life. That's the image engraved on me, I haven't erased that image from the photograph. I know that in Japan this type of life, this type of culture really still exists, without being influenced by Westernism.

There was in Japan, there still is in Japan, when there's a large family, the parents get everybody together and say, "Please, when you go out to work never dishonor the name of the family." This was also used in Brazil. In . . . the jobs I've worked, the programs [and] trade unions in which I've participated, I've always carried with me this word, try never to dishonor the name of the family.

Daniel: Did [your parents] talk about their youth in Japan?

Eduardo: No, because their memory couldn't recover their adolescence, just a few points that marked it. [I remember once] when my mother asked my grandmother to buy bananas, and my grandmother said that she would not have had this opportunity in Japan.

Before I left for Japan I asked my mother if she'd like to come. She said no, maybe one day she'd come on a holiday, but to stay, she didn't want to stay here. Now I know exactly why. She comes from a very rural family here in Japan, so she always wanted a comfortable life, and in Brazil she discovered that this life really exists, and that what isn't lacking at home are fruits . . . bananas, oranges, which she eats in great quantities, without worrying about tomorrow. I asked her, what's the memory she had of Japan. There's a peculiar word, to say "cramped," it's *semai*. Japan is very cramped. It seems like she imagined that in the future she could go to a country where she could breathe.

Maybe she wouldn't want to return to the place where she used to be, but she'd want to see exactly what Japan transformed itself into after the scarcity of fruit, after the scarcity of food.

And so I'm making exactly the reverse journey that they made, they went to Brazil and I'm returning [to Japan]. Maybe it's a source of pride for them that in Brazil a seed grew and this seed is returning home. Clearly, I'm not going to stay here long, but I only want to bring the message that Japanese people are fine over there, just as they're fine here, so there should be a link between Brazil and Japan. Yes, this link, very great and very strong, exists.

## Moment 2 (1990): Gaijin in Japan

Eduardo: As soon as the airplane took off, I felt a certain fear. I had hope
for [a positive] change, but I was afraid of what was going to happen. Maybe a moment when things could get out of control. You're a
little lost here, not knowing how to say anything, not knowing how
to write, or ask for help.

Daniel: Describe your first days here, if you remember.

Eduardo: I landed at Narita airport [in Tokyo]. It was really frightening, because there were a lot of Japanese people *(amused)*. I had to
wait, me and four Brazilians. I sat there lost in the airport, and then
came the person [from the broker], and this brought me a little feeling of security.

    I was one of the pioneers. And when I was sitting there dazzled by
the new world, with so many people who were different, even though
I belonged to the [same] race, for me it was a terrific scare. I went
into Tokyo. . . . I'd never seen a megalopolis like that, it frightened
me a lot. Just when I was going to get out of the van, the Japanese
man asked me to wait inside. I saw him go into an office, talk with
four people, and one of them looked out, through the window, and
approached more closely. Then he said, *"Muito prazer* [pleased to
meet you], my name is Onoda." In Portuguese. So I saw that he was a
Brazilian, and this made me feel more calm. We then went to Yokohama, [where I] stayed for a day and a half. It was a dormitory for
Brazilians who were arriving, and so it was, today you go to Yokohama, you go to Nagoya, they were distributing people. And I was
selected to come to Nagoya.

Daniel: Everything was already—

Eduardo: Already determined. So I came here to Homi. There were so
few Brazilians here that it was common for the Japanese to stop and
stand there looking, whispering among themselves. Observing you,
like you were an alien.

Daniel: But how did they know?

Eduardo: Precisely by your style of dress, by your posture. Brazilians
gesture a lot with their hands when they talk, they talk a little louder,
laugh loudly. I felt like I was a, a spectacle, walking around Homi,
because wherever I went people stopped. They inhibited me, they
made me nervous. But you get used to it. Maybe with all this time
I've been here, it's helped me to control a certain fear I had, a terror
of things going out of control.

[At the beginning] I was illiterate, I couldn't read, I couldn't write, I couldn't speak. . . . so I was practically an expert in silent movies, like Chaplin. But little by little I learned the language, I learned their customs, I kept on learning and, today, here I am.

When I arrived here, I saw myself as a foreigner, I couldn't tell if I was a Brazilian or an American or an Italian, at that time I was a foreigner. I was different. Because when someone just arrives here, at that time, when people would stop and look at you, sometimes you would feel so strange that you couldn't exactly remember your nationality.

## Moment 3 (1991): Japanese in Japan

Eduardo: I was thinking [in May 1991] that if I went back to Brazil and if the economy had gotten better maybe I would stay there. The good-bye party here, even in Japan, you leave here and go to a neighboring city, some people feel a friendship, that it will be a while before you meet again. But I was going back to Brazil, which is nineteen thousand kilometers from here, so they would never see me again. Maybe some even thanked God for that *(both laugh)*, that I was going away—

Daniel: I doubt it *(both laugh)*.

Eduardo: Well *(laughs)*, so, the hanchō went, the foremen, and some Japanese [workers] that I knew. Some who didn't talk to me much went because it was a good-bye party. It's usual for [the hanchō] to give a speech, and Japanese people, when they give a speech [because] someone is leaving, the first thing they say is, *Anta no karada wa, ki o tsukete*, meaning, Take care of your body. People say, "Be careful, take care of yourself." That's how they talk. *(Clears throat.)*

At that moment I stopped being a Brazilian, I was a Japanese, it was like a group of friends who would never be separated. At that moment I felt I was a Japanese. At that moment I had a very strong desire to stay. I felt very good to be treated like that. At that moment you think, Hey, I always thought no one was paying attention, but everyone's paying attention now. Everyone knows you really exist. And so I began to understand that there are certain situations in which you're pushed to the side, but this doesn't mean that you're no longer being watched by them, that is, it doesn't mean that when you're sitting at the table, you don't exist for them.

Daniel: So on that occasion you became a Japanese?

Eduardo: Yes, it was at that moment, I think it was only at that moment. That day. It seemed the differences were put aside, it seemed you were no longer a Brazilian, so everyone treated you really like . . . like a . . . friend. And so it was at that moment that I really no longer felt like a stranger.

Daniel: When you say that you felt Japanese at that moment, you're saying what exactly.

Eduardo: That there was no difference at all. There had been this barrier that I talked about. [But this was a group] without rank. There was neither a general nor a captain nor a colonel. Everyone there was a worker. There was no distinction of hierarchy.

At that moment I didn't feel strange, I didn't feel different. You're an American, a Brazilian says, "We're friends," there doesn't exist anymore either an American or a Brazilian, it's like that. There were neither Japanese nor Brazilians there, everybody was the same.

Daniel: Was it that you felt Japanese or was it that you felt, let's say, a human being—

Eduardo: Right.

Daniel:—among a group of human beings.

Eduardo: Human beings. Everybody was united, there was no difference at all, at that moment, nobody treated you like . . . a person of a different color. You were the same color as them.

Daniel: Yes, but you *are* the same color as them.

Eduardo: I'm their color. I'm yellow. *(Laughs.)*

## Moment 4 (1992–present): Brazilian in Japan

Eduardo: With the [June 1990 change in visa regulations] the great mass of Brazilians started to come. I also took advantage of this [change] to see what Japan is like, to get to really know the culture, the food, only it left me wanting certain things. Relations in Japan, Japanese people, they're very cold, and that's something my father, I don't know if he was afraid to say anything but he hid that part, the coldness. For you to have contact with a Japanese you have to win him over first, and in that winning him over you have to hide your feelings. You have to never think about going home, you've got to just think about work. And Brazilians are very different, because a Brazilian thinks about things at home, the family, his parents. In some situations, you can't see inside [Japanese people], it's a very thick wall, so I can't manage to visualize them. That's what makes them cold.

Sometimes they're really rude, sometimes they're really serious, but I think all that's normal here. The older Japanese were accustomed to this, it was a custom to speak in a loud voice, to yell. But sometimes this doesn't bother me, what's important is that the Japanese have a certain vision, I won't say whether it's correct or not, but it's a different vision, and I for my part am still . . . quite Brazilian. I like human warmth [*calor humano*], I like people who are responsive.

Eduardo: Today I'm a Brazilian. I managed to identify myself. After two or three years, you manage to recover your identity. So I am Brazilian.

Daniel: I never expected that. That in the beginning you simply feel like a gaijin, a gaijin from any old planet or country or something—

Eduardo: Or from the world beyond.

Daniel: From the world beyond, and so with time, instead of becoming Japanese you became more—

Eduardo: Brazilian.

Daniel: Brazilian. Why that, huh? Why do you think you didn't become more Japanese?

Eduardo: With time I had to . . . know exactly where I came from. The [Brazilians] were all telling me, "The first thing you should never hide from anyone is that you are a gaijin, you are a dekassegui, you are a Brazilian." No one ever told me, "You have to be a Japanese. You have to be like them, you have to behave like them." Even if they told me I had to be [Japanese] I think I wouldn't accept it.

Daniel: Why not?

Eduardo: Mmmmm . . . I'm very much a patriot, I'm very proud. It's funny, in Brazil I feel Japanese. . . . In Brazil, [nikkeis always] say, "You're Japanese."

[There] I tell myself, You're Japanese. And in Japan now I tell myself that I'm a gaijin, I'm a *burajirujin* [Brazilian, in Japanese]. Maybe with their help saying that I'm a burajirujin, I recognized myself as a *brasileiro* [Brazilian, in Portuguese]. So I think I never identified myself with [being Japanese], only by my features, they're traces that my parents couldn't manage to hide *(amused)*.

Daniel: And when you go back to Brazil, you'll again be—

Eduardo and Daniel: Japanese.

Eduardo: I'm like a person without a country in Brazil. But I've grown accustomed to that. If I really thought that here I'm Japanese, and there I'm Japanese, and if here I wasn't accepted as a Japanese and there I wasn't accepted as a Brazilian, then I'd . . . I'd feel pretty hopeless. But I'm Brazilian here, and Japanese there. Maybe a Brazilianized Japanese, like people say. But over there in Brazil I'm going to have a lot of human warmth, even being Japanese.

Daniel: How to say it. Now you're a Br—

Eduardo: Brazilian.

Daniel: Brazilian in Japan. And before you were a Japanese—

Eduardo and Daniel: In Brazil.

Daniel: And it might be that in the future you'll again be—

Eduardo and Daniel: A Japanese in Brazil.

Eduardo: Like that time [I went back to Brazil, in 1991], really I felt Japanese here, but I thought to myself, Why would a Brazilian try to be Japanese? Is it really going to change anything in my life? Maybe I could keep being Japanese, a Brazilian naturalized Japanese, but I'm not going to have my own life, it's going to be a limited life, a completely closed life. . . . Maybe it wouldn't have much charm [*graça*], much feeling. Things here, I've noted that people do things . . . because of obligation. However much they might one day want me to stay, I'll respect [their wish], but I won't accept [it], because it's a . . . it's a different universe. Your behavior is gaijin. They want you to be a *nihonjin* [Japanese]. Well, I as a Brazilian, I'm not going to pass the rest of my life eating sushi, and maybe *misoshiru* [miso soup], *yakisoba* [fried noodles] . . .

### Truce-seeking

In allowing Eduardo Mori to describe how he has grappled with others and with himself over his own identity, I am trying to let go of my proclivity, as a social scientist, to explain him. History, culture, and social relations confront us all with concrete situations, but they do not manufacture us. We make and remake ourselves, as does Eduardo, through our engagements with those situations. We are not autonomous agents, but neither are we clay molded by history.

Describing the living of human lives offers challenges to the ethnographer, for both the circumstances of a life and one's engagement with those circumstances must receive their due. To complicate matters further, people can sometimes change their own circumstances. Migrating from Japan to Brazil, or Brazil to Japan, one plunges into new and radically unpredictable situations. Lives are collisions between historical conditions, biography, and agency. As Baldwin writes, characterizing his efforts to come to terms with being a black man in the United States: "Truce . . . is the best one can hope for" (1990 [1955]:5).

I doubt that human truce-seeking can be fully theorized, for every human's truce is different. Theory's great overlooked service is to constitute the unexpected—to enable the flashes of surprise latent in any encounter with the world. If our abstractions are not to ensnare us, dulling awareness and sensibility, we must strive to see beyond them, into what Sapir called "the nooks and crannies of the real" (1949 [1939]:581). For this difficult enterprise we need the openness required to witness the uncommon, the unknown, the unforeseen. To end this chapter, then, and to frame those that follow, let me advance, albeit gingerly, yet another metaphor, as a spur to the imagination.

Once I asked Hiroshi Kamiōsako, a Japanese friend who is a Kyoto kimono designer and painter, to take me to a temple he liked that was off the tourist track. We visited a small Zen temple in the city's northern suburbs. The temple had a garden of raked gravel, rocks, and clipped bushes, behind which was an earthen wall and a vista of Mount Hiei in the distance. In the middle ground, just beyond the wall, cedars rose on either side of the far-off peak. The garden's elements were primordial earth-stuff, vegetation, an ancient nonhuman landscape. In such a garden, the careful choice, placement, and framing of natural materials produces a subtle, yet stunning, effect. I am not educated in Zen, nor in the esoteric meanings of Zen gardens. For me, an effective Zen garden has a visceral impact, an earthy, almost tactile specificity.

In such gardens, material and artist are inseparable: one would certainly not want to describe a Zen garden as a product of nature, nor as solely a human creation, nor again as, say, 50 percent natural and 50 percent human. A Zen garden depends for its effect, for its very existence, on the contrast between human engagement with nature and nature's nonhuman intransigence. Subtract either element and you destroy the garden.

Similarly, a person must make a self, and a life, from intractable materials—the conditions of one's birth and the vicissitudes of one's journey through the world. Lives are not aesthetic creations, but they share with some such creations the important fact of irreducibility. The idiosyncratic apprehension and use of unalterable circumstances make persons absolutely unique, despite their immersion in what is in a gross sense the same world.

And perhaps, as the effect of a Zen garden cannot easily be captured in language, such human creations as selves and lives also escape our attempts to couch them in terms of consequence or volition, the most readily available linguistic resources for the description of human action in the world. Some Zen gardens resemble one another, as do some lives, generated as they are out of similar materials and under similar constraints. But in an important sense a particular life, like a particular Zen garden, is an obstinate singularity. To be fully appreciated, it must be taken on its own terms.

I do not wish to push the aesthetically freighted analogy too far. Too often the materials from which selves must be formed are unyielding, unpromising, unsatisfactory, even alien and painful. Selves are often the products of urgent necessity (Wikan 1995); alternatively, they may have a tentative, nostalgic, or longing quality. And selves, unlike scrupulously planned and carefully preserved gardens, are haphazard, subject to accidents, and always unfinished.

But occasionally a self achieves a state of suspended tension, a point of abeyance, suggestive of a Zen garden. If home is, especially in these days of transnational lives, less a physical space than an existential truce, then perhaps Eduardo will someday find a home in the world. I close with a fifth moment in Eduardo's identity path, an imagined opening to the future strongly tinged with yearning.

### *Moment 5 (the future): Brazilian in Brazil?*

Daniel: Is it more . . . comfortable, let's say, to be a Brazilian in Japan or to be a Japanese in Brazil? Do you understand the question?
Eduardo: Mm-hmm. It would be easier for me to be a Brazilian in Brazil.
Daniel: Brazilian in Brazil.
Eduardo: In Brazil.
Daniel: Is that possible?
Eduardo: It's possible. Eh . . . In Brazil . . . I never had anything like . . . anything as rigid as it is here. What hurts you a lot is this very great rigidity. A Brazilian lives a more unruly life, without any rules, but to be sure with a certain limit. A Japanese, he's got rules. Because I'm not much for rules, I'm really Brazilian, and so I think I feel comfortable at home, in Brazil.

Because in Brazil . . . we've got Japanese, we've got Germans, we've got Italians, we've got Americans, we've got Vietnamese, Chinese. So there, a Brazilian, when he meets a Chinese friend, he'll never fail to say, "Hi, how are you doing, how's everything?" I really miss that here. That intimacy, that really comfortable thing in the sense of saying, "Hi, how's it going, how are things, how's your family?" And a Japanese person no, a Japanese only says "Good morning," a "good morning" like, of the factory, really forced. It's that obligatory greeting. With us it's different, we ask with warmth.

I miss that, I miss Fridays, when we leave work and head for a bar. Drink a beer, relax a little. There was always a person to sing a samba, samba is also a product of Brazil, it corresponds to a certain human warmth that's also a thing of Brazil. I miss Brazil, so I think what I'd rather do is really to go to Brazil, to be a Brazilian in Brazil instead of a Japanese here in Japan.

I only have the feeling that one day I'm going home, whether I'm Japanese or Brazilian at home, of this I have complete certainty.

# Elena Queiroz de Assis Takeda

## *"I defeated them all"*

### *Living inside the factory*

Shortly after returning to Japan in July 1995, I took the subway into Nagoya to visit Restaurante 51. As I was sipping an Antártica, a flyer, printed in Portuguese and Japanese, caught my eye. Entitled *Festival Cultural do Brasil* (Brazilian Cultural Festival), it announced a free event in Nisshin, an eastern suburb. A photo showed a man in a tropical shirt spinning a tambourine and four women in scanty Carnival attire. The festival was to feature bossa nova, a show of summer fashions, a local samba school, and bingo. I noted with disappointment that the date, June 4, had passed. But something else on the flyer gave me a jolt. "All proceeds from bingo," it read, "will be donated to the Professionalizing School for Indigenous Peoples of Amazonia." And there was an ad at the bottom for the "Amazonas Camping Hotel," located in Manaus.

I realized that I was looking at an announcement for Elena Takeda's farewell party. Elena had sent me an invitation, but because of my teaching responsibilities in Santa Cruz, I could not get away in time. Elena was now back in Brazil. I felt as though I had seen a ghost.

A year earlier, within forty-eight hours of landing in Japan for a summer of preliminary fieldwork, I had met Elena Takeda. I was staying with Mayumi Sawada,[1] a Japanese woman who lived in Nisshin. Mayumi ran an English school, but one evening a week she offered a Japanese class, taught by volunteers, for South Americans. Through this class she had come to know Elena, and she offered to introduce me to her. Mayumi knew I wanted to meet Brazilians; Elena would be the first.

Elena's family had no telephone, so we went unannounced, on a torrid, hazy Saturday afternoon. I still felt disoriented from changes in time, climate, and surroundings. Through the window of Mayumi's air-

[1] Her real name.

conditioned Toyota I watched the faded suburban greenery, punctuated with motorcycle dealers, pachinko parlors, and discount houses, slide past. Turning off the highway, we entered the grounds of the Chubu Iron Company and parked near a shabby two-story building crammed with minuscule apartments. I stepped out into air so heavy it seemed almost liquid. A striking dark-haired, brown-skinned woman in her twenties opened the door to apartment 203, and we entered a stuffy kitchen in a state of disarray. There was a table, big enough for four or five people to squeeze around, a refrigerator, a two-burner gas stove, and a sink piled with dishes. A fan wobbled and churned, distributing currents of heat. The adjacent living room, scattered with plastic toys, was furnished with a black vinyl couch. An infant boy was crawling on the tatami floor.

Elena greeted Mayumi effusively in Japanese and called upstairs: *Bā-chan, bāchan* ("Granny"). A slight, older woman, about sixty, descended. Barefoot and clad in a plain white dress, she hailed Mayumi, who gave her a bag of fresh vegetables from her father's garden. The granny seated herself at the foot of the narrow stairway. She was a nissei who, Mayumi told me, spoke fluent, if countrified, Japanese. Mayumi presented me simply as her *Amerika no tomodachi*, American friend. Elena wiped bits of leftover food from the table, placed some forks and meat-filled crepes upon it, and produced a can of Schlitz—"American beer"— for me. When directly introduced to her, I said *Prazer*—informal Portuguese for "Pleased to meet you." Her jaw dropped and she became excited. An American in Nisshin who spoke Brazilian was a novelty.

Elena was married to Granny's son Horácio. Ivan, the infant, was their child. Also living in this apartment were Granny's daughter Mika, Mika's husband Romeo, and their four-year-old daughter Ariane. Ariane appeared and lay down silently on the stairs next to her grandmother, who stroked her hair. Horácio, Mika, and Romeo were absent, working overtime in the adjacent factory.

Back in Brazil, Granny informed me, she owned a plantation, currently administered by a manager. Her husband, an issei, died long ago. Then the soil began to give out. Unable to continue growing coffee, Granny started raising chickens and pigs. She described herself as uneducated, but stated proudly that all four of her children had gone to university in Brazil. Like Horácio, formerly an engineer for Coca Cola, and Mika, a pharmacist, they were all now doing manual labor in Japanese factories.

This was Elena's third year in Japan. She told me that Ivan, fourteen months old, had been born prematurely, weighing just a kilo and a half at birth. There had been an Rh problem of a type exceedingly rare in Japan; the doctors had decided for safety's sake to perform an early Cesarean section. They told her she could not bear any more children. She had wanted six. Elena's natal family, petty merchants in São Paulo and Amazonia, were not of Japanese descent. Hence none of her blood relatives were living in Japan, and she missed them intensely. But she praised Japan as a wonderful place with kind people. Though some Japanese might be prejudiced, she observed, "if they see a hungry person they'd give him food, even if he were a *preto*," a black person.

I stopped by Elena's apartment several times during my summer 1994 fieldwork, and on occasion she visited me—accompanied by her son, but without her husband—at Mayumi's. We quickly developed a friendship. From the moment we met she was eager to help me. Someone should, she insisted that first afternoon, document the sufferings of Brazilian workers in Japan. The next day, Sunday, Mayumi, Elena, Ivan, and I drove into Nagoya. We stopped at the Osu Kannon temple, where Elena gave me coins to toss into the wooden receptacle as an offering to the gods. We then entered the nearby shopping arcade, and she introduced me to Restaurante 51. I offered her and Ivan something to eat and drink, but she adamantly refused. Instead, she treated me to a guaraná. And to my astonishment, within a week she had arranged for me to tour the factory in which she worked.

### Chubu Iron Company

> I never thought that there could exist a place as dirty *(laughs)* as this
> factory. For me, this place, at first sight, I thought it was the end of
> the world, the ruins of the end of a war or something *(laughs)*—
> those old machines full of grease, all that pollution. Somebody starts
> out white and clean and by the end of the day they can't even see
> themselves. We're all black inside from the pollution. Ahh *(inhales)*
> . . . it was terrible. I'd never even washed a dish in my life. In São
> Paulo, I had a very peaceful life. . . .
> —Elena Takeda

The Chubu Iron Company was founded during World War II. Its Nisshin plant, dating from the 1950s, manufactures cast iron and metal auto parts, sending its products to Toyota Motors, which buys most of the plant's output, and to Nippon Densō, a Toyota subsidiary. Directly or indirectly, the company is therefore entirely dependent on Toyota. Chubu has won a Toyota quality-control prize.

Of Chubu's 589 employees in June 1994, when I visited the factory, 71 (12 percent) were foreigners, who are supplied through an intermediate company, the empreiteira Daiichi Kōgyō. Of the foreigners, 70 were Brazilian and one was Peruvian. Eighty-six women—eight of whom were foreigners—worked in this factory. Chubu hired its first three foreign workers in July of 1990. The number rose rapidly until 1992 but then flattened out, owing to the Japanese economic slump that continues to the present.

Elena had interceded with the company managers to permit me to visit the foundry and machine shop. On the Thursday after our first meeting, I arrived at her apartment, accompanied by Mayumi, just before noon. Granny was out front, with Ivan strapped to her back. Ariane was collecting crickets and cicadas in a plastic insect box of the kind popular with Japanese children. Soon Elena appeared, in her green work uniform, and led Mayumi and me to a lunchroom the size of a large gymnasium, with rows of tables. Workers selected from the food items offered (noodles, tofu, cutlets, rice, miso soup) and poured cold green tea from thermoses. Brazilians sat together, eating quickly and then going outside to talk and smoke before returning to the clamor and repetitive motion of the shop floor.

Elena and a manager who spoke a little English accompanied me through the factory. About two-thirds of the foreign workers are employed in the machine shop, with the remaining third in the foundry. The Nisshin plant bears little resemblance to, say, a Toyota Motors factory, with its complex robots, air conditioning, and immaculate, stately assembly line. Indeed, it bears little resemblance to photos in the Chubu Iron Company brochure. The buildings—greasy, noisy, fetid, dust-filled, and hot—show their age and devotion to heavy industry. In the foundry, our first stop, the temperature was well over 100 degrees. Sparks fly and conveyor belts clank; a heavy burning smell hangs in the air. Workers wearing hard hats and masks rarely speak. The noise makes it impossible to converse, and in any case the dangerous work of pouring and casting molten metal demands one's full attention.

The machine shop is cooler, but the hissing, pounding, and rattling is even louder. The workers in this area, where parts cast elsewhere are automatically machined to specification, wear no hard hats or masks but do use earplugs. Elena told me that there are nevertheless many cases of hearing loss. The machine shop demands routine, unskilled labor. Though she was currently one of the few women assigned to the foundry, Elena had previously worked here. It had taken her only three or four hours, she said, to learn her job. Our guide added that training for most jobs performed by Brazilians takes a day, or at most a week. The Brazilian workers we passed were too busy to do more than nod or murmur a greeting.

After the factory tour, we retired to a conference room, where I was able to talk with company representatives. A woman brought *oshibori* towels and iced coffee. Such social occasions in Japan are usually formal, but I was struck by Elena's relaxed way with these men. Though she was a manual worker, a woman, and a Brazilian, she joked and bantered easily with them. The fact that she had been able to arrange my visit was itself extraordinary. It dawned on me then—and the feeling was to intensify later—that I had happened upon a most unusual person.

## Meat every day

In August 1994, I interviewed Elena in Mayumi's house. She came, as usual, with Ivan. I dived into the conversation uncertainly. The research was hardly underway; I had been in Japan a short time, and did not yet know what I wanted to know. Elena was the first interviewee of my Japanese fieldwork. I hoped eventually to get around to the topic of Ivan's birth, which I knew had been a dramatic, difficult event, but first I simply aimed to put her at ease, letting her tell the story of her early days in Japan.

Daniel: I just want to hear what you have to say. So, for example, you can start with your decision to come to Japan.

Elena: My family, eh, after I married, I don't know what to say *(laughs a little nervously)*, my husband didn't have any money. My family was against the marriage for that reason, so my husband said, "Then let's go to Japan to earn money to buy a house, so we can be independent," and then . . . we came to Japan to get some money together *(laughs)* . . .

Daniel: And your arrival?

Elena: I thought [beforehand] that Japan was a paradise, clean, beautiful, but the shock I had in Tokyo was . . . it was the same as São Paulo. I had seen on television that the Japanese were going to finance the cleanup of the Tietê River in Brazil, but meanwhile, the first thing [I saw] in Tokyo was a polluted river. I mean—

Daniel: From pollution to pollution.

Elena: And afterwards, all the new cars, and . . . very polite people, they don't cut into line, [they always say] *"Sumimasen"* ["Excuse me"], they let you go ahead. There are no muggings. I left my purse in a supermarket, and the man ran after me to give it back, with everything inside *(laughs)*.

Daniel: Did you [stay] in Tokyo [when you arrived]?

Elena: No, we went to Kameyama. . . . There was a Bolivian who gave us a great job, housing with everything, total comfort—

Daniel: Kameyama, where's that?

Elena: I don't know.

Daniel: But near Tokyo.

Elena: No. It's far away. We arrived in Tokyo in the afternoon, and got there at eleven at night. They picked us up in a van. We had paid our own passage [to Japan]. Most people don't have enough money for that. So we went there, *nossa* [an exclamation[2]], total comfort, eating meat every day, a circular refrigerator that I've never even seen in Nagoya. It swivels. If you want a dish you turn it around and grab it.

[We were living in] absolute luxury. We'd heard that here you led a hard life, you didn't eat meat, there weren't any beans, there were no comforts at all, worse than the life of the lowest unskilled worker [*bóia fria*] in Brazil. So I was astonished. On weekends we went to the beach. We'd say to the Bolivian, "This isn't possible, we didn't come here to lead a life of luxury, we came here to suffer, to earn money, to save," and he'd say, "This is all covered by the empreiteira, you came here to work hard and you have to eat well, eat meat, eat *sashimi* [raw fish, a delicacy], and go out at night." He'd take us to a sunakku, to a karaoke bar, he'd offer us things.

Daniel: Just so I understand, you were staying in a—

Elena: Rented house. There were just two people [in the empreiteira], a Japanese and a Bolivian. This Bolivian, he spoke nihongo [Japanese].[3] The Japanese [owner] was being scammed by the Bolivian, the Bolivian was a swindler. [The enterprise] was managed by the Bolivian. The owner didn't understand anything we said, he didn't know Portuguese. He only understood what the Bolivian said to him, and the Bolivian, he had been a drug dealer or something down there in Bolivia.

Daniel: Where did you work?

[2]Short for "Nossa Senhora," Our Lady (i.e., Mary).

[3]The Bolivian, bilingual in Spanish and Japanese, is presumably a nikkei, though Elena does not say so.

Elena: I worked in a factory that made drinking glasses. The job wasn't terrible, it was hot, we worked hard, it wasn't dirty or very heavy, but it paid much less than where we are now. We had told the Bolivian, "We don't want all this luxury, we want to save money, because we want to take it to Brazil." So then came payday. The Bolivian paid me 12,000 yen [about $120], my husband 60,000. The truth is we expected to get paid 600,000, for working forty-five days. He deducted 80,000 for the telephone. I only called Brazil once. I mean, all those comforts that he said were covered by the empreiteira, he collected everything from us. Well, forty-five days, we couldn't accept a salary like that, so ... He said, "If it's not OK with you, then leave."

Daniel: Who [exactly] was there?

Elena: Three couples, me and my husband, and his sister [Mika] and brother [Arturo], everyone married. [Mika] had left her job [in Nagoya] because [in Kameyama] it was [supposed to be] *really good*, eating meat every day, right *(said sarcastically)*.

Daniel: So after getting paid, you all left?

Elena: We all left.

Daniel: They didn't keep your passports.

Elena: They tried to keep them, but we said, "If you don't give them back we'll call the police." I told my husband, "This is something I can't stand, because I'm a descendant of people who work in commerce and I like things done right, this isn't right." My husband said, "But we're in Japan, this isn't Brazil, if you complain here they'll arrest you." All the nisseis, they're so *afraid*, they just put up with everything. . . . But then my brother-in-law blew the whistle, he said [to the Bolivian], "This is the situation, whether you like it or not."

Daniel: And after that you went to—

Elena: Nagoya. Direct to [the empreiteira] Daiichi, the biggest, I think, in Japan. [Romeo and Mika] already knew Daiichi. When they came [to Japan], they paid three months' salary [to Daiichi] just for the ticket. It was robbery, it was a *mugging*. All the nisseis who came here three years ago went through that. They couldn't call Brazil, they ate the cheapest food, chicken. Fruits and vegetables, only in season, the first three months. That Bolivian had told us to leave the number of our bank account, he would send the money to the bank. We're still—

Daniel: You're still waiting. But what money was that?

Elena: We didn't like [losing] 80,000 [$800] for the telephone. How much is a call to Brazil, how many minutes did we talk. An hour? An hour isn't 80,000. I told my husband, "You've got to at least talk to him about this, if you don't I will." I didn't know nihongo, nothing, but I could speak a little Spanish. I know a *malandro* [scoundrel] when I see one. Just by his manner I didn't like him.

[Once] we went to a karaoke bar. ... [The Bolivian] ordered Cokes for everyone. I said, "I don't want a Coke" *(laughs)*, and he told my husband that I had to have a Coke, as if I was obliged to drink something I didn't want to drink. When we got home, [the Bolivian] called a meeting. He was like a Mafia boss, he sat at the head of the table and talked in a voice intended to make us all bow our heads and listen to him. My husband said, "If my wife doesn't want to drink Coke, she doesn't have to drink Coke." So [the Bolivian] saw he wasn't dealing with the same fools he was used to dealing with. I mean, we were fools but not *so* ignorant as all that.

The Coke [affair] happened during the time when we were taking trips to the beach. We never thought we'd be eating beef, because we knew that beef here costs a fortune. We were eating more beef than in Brazil. My husband wanted to give up his beer and cigarette habits, because here in Japan [the prices] are absurd. He was smoking and drinking more than in Brazil. The Bolivian brought [the stuff].

Daniel: He was paying for it, and afterwards deducted it from your salary.

Elena: He deducted it, an absurd amount. His dream was to be the boss of a Mafia gang, the way he sat at the head of that table, Daniel. ... He was talking *rarara* [gruff sound], like that. My [other] sister-in-law, [who is] Paraguayan, was like this with him, she spoke Spanish with him. They got together to run me down. I had to clean the whole house for everyone, because my [Paraguayan] sister-in-law had had an accident two months earlier. It didn't seem like anything was wrong with her anymore, but she knew that I was coming, me being a gaijin [that is, not a nikkei], and gaijin, for nisseis, are domestic servants. That's what they have in their heads, they don't see a person, they see a maid. Plus this Bolivian was living with us, and his nephew was living there too. There were three couples plus two men. [The Bolivian] said, "Men don't do housework, just women." And my husband said OK.

Daniel: And then you confronted the Bolivian about the salary?

Elena: No, we asked for an explanation. We didn't confront him because we knew he wasn't ... He had shown us old photos of himself, his appearance had changed *(Daniel laughs)*. One photo with a mustache, another with a wavy hairdo, another with straight hair, one thin and another fat *(both laugh)*. No, Daniel, I didn't trust him from the moment we arrived.

Daniel: And his explanation was—

Elena: That my husband was the oldest in the family, that he had to pay the biggest part. But he's not those people's father, he's my husband. So we wanted to get [the rest of the money]. And he was telling the [Japanese] owner exactly the opposite of what we were saying. He thought we couldn't understand anything. I really couldn't understand but my brother-in-law and my husband understood some of it.

[The Bolivian] sent us away, [and we never received the money]. Later we heard that he was going to Bolivia or Brazil to get Brazilian and foreign women to set up a house of prostitution here. So he's really a mafioso, isn't he.

## Bad blood

After forty-five days, Elena and Horácio, together with Mika and Romeo, left Kameyama. The empreiteira, Daiichi, placed them in Homi Danchi, where they stayed a short time before moving into Nagoya.

Daniel: Why did you move from [Homi Danchi]?

Elena: Because of the empreiteira. For example, I go to an empreiteira, I want work, but there's no apartment available. So they stick me wherever there's a place. As soon as another apartment closer to the factory is vacated, they stick me in that one. [At Homi] we were far away, my husband and I had to spend an hour getting [to work] every day. So then we [moved] closer, it was fifteen minutes, and now we're inside the factory.

We spent fifteen days [at Homi]. Then we went to live in Hirabari [a Nagoya neighborhood] in an apartment a lot smaller than this one, me, my husband, my brother-in-law, my sister-in-law, [and] my brother-in-law's father. Really tiny ... cramped. We stayed there two years. [We've been here] seven months.

Daniel: And the Paraguayan woman?

Elena: She and [her husband, Arturo] went to work in pachinko. They live far away, in Nagano [prefecture]. When we meet, it's [always] "*My love*" [spoken in English], you know how it is. . . . Ai, how I miss her *(sarcastic)*.

Daniel: Living there, with Horácio's family. What's it like?

Elena: ... There's really a lot of prejudice. ... It's like black people. You've heard of Mandela, the struggle of Mandela. Well, in that house it's like being black in Germany. Unfortunately, it's their bad luck that wherever I throw myself, I do well. I don't try to get anything, things come to me. This terrifies them, I think it's great *(laughs)*. I think I'm the only Brazilian who participates in the *Fujinkai*, an association restricted to Japanese housewives. My mother-in-law [tried to get in] and they didn't accept her. In this club I taught them how to cook Brazilian food. I was on television here twice.

Daniel: I'm interested in [Ivan's] story.

Elena: I got pregnant [while I was] working. I'd [commute] by bicycle. There was a big hill [between Hirabari and the factory], and sometimes I couldn't make it, I'd have to continue on foot. I couldn't stop working, because the minute my son was born I'd have to stop, and then my husband wouldn't be able to save any money. So I wanted to work as long as possible. My mother worked until her ninth month, why wouldn't I? [I did so] by instinct, on account of my Brazilian roots. Heavy work and everything ... Mmm *(laughs softly, voice falls)*, at home, my husband was drinking, arguing, doing horrible things.

Daniel: Because ...

Elena: ... I don't know, we never agreed about anything.

Daniel: Mm-hmm.

Elena: These days, I can put up with it a little better. I'm not in Japan any longer on his account, but on my own account. I want to see things, and understand what's going on here, the people here. ... But I ... suffered a, a ... disillusionment. He [Ivan] got hit when he was in my stomach *(laughs)* ... eh ... Those kinds of things, right?

I went to the doctor, the doctor said, "You want to have a child and you want to work. Either do one thing or the other." I thought, Are you going to follow the doctor's orders or your own? I *can* decide *my own* life and my son's. So then he did all the examinations. He said, "Unfortunately, you really can't have this child, first because you're working, and now because you have a problem of Rh-negative, you're risking your life." I said, "But I *want* to have this child, just explain the possibilities to me." The empreiteira didn't know I was pregnant yet. [The doctor] said I had a blood problem and it was dangerous, I could die and my son too. [He asked] if I wanted to get rid [of the fetus]. I said, "No, I want to have him and that's that." Then I explained it all to my husband. And I kept working.

Daniel: [The factory eventually] found out.

Elena: After I really decided to have the baby, they did. . . . I was three months pregnant. And then they made me do work that was worse and worse.

Daniel: How come?

Elena: Because when you're six months pregnant, at the most, you have to leave, another person comes in [to take your place]. I learn jobs quickly but there are people who don't. So they were already putting other people in my place to learn my job. They didn't need me anymore, so they made me do jobs that other people wouldn't do, sōji, cleaning, the worst.

Daniel: So it's "Out!," end of conversation.

Elena: *Bye bye* [in English]. And in my case it was terrible, because I'd dedicated myself to my job. A Brazilian [that is, a non-nikkei] has to work a lot harder than a nissei to be able to . . . have some value, not to be fired. So I sweated blood, I was working just like a man, a man didn't do the work I was doing.

Daniel: Did they cut your salary?

Elena: No. The same salary and the worst job. They'd hire [a man] to do the easiest work I had been doing, they'd pay double the salary, because a man makes 40 percent more than a woman. All right. When I went to the doctor, I'd go in the morning. After lunch I'd return to work, so as not to lose the [monthly] bonus, if you don't miss a day you get a bonus of 20,000. I'd work till ten at night, because you have to work eight hours a day, if you work seven you lose the bonus.

Daniel: Were you feeling sick?

Elena: No, I wasn't feeling anything. My problem was my blood. Because my Rh was negative, and my son's was positive, they don't mix, so my body was creating antibodies against his body, wanting to expel him, do you understand? So I had to do tests every week to see if the level went up. I knew that it would, but they might still be able to save his life. At five months they can't save him, [but] at six months and a few days they can. We were really pulling for it, that of the nine months, we'd get to six.

One day, the doctor said, "You're going to be operated on now." I said, "*Really*" *(eyes widen)*. My dream was to have a normal birth, I wanted to be a real mother. . . . He said, "It's going to be a Cesarean, and it's going to be now." And I was going to wait till the sixth month, to buy the little clothes. He said, "You've got two hours." I said, "I can't be operated on [now], I have to talk to my husband, I have to tell them at the factory." He said, "I'm going to do a new blood test. It takes two hours to get the results. This is an emergency, from 94 it went to 1,020, that's an impossible level." It frightened everyone in the hospital, a bunch of faculty came to study [me], I was just like a guinea pig there.

I had two hours, so I went right to the factory [and told them], "I'm not coming back." And I let my husband know I was going to be operated on right away. Then I went to the supermarket, I had to get some thongs and a nightgown, whatever I passed I grabbed, by then I was running. At the hospital, the doctors were scared, because they never had a case like that, they didn't know of a case of a [mother who was] Rh-negative with a baby who was positive. Japan is positive, Rh-positive.

Daniel: Everybody.

Elena: Everybody. Rh-negative doesn't exist. So . . . then there was a meeting at the hospital, "Let's do some tests," and it was postponed till the next day. Then [they said], "Let's examine the baby," taking his blood through my belly. They stuck a fifteen-centimeter needle in my belly, *Gomen nasai, machigai,* "Sorry, I made a mistake, one more time" *(laughs)*. Three times like that, they finally took some blood from his umbilical cord. Usually they take amniotic liquid, but [the doctor] took it from the umbilical cord, he was messing around, it was difficult.

They did the test and saw they didn't have his blood type in the hospital, and when he was born he was going to need [transfusions]. [It had to come] from another hospital in Nagoya, blood for my son and for me too, because I had a bad anemia. So . . . waiting, waiting, waiting. I couldn't eat anything, because of the surgery, just IV serum. It was postponed two days. Then, "OK, let's do the operation." But where was the empreiteira? I needed someone to sign the paperwork and translate the papers for me so I could sign them, because it was a case of life or death. The empreiteira didn't show up. No one . . .

Daniel: Did you call—

Elena: I called five times. They said they were on their way, but they didn't show up. So I thought, "There's no alternative, we've got to operate, let's go." ... My husband said he wanted to come [to the hospital] to wait. I said, "It's not necessary, if I die, you won't be able to do anything, and if I wake up, after two hours of operation, it [still] won't help anything. Stay at work, it's better."

I was only able to see my son two days later, I went three days without eating. The second day the nurse said, "Let's go to the bathroom." It hurt like hell, I couldn't do it, so she said, "I'll help you." And on the way back I got dizzy, I thought she would steady me. But she didn't steady me at all, she let me fall. I fell down, I passed out, they called for help.

[I stayed] in the hospital fifteen days. My son, after all that ... he was so tiny, he looked like, with bandages on his eyes, a computer attached to his heart, blood ... The doctor said that the blood transfusions had burst a vein in his head, that he might not be a normal child, probably he would have vision problems. But till now, everything is fine.

Daniel: Elena, what do you think after three years [in Japan], the good and the bad, let's say.

Elena: I defeated them all *(laughs)*. I have to carry everyone on my back. Alone. My husband is a husband in name only, he never helped me in any way. I'd get home pregnant, tired. To give me a massage, or some support, nothing, he never did anything. Not ... moral support, or anything like that. I don't know how I'm still able to carry on.

Something stops me from changing the situation, I know I could change it easily. I could simply go away and that's it. I ... I'm not ... I cast my lot into this here, it has to work out, do you understand, I thought, I'm going to get married and it has to work out, so ... eh ... I went against my family because of that. My family was exactly right, but ... he has to straighten out. Either he will have to be with me or he'll have to stay behind, he has to learn this.

## Neither of the two sides

Elena mentioned her difficult pregnancy to me at our very first meeting. It is the central event of her stay in Japan, of her entire life. That pregnancy is a high-stakes drama of self-affirmation, played out with and against the doctors, the factory, her in-laws, her husband, her own body, and her self.

Elena's loneliness and her sense of estrangement from her nikkei relatives are evident. She accompanied Horácio to "his" country, Japan, where she was an outsider, ignorant of the language and culture. She had to live among his relatives, who sometimes treated her with prejudice and disdain. In Kameyama, she was pressed into service as a housemaid. Even the granny, she once told me, "swallowed" her without enthusiasm, like bitter medicine. Her husband provided no emotional or practical support, and she even alludes to instances of physical abuse.

Elena's sense of difference takes a literal turn in the narrative of her pregnancy. Elena has no Japanese blood, which endangers not only her own life but that of her unborn son. Her Rh-negative gaijin blood comes to symbolize her alienness and alienation from those around her, but also spurs her determination to transcend the obstacles that it, and they, place in her path. Despite the mortal danger, the entreaties of her doctors, the demands of the factory, and the weakness of her husband, she persists in the pregnancy and gives birth to a son. In the end, as she puts it, she "defeated them all."

The birth of Ivan was a revelation and a triumph. Elena understood that she could, if necessary, stand alone. She was no longer living for her husband; their relationship now hinged on whether he was able to straighten out, to accommodate himself to her needs. Nor did she need him to mediate between her and Japan. "I want to see things," she says, "and understand what's going on here, the people here." In the beginning, she understood no Japanese; she was forced to ask Horácio to intercede on her behalf. Now, speaking flawed but flowing Japanese, she moved in Japanese circles, such as the Fujinkai, that were closed to her nikkei relatives. She appeared on Japanese TV; they did not. She was the one who was able to prevail upon the factory officials to permit my visit. With those officials she had respect and credibility. Elena had come to terms with Japan. Of her family, she was the only one who had thrown herself fully into Japanese life.

Despite her physical tribulations, her family troubles, and her emphatic lack of Japanese blood, Elena did not turn her back on Japan. In fact, her self-assertion in the face of these difficulties was what permitted her to forge a relationship with Japan, on her own terms. Owing to her curiosity, her personal magnetism, and her fearlessness, she cultivated Japan within her. In the end, she was more comfortable with Japan—one might even say, more Japanese—than the vast majority of nikkeis I met during the fourteen months of my fieldwork.

Elena once wrote me from Amazonia, referring to the sayonara party I had missed. "It was a great pleasure to give thanks for having gotten to know the other side of the world, the other side of life, and for having proved to myself that I belong to neither of the two sides." She had staked out a place between, or beyond, Brazil and Japan, inhabited by herself and Ivan and, perhaps, the wild things of the forest.

## Caimans and colored parrots

Around 9:00 the night before I left Japan in August 1994, there was a knock on my door. It was Elena, who had come to say good-bye with Ariane and Ivan. She had brought some KFC chicken and some small presents from her recent trip with the children to Mt. Fuji and Disneyland. Elena told me that Ivan had fallen sick some days earlier: he had fainted, his face turning purple. An ambulance rushed him to the hospital. They thought that maybe he had choked on something. She had been afraid, and did not yet seem relaxed, though Ivan looked to have recovered fully. She gave me copies of photos she had taken the day we went to the Osu Kannon temple. I sensed Elena didn't want to go back to her apartment; she seemed sad. She urged me to visit her in Brazil. She finally took her leave just before 11:00. There was work early in the morning.

Elena and Ivan returned to Brazil shortly after the 1995 good-bye party in Nisshin. In early 1996, I received a long letter from Manaus, describing her re-encounter with Brazil. When the plane touched down in São Paulo, she wrote, the entire crew applauded the end of the marathon voyage. Elena, carrying Ivan and a backpack and pushing two carts of baggage, hoped to pass easily through customs. She headed for a middle-aged blond woman who she thought might be sympathetic. Instead, the woman demanded: "Give me $100 and you can go through."[4] "I don't have it," responded Elena. "Then put the bags on the rack and open them up." She did so, observing, "I've been in Japan four years, and according to the consulate my baggage can enter as used goods." At which the woman snatched one of Ivan's toys, saying, "This is new; I'm going to keep it." In the end, wrote Elena, the customs officer "managed to leave me speechless. I lowered my head and began to cry. The first thing that came to my mind was that after so much saudade for my homeland, all that I had hoped to hear was 'Welcome home.'"

[4]Reports of such extortionate demands are common. Returning dekasseguis are also wary of being followed from the São Paulo airport, as they are conspicuous targets for thieves.

After a month's stay in São Paulo, she and Ivan traveled to Manaus. Horácio was due back in a few months: "I don't know how that will be." Elena and her brother had begun work on the Amazon Camping Hotel. Elena hoped to tempt Brazilian and foreign tourists with "ecological camping." She wanted especially to attract Japanese, who would be thrilled at the glories of the Brazilian rain forest.

One day, exploring the nearby terrain, she and a guide climbed a wooded hill. At a spring, the guide whispered to her, pointing at a caiman lying motionless before them. "When I saw that caiman," she wrote, "I was as paralyzed as he. Some kind of enchantment rooted me to that spot."

The caiman is not the only wonder of the forest. "From time to time, groups of colored parrots with enormous tails fly by. In the late afternoon, before dinner, I lie in the hammock watching small birds of every color and shape."

# CHAPTER 8

# Bernardo Kinjoh

## *"All the doors would open"*

### *The honey trap*

Building 24, the largest in Homi Danchi, is a scarred warren rising to eleven floors. On a cool Sunday afternoon in March 1996, I take the elevator to the sixth and follow an open corridor past identical doorways to the apartment of the Kinjohs, a family I know through their son Júlio, a student in the Kokusai class. Júlio, about to graduate from Homi Chū, is a regular visitor to our apartment, for Maria has been helping him with English. Bright and hard-working, he has gained admission into a technical high school in Nagoya, where he will be the first Brazilian in its history.

I check the number and knock. Dália, Júlio's younger sister, opens the door, ushering me into the small, spare apartment. Selene, their mother, is preparing lunch. I decline her offer of food, for I have just eaten, but the soup smells delicious. I sit at the kitchen table with Júlio, trim and sporting a crewcut, and his father, Bernardo, a chunky man with beard and mustache. Selene brings me an orange soda. Dália shoos the family's white mutt, Chiquita, into another room.

I am here because Júlio, like several other third-year Brazilian students at Homi Chū, has agreed to an interview. I explain that graduation from middle school is a moment of passage. Bernardo invites me to ask Júlio whatever I want. As she moves around the kitchen, Selene eavesdrops, as does Dália, who posts herself at the doorway to the living room. With everyone present and listening, this will be, intermittently at least, a family interview.

Júlio begins by talking of his life in Brazil, where he attended school until fifth grade, in classes that were, he says with a touch of amused nostalgia, always in a state of uproar. He also studied afternoons at a Japanese school. There he practiced the syllabaries, though he did not learn spoken Japanese or kanji, the Chinese characters indispensable to Japanese writing.

He came to Toyota with Selene and Dália directly from São Paulo in January 1993, about six months after Bernardo. Shortly after the family had settled in, a teacher from West Homi Grade School visited their apartment, inviting Júlio to attend classes. Because there were only three weeks left in the school year, as a sixth-grader he spent the whole time preparing for commencement. "My friends," he laughs, "were really teasing me because I had just got there and I was already graduating."

Soon thereafter, Júlio found himself in the first-year class at Homi Chū. Because he could not speak or understand the language, some of the Japanese students ridiculed him, on occasion surrounding him and taunting him belligerently. "I couldn't respond," Júlio laments. "There were times when I got furious. [But] suppose I would fight at school, and [the teachers] yelled at me. There would be no way for me to defend myself; whether I was right or wrong, the blame would be sure to fall on me." He ignored the tormentors as best he could.

Of the ten or so Brazilian students who entered Homi Chū with Júlio, half quit school before finishing the third year. When I ask him whether he too ever thought of leaving school for the factory, he takes a breath.

> During my third year, I wondered whether I should work or not. Each has its good side and bad side. Work is bad because you end up working all day, but in compensation, at the end of the week, during holidays, you've got money to go out. As for studying, the bad side is that you don't have time to go out, but in compensation you gain experience and knowledge. I wanted to be a person with a lot of knowledge. . . . I wanted to have a profession so I wouldn't have to pinch pennies.

Júlio has learned an astounding amount of Japanese in the past three years. Still unsure of his language abilities, he looks forward to high school with a mix of apprehension and determination.

> It'll be like middle school [all over again], like the first day. I don't know anyone, I'll have to make some friends. But I'm not going to have the same insecurity, not knowing how to say anything, not knowing how to defend myself. Anything I don't know now, at least I ask questions. But I'll really have to work hard.

He knows he might face discrimination. But, says his father, "His spirit is prepared." Júlio echoes: "I'm going to raise my head and go forward."

I close the interview by asking Júlio about his future plans. The conversation takes a surprising turn.

Daniel: Are you thinking about going back to Brazil?

Júlio: Not now. I'm thinking about finishing high school here, and [then] I'm going to leave [Japan] to study in another country.

Daniel: In another country? Such as . . .

Júlio: For example, I'm thinking of going to England or Australia . . .

Bernardo: When the time comes, I'll go around to the embassies, to see if [he] can get a scholarship. He'd go alone, because by then he'll already be an adult, he'll have responsibility for himself, he'll be able to leave his mom and dad *(everyone laughs).*

Daniel: But how did you get to thinking about this, Júlio? It's not everyone who says, "[After] high school I'm going to Australia or England." Why England?

Júlio: I want to learn the languages that are most widely spoken in the world. I already know Portuguese, and I'd like to keep learning Japanese, and learn English. If I learn English, French would be easier, and the rest . . .

Bernardo: It would be a great thing, because [he could say], "I'm a [Latin] American, I studied in Asia, and I know Europe," which is the cradle of civilization. Then he'd be complete, he'd know just about the whole world, all that would be missing would be Oceania. His cultural level, his level of instruction, would be terrific.

Daniel: And with that, he'd have a lot of doors open, wouldn't he . . .

Bernardo: Yes, all the doors would open.

Daniel *(to Júlio)*: Personally, I think you're doing the right thing, instead of going into the factory now.

Bernardo: We always try to explain that if he goes into the factory, he's going to spend his whole life as an employee. But [if] he studies, he'll open other doors. If he goes to work now, he'll be very limited, he won't learn much. Most of the doors in front of him will close. He'll just be living a life of working, and then getting married, having a family, and dying *(laughter from Bernardo, Júlio, and Daniel).*

Daniel: Not so fast as that, I hope, but—*(Daniel and Bernardo laugh)*

Bernardo: Not so fast, but—

Daniel: But it's true, because to go into the factory now, at Júlio's age,

well, it's appealing because you can make some money, except that you're exchanging a future—
Bernardo: Closing a lot of doors—
Daniel:—for money now, and I think it really isn't worth it.
Bernardo: If you think it through, it's not worth it.
Daniel: And twenty years from now, a person looking back is going to think, Well, I made a mistake—
Bernardo: I failed to open a lot of doors, that's the hard part.

With Júlio's mention of his future plans, the tiny apartment suddenly opens onto the world. I have a minor epiphany: the Kinjohs have a different sense of possibilities from any other Brazilian family I know in Japan. Bernardo seizes upon my casual reference to open doors, turning it into the dominant motif of his subsequent comments and the basis for our collaborative endorsement of Júlio's decision to continue his schooling.

That afternoon, reflecting on the life chances of teenagers, I realized that Bernardo and I shared a view of biographical time as a series of branching paths. We had sons of roughly the same age, enrolled in Japanese schools. But Júlio's situation was more precarious than Eli's. Eli had the security of a pending return to an American high school, with good prospects for admission to a decent university. All doors were open. In contrast, Júlio was already forced to make difficult, consequential decisions, with no assurance whatsoever of success. His choices now would forever cut off certain later options. Júlio's life paths branched sooner and more radically, demanding of him a maturity beyond his years.

I knew that Bernardo was enlisting me as an ally in the battle for his son's (and, indirectly, his daughter's) future, and I willingly joined forces with him. With dismay, I had been watching Brazilian teenagers, frustrated and lost at Homi Chū, leaving school for Japanese factories. I understood why they did so, for school life was regimented, enervating, demanding, and culturally alien. To adolescents with few resources or diversions, work made more sense and had more appeal: the factory meant money and freedom. The students had siblings and friends who were drawing what seemed to them huge paychecks, buying motorcycles, stereos, and cellular phones and going to discos on Saturday nights.

But I worried about the teenage workers. Unlettered, undereducated, and foreign, their futures in Japan, in an economy that put a premium on skill and in a country that put a premium on belonging, were dim. I had come to see the factory as a honey trap, a seductive dead end for Brazilian youngsters.

And what would they do if they returned to Brazil, five or ten years down the road? In Brazil an even harsher economic climate prevailed, and lack of education would probably condemn them to the margins there. I hoped I was wrong, but it seemed to me that the Brazilian children going into the factories might never escape the lowest and most dangerous jobs. They would gain few useful skills on the shop floor. Either they would remain in Japan as foreign guest workers—as long as the Japanese economy needed them—or they would bounce back and forth between bad situations in Brazil and Japan, never at home or secure in either country. Indeed, difficulty readjusting to life in Brazil had, by 1995, acquired an informal clinical diagnosis—síndrome de regresso, returnee's syndrome—and shuttling across the blue hemisphere, between factory job in Japan and disappointment in Brazil, was already a dreary, well-established pattern for many nikkeis.

So I admired Júlio's resolve and his audacity; I wanted to encourage him. And I thought he had a chance, for the perspective fostered within his family was both enabling and realistic. I was later to understand more clearly how Bernardo himself had built a life, and a self, out of this seize-the-day vision.

### Brazil to Guinea-Bissau to Japan

On a May evening in 1996, I am again in Building 24, at the Kinjohs' door. Selene calls out through the window by the sink, dries her hands, and welcomes me. Bernardo and I seat ourselves with Budweisers at the kitchen table, a tape recorder positioned between us. This time I want to hear his story. Júlio greets me and returns to the tatami living room to watch television; Dália is out. Selene is preparing a hot snack, filling the apartment with the savory aroma of beef frying with onions and garlic. Chiquita scampers about as we talk.

Bernardo moved to Japan in August 1992 following a series of personal economic disasters. Selene and the children joined him soon thereafter. In a daring move, Bernardo quit the factory and became an independent carpenter and builder. Selene then left her job at Kawamatsu Electric, where she had been making battery chargers, to work alongside Bernardo.

Self-employed Brazilians are rare in Japan. The leap to independence from the factory is just one manifestation of Bernardo's confidence and practical initiative. All Brazilians in Japan seem to have plans for their return to Brazil, but these are mostly either consumption-oriented (buying a house and a car) or pie-in-the-sky (opening a business of indeterminate nature). I often felt that Japanese factory life spurred fantasies that held little hope of being realized or of significantly bettering the worker's long-term prospects. The gap between actual daily grind and imagined fabulous future could be breathtaking. Selene and Bernardo, in contrast, take carefully calculated risks, looking constantly to wedge openings to the future. Júlio's thoughts of an education overseas reflect his parents' values, their expectations, and their expansive vision. That vision extends beyond the apartment, beyond the factory, beyond Japan, beyond Brazil, beyond the blue hemisphere. The Kinjohs are not romantic One-Worlders, but pragmatic cosmopolitans.

At the same time, Bernardo acknowledges that anywhere can be found in oneself. His roots are, he recognizes, Okinawan, Japanese, Brazilian. These are powerful, and meaningful, identities. But a self is not just a determinate product of birth or upbringing. Willing to jump into the world, Bernardo also opens himself to it.

As we talk, Selene listens and occasionally interjects a comment. Júlio also eavesdrops from time to time. The mood is relaxed and amiable. Bernardo begins by describing his life in Brazil.

Daniel: What were you doing before you came to Japan?

Bernardo: I worked with projects, it could be construction of dams, hydroelectric plants, nuclear plants, international airports, highways, bridges, heavy engineering, involving a lot of government money, multinational loans. I spent twenty-two years in the profession. There was work in foreign countries too, Angola, Mozambique, Nigeria, Guinea-Bissau. And South America.

Daniel: So you're an engineer—

Bernardo: No, I'm not an engineer, I'm a project planner. I worked together with the engineers, [their designs] have to be executed, so getting them down on paper, that was my job.

Daniel: So starting from the plans of the engineers to the termination of the project.

Bernardo: Yes.

Daniel: How many people you needed, which materials, how much time each step—

Bernardo: That's it, all the steps.

Daniel: Where did you learn this skill?

Bernardo: In life.

Daniel: In life?

Bernardo: In life, twenty-two years.

Daniel: You didn't study this in school or . . .

Bernardo: No, I was trained in mechanical design, but I never exercised my profession, I fell right into civil engineering. Because the engineers were my colleagues, they were college professors, I'd attend classes as an auditor. [The professor] would say, "Kinjoh, don't you want a degree? It would be good for you," and I'd say, "I don't want a degree, I want to learn." So I'd go to the classes that interested me. The students would say, "Hey, you're really old to be here in school *(Júlio laughs)*. You're a tourist here, because sometimes you come, and sometimes you don't."

You keep practicing your profession and you keep learning, learning from the professors, from the great masters, those who I consider really *engineers*, because there are engineers and then there are *those engineers*, that you take your hat off to and respect. And I read a lot of books, books in English, books in French, because I had to take ideas from wherever I could, how to do things, what's the equipment like, what's the plant like, what's the generator like, what's the turbine like. They'd say, "We're constructing a hydroelectric plant in France," or wherever, so they'd send the catalog to me. I'd study the catalog and try to make something similar, changing the dimensions. When I didn't know a word, I'd get the dictionary. Lots of words I understand, I just don't know how to pronounce them.

Daniel: Were you working for yourself or for a company?

Bernardo: Until 1979 I worked for [various engineering companies]. In '79 I opened [my own] office. I'd been an employee and now they became my clients.

Brazil, it's very unstable, it's an up, down, up, down, one minute you've got work and the next you don't. The companies suffer a lot with all this, so I thought, Hey, I'll open an office, a small one, just to deal with engineering projects. If I need more people I'll simply contract them, free-lancers, engineers, planners, designers, typists, whatever is needed. This will save the company from having to hire someone and afterwards be stuck with some lazy person with no work to do. I'd serve as the lungs of those companies. I'd get projects from each one, sometimes a dam, sometimes a hydroelectric plant, a renovation, a highway, a railway.

Daniel: So you functioned as a subcontractor?

Bernardo: Yes, subcontractor. In '79 I said to myself, Now it's do or die, like here in Japan, you're going to leave the factory and it's do or die. The office was in São Paulo, very near them. Everything depends on contact.

Daniel: And how many people worked in the office? Just you?

Bernardo: Selene too. There were days, months, that it had eight, ten persons working, sometimes it had four persons, because it depended on how much work there was.

Daniel: So, from '79 until when—

Bernardo: 1990. [That was when] I went to Guinea-Bissau.

Daniel: How come?

Bernardo: Because I was sick of the economic policy of the government. [Brazilian president] Collor took my money, and I had to pay the employees, I had to pay my debts. He decreed a bank holiday on the 15th of [March], 1990, when he took office. Everything you had in the account over 50,000, you'd be forced to lend to the government. He, the government, would return it a year later, with interest and cost-of-living increase, except he left you with [only] 50,000 in the account.

Daniel: 50,000 what?

Bernardo: Cruzeiros.

Daniel: Cruzeiros. *(Both laugh; Brazilian currency has changed names so many times in recent years, it's difficult to keep track. Collor changed the currency from cruzados to cruzeiros.)*

Bernardo: It would be enough to fill the gas tank of my car two or three times, that's all. So I had to negotiate a lot, to meet my obligations, whatever I could pay in cruzados I paid in cruzados and not cruzeiros. It's confusing, they took away some zeros, cut everything, all I know is I ended up with 50,000 cruzeiros in the account, it wouldn't even be enough for one month.

Everyone [was] hopeful, saying, "Look, this plan is going to work." Three months later I was in Guinea-Bissau.

Daniel: How did that happen, someone who isn't thinking about Africa suddenly goes to Africa.

Bernardo: A guy came up to me and said, "Such-and-such a professor suggested you, wouldn't you like to work in Africa?" He was a Guinean. He was going to university in Brazil. So I [went to] Africa, I saw what the conditions were like. I ended up on the doorstep of the Brazilian embassy. I asked for help. They said, "We're still brand new here, our ambassador just took office." They wanted a lot, and were willing to give little, in other words, 99 percent of the work would be mine and they would get the glory.

I thought, I'm not going to be exploited, so I started off on my own. There was an office of the United Nations there, the program for industrial development. My idea was to open up in Guinea-Bissau, but [staying] in permanent contact with my colleagues, the engineers, the masters in Brazil, so I could have their technical support. [The UN] thought the idea was interesting, so I filled out various forms.

Daniel: It was going to be a dam project?

Bernardo: Everything having to do with the development of the country.

Daniel: It's one of the poorest countries in the world, isn't it?

Bernardo: Yes, they live by ... aid, donations. It doesn't have any infrastructure on which to build an industry, nothing, basic sanitation zero, electricity zero. The capital's supplied by generators, diesel. This is a contribution of the French government, there's a TV station, a donation of Portuguese TV. There's a radio station. There's a telephone system that was a donation of French Telecommunications. There's the International Bank of Guinea-Bissau, the only bank they have.

I had to run this whole marathon, to be able to get some projects. I had to do interviews with eight functionaries, but those eight weren't there, so I had to wait a month, then one came, and after two more months came another one, with me desperate to get to some result. After eleven months I thought, This isn't going to work.

My project really couldn't be done like arriving in Guinea-Bissau and opening ... a *bar*, right. No, I depend on funds to carry out projects, except [in Guinea-Bissau] funds don't enter by the normal routes, as in Brazil. The process is very slow, and I had to wait for a reply from the United Nations, that would come from New York, and go to Brussels, and from Belgium it would go to Vienna. And from Vienna it would go to the Ivory Coast. From the Ivory Coast it would go to Guinea-Bissau. To this very moment I've never received a reply. I thought, Forget it.

Daniel: So eleven months just awaiting responses.

Bernardo: Exactly. And working. It's a poor country, so a technology of Japan, a technology of the United States, is no good for Africa, because they're very backward. Now a country like Brazil, we're at a lower level, so it's much easier for [Guinea-Bissau] to adapt that technology to its own technology. It's even lower, it's at zero.

For example, there's no way to make a great highway, to move products from the interior to the center, and have it asphalted, because it's not going to last, there's no way to maintain it. But if you want to make a system where each region does its own maintenance, the minimal engineering for that exists, how to make gutters, how to avoid a low-lying place, to prevent it from becoming a mire, so you can have normal traffic. It doesn't have to be asphalted, simple gravel takes care of it. I did some work for them there, but I didn't get paid anything, so I thought, Working for free is no good.

Daniel: Where were you living?

Bernardo: In a hotel.

Daniel: A hotel, like . . .

Bernardo: Like a fifty-star hotel. *(Daniel, Bernardo, and Selene laugh).* From my room you could see about fifty stars *(all laugh again).* There were various foreigners [in the hotel], there were Dutch, there were Germans, there were . . . Swedes, French, and me, and Brazilians, and Americans too.

Daniel: And everybody drinking on the hotel patio, or something like that—

Bernardo: Yes, that kind of thing.

Daniel: And so you decided to go back to Brazil.

Bernardo: Yes. Then I worked three more months [in Brazil], same work as before. I managed to earn $500. I thought, This is crazy, three months to earn $500, the thing is if I went to Japan and tightened screws, I would earn more. [A friend] told me, "Kinjoh, no way are you going to tighten screws, you won't be able to stand it," and another said, "It's a waste for you to throw out twenty-two years of your profession." Well, right . . . but it's just that in Brazil I'm an executive . . . with no money, and in Japan I can be a factory worker with money. And there was also the chance for my children to study at the level of the First World. So my wife convinced me, "Let's go to Japan."

### Spider webs

Bernardo: When I came here [in 1992], the first job I got was a construction job, making log houses, Canadian style. In Saitama-ken, near Tokyo.

Daniel: Did you have any experience doing that?

Bernardo: No, just guts. The first day they put a hammer in my hand and said, "Turn around, go over there up on the roof," and so I went to the roof. My big problem was understanding what was written down. I still don't understand what's written, but I look at the drawing and figure out what has to be done. I had spent many years doing this. [At the end of 1992] I came here [to Toyota], because for one thing I [brought] my family over, and for another, the company went bankrupt.

I arranged a job with [the empreiteira] Ueyama. I went to live in Ueyama's ryō, just long enough to go through the procedures to rent the apartment. My wife and children were staying in my brother-in-law's apartment [in Homi building 23]. On weekends I'd visit.

Daniel: And you were working at Tōsei, at that time?

Bernardo: Tōsei, uh-huh. One year and eight months at Tōsei.

Daniel: Describe that job.

Bernardo: It was a job that was really ... mechanical. You grab some blanks, place them in the press, push the button and the press comes down, take out the [piece], trim the sharp edges and throw it in [a bin] there, then they take it away. All this is just a question of practice. In the beginning it was good because my objective was to reach the daily quota, which was hard to do. Afterwards, when you get the hang of it, it's a game. Your brain grows spider webs, it doesn't function at all anymore. You think, If I do it this way, it might go more quickly. There's nothing else to think about. I was always hoping that the machine would have some little problem.

Daniel: *(laughs)* How come?

Bernardo: Because I'd go behind the machine and mess around with the wires.

Daniel: A problem with the machine is a kind of entertainment?

Bernardo: It was entertaining for me because it helped pass the time. Just making the daily quota gets boring, come over here, run there, run here, run there, trim the edges, come here, go there, I mean, it's just a rat race. You'd move your legs around to walk and move your arms around to trim the edges, putting pieces in the press and pulling pieces from the press. I'd figure out anything to distract myself.

Daniel: Wasn't it possible to daydream, to make plans, or let your mind go on vacation?

Bernardo: No. .... If you daydream too much, you'll burn yourself, so you have to pay a certain amount of attention. It's just pay attention, stay there. *TAAAAAA*, I got shocked, so you know you can't mess around with that thing or you'll get a shock. It's the only reasoning you do, to not do such and such, if I put my hand there I'll get burned, so I don't put my hand there.

Daniel: So you would go into the factory, becoming a sort of robot for—

Bernardo: Exactly, like a robot, it's an automatic, mechanical job.

Daniel: For eight hours, and afterwards zangyō?

Bernardo: There was always zangyō, in that section. Three hours of zangyō.

Daniel: So eleven hours a day doing that. Wasn't it tiring?

Bernardo: In the beginning it tires you physically, then you get used to it. When I was working in Brazil, my fatigue was mental. Here no, the fatigue is physical. I can only say that if you sleep well at night, the next morning you're fine, you recuperate.

Daniel: Coming home, was it possible [to find] time for relaxing?

Bernardo: Taking a bath ... My relaxation was to try to get rid of the smell of Tōsei. The vapor gets impregnated in your skin, in your hair, in your clothes. . . . It's a terrible stink. I got used to it, but my family didn't. They complained of the bad smell, right, *bem* [darling]?

Selene: Yes *(laughs)*, it would come up the elevator . . .

Bernardo: They'd know beforehand that I'd arrived.

Selene: It was incredible, Daniel, it's true.

Daniel: Why did you decide to leave [Tōsei]?

Bernardo: ... I thought about it like this. The automobile industry is going to have a big decline, so overtime is going to fall off. I thought, Look, I'm not going to go through another suffocation [like in Brazil], I'll look for some other work that I'd like doing, that at least has some relation to me. So I went to look for a job as a *daiku* [carpenter]. I went to the city hall, and they suggested this firm to me. [The woman in the office] asked if I had experience, if I spoke Japanese. I said, "Almost nothing, but ... I understand a little, and if there's a blueprint then there's no problem, I can interpret the drawing and I know what to do." "Oh, well, if it's like that, let's see if we can manage something." Then she called the firm. I got hired. I was the first Brazilian daiku there. He took me to some buildings they were making. Then he said, "Your equipment is over there." I went over to the truck and took my hammer, saw, everything I needed. My first job, I was told to fix some things a client had complained about, so I went there and saw what was wrong and began to fix it.

Daniel: And you had experience as a carpenter in Brazil, or . . .

Bernardo: I had done it as a hobby, I'd make a shed, I'd make the furniture for the house, so I had a notion.

Daniel: And this job was better [than Tōsei]?

Bernardo: In the beginning, it wasn't good, not in terms of salary. But you have to start somewhere. So I worked there six months, and then I thought, Now I'm going to work for myself. In those six months I began to buy the tools I thought I'd need. A little bit here and there. My wife complained because she was afraid I might go to work on my own.

[When I did so] I began with an empreiteira, subcontracted, with them as the responsible party, because here in Japan I'd have to have a course of study, I'd have to have at least high school to be able to practice that profession, a specific course on cabinet-making and carpentry.

Daniel: Didn't you think it was risky to work on your own here as a carpenter? *(Bernardo shakes his head.)*

Selene: My husband has always been like that; he always puts us at risk.

Bernardo: That's why she didn't want me [to quit].

Daniel: And it's working out?

Bernardo: It's working out, thank God. [I also work for] another empreiteira that makes another kind of house.

Selene: It's another kind of material.

Bernardo: She does the same thing, she gives me a hand.

Selene: I'm the only woman, it's more for men . . . it's strange.

Daniel: It's better than the factory?

Selene: Well, it's better because I work with him, but . . . it's . . .

Bernardo: It's heavy work.

Selene: I've gotten used to it, but it's really heavy.

Daniel: Yes, but at least, I imagine that you don't have a boss, and the hours you can . . .

Selene: Yes, we can make our own hours.

Daniel: Do you usually take a day off?

Bernardo: Sunday.

Daniel: Uh-huh, every Sunday.

Bernardo: When we can.

Daniel: When you can, uh-huh.

Bernardo: Normally, we can't.

Daniel: How much longer do you think you'll stay here in Japan?

Bernardo: . . . Maybe four more years, five years.

Daniel: For the kids—

Bernardo: Yes, to get them on their way.

Daniel: And then?

Bernardo: . . . Go back to Brazil. If things go well, retired. I mean, retired financially. I'm not going to stop [working], but I'm not going
to run after money anymore. I'm going to live more easily.

Daniel: Do you miss your profession?

Bernardo: Very much . . . I miss it very much. [But] for me to practice my
profession again in Brazil, I'd have to bring myself up to date. In
Brazil every month I got the technical journals, but here I don't.
There's no way . . . so I'm very much out of date. Here in Japan I have
no way to deepen my knowledge.

Daniel: Do you still have contact with colleagues in Brazil?

Bernardo: Sometimes I'm in touch with them, but the response is always
the same: "Stay right there because things are lousy here."

Daniel: I think this is one of the hardest things for many people here in
Japan, to leave your profession behind.

Bernardo: It's really an awful thing.

## *Dual nationality, unofficially*

Daniel: Bernardo, do you think of yourself as a Brazilian, or what . . .

Bernardo: Always.

Daniel: Not as a Japanese?

Bernardo: As a Japanese too. I love Japan, because my blood is Japanese, and I love Brazil because I was born in Brazil. Officially I don't
have dual nationality, but in my heart I do.

Daniel: Is it possible for you to feel at home here in Japan?

Bernardo: No. Not like that *(softly)*, not at that level, to feel at home in
Japan I would have to know, and understand the Japanese [lan-
guage? people?], and I don't. . . .

Daniel: You think language is the obstacle?

Bernardo: No, it's . . . it's the lack of time too. You need a much longer
time, you need to dedicate yourself much more for you to assimilate
the culture. There are three thousand years of history, of culture,
you can't swallow it all at once. You've passed your whole life in
Brazil, with other customs, another tradition, and suddenly you
come to a country that you've only heard talked about, by your parents and grandparents. But it was a set of customs they had ninety
years ago . . . from the time they went to Brazil. From then to now

there was a second world war, the customs changed, the way of life changed, because the Japan of today, it's in the First World, for what ... fifty years? Before that it was ... maybe worse off than Brazil ... in social terms, in political terms. ... So much so that my grandparents went [to Brazil] to make a life, because [Brazil] was the land of *(laughs)* the future.

Daniel: And coming here, do you think that you discovered, eh ... a part of yourself that's Japanese?

Bernardo: ... No, I already had that in Brazil, because my wife's parents were Japanese. We were very close, the relatives too. We'd go to parties, Japanese style, we don't do typical Brazilian parties, in Brazil when we have a party we have those typical Japanese dishes, more ... inclined toward Japan, more like Japanese customs, but the customs of the era of my grandparents, of my ancestors.

Daniel: So in Brazil, you already knew Japan, but a Japan of times past.

Bernardo: Right, the Japan of times past.

Daniel: And coming here, it's hard to find the words, but did you find a part of yourself, that you didn't know before?

Bernardo: Look, in any country you visit other than your own, your ... country of birth, you always find something inside, that you adapt to yourself, it doesn't necessarily have to be Japan. Portugal, Spain, France, the United States, any country you visit you're going to find something that you assimilate into yourself.

Daniel: Yes, I agree.

Bernardo: Just as in Japan, I've assimilated lots of things, I've learned lots of things, I've managed to identify myself.

Daniel: What would those things be?

Bernardo: ... It's the respect, here. I think this is admirable, the car goes into the other lane to avoid a bicycle or to avoid a person who is walking in the street. I think this is incredible. If you were in my country, in Brazil, they'd say, "Hey, you want to die?" Right? Or "Get out of the street," something like that, or "Go wash dishes," or "Women shouldn't drive cars," those absurd things. And here no, people, the great majority, 99 percent, they have respect. In Brazil, in my country, unfortunately it's the opposite, it's 99 percent who don't have respect and 1 percent who do.

Another thing I like is the organization of the state here, of the city, it really works. Sometimes you have ¥300 coming back to you, something they collected too much for, a tax, so you think, I'm not going to go [to city hall] because just in train fare I'll spend 900. So they give you a little time and then they take the money and put it into your account *(laughs)*. They send a letter saying, "We're sending the ¥300, it's deposited in your account." Hey, in my country this kind of thing doesn't happen *(laughs)*, if there's a return of money you've got to go there and get it, if you don't it goes into some box. Here they return it because it isn't their money. This, I think, is respect.

Daniel: [Are there] things you miss about Brazil?

Bernardo: Freedom of communication, of expression. Here you are part of a society, and this society demands a lot from you, with its rules. In my country, in Brazil, you've got much more freedom, you can shout, yell at people until ten at night. If your neighbor objects, you stop at ten. If your neighbor doesn't say anything, you can go on till eleven, midnight, five o'clock in the morning. Sometimes your neighbor comes over and says, "Hey, let me into the party too, you didn't invite me but I'm inviting myself," there's that kind of freedom.

### *An open identity*

No wonder Bernardo seized upon my image of open doors to the future, of biographical time as branching paths. His own career reveals him as a man who creates and exploits openings. He strikes out on his own as an engineering subcontractor, attends lectures at the University of São Paulo when he finds them useful, heads to Guinea-Bissau after the collapse of his business in Brazil, goes to Japan when the African venture fails, leaves the factory to take up a career as carpenter and builder. He turns back when he hits dead ends, moves forward when opportunities present themselves. When his profession of twenty-two years becomes untenable, he simply abandons it—as painful as that is, there is no realistic alternative. Above all, then, he presents himself—and there is no reason to doubt the accuracy of the picture—as a pragmatist attentive to the world and ready to find in it sources of survival and satisfaction.

I think Bernardo's stance toward himself has this same openness. "Officially I don't have double nationality," he says, "but in my heart I do." The mix of Japanese blood and Brazilian birth presents no problem, but rather a chance to extend himself in two directions. Japan for Bernardo means "respect," civility in interpersonal transactions and in transactions between state and citizen. Brazil means "freedom of expression," a fluid, outspoken personal engagement with others. Perhaps there is a latent contradiction here, in the sense that "respect" and "freedom of expression" potentially conflict. I am sorry I did not ask about that. In the interview Bernardo himself gives no sign that he sees such a contradiction. For him, living in a foreign country offers possibilities for self-discovery: "You always find something inside. . . . Any country you visit, you're going to find something that you assimilate into yourself."

Bernardo has an open identity. Without losing a sense of himself, he can adopt other points of view, engaging in a sympathetic dislocation of perspective. He finds in others resonances of himself, and vice versa. This openness is perhaps most evident in Bernardo's discussion of yet another aspect of himself, his Okinawan roots.

## Cultural relativism as identity practice

Both Bernardo, a sansei, and Selene, a nissei, are of Okinawan descent. Historically and culturally, Okinawa occupies a distinctive, subordinate place within the Japanese nation (Taira 1997).[1]

An autochthonous state arose in the Ryukyu Islands south of mainland Japan, eventually consolidating, by the end of the fifteenth century, into a coherent kingdom whose seat was Okinawa. A tributary state of China engaged in long-distance trade, the Ryukyu Kingdom flourished for a period but by the seventeenth century began to suffer growing pressure from Satsuma, a feudal province of southwestern Japan. Japanese territorial ambitions culminated in the annexation of Ryukyu—"the first foreign country absorbed by imperial Japan" (ibid.:143)—by the Meiji state in 1879.

Okinawan customs and the Okinawan dialect differ substantially from those of the mainland (*Naichi,* or *Hondo).* The Okinawan economy has long been fragile, a reason why Okinawans emigrated in large numbers to South America in the early twentieth century. And Okinawa's relatively recent association with Japan brought immense

[1]A former provincial governor, Junji Nishime, once noted: "Although vis-à-vis Americans, Okinawans insisted that they were Japanese, they felt that in Japanese society they were a different kind of people . . . from the Japanese" (cited in Taira 1997:165). "Japanese" when under American rule, "Okinawan" when subordinated to Japan, Okinawans resemble nikkeis in their contextual apprehension of national identity. But instead of people moving from one nation to another, in the Okinawan case the national jurisdiction has been replaced.

tragedies in its wake. The site of a World War II battle in which civilian casualties were extraordinarily heavy, Okinawa was the only Japanese home island to be invaded. To many Okinawans today, that calamity had overtones of a sacrifice at the hands of Imperial Japan. Its sequel was more than a quarter-century of heavy-handed American occupation, which fueled a successful movement for reversion. Nevertheless, because it is convenient for both the United States and Japan, Okinawa today bears the burden of hosting huge American military bases. The bases, and crimes committed by U.S. servicemen stationed on them, continue to trigger massive and acrimonious protests in Okinawa, as in 1995–96, following the rape of an Okinawan schoolgirl by American soldiers.

During a brief visit to Okinawa in August 1994, I discovered that the currents of difference between Okinawa and Hondo ran deeper than I had imagined. In particular there was, among Okinawans I met, including those who had grown up in South America, a lingering resentment of the island's singular, terrible fate during the war.

Southern Okinawa is beautiful, a tropical landscape of serene villages, narrow lanes running through fields of sugar cane, and rugged, rocky coastline. The sea shines in stunning hues of blue and green. The land is riddled with caves, hideouts of Japanese soldiers and civilians during the Battle of Okinawa. Refusing to emerge at the behest of the Americans, the cave-dwellers were customarily torched with gasoline. At Itoman, the Himeyuri Peace Museum recounts the battle, focusing on the deaths of about two hundred student nurses caught in the fighting and killed in the caves. This museum is the strongest indictment of Japanese militarism I saw in Japan, holding the wartime government responsible for sacrificing Okinawans to slow the American advance to the mainland. Its displays suggest that the women, indoctrinated by the militarist educational system, were used by the army, sucked into the greatest danger, and then abandoned to their fate. The slaughtered student nurses, portrayed here as innocent victims of imperial deceit and cynicism, would seem to be a metonym for the people of Okinawa.

My friend and guide, Rosa Shimoji,[2] an Okinawan woman who had grown up in Bolivia, told me that people from Hondo rarely come to this museum, and when they do, they hurry through. I recalled the comment of a Japanese friend in Nagoya who, when I mentioned I was traveling to Okinawa, inquired: "Why? It's a sad place." Her words echoed those

[2]Her real name.

of a middle-aged German woman I met on a train north of Munich, in 1967, when I said I was going to visit Dachau.

Tensions between Okinawans and mainlanders persisted among immigrants to the American countries, reproducing social divisions and marriage taboos. These prejudices have eased over time. Nevertheless, unlike the nikkeis I knew whose families had emigrated from Hondo, many of whom seemed only weakly interested in their places of ancestral origin, nikkeis of Okinawan descent showed a strong sentimental attachment to Okinawa and Okinawan ways. As is true of marginal people everywhere, difference weighed more heavily upon them than it did upon those at the center, often contributing to a more nuanced and ironic view of human affairs. At times, marginal positions encourage bitterness and hostility, but that is not the only possible outcome, as Bernardo Kinjoh demonstrates.

During the interview at the Kinjohs' in March, Bernardo and I discussed Okinawa. I broached the topic gingerly.

Daniel: This question is a little delicate, because of my ignorance, but is there a problem between Okinawans and Japanese from Naichi?

Bernardo: Yes, there is. Just as there's a problem with people from Okinawa, there's a problem with people from Hokkaido, there's a problem with people from Kyushu, so . . . It's like in Brazil, in Brazil we have *paulistas* [natives of the state of São Paulo], and we have nordestinos [natives of the Northeast]. The nordestino, he's considered to be of an inferior level. He's considered to be of a low cultural level, so Okinawans, people from Hokkaido, people from Kyushu, are considered to be of a low level in relation to [people from central Japan]. We're aware of this, so we try to deal with people in the best possible way, because [prejudice] doesn't lead anywhere.

Daniel: Yes. When I went to Okinawa last year, I didn't know much about Okinawa. I was talking with Okinawans, who said that their relation with Japan, they called it Japan, like they were from another country, they said, "We sometimes have problems there [in Japan]," such as discrimination.

Bernardo: Usually that type of discrimination comes from ignorant people, people of less culture.

Daniel: Ah, it must be like that.

Bernardo: So when [people] get a little more knowledge and maybe change their point of view, they won't make that type of segregation. I work a lot in the street, I deal directly with Japanese people, so sometimes we encounter this, but we turn the situation around. The second time we meet [them] they're already starting to want to converse, to learn something more. . . . But you sometimes run into this kind of thing, yes.

Daniel: I knew about this problem in Japan, but I didn't know whether it was, let's say, exported to Brazil.

Bernardo: Among the older generations, yes. Among the isseis there was a certain discrimination, as there is here. But look, the thing evolved, the new generations were arising, and so, living along with Brazilians, they were forgetting that stuff a little, and today you don't find this deep-rooted business, Hey, that person is from Okinawa, that person is from Hokkaido, that person is from Kyushu. In truth, all the people who immigrated were poor people who didn't have anything and went to Brazil to try to better their luck. And usually those people were [from] Hokkaido, Kyushu, and Okinawa. Even so, there was still that rivalry, that prejudice, but with the new generations it isn't as strong anymore.

Daniel: It's a good thing, because there in Okinawa, maybe because of the experiences during the war—

Bernardo: Mm-hmm.

Daniel:—people have a lot of resentment. People there, it seemed to me that they felt used, right—

Bernardo: Mm-hmm.

Daniel:—by the Japanese Empire, so because of those terrible experiences—

Bernardo: Because of the geographical distance, the extremities really are the pawns in the chess game. They're the ones to go first, to be sacrificed in favor of the pieces of greater value, as in the chess game in which central Japan [said], "Let's leave the pawn," which would be Okinawa, "[open] for . . . possible attacks," but keep the center [safe]. Once they lost Okinawa, [they said], "Now let's give up." The residents of Okinawa feel resentment over this.

Bernardo recognizes discrimination against Okinawans, yet he refuses to single out his own group as uniquely persecuted or injured. He immediately counters my effort to draw him out on the issue of anti-Okinawan prejudice by pointing to a parallel between Okinawans and people from Kyushu and Hokkaido, the outlying islands of mainland Japan. He makes a further connection with the situation of nordestinos in

Brazil, victims of paulista prejudice. This is, indirectly, a self-criticism, for Bernardo is himself a paulista.

He observes, however, that despite prejudice within Brazil, the country had a softening effect on distinctions made by the Japanese immigrants: "Living along with Brazilians, they were forgetting that stuff a little." Here is an endorsement of trademark Brazilian values, the permeability of ethnic boundaries and the attenuation of ethnic assertiveness and self-segregation. He goes on to note that the immigrants to Brazil, regardless of their origins, were equally marginalized and impoverished in their homeland. Acknowledging Okinawan resentment, he nevertheless casts the Battle of Okinawa in strategic terms, as an injustice perpetrated by those at the center protecting their own interests rather than as a product of virulent ethnic hatred. Even where he encounters prejudice—on the street, in his job—his impulse is to deal with it, to turn it around by example and by persistent effort.

For Bernardo, ethnicity both sets him apart from and renders him the same as others who belong to different groups. He is, not just in theory but in his personal practice, a cultural relativist. But he is no fragmented postmodern man. Aware of his own origins, appreciative of the ways of others, willing to become other than he has been, he never loses himself as he follows the inner pathways that open up as he makes his way through the world.

### Big sky

Maria, Eli, and I spent a long summer vacation overseas in 1997. When we returned to Santa Cruz, there was a fax waiting from Júlio Kinjoh, from Japan, dated several weeks earlier. He had been selected to spend a year in the United States, as a participant in the Youth for Understanding international student exchange program. I was not surprised. I called Júlio in Sedona, where he was living. We spoke in Portuguese; his English was not yet fluent, but he said he was doing well. The classes were not too hard, and he was a star on the school's soccer team. Arizona was different from Toyota, he said, in what was surely an understatement. The move from his parents' narrow apartment in Building 24, steaming amidst the danchi's white concrete and the neighborhood's green rice fields, to a ranch house in the ochre desert under the big sky of the American southwest, had to be a shock. And Red Rock High, I was very sure, bore no resemblance, in architecture or in atmosphere, to

Homi Chū or to Júlio's technical school in Nagoya. But after all, Júlio was already a veteran of global migration: who was better prepared than he to cope with the surreal change?

I wrote Júlio's parents, reassuring them. Bernardo and Selene phoned one Sunday from Homi Danchi, to *matar saudades*, to kill feelings of distance and loneliness. This was, Bernardo observed, a fabulous chance for Júlio to learn English.

On his way back to Toyota City in June 1998, Júlio spent two weeks with us in Santa Cruz. He brought a portfolio filled with his striking drawings of people and places in Arizona, explaining them in fluent, colloquial English. At the turn of the millennium, we received a New Year's card, wherein Júlio announced that he was to enroll in a polytechnic university in Melbourne.

# CHAPTER 9

# Miriam Moreira

## *"I lived there, I was born there, I grew up there!"*

### Another country

The first Brazilian middle-school students I met were Miriam Moreira and her younger sister Tamara, the girls who entered Homi Chū the same day as did Eli. I liked them from the start. Tamara is more spontaneous than the reflective Miriam, but both are friendly, vivacious, and amusing. Occasionally they would wangle their way into my group at school. I was a lax "teacher"; we hit it off, and our conversations strayed agreeably far from academic matters.

The sisters' background was unusual. Most nikkeis I knew (and most of my Japanese acquaintances) had little interest in organized religion. But this was a missionary family. Tullio and Marina Moreira came to Japan in 1991. Their five children moved in with Mr. Moreira's older brother and sister-in-law, who lived in Indaiatuba, a few hours from the family's home in Guarujá on the coast of São Paulo. After seventeen months spent working in Japanese factories, Tullio and Marina fetched them. Upon returning to Japan with the children, the Moreiras took up their missionary work in earnest.

Tullio, a pastor in the Assembly of God church in Brazil, now headed a nationwide Japanese evangelical organization that ministered mainly to Brazilians. A non-nikkei, he spoke little Japanese. Marina spoke even less, though her father had been born in Japan and her mother was a nissei. Marina now cared for the two youngest children, aged six and eight, at home. The Moreiras' oldest daughter, eighteen, had recently gone off to Lisbon to study in a missionary high school.

The Moreiras lived in Building 141, a Kōdan high-rise that (to their annoyance) overlooked the bustle of Homi Praça and the Meitetsu supermarket. On a February evening in 1996, Miriam ushered me into an immaculate living room that doubled as the pastor's office. Heavy furniture and office equipment rested on a plush new baby-blue carpet. Miriam, due to graduate from Homi Chū the following month, was my intended interviewee, but Tamara was curious and eager to participate, so she joined us. The girls banished their six-year-old brother Moisés, who had been watching television, to a bedroom. Marina sent in a demitasse of strong, sweet Brazilian coffee for me. Later, when the interview was over, she brought some fresh homemade pudding topped with grated coconut, and we all chatted together for another hour.

The sisters talked in relays, completing or augmenting each other's thoughts. They had passed through many dramatic events together, jointly working through their unusual experiences, mortifications, and frustrations. They spoke of partings, reunions, loneliness, bewilderment.

Teenagers inhabit another country, more distant than any on earth. Children present a special ethnographic challenge. We ethnographers can view our own childhoods only in retrospect, with the eyes of adults. This biocentric distortion may be more difficult to overcome than most ethnocentric prejudices. Our adult state seems the inevitable culmination of a developmental process. We know the outcomes all along the line; we sense a spurious inevitability in who we were at any moment. It is hard for us to project ourselves into a childhood state where tomorrow was a mystery, and riddles of friendship, competence, morality, dependency, and attractiveness were terrifyingly unresolved. The child's perspective, fraught with uncertainty, lack of control, and the contradictory anxieties of both limitation and possibility, is, in a word, alien.

Interviewing Japanese-Brazilian teenagers confronted me with multiple forms of alienness—age distance, cultural distance, and, since most of my interviewees were girls, gender distance.[1] I relished the chance to grapple with their unfamiliarity. I found my young friends fascinating, and I felt privileged to be admitted into the anterooms of their lives. I was struck by their flexibility and bravery when confronted with unknown and unpleasant situations not of their own making. They were, in equal measure, fragile and strong. Their stories were poignant, frightening, sad, and inspiring. It is difficult for me to use more measured terms when writing of these young people, because their experiences were so intense and they spoke of them so vividly and directly.

[1]I found it much easier to interview Brazilian girls than boys. Júlio (Chapter 8) was an exception. Most of the boys seemed to have less patience with me, and less willingness to probe their own feelings, than did the girls.

Like others, Miriam and Tamara recounted highly charged events engraved in their memories: the joyful reunion with parents; the dreaded first day in a hostile school; the taunts, stares, and deceptions of classmates; the blows of others' ignorance. They passed through the fires changed, but remarkably intact.

## Waiting, alone

Daniel: What did you think when your parents [left]?

Miriam: It was hard, because we're a very united family. My parents always gave us a lot of attention. Our aunt and uncle are also good people, but it's just not the same thing. So we missed them, but we asked God, and God consoled us. [Our parents] knew they had left us in good hands. In Brazil, there's a lot of . . . Our friendships started to influence us, because of our age, to take us to the other side, even more because we were so far from our parents, so I'm very grateful to God because He always protected us, He never let us be influenced.

Daniel: What were their plans?

Miriam: They would come back, and—

Daniel: Within what period?

Tamara: Three months, more or less.

Daniel: And what happened?

Tamara: We stayed there [a long time].

Miriam: Man's plan isn't the same as God's plan. We don't know what's going to happen tomorrow, only God knows about tomorrow.

Tamara: When they returned to Brazil [in 1993], they said [they were taking us to Japan], only we thought that when they came back to Brazil, then we'd—

Miriam: Live in Brazil.

Daniel: In the beginning, you didn't want to come here?

Miriam: No. *(Tamara clicks tongue in agreement.)*

Daniel: Why?

Miriam: I knew that Japan was a country like, here you're stupid. I had a lot of friends [in Brazil], I was going to take courses in languages, in computing. And then I got the news that [I would have to] leave all that, to go to Japan, to feel like an ET.

Daniel: What was the image you had of Japan?

Miriam: The image I had was that Japanese people were very kind, they were very polite, I thought it was . . . a paradise in terms of, that

there wasn't much violence. . . . I knew there were a bunch of chopsticks, those things that everyone knows. Houses right on top of one
another.

My father had sent photos, I thought there would be pretty
houses. I got here . . . the first thing [I saw], when I went to the bathroom, was that hole. *(She is referring to a Japanese-style toilet, set
directly into the floor.)* I thought it was absurd, because in Brazil I
thought [Japan was] a First-World country . . . but it was totally different . . .

Miriam: When my parents went to Japan [we lived in] Indaiatuba with
my aunt and uncle, a year and five months far away from my parents.

Daniel: [In that Indaiatuba school] did you have a group of friends?

Miriam: In Brazil making friends is the easiest thing in the world, because people come right up to you. It's the opposite of here, because
here, if you don't try to make friends, they don't approach you. It's
like . . . human warmth, there [in Brazil] it's really like that, the people are really friendly.

Daniel: What do you mean, human warmth?

Miriam: Like . . . *(small laugh)* you're a new student, so everyone wants
to show you the school, "Come here, this is such-and-such a place,"
then one person introduces herself, then another, they make friends,
the friendship grows and grows. . . . They don't leave you to one side.
Sometimes you're behind in your studies, so the teacher gives someone permission to help you. And even more when, for example I'm a
foreigner, well, I'm not a foreigner, I've got a Japanese face, everyone comes up to me, it's the opposite of here *(laughs softly)*.

Daniel: How is it here?

Miriam: Here, when you arrive . . . To tell the truth, I never expected
such a shock, because . . . right away you feel like an ET, deaf, dumb,
and illiterate, because you don't understand anything they're saying.
Sometimes they gather around you and stand there whispering in
each other's ears, "Who could it be?" In Brazil they come and ask
you, and then a conversation begins, but here, they have a mania for
standing there whispering, and looking at you kind of, and you feel
sort of . . .

## Reunited

Daniel: When your parents [returned to Brazil] to get you, tell that story. *(The girls laugh.)*

Miriam: Ah . . . I think it's better I don't tell you, in a minute I'm going to start crying, right here *(she and Tamara laugh)*. . . . It was super-emotional, because . . . it was hard, [they] left five children in Brazil. The smallest, the baby, was how old?

Tamara: He was a little over two.

Miriam: [My father] always sent photos, videos. My uncle would say to [Moisés], "Your parents are in Japan, I'm your uncle." Because a lot of people here in Japan have a problem. When you leave a small child, and you return, [the child] says, "That's not my father," and it's a tremendous shock. We showed the pictures to Moisés, "Look, Moisés, that's your father." My father was afraid because he'd heard that children didn't recognize their parents anymore when they returned. [But] when [he and my mother] arrived [at the airport], we didn't even wait for him to go through the gate, we all ran crying into his arms. *(Voice wavers.)* It was super-emotional. Everyone was watching, but . . . we couldn't control ourselves, it was super-wonderful.

Afterwards we all went home happy, we had a big party. We'd prepared all those delicious Brazilian foods. *(Laughs.)* Roast pork, lots of different fruits, a bunch of things.

Tamara: We'd asked them what they couldn't get in Japan—

Miriam: Whatever they couldn't get in Japan, [we got]. These days there are Brazilian products [here], but before they really couldn't get them.

Daniel: And how long did they stay in Brazil?

Miriam: Two or three months, to do all the paperwork for our passports [and] documents. [During that time] we traveled all around Brazil to see friends and relatives. Then we returned to São Paulo.

Daniel: How did you feel when it came time to leave [Brazil]?

Miriam: *(laughs)* Ah, I was, we . . . My heart was in my mouth.

Tamara: Yes.

Miriam: We had a big good-bye party for the people in the church, our good friends.

Tamara: Everyone came to the house—

Miriam: And called us at home, they came to the house, gave us presents, and there was a lot of crying *(amused, nostalgic tone)*.

Tamara: There was crying every day.

Miriam: Every day my head was this size *(demonstrating with hands)*, all swollen up.

Tamara: And the last day, everyone came.

Miriam: The last day, nossa . . . I don't even like to talk about it, in a minute I'll start crying right here *(Miriam sniffs, Tamara laughs)*.

Daniel: You didn't want to go to Japan?

Tamara: I thought I wouldn't have many friends. . . .

Miriam: I thought there would only be Japanese, Americans, and I don't know how to speak their languages. . . . I was always imagining, What's it like there, how are they going to receive me, will it be the same as in Brazil? [Maybe] everyone will tease you because you're a foreigner.

## *Joys and disappointments*

Daniel: Tell me about [your] arrival in Japan, the first day.

Miriam: We went straight home. We arrived at night, and then went to see the house. I thought it was really strange because I wouldn't have imagined a wooden house, with a bathroom like that.

It was a two-story house. . . . Down below there was a small kitchen, a living room, and then the *furo* [bath]. Upstairs there were just two bedrooms. And that was where we slept. We five children shared those rooms. My father and mother used the living room as a bedroom. So we didn't have a living room.

Daniel: Was this what you expected?

Miriam: It was really different.

Daniel: How?

Miriam: In Brazil, a wooden house is a shack. Here it seems a wooden house is a thing for rich people. I expected it to be one of those superbeautiful houses, one of those *mansions*, with those verandahs.

Daniel: You were expecting a Brazilian-style house, but of the First World?

Miriam: Right. [But] it wasn't. [It was] terrible . . . and it was very small. I was really amazed by the stove. In Brazil, my stove had six burners, and here it only had one *(laughs)*. Horrible.

Daniel: Was there anything, let's say, magnificent, there in that house?

Miriam: . . . There was . . .

Daniel: What?

Miriam: My parents *(all laugh)*. Just that. My parents.

## The reality of a Japanese school

After a month, the Moreiras moved to a new neighborhood in Nagoya. The girls had to change schools. Unlike Miriam's first Nagoya school, the second had no Brazilian students.

Miriam: In the [second] school, I felt a kind of discrimination. The first day I had to go in front of everyone and introduce myself. The teacher spoke to me and I couldn't understand what she was saying. I looked her in the face, I looked the others in the face, [I thought], What's she saying? At that moment I just wanted to cry, inside I was really crying but I kept quiet, I didn't know what to say.

Daniel: Everyone watching, expecting something, and you not knowing—

Miriam: Everyone watching me, expecting something, and everyone sitting there talking [about me]. I was even trembling a little. In the first school I had three interpreters, I thought, Japan is the greatest. But then you confront the reality of a Japanese school, alone. When I went to talk with the principal [when I enrolled], I could feel that he was cold. I thought, "I don't want to go there," I cried a lot. We took an interpreter with us. She asked if there weren't some Brazilians in the school. [The principal] said, "There aren't any." I got super-sad when I heard that *(voice drops)*, I thought, I'm going to have to be the first.

But I got happy that same day, because I managed to get through the difficulties. I thought, Me being the first foreigner here, if more foreigners come I can help them. Because, if you go through that, you know just how bad it is.

Daniel: And what is the reality of a Japanese school?

Miriam: Without Brazilians?

Daniel: Yes.

Miriam: Ah, horrible *(laughs)*. ... You sit there in the chair without knowing what to do. The bell rings, you don't know what it's for. Sometimes the people go to PE, you don't know what it's about. They don't come and call you, saying, "Let's go, now we're going to have such-and-such a class." They leave you there, and then you're all alone.

Daniel: The first day, [did the teachers help you out]?

Miriam: She spoke English a little bit with me, she spoke strange English. I thought, I wonder if she doesn't know how to speak English? I think she's asking me to introduce myself. So I went and said, *"My name is* [spoken in English] such-and-such.*"* I introduced myself in English, because in Brazil you learn [to do that]. She saw that I was trying, that I wanted to learn, so she helped me a lot.

Daniel: And the students?

Miriam: Pretty soon they'd come up to talk with me, some of the girls, and I wouldn't understand. That would get them annoyed. I'd just stand there looking at them, not saying anything. They'd get furious.

Daniel: Furious?

Miriam: Yes, because they don't have any patience. But I stayed late at school, looking up words [in the dictionary]. A month went by, and I went up to a little group of them, and said *Ohayō* ["Good morning"]. They said, "Ah, she learned to say ohayō." I had a little list, I carried around some phrases, and would talk with them, except whenever they were talking I didn't understand anything *(laughs)*. I just knew the phrases I'd memorized. With time I made a lot of friends. Bit by bit you conquer their friendship, they see the effort you're making and then they come to help you. In Brazil, the first day they come to help you. Here you have to show them your effort first.

Tamara: [There were two boys], these two were friends, and the one in front of me didn't like me, and the one at my side also didn't like me. ... One day, when the bell rang, the boy at my side kicked my notebook, and then the boy in front grabbed it, and then the two of them kicked it back and forth. I saw they didn't want me sitting near them. The teacher told [them] to teach me Japanese, but they didn't want to. What I thought was really bad was when they'd say, "This is called such-and-such." I'd copy it down, I mean, they were teaching me bad words, swear words.

Miriam: They would say swear words, with us thinking it was the name of a person. They would say, "His name is *Baka* [Stupid]," so I'd say, "Nice to meet you, Baka."[2]

Tamara: I went to look up what they were saying. But I didn't find [most of] those words in the dictionary—

Miriam: Because they're not in the dictionary *(laughs)*.

Daniel: What words?

Tamara: Baka, *hentai* [weirdo], *sukebe* [lecher], those things.

Daniel: Did they also say those words to you?

---

[2]The insult "stupid" is stronger in Japanese than in English.

Tamara: One boy always called me baka, baka I knew was "stupid," because it's in the dictionary. I'd look him in the face like this. Then
everyone kept calling me baka. Once a boy said to me, "You're
baka." So I said, "I am, I'm baka." They looked at me amazed, and
said, "You're baka." So I said, "Yes, I'm baka, thank you for calling
me baka," and afterwards they never called me baka again.

Daniel: *(to Miriam)* And did this also happen to you?

Miriam: With me it was a little different. During sōji, I didn't know how
to do it right. I'd grab the *zōkin* [the rag used for cleaning], first I'd
look at what they were doing so I could copy it, and they'd say,
"Gaijin baka." And I'd stand there watching them. ... Later a girl
taught me how to do [sōji], because after I started making friends,
the girls started to like me. I didn't speak, but I pointed, with a gesture, or with a word in English, I always found a *jeitinho* [an improvised way], that Brazilian jeitinho always works *(laughs)*. So when
the boys called me baka, [the girls] taught me how to say, "No, I'm
not baka, I'm learning nihongo, I'm learning more than you are.
You're baka, because you don't know how to speak Portuguese or
even English, you just speak Japanese." I looked up in the dictionary
how to say this in Japanese and I got [the girls] to teach me to perfect
the sentences. ...

### Carnival, soccer, favelas, and Indians

Tamara: One time I brought photos [to school], because they wanted to
see Brazil. [I said], "I lived there," and they said, "What are you
talking about, that's not Brazil, that's America [the United States]."
I said, "But I've n-never been to America, if I'd been to America I'd
know how to speak English" *(everyone laughs)*. "That's not America, that's really Brazil." They said, "No, it isn't Brazil," and I'd say,
"Yes, it's Brazil," and they'd say, "No, that's not Brazil." I said,
"But how can you not believe me *(laughing)*, I've always lived in
Brazil." I asked myself, Why don't they believe that that's Brazil?

Daniel: They were photos of—

Miriam: Of Guarujá, São Paulo, like that. [Photos] of the buildings along
the beach at Guarujá. They think the beaches just have jungle. They'd
say, "No, this doesn't exist in Brazil." I said, "What do you mean, I'm
a Brazilian, I lived there, I was born there, I grew up there"—

Tamara: I said, "Brazil isn't just the Amazon." They ask a lot of questions about the Amazon.

Miriam: They'd ask if there were bathrooms in the houses *(both girls talking at once)*. So I'd say, "We have bathrooms." Then they'd say, "And are there doors?" I'd say, "Nossa." Each question was—

Tamara: They'd ask if there were toothbrushes in Brazil—

Miriam:—stupid—

Tamara: [A Japanese friend] asked my mother—

Miriam: So [my mother] said, "No, in Brazil we grab a stick *(she and Tamara laugh)*, there in the Amazon we grab a stick, and we do this *(holding the imaginary stick still and moving her head back and forth)*. We move our head back and forth and that's how we brush our teeth" *(both girls laugh)*. The Japanese woman said *(sucking in her breath, in feigned wonderment)*, Hontō? [*Really?*] So [my mother] said, "Yes, hontō, it's true."

They imagine that Brazil just has jungles, the Amazon River, Indians, *favelados* [slum-dwellers], thieves. There's a [Japanese-Brazilian] singer named Márcia [who is a television star in Japan]. [She] was [on] a program they used to have, [featuring shows from various] countries. She presented the [Brazilian] program *Aqui Agora* [*Here and Now*], and *Aqui Agora* had shown police running after some thieves and firing, killing people. The thief ran this way and that, and everyone [was] running, frightened out of their wits, and in a *favela* in Rio de Janeiro.... On TV, it showed *all over* Japan. I walked into school, [people said,] "Hey, did you see what was on television?" I got super-sad. I said, "It's not in all of Brazil, just in some regions from time to time."

Then I tried to explain to them, that ... for example, here in Japan, when an earthquake happens, it doesn't mean that it happened in the whole country, it was just in one place. But in other countries, when the Kobe earthquake happened ... In Brazil the news they showed was that ... They called us here, "Nossa, it ruined all of Japan." But it was just in one place. Well, they think that Brazil is just Carnival, soccer, favelas, and Indians. Just that. That's Brazil *(spoken softly)* ... unfortunately. And we don't know how to explain because they don't believe us. I showed them so many photos, beautiful ones, my house has a swimming pool behind it, a barbecue, and they didn't believe it.

Daniel: They just said that—

Miriam: "It's the United States," because the only thing [they know] is the United States, England ... those countries, France ...

## *Japonesinha to gaijin to brasileira*

Daniel: In Brazil, did they call you . . . Japanese?

Miriam: "Little Japanese girl" [*japonesinha*].

Tamara: "The little Miss Mestiças" [*as miss mesticinhas*].

Miriam: It's only because of our eyes *(laughs)*. . . . I mean . . . I don't think there's anything Japanese about us, we're really Brazilian, it's just that, compared with [other Brazilians] . . . I think it's because of my mother.

Her father is Japanese, born here. At the age of six he went to Brazil, because of the war. There was a group of Japanese there, escaping the war, but they didn't want to mix with Brazilians. My mother said that her father would [call the Brazilians] "gaijin." She [finally] came to understand what a gaijin was once she got to Japan. [In Brazil] she thought that [a gaijin] was a Brazilian.

But because she attended school [with Brazilians], she only spoke Portuguese. As she grew up, she started to think, I want to be around Brazilians, because she got that caring, that love [from them], and saw that it was different. She started to learn about Brazilian culture. She wasn't allowed to [go out with Brazilian friends] because of her father, [who insisted], "You can't mix with Brazilians." But then she did start to go around with Brazilians, and when she grew up, she married a pure Brazilian *(laughs)*.

Daniel: Are you still japonesinhas here in Japan?

Miriam: *(laughing)* We're gaijin.

Tamara: Right.

Miriam: However much you have a Braz-Japanese face, really narrowed eyes [*olhos bem puxados*], [this kind of] hair *(touching her hair)*, you can have everything on the outside. But inside yourself . . . just like Mrs. Mizutake[3] [one of the bilingual teachers] said, you're Brazilian, and they don't see you as a Japanese, no way. They see you as a foreigner. That's why you're called gaijin in Japan. . . . We don't even have our own what's-it-called . . . our nation [*pátria*], because in Brazil we're called japonesinhas and here we're called gaijin, so it's . . . *(laughs)*

Daniel: Well, let's see. In Brazil, they call you—

[3]Naomi Mizutake (Chapter 14).

Miriam and Daniel: Japonesinha.

Daniel: Here, they call you—

Miriam: Gaijin. *(Tamara laughs.)*

Daniel: But how do you feel inside?

Tamara and Miriam: *(echoing each other in a soft cascade)* Brazilian.

Miriam: Because in Brazil it's more, like, just talk, just joking, but here they call you that in reality. In Brazil, sometimes there's the [hymn] of Brazil.

Tamara: I almost forgot *(laughs, sings haltingly the beginning of the Brazilian national anthem).*

Miriam: Our friends would sing [the anthem] exactly right, they would raise the flag, and then they would stand there teasing us [to the same tune], *O japonês tem cinco filho* ["The Japanese has five children"] *(dissolves into laughter and confusion).*[4]

Daniel: Who used to sing this?

Miriam: *(both laughing)* Some Brazilian boys we knew . . . They'd come up close to us and start to sing.

Daniel: But was this for, I don't know, to provoke you, or . . .

Tamara: No, not at all—

Miriam: They're really jokesters, they know we take everything as a joke. But in a certain sense—

Tamara: They thought we were strange—

Miriam: No, not strange—

Tamara: They think we're different.

Miriam: They wanted to make friends with us. . . . Brazilians try to make friends through joking around.

Tamara: The young guys at Homi, I think it's the same thing, always with the jokes. To make friends.

Daniel: But then, on the inside you feel—

Miriam: Brazilian.

Daniel: And what exactly is a Brazilian? I don't understand it very well.

Miriam: *(soft laughter from both)* Ah, you've got human warmth. . . . You've got various cultures inside you, because you live together with Italian descendants, various descents. In my class each one had a [different] descent. But we'd talk to each other, we'd visit their house. It was different in their house, the mothers and so on. It was fun, it's just

---

[4]This mocking song has any number of variants that enumerate the negative qualities of the "five children."

that, I was the only one who was different. My face was completely Japanese, [but] I had a Brazilian culture. They were all mixed up, Portuguese, French, [and so on].

## Miriam displaced

Miriam's identity path—from *japonesinha* to *gaijin* to *brasileira*—bears a strong resemblance to Eduardo Mori's. Nevertheless, she negotiated that trajectory on the basis of her particular life experiences, and she appropriates the meanings of those categories in terms that sometimes resemble, and sometimes diverge from, those of Eduardo.

One's self ordinarily rests unremarkably in a known environment, oriented toward known others and known surroundings. When displaced from this familiar environment, the self becomes disoriented, and therefore available for conscious reorientation and reworking.

Away from home, in Indaiatuba, Miriam finds herself enmeshed in a benign but less secure relationship with her aunt and uncle, with feelings of longing for her absent mother and father. She reorients her self in a well-understood direction, toward a relationship with God, who protects her and gives her the strength to resist the malign influences of her peers. Her self-in-Indaiatuba requires attention, her own imaginative intervention to create an environment in which that self can feel secure.

Entering a new school there, she is grateful for the warm reception she receives from her colleagues, despite their joking about her Japanese appearance. Her awareness of her quasi-ethnic difference (as a "japonesinha") emerges strongly against the background of this new environment. But unlike Eduardo, Miriam has always felt "Japanese" to be more a false label given her by others ("it's only because of our eyes") than a substantive self-identification, for she was raised in a household that neither propagated Japanese customs nor affirmed Japaneseness. In Indaiatuba, her "Japanese face" draws attention, but that attention, she feels, brings others close to her, willing to befriend and aid her.

In Miriam's view, her Brazilian classmates accept her despite her unusual appearance. In contrast, she suffers painful rejection and isolation in the all-Japanese school in Nagoya, where she is labeled a "stupid gaijin." This label too is one she does not internalize, though she resents it tremendously. The barriers between Japanese and Brazilian seem to her regrettable and unnecessary. She sets out to show that she is neither stupid nor so different, staying after school to study Japanese and, as she puts it, "conquering the friendship" of some of the Japanese girls who initially rejected her.

These contrasting experiences lead her in retrospect to identify acceptance of difference with "human warmth," and "human warmth" with Brazilianness. The Japanese by implication—and the school principal explicitly—seem "cold." Brazilianness thus characterized is a quality she can easily identify with, by virtue of her accepting personality—she wins over the Japanese girls by sheer effort and goodwill—and her mixed descent. She owes her physical existence to her mother's revolt against her own immigrant father's ethnocentric ban on mixing with Brazilians. "Brasileira" is thus a category Miriam can readily assimilate into herself.

The episode of the photos is particularly shocking and significant for both Miriam and Tamara, who experience their colleagues' skepticism as unwarranted and injurious. The Japanese students reject the girls' effort to reveal themselves, to win acknowledgment, treating the photos as fraudulent. The house in Brazil, representing Miriam's and Tamara's intimate past, is denied. The ignorance and insensitivity reinforce the girls' connection to Brazil, underlining the inner distance between them and the Japanese students. For Miriam and Tamara, as for the patrons of Restaurante 51, Brazilianness becomes secret knowledge, clung to and harbored in defiance of any outward accommodation.

The *Aqui Agora* television program has a slightly different, but analogous, effect. For Miriam's Japanese acquaintances, the police chase is a metonym for Brazil, authenticated by virtue of the program's Brazilian origins and its introduction by a famous nikkei entertainment figure. Yet Miriam knows that her country and the life she led there cannot be reduced to a lurid, violent, tabloid spectacle. Powerless to refute or explain the images, again she is left with secret knowledge, and the gap between her and Japanese others further deepens.

When all is said and done, Miriam, like Eduardo Mori, is almost, but not quite, settled into a Brazilian identity. The labels—gaijin in Japan, japonesa in Brazil—leave her wondering if she really has a nation. Unlike Eduardo, she has never flirted with a Japanese identity. Nevertheless, the alliance of a disparaging ethnic rhyme with the Brazilian national anthem is, I think, troubling to her, though she dismisses the schoolboys' behavior as mere joking. For in Miriam's idealized Brazil, appearance would never be an issue. Brazilianness is an inner quality, human warmth, that pays no heed to physical type. Perhaps we could say that Miriam is, by her lights, a true Brazilian, and that it is the Brazilianness of Brazil that is in doubt.

Miriam will, I think, remain a true Brazilian in this sense, but Brazil, in its more standard, concrete cultural forms, may slip away from her. We ended our conversation with a look into the future.

Daniel: Just one more thing, Miriam. What are you going to do now that you're graduating from the chūgakkō?

Miriam: Well, my future . . . To tell the truth, I don't know what my future will be, because only God knows what tomorrow will bring. But what I think, what I want, is to study languages, I want to learn to speak English, French, Spanish, and [to study] computing. I'd like to work, but my parents don't want me to. [My father] said, "You're going to study music, computing, and languages."

Daniel: Here in Japan.

Miriam: Here in Japan.

Daniel: Because once you told me—

Miriam: I was thinking of studying in Europe, but . . . Well, my sister is there, and she . . . Well, it's pleasant there and everything, but it's hard to be far away from your parents, alone, studying, they've got problems and I want to be together with them.

Daniel: So for now, you're thinking of staying here and taking private lessons.

Miriam: That's right.

Daniel: And do you know when you're going back to Brazil.

Miriam: No. *(Laughs softly.)* No. We've got a house there, but . . .

Daniel: And . . . high school?

Miriam: Well, I really don't know about high school. . . . If I had stayed in Brazil I would graduate.

Daniel: Did you think of going to kōkō [Japanese high school]?

Miriam: I thought about it, but it's just that, on *tests* I get good grades, the teachers all say, *Sugoi!* ["Wonderful!"], but I don't think it's sugoi, because I memorize these things, I don't learn them. Sometimes [when I use the bilingual dictionary] there are even words in Portuguese I don't know. So it's very hard to learn. I get some things, but it's really hard. I stay late after school, pushing myself, because I want to show that not all Brazilians are vagabonds, everyone has to put forth an effort. . . . [I do it] for myself, because I know that in the future I'll get something out of all this. There are books in Portuguese at school, but when I grab one to read, I think, Nossa, it's so hard, and sometimes I ... Because I stopped [Brazilian school] in fifth grade, so ... I studied just a little bit, right?

Daniel: Fifth grade, [in Tamara's case] fourth grade, there wasn't much chance—

Miriam: There wasn't any chance to study Portuguese.

# CHAPTER 10

# Catarina Noriko Iemura

## *"If it was up to me, I'd never leave Japan"*

### Bye bye, Japan

It was a school Saturday in February, a half day. Maria and I had arranged to meet everyone at Homi Station at one o'clock. Snow fell and melted into the grimy platform. The girls had changed out of their uniforms into jeans and jackets—everything in shades of gray, inadvertently matching the sky. Catarina was wearing a brand-new pair of black sneakers. The train churned through bare fields. It was crowded, as it always is when the weather turns bad and the roads get slick; steam bloomed on the windows. Just outside Toyota Station, in the covered walkway leading to the Sogo department store, we joined up with Rieko, the only Peruvian girl at Homi Chū, her mother Hermina, and Rosa Kitagawa (Chapter 12), a bilingual teacher employed by Aichi prefecture. Rosa embraced and kissed each of the girls. This was to be Catarina's sayonara party. The following Tuesday she was flying to São Paulo, for good.

We walked to Denny's, ten minutes from the station. Fluorescent-lit, decorated in pastels, the chain restaurant affects a vaguely American style. But the only unambiguously American dish on the menu was "jambalaya," a risky order. I chose the *yakiniku* plate: strips of beef with miso soup, rice, and radish pickles. Others ate Japanized versions of hamburgers, spaghetti, or cheese casseroles. We toasted Catarina, clinking coffee cups and glasses of soda. Rosa took photos, the girls joked around, and the sleet turned to rain.

Crowding under umbrellas, we walked back to Sogo, where the girls shopped. They took more pictures at the fountain on the eighth floor. Then Maria and I gave Catarina good-bye hugs and wished her happiness. She seemed sad. Maybe the dreariness of the day had seeped into the gathering. Rosa went home; the girls left; Maria and I chatted in

Portunhol[1] with Hermina in the Sogo coffee shop. Outside, the sky was a darkening slab. The rain turned to sleet. By the time we got back to Homi it was again snow.

### Mysterious ailments, migraines, and discarded dreams

I first met Catarina's mother, Regina, and stepfather, Santos, in the fall of 1995 at the Sunday Japanese class offered by the Toyota International Association. One morning they offered Maria and me a ride home. On the way back to Homi Danchi we got lost. I tried gently to get them on the right track, but they had ideas of their own and I did not want to insist. We drove around furiously for an hour or so, passing Denny's several times; it became almost a joke. They said this always happened, since everything looked the same and there was no hope of reading the street signs. They didn't seem to want to ask directions.

Regina and Santos had been living in Curitiba, capital of the southern state of Paraná, before coming to Japan a year earlier. Santos, a *paranaense* who described himself as descended from Germans and Spaniards, had been a cigarette salesman in Brazil. Regina, also a native of Paraná, had been a student. They had moved to Homi recently, after stints in Chiba and Mie prefectures. Regina was currently making "auto sensors"—she couldn't say exactly what they were used for, but she thought they were exported to the United States. Santos worked in an instant rāmen factory. He never ate rāmen anymore. Santos estimated that they might stay in Japan five more years, but it seemed to me that he pulled the number out of a hat. Until someone bought a ticket, you could not be sure when they were going. By autumn 1995, I knew that "maybe next year" usually meant "I have no idea."

As we were circling aimlessly through the streets of Toyota, Regina told me that she had a thirteen-year-old daughter, Catarina, who was studying in an apartment at Homi Danchi. Some Brazilians sent their children to this "school," run by a nikkei woman, so that they wouldn't lose their Portuguese. The woman had told Regina that the school was recognized by the Brazilian Ministry of Education and Culture (MEC).

By November, Catarina had transferred to Homi Chū, where I worked with her on elementary Japanese. Regina and Santos had begun to suspect that the apartment school was not really approved by MEC

[1]An improvised mix of Spanish and Portuguese.

when the teacher could not produce the certification. Regina did not look well to me. One day I called to ask how she was feeling. She told me she'd been suffering from headaches and fatigue. The doctor had first said it was low blood pressure and had given her some medication, but it had not helped. Another time the doctor said it might be a brain problem. Now he said there was no physical cause. During the past few weeks Regina had missed some work, even though she needed the money. She thought her problem might be "stress," a common complaint among Brazilians who work in Japanese factories. Like many Brazilians, she did not trust Japanese doctors. She had gotten contradictory diagnoses—they sounded to me like the airiest of conjectures—and now the official position seemed to be that nothing was organically wrong.

About a week later, I heard someone call my name at the Meitetsu supermarket. It was Regina. She looked tired and pale. She wasn't sleeping well. She said the doctor now told her she had migraines. She showed me the pills he had given her, but they meant nothing to me. She had stayed home from work that day to go to the clinic. They had done a tomography, blood tests, and blood pressure measurements; everything was normal. What she really needed, she said, was to take about two weeks off work, but there was no way for her to do that. Regina thought that the terrible, constant din of her factory might be contributing to her problem. She didn't know how much longer she could take it in Japan. Life here was "strange"; there was no time; everything was difficult.

I told her that Catarina was doing well at school. She said Catarina studied Japanese every night; she often had to beg her daughter to do something else. Regina felt bad because she was so tired when she got home that she could not talk much with Catarina. She repeated several times that she did not want Catarina to go into the factory. Catarina's education was important: if she went into the factory, what could she look forward to? She hoped Catarina could go to high school here in Japan. I did not voice my doubts. However much Catarina studied, it would take a miracle for her to learn enough Japanese to pass a high-school entrance examination.

Catarina herself abandoned this dream as the school year wore on, reluctantly preparing to return to Brazil. Several days before her sayonara party, she visited our apartment for an interview. She wore a green sweater and jeans and carried a backpack and a disposable camera. I offered her an orange and some crackers and cheese; she ate a little of everything. She likes green tea, so I made a pot. She took photos of Maria and me together, and of each of us separately. She said she did not want to go back to Brazil. The interview was wrenching, as I had suspected it might be. Catarina has had anything but a settled or calm life. For much of our conversation she was near tears. She is an appealing girl, sometimes enthusiastic and sometimes sad, with many problems not of her own making. I retreated as tactfully as I could from the most searing topics, but it was also clear to me that she wanted someone to listen to what she had to say. I offer these passages to readers because I think that her compelling testimony, a vivid portrayal of her attempts to find serenity and meaning in the midst of the uproar around her, deserves a wider audience. Too often we—parents, relatives, teachers, anthropologists, researchers—treat children as adjuncts of adults, or as lesser beings. Catarina outshines the adults who made the world in which she is forced to live.

Catarina was born in Curitiba. Her father, who lives in Brazil, is of German descent ("tall and blond") and during the past few years has had little contact with her. Catarina resents the fact that his surname appears on her official documents. She prefers to use Regina's Japanese family name.

Regina's parents, both nikkeis, are divorced. Her mother lives in Paranavaí, Paraná; her father, a retired military officer, remarried a much younger woman and now lives in rural São Paulo. After her own separation, Regina returned to Paranavaí with Catarina, then three. When Catarina was ten or eleven, Regina moved back to Curitiba. She married Santos, and the two migrated to Japan. Catarina stayed in Paranavaí with her grandmother, her teenage uncle Hélio, and her aunt Lúcia, a woman in her twenties who has, according to Catarina, "a problem in the head."

By the beginning of 1995, Regina could no longer stand the separation from her daughter. She went to Brazil to fetch her. Catarina was afraid to go to Japan but had no choice. Arranging all the papers—the passport, the visa, the authorization from Catarina's father—was nerve-racking, for Regina had nonrefundable tickets with a set departure date. Through tearful entreaties and "with God's help," she said, they got the visa just in time.

Catarina and I began our conversation by talking about her boring, turbulent life in the household of her grandmother, during the period after Regina had moved out.

## At "home," in Brazil—then

Catarina: My life in Brazil was . . . very dead [*parada*], I didn't do hardly anything. I went to school in the morning, till noon,[2] I went home, there were times when I helped my grandmother. Later on [in the day], I studied, things like that, I . . . it was boring. But after I came to Japan, it got a lot better.

Daniel: I've never been to Paranavaí. Can you describe it for me?

Catarina: It was a small town, a good town, well, on the one hand it was good, but on the other hand no. Because it had some thieves *(laughs)*. But there weren't all that many. I had a lot of friends there, from time to time I'd go out [with them]. Here I also go out, but not so often. In my street there was always some kind of commotion *(laughs)*. The boys would be making a commotion, they would provoke me.

Daniel: What were they doing?

Catarina: They would stand around bothering people, swearing. And there was also a little thief who lived on that street. It really would have been better for me to come to Japan [sooner]. I liked[3] it more [here], but now I'm going to have to go back to Brazil. It's a shame *(soft laughter)*.

Daniel: What was the house like?

Catarina: There's a house in front that's [my grandmother's], it's enormous. My mother and I lived in back. [My grandmother] is a Spiritist, [she has] a center there upstairs. She's a *mãe de santo* [a "mother of the saints," leader of a religious group], she helps people. . . . She gives blessings.[4]

There were always meetings. I didn't participate. I really didn't like it *(laughs)*.

Daniel: Were there always people coming and going to consult with your grandmother?

Catarina: Always. At seven A.M. there were already people there.

Daniel: Every day?

[2]Brazilian schools offer morning and afternoon sessions. Students normally attend classes for just half a day.

[3]In this interview, Catarina often uses past tense in speaking of her life in Japan. By the time of the interview, she had gone liminal.

[4]Catarina described her grandmother's practice as a mixture of Umbanda and Candomblé, two Afro-Brazilian religions. A mãe de santo typically offers *consultas*—advice and ritual curing.

Catarina: Every day, I hardly could talk with her. She didn't have any time for us.

Daniel: What was the school like there?

Catarina: The school was really close by. It was a public school. One of the teachers, Clementina, had been my mother's teacher, and my uncle's, and now she was teaching me. Now she's the vice-principal. I liked that school.

Daniel: What year had you finished there?

Catarina: I was just starting seventh grade. Here it would be ichinen. It was the fourth day of classes. I didn't know my mother was coming to get me. It was a surprise *(soft laugh)*.

Catarina: My grandfather [that is, mother's father] used to get mad at my mother. He wanted to kill my mother. My own uncle Raimundo [mother's older brother] wanted to kill my mother. He would just fight [with everybody], I don't know why.

   When he visited he'd come armed. Once my mother took [his gun], because if she hadn't, he would have killed her. That day there was a big commotion. My uncle fixed on my mother, he ran after her, he had a revolver, he had once been a policeman. I was taking a shower, I didn't know anything. When I came out, I saw everyone fighting, my mother was there in the bedroom with my grandmother, held prisoner, because he wanted to kill [them]. I didn't know what to do, I ran there too. My mother still doesn't talk to Raimundo. My aunt is worthless too, the one married to him, she's also fought with my mother, an ugly fight. My mother once hit my uncle, that kind of thing.

Daniel: And does Raimundo still have contact with the family?

Catarina: He does, yes. He didn't use to be like that. He used to be fine, he'd talk with my mother, they got along well when he was young. A year ago, he and another guy were partners in a snack bar, but it didn't work because someone robbed the lanchonete. He suddenly changed. He's unemployed. My grandmother keeps giving him things, because he's not working. He doesn't do anything, he changed a lot.

   Sometimes my mother would give me money, and he'd take my money. I don't know how he found [it]. My aunt [his wife] would steal my clothes.

   My cousin Joceline, who is their daughter, she's going to be seven in December. I really like her, she's suffered too, she almost died. The girl was small, [my aunt] gave her a kick in the back, it almost killed her. That day there was a fight. My mother hit [the aunt]. So . . . they've never spoken since. Every time they meet they fight.

## *Off to Japan*

Daniel: Could you explain to me about coming to Japan? One day your mother told me, but it was pretty complicated, right?

Catarina: It sure was *(laughing softly)*.

Daniel: Well, first, why did you decide to come here?

Catarina: I didn't decide to come to Japan *(laughs)*.

Daniel: So then tell me, in your own way.

Catarina: OK. Right from the start. My mother and my grandmother always fought. [My grandmother] was always beating it into my head that "Japan is no good," "You won't get along there," "The school is awful," "They'll mistreat you." I'd just sit there thinking. I'm a rebellious person. I'm a little bit rebellious, but now I'm getting better. Then my mother would say, "No, it's not like that." Over a year ago, she was asking me to come to Japan, and I didn't want to.

There were also times when me and my grandmother would fight. Sometimes she'd be mean to me and my uncle. My aunt [Lúcia] has problems, and [Hélio] would hit her, then she'd grab him, she isn't right in the head, she'd say we did it, and then [my grandmother] would lay into me and Hélio. And Hélio would also get disgusted, angry. He's sixteen now. . . . There were times he would cry, then he'd quiet down, he'd say to me, "Don't tell anyone," because we were really close to each other, we were always together at school. After I came here I've been really missing him.

When my mother came to get me, I didn't know about it. She [must have] called [my grandmother] a few days earlier. My grand-mother told me, "I think she's coming to get you." I didn't know what to do. Because [my grandmother] is a Spiritist, she was sure to know [these things]. I thought, I wonder if it's true. . . .

So then, on the fourth day of classes, when I had a free period, my mother showed up in front of the school. I was shocked. She had my grandfather's car. I looked at her. It was a long time since I'd seen her, I thought she looked strange, she was strange, she was laughing. I was rooted to the spot. I was afraid *(small laugh)*. Then I looked at her, and I said, "*Mãe*" [Mom]. She said, "Yes, it's me, I came to get you." I said, "I'm not going, forget it," and we started to fight. Then my mother went into the school to talk with the principal, to get my papers to take to Japan.

I was crying. I didn't want to go away with my mother, no way. I ran away. She came after me, I made a huge scandal, ai, it's so embarrassing, even today I'm sorry about it *(laughs)*. I didn't know anything about Japan, after my grandma said so much stuff . . . she didn't even seem like my mother's mother. . . . That's right. But after I went to Japan, I saw it wasn't like that. I like it here now and I don't want to leave *(soft laugh)*.

Daniel: What kinds of things was your grandmother saying, exactly?

Catarina: She'd say, "Japan's no good," she said a bunch of things about my mother, she'd say, "Your mother cut classes," that my mother never liked to study. "Ah, you're going to be just like her, if you stay around her" . . . I didn't know where I stood. . . .

Daniel: You were in the middle—

Catarina: Right.

Daniel: Of those other people.

Catarina: Divided. There were people who said a bunch of things about my mother, and about me. I got tired of that, but I put up with it, I *had* to put up with it. I didn't know if what they said was true or a lie. They said a lot of things to me, stupid things. . . . They even said . . . that my mother was worthless, that she would rather be with my stepfather than with me. [My mother] would call [us in] Brazil and I wouldn't talk to her. . . . I'd say I wasn't there, or that I'd gone out. . . . I never talked to her, but one time I did. I said that I wanted *(clears throat)* to finish eighth grade [in Brazil], but she wouldn't let me. She came to get me. And I saw it wasn't like [they had told me], she explained everything.

Daniel: How was [your flight]?

Catarina: During the takeoff I got sick because I'd never flown in an airplane. Then we got to Japan and it was strange for me because I didn't know anything. I didn't know how to eat with chopsticks. The very first day we left the airport and went to eat rāmen, I couldn't figure out how to do it, I was ashamed, but afterward I got the knack.

My stepfather and a friend of his were there. They had left work in their uniforms. They picked us up in a van. In the beginning I got along well with him, but then it got worse.

Daniel: And you went to Chiba prefecture, right?

Catarina: Yes. My mother wanted me to start [public] school. But where I lived there weren't many Brazilians, I was afraid and wouldn't go. My mother's boss arranged [for me to enter] a [private] language school. So then I started to study nihongo, and I began to meet a lot of people, I met Americans, Koreans, Chinese, an Indonesian, ah, I liked it. Things got better.

I just stayed there a month, because after a month we moved, [my mother and stepfather] had arranged jobs [in Mie prefecture], to work in the Brother factory.

Daniel: Did you go to school [in Mie]?

Catarina: Not there, that's really not a good place. We practically lived ... in a *cortiço* [a slum tenement] *(laughs)*, ah, that was horrible, the bathroom and everything. There were only Peruvians there, illegals.

Daniel: It was a factory dormitory?

Catarina: Yes. They had told us it was a beautiful house, my mother believed it. That place had two floors, the stairway was practically falling down. There was a kitchen, bathroom, and furo, upstairs there were two bedrooms, it was horrible, sickening. There was a green carpet, but it was old, everything stank. [We lived there] two months.

Daniel: Were there other kids living there?

Catarina: ... Yes, sort of. ... The only one really [living] there was a Peruvian. I think he was sixteen. I actually tried to talk to him, but it doesn't work with Peruvians, they're a pain. There were some Brazilians who lived there. They were fine. Not in the cortiço, across the way was an apartment building. They talked with us and everything, I even was going to return to Brazil with them, except ... it didn't work out, now I'm going back before them.

Daniel: So you didn't go to school there?

Catarina: No, I stayed home all day long.

Daniel: Uh-huh, doing ...

Catarina: Nothing *(laughs)*. Like, sometimes I'd listen to music, [or] study nihongo, in Chiba I'd learned katakana, hiragana, I didn't know kanji. It was here that I learned kanji, at Homi Chūgakkō. ...

Daniel: So it wasn't a life that was very ... agreeable.

Catarina: It wasn't *(small laugh)*. It really wasn't.

Catarina: [We came to Homi] I think it was in month eight [of 1995] ... ai, what day, I think it was day seven.

Daniel: Seventh of August?

Catarina: Yes, that was it. After being here for a while, I forgot the [Brazilian words for the] months.[5]

At first, we were in 142. We didn't even stay there a week, because we couldn't stand it, it's terrible. Down below there was a *commotion*, a bunch of young punks [*moleques*], all Brazilians. The nihonjin complained because they turned their music all the way up, you can't do that.

Most of the people [in that building] are Brazilians, we really couldn't stand it. Even though I also am one *(amusement in voice)*. They're really troublemakers. And there are also thieves in 142. They broke into the apartment of a friend of my mother's. He rang the bell of this girl's apartment, and pushed his way in. Luckily she had someone with her, because she lived with another woman. And he left.

In 142 there are bikers, it was no good. The day I arrived at Homi I already wanted to leave. But after we moved to 128 it got better. Now in 11 it's gotten a lot better. It's just that 11 is dangerous because when you go by Family Mart [a convenience store at the foot of the Ken-ei apartments] there's a bunch of furyō. They hang around there, one time when I was leaving they started to follow me. I walked slowly, because if I ran they would run too. They were boys, and I was alone. I never went there alone again. It's very dangerous there.

Daniel: Worse than Brazil?

Catarina: Ah . . . I guarantee it *(small laugh)*.

### At "home," in Japan—now

Daniel: [To leave Brazil,] there's a lot of paperwork. [You] also [needed] a document from your father . . .

Catarina: That was the hardest, because he didn't want to give it to us. I still don't talk to him, [I haven't] since I was little. I don't think I've told you that before. He never talked to me, we haven't seen each other for a long time. I never got along with him. I can't bring myself to call him "Dad." Now I've got my stepfather, only I can't call him "Dad" either. I never had a father. Sometimes there are fights at home, I can't bear them anymore. I decided that I'm going to leave here. I told them, "It's better for me [to go] than to be in the way here." It's no good. I never had a father.

[5]In Japanese, the months are named *ichigatsu* (one-month—that is, January), *nigatsu* (two-month), and so on.

Daniel: These situations, as you know, they're always a little difficult—

Catarina: They are.

Daniel:—when there's a stepfather, stepmother, well, you probably know other people—

Catarina: Yes, I do.

Daniel:—in difficult situations because of this. Here in Japan life isn't easy—

Catarina: Ah, it really isn't.

Daniel:—and often the adults have problems too.

Catarina: They do.

Daniel: And unfortunately, sometimes they involve their children—

Catarina: It's true. That's what I tell my mother. Sometimes they fight and my mother vents her anger at me. That makes me mad, and I tell her that. Sometimes she understands, and sometimes she doesn't. But then she thinks about it, she feels sorry and comes to talk with me, except by then it's too late, there's already been another fight.

Daniel: Yes, it's really very hard.

## A point of rest?

Daniel: When did you start school [at Homi Chū]?

Catarina: I started the twenty-sixth of month ten.

Daniel: So you spent over two months here without going to school?

Catarina: Without going to school.

Daniel: Doing what?

Catarina: I stayed at home and studied. Sometimes I helped out, cleaning the house, there was always dinner, because I had to make dinner. . . . Afterwards they put me in school. . . . The first day was bad.

Daniel: Can you describe your first day of school to me?

Catarina: Marly took me. Then I went with my [homeroom] teacher, the *tannin-no-sensei*, Wada-sensei, to room 26. There were Brazilians there. Sebastião was by my side. I'd say things to him [in Portuguese], and he'd speak [Japanese].

The first day was bad, I didn't understand hardly anything. I didn't know what to do. There was that Peruvian girl [Rieko], she helped me a lot. In the first days the English teacher kept asking me to say things in Japanese. I just sat there, I didn't know anything.

Daniel: And the Japanese students, how did they treat you?

Catarina: The first day, there was a boy [sitting] behind me, I didn't understand what he was saying, and he started to shout at me. Then the

Peruvian girl came and told me [what he was saying]. He was in my group, for *kyūshoku* [lunch] and everything, [I did] everything together with him. That boy was obnoxious, nobody in our homeroom liked him. [In the beginning] he said he didn't like me, then later he started to try to talk to me. I wouldn't talk to him, I just made faces at him. I remembered that during the first week he'd just been bugging me.

Now there's another boy, Tanaka-*kun*, he's the funniest boy in the school, he's in my group.[6] Hiroyuki teaches him Portuguese, and then he comes to talk to me *(laughs)*, [he says] *Tchau, Bom dia*—those things. He's great, he was like the only person who I've gotten along with, nihonjin, but then I started talking to the others and it got better, now everyone treats me well.

Daniel: And the teachers?

Catarina: I got along well with them too, I don't have any complaints about them. Well, yelling is normal, because they all yell, when everybody's making a lot of racket, but I think that's fine.

Daniel: And did the teachers hit the students?[7]

Catarina: That happened in my class, it really scared me. [The teacher] hit a nihonjin. The boy isn't quite right in the head, [the teacher] hit and kicked the boy. That's when Sebastião stood up. "You can't keep hitting him, if you're going to hit him, why don't you hit me," confronting the teacher. And [Rieko], the Peruvian, just kept looking at me. I didn't say anything.

Daniel: So Sebastião confronted the teacher?

Catarina: He confronted him.

Daniel: How amazing. . . . And that didn't cause a problem with the teacher?

Catarina: The teacher didn't say a word.

Daniel: It's something so rare it's scary, isn't it.

Catarina: It's really scary, it's worse than scary. I remember that after everything had quieted down, [Sebastião] asked us, "Don't tell anyone about this, because if you do the boys will tease me, because I defended [him]."

Daniel: How would you compare [Homi Chū] with your school in Brazil?

Catarina: Well . . . comparing them, even though things are hard, I pre-

---

[6]The suffix *kun* (Mr.) is sometimes used to refer to or address young males.

[7]Brazilian students often told me of such events, which they found shocking.

fer it here, I wish that schools in Brazil were like [these]. To stay all afternoon at school [as we do here], I'd really like it.

Daniel: If you could change something in the school here, however you wanted to, what would you do?

Catarina: Me, change something? I wouldn't change anything, it's fine as it is *(laughs)*.

Daniel: So really, as far as school goes, you're satisfied.

Catarina: I am, yes I am, I'm very satisfied.

Daniel: And do you think you learned a lot here?

Catarina: I really learned a lot. In Brazil I wouldn't have had the chance to learn so many things.

### Brazilian or Japanese?

Daniel: Do you feel more Brazilian or more Japanese?

Catarina: *Ih!* [exclamation.] It's a hard question *(laughs)*. Well. Ah, I feel both of them at once *(laughs)*, both of them. I feel like, yes, brasileira and nihonjin *(laughs)*.

Daniel: And in Brazil how did you feel?

Catarina: In Brazil, nothing, just Brazilian *(sighs)*. There, it was just Brazilian. I didn't do hardly anything, I went to school in the morning, things like that *(spoken in a sad voice)*.

Daniel: Did people call you "japonesa" there?

Catarina: In the private school, from preschool to third grade I went there, I had that problem a lot. They called me "japonesa," me and my friend, because she was also a nihonjin. We went around together all the time, the two *descendentes*. The others would say, "Hey, japonesa," things like that. But afterward [in the] public school, I never had [that problem].

Daniel: You didn't feel yourself to be a Japanese-Brazilian, just a person?

Catarina: I didn't feel anything.

Daniel: And coming here, that changed?

Catarina: Ah, I think I changed *(clears her throat)*.

Daniel: Can you explain it to me.

Catarina: Ai, well ... my God ... I feel, I don't know how to explain it. ... Well, it's like in Brazil I'd never have the chance to know anything about Japan. There I didn't feel anything, as I said, but now in Japan, I had the opportunity to learn about Japanese culture. I know something [about] kanji, hiragana, katakana, how to talk a little, I could understand what they said, I'm starting to adapt to the people in my classroom. Now that I'm starting to go around with nihonjin, I'm leaving for Brazil, that's going to be a real drag for me. Even today I'm going somewhere with a nihonjin. And the Peruvian girl is also coming with us. . . . It's a real shame, because I like it here, the people, I'm starting to talk with the girls in my homeroom, it's too bad.

Daniel: I think you described yourself as one part Brazilian and one part Japanese. What's the Brazilian part?

Catarina: The Brazilian part . . . I really don't feel very good about it. I'd rather be more nihonjin.

Daniel: The nihonjin Catarina, what's she like?

Catarina: She's fine, I like that part. I'm very talkative. With the kids, right. I don't know if I talk a lot but when the time comes to talk I talk. . . . well, that's it *(laughs)*.

Daniel: And the brasileira Catarina, what's she like?

Catarina: The brasileira Catarina, she likes to go to *festas* [parties] a lot, every birthday that there was in our street we'd have a festa. That was really great. There were times we'd go to a movie. All that I liked a lot.

Daniel: So that Catarina likes birthday parties. Doesn't the Japanese Catarina like them?

Catarina: Ah . . . I don't like them much, here in Japan. After I came to Japan I found those festas strange, I prefer the festas of Japan.

Daniel: Such as?

Catarina: Like *hanabi* [fireworks], those I like. There are a lot of festas. Well, I don't know all the festas, but the ones I went to [here] I liked a lot. I enjoyed myself, with the nihonjin.

Daniel: Mm-hmm. And is being among nihonjin different from being among Brazilians?

Catarina: It's different.

Daniel: How?

Catarina: Well . . . among nihonjin you learn a lot, they teach you a lot, culture and things like that. But with Brazilians you don't learn anything because they're Brazilians, it's always the same thing. Yes, that's it.

Daniel: How is it the same thing?

Catarina: The same thing, like, you talk, it's just talking, shooting the breeze [*jogando papo no ar*], that's the dumbest thing there is.

Daniel: Don't Japanese people shoot the breeze?

Catarina: Well, not with me, but with others, they must. But they teach me a lot of things, because I'm a Brazilian, I'm not a nihonjin, they teach me a lot of culture. Another time we went walking in a park, I really liked it. We also went to an *onsen* [a hot spring], those things.

Daniel: Do you think in time you could be accepted in Japan as a japonesa?

Catarina: Yes.

### Going "home" to Brazil—next week

Daniel: Well . . . [now] you're leaving Japan, Catarina.

Catarina: I don't want to work here. Someday I'll have to work, but I want to finish school. I want to study languages, things like that. . . . So one part is studying, and a little bit is the [strife in my] family, but it's more because of studying.

Daniel: Why is it you don't want to go into the factory?

Catarina: The things that they say, in the factory it's one person trying to take advantage of the other, those Brazilian things . . . Work here, no way. I'd rather study, I always wanted to study, to do something, to be someone in life.

Daniel: And life in Japan in general, how is it different from Brazil?

Catarina: Well . . . the situation. Ai, there are a lot of things there, people say there isn't much inflation now, but there is, prices going up . . . Those people in the street, poor people, those beggars, those street children. Here there isn't so much of that, here there isn't any, to tell the truth. Things like that I really don't like about Brazil.

I'm going to find it strange because I've been here for a year. When I get back to Brazil I won't know what my friends are saying, I'll be out of it. Later on things will get better. But I prefer it here, the level of studies here is higher. But for me, there's no way I can enter kōkō. . . . If I could, I would.

Daniel: Looking toward your return to Brazil, what are you going to miss?

Catarina: I'm going to miss the school, my parents, the teachers, you, because you're really OK *(she laughs)*—

Daniel: Thanks!

Catarina:—my friends . . . I'm going to really miss the culture here. For sure I'm going to study nihongo. I'll study *eigo* [English] too, I want to study languages. I'm going to miss this place a lot, because I won't have the opportunities I had here. If it was up to me I'd never leave Japan.

Daniel: And what do you miss here about Brazil?

Catarina: ... Well ... to tell the truth, nothing at all. I'm not the same person anymore. ... In Brazil, I won't have time for myself, I really don't want to have any time for myself. I want to study a lot. Here my mother gives me attention, even though she works and everything she has time for me, but my grandma never had any time, that was really bad.

Like I said, I was rebellious, in that way I changed a lot. I would think things like, Ai, my mother doesn't like me, that's what I thought about all the time.

Daniel: So you were able to understand your mother's situation a little better, here?

Catarina: Yes, I could understand it much better.

Daniel: Will you live again in your grandma's house?

Catarina: Yes.

Daniel: And you'll go to school there in Paranavaí.

Catarina: That's right, to the same school I was in before.

Daniel: Well ... what do you think about your return, how do you feel?

Catarina: *(sighing)* Ahh, well. Those same things are going to happen. So it'll be the same life I had before. I won't get hardly any attention *(small sigh)*. ... I know that *(voice falling)*, that I won't get *much* attention, it's going to be like *always*, my aunt has problems, she's always provoking me, things like that, everything will start all over again. ... That's what's bad, that I think about most, that's what I'm afraid of.

The boys also used to provoke me. I fought a lot with them, I don't like them much. I feel sorry for Lúcia, but sometimes it's no good, she keeps provoking me, but all right, I keep quiet because she has problems.

Daniel: Yes. I know how hard it is not to get into arguments.

Catarina: Yes, it is.

Daniel: People provoke you but—

Catarina: It's true.

Daniel: It's better not to get into it—

Catarina: It's better not to get into it.

Daniel:—and keep—

Catarina: But they keep saying bad things about me, I can't stand that *(laughs softly)*.

Daniel: Yes, that's hard, it's hard to put up with it.

Catarina: It's hard. For sure they're talking about me a lot when I'm not there. When I was in Brazil, I almost moved to my godfather's house. He wanted me to come, and there was a fight. My godfather told my grandmother that it wasn't working out. My mother wanted me to live [with my godfather], because she didn't want me to stay with my grandmother, so that the same thing wouldn't happen to me that happened to her, because she suffered a lot. But it didn't work out. My godfather, I still talk with him, except my godmother doesn't much like my mother. She's kind of—

Daniel: Does [your godfather] live there in Paranavaí?

Catarina: Yes, in Paranavaí.

Daniel: You've got a reasonable relationship with him.

Catarina: I do, he's fine, I like him a lot, and also his children—

Daniel: You could visit him at his house.

Catarina: I could, I always used to go to their house by bicycle.

Daniel: I think that's important, to have people—

Catarina: Yes.

Daniel:—that you can visit, to be comfortable with those people.

Catarina: Yes.

Daniel: And then knowing that you also made friends here in Japan—

Catarina: Ah, that's bad too.

Daniel:—who will think about you.

Catarina: Well, what will they think, what will they call me, when I get there, because the boys of my street are like that. Because I traveled overseas, when I arrive for sure they're going to start calling me "japonesa." They'll call me that, I'm sure, because I know them very well, but afterwards, as time passes, they'll—

Daniel: It will pass.

Catarina: It will pass, there's no problem because it won't bother me. I'm really, there's nothing you can do about it *(laughs)*.

Daniel: Well . . . well, I hope that everything goes well—

Catarina: Ai.

Daniel: It's possible that there will be problems, life is like that—

Catarina: I'll have them, of that I have no doubt *(laughs softly)*. I feel so good now, but when I get there my grandma is going to ask me a bunch of things, how come I'm returning. [I worry that] she'll start up with the stupid things again about my mother. . . . I'm going to have to put up with my aunt. . . . I know I'm going to have to put up with a lot yet.

Daniel: But at least you know what to expect and you're a year older, maybe it will be . . .

Catarina: Yes, OK.

Daniel: Well, you must know that adults are, really, sometimes very ridiculous, and they say *(Catarina sighs)* a lot of stupid things.

Catarina: In my family it's like that.

Daniel: Yes, but it's not only your family—

Catarina: Yes, I know that.

Daniel: —but adults are like that.

Catarina: I know.

Daniel: Sometimes kids think, Well, adults know a lot about life and everything, but a lot of times it's not true—

Catarina: Yes, that's right *(laughs)*.

Daniel: —because adults also have big problems—

Catarina: Right.

Daniel: —and don't know how to think about them—

Catarina: Yes, I know.

Daniel: —and they say ridiculous things, right—

Catarina: Right.

Daniel: —and well, if you can manage not to pay attention to those ridiculous things, good, but I know that sometimes—

Catarina: It bothers you a lot.

Daniel: It bothers you, it's hard, mainly when they're talking about you, or your mother *(Catarina sighs)*, but, well . . . It's really their problem. . . . Understand.

Catarina: Yes, I do understand.

Daniel: Do you know when your mother will go back to Brazil?

Catarina: I don't know. It's going to be a long time before I see her. She says she wants to stay here two more years but I know it's not that way. Because she's not going to be able to get the money together. But now I'm going back to Brazil. I was here just a year. I guarantee that she'll stay here about five more years. . . . She'll leave her present job and get another, things like that.

Daniel: That's what it's like here, no one really knows, I just know she wants to leave, but . . .

Catarina: Yes, except she says it's not possible to go back to Brazil for the time being. This year she doesn't want to go back.

Daniel: Well, I don't really know. .... You'll be able to throw yourself into your studies, you'll learn a lot of languages—

Catarina: That's what I really want.

Daniel:—and maybe the next time we meet we'll speak ... English, right—

Catarina: Right *(she laughs, then Daniel).*

Daniel:—or another one—

Catarina: Right.

Daniel:—who knows, French *(they laugh)*—

Catarina: French, do you know how to speak that?

Daniel: Ah, no, I don't speak it well. Just—

Catarina: I studied French, but I forgot it.

Daniel: But you'll learn English, I think English will be very easy—

Catarina: Yes.

Daniel:—for you, after learning Japanese.

Catarina: Yes, nihongo, I'm going to learn nihongo, eigo, and then Spanish.

Daniel: That will be really great.

Catarina: I'm going to learn a bunch of languages, I want to learn a lot.

Daniel: And with those languages you'll have a future there in Brazil, you can go to university, and who knows what.

Catarina: I already know what I'm going to do, all the courses, I've decided everything.

Daniel: Well, Catarina, would you like to say anything else?

Catarina: No *(laughs).* Well ... Uh ... *(laughs)* something else to say. At this moment when I'm going back to Brazil, leaving people here, [I want to say] it was great meeting all of you too, meeting Americans who speak Portuguese *(both laugh)*, and nihongo. I liked it a lot here, meeting all these people who were really different, who I never thought I'd meet. .... Yes, that makes me very happy, I met a lot of people, Koreans, like in Chiba, nihonjin, from my class, I liked them.

Daniel: Mm-hmm. And that will always be with you.

Catarina: It will. For sure *(laughs softly).*

## Full circle—but not quite

This interview, as I am sure the reader noted, left me periodically at a loss for words. I had the constant sense that the ground could open up at any moment, and it occasionally did, leaving us on the edge of an abyss of uncertainty and fear. I tried to offer simple reassurances, inadequate as I knew they were. I am Catarina's friend; I wanted to acknowledge her fears and yet to help her feel that things might work out. Transcripts are brutal: I find my words clumsy and insufficient. Nevertheless, once we had plunged into the conversation, it would have been wrong, I believe, to cut it short or retreat abruptly. It was important for her to have her say, and for me to listen and provide what encouragement I could.

Ethnography, if it is to address the worlds of others in a serious way, is sometimes risky business. You see things you might not wish to see, and find yourself caught up with others in ways that demand your engagement as a human being as well as a professional. The neat exploration of neatly defined topics is sometimes not an option, as research objectives are overwhelmed by more compelling and encompassing responsibilities.

Catarina finds herself propelled from one precarious situation to another, never quite able to find a place of shelter from the human maelstroms that swirl around her and sometimes catch her up. To her, the commitments of the adults closest to her seem always equivocal, unsatisfying. In her eyes, she has no father; she has a mother who cares for her and yet cannot provide fully for her needs; she has a grandmother with all-consuming religious involvements and a sharp tongue; she has an aunt who has "a problem in the head." There are hints of affection in her references to her teenage uncle and godfather, but her comments on her life in Brazil convey an overwhelming impression of emptiness punctuated by episodes of verbal and even physical fighting. Even worse, perhaps, is the tug-of-war on her emotions generated by the insults and criticisms directed at those close to her by others close to her, leaving her, as she pointedly observes, "divided."

The phrase "human warmth," which most of my interviewees strongly associated with Brazilians, never once appears in the transcript of my conversation with Catarina. Perhaps this is because Brazil is not, for Catarina, "home," if by "home" we mean a place where one feels at ease, secure, welcome, surrounded by people upon whom one can rely for protection and love. In this sense, there is no "home" anywhere in Catarina's account, neither in Brazil nor in Japan. She is adrift.

Being adrift, she clings desperately to certain pieces of herself that make life bearable—most notably her desire to learn, manifested in her devotion to her studies, her infatuation with languages and cultures, and her final reluctant decision to return to Brazil. One should not underestimate the institutional attractions of school for students living in disturbing or chaotic conditions. Homi Chū, so often the object of intense criticism by the Brazilian teenagers I knew, is for Catarina a refuge, despite its own episodes of violence. After a difficult start, with the support of teachers and a few friends, she has acquainted herself with Japanese ways and begun to connect with a few Japanese students. The all-consuming nature of middle-school life, with its long days, brief vacations, and excruciatingly detailed organization, is for Catarina liberating, for it offers relief and distraction from the difficulties and anxieties of family life that have always tormented her.

Moreover, her world has expanded immeasurably. She has made Japanese friends, a Peruvian friend, and has met Koreans and Americans, people very unlike the irritating boys in her street in Paranavaí. The world is bigger than Catarina ever dreamed it was, and it contains people more sympathetic than she ever imagined. Romanticism and denial color her view, but her enthusiasm for other people and other ways distinguishes her markedly from most of the Brazilian adolescents in Homi Danchi. The unknown world out there offers hope, in contrast to a known world that has offered so little.

Given Catarina's turbulent biography, the question of ethnic identity shrinks in significance, or perhaps takes on an unusually personal cast. Is she Brazilian? Is she Japanese? The question is hard for her, in part because, I think, it does not address the issues that are most central to her. She seems to reject Brazilianness, but Brazilianness is a surrogate in her account for the frustrations, annoyances, sadness, and emptiness of her life in her grandmother's house in Paranavaí. By moving out from family, street, and neighborhood (and, by extension, from the nation), she finds a self that she likes, that has some promise. Japaneseness, of which she approves, stands in for her newly acquired knowledge, for human contacts that are not dangerously volatile, for organized days and relief from the ingrown oppressiveness of family conflicts. I think she does not care much if she is a Brazilian Catarina or a Japanese Catarina; those are my inventions. She would rather be a Catarina-at-home, in Brazil or Japan; but adrift as she is, she prefers to be a Catarina-learning, a Catarina-extending-herself.

In fall 1996, I received a letter from Paranavaí. It came in an envelope, decorated with cute drawings and mangled English. I inferred that Catarina must have taken Japanese writing materials, which often feature such gibberish, with her to Brazil. Inside, on stationery headed by little monkeys at sea—"At the tip of the boat, they flagged in their friendship"—Catarina had written a message in her flowing hand. She asked about Eli's studies, Maria's work in the adult school, my book. She said she was well, but mentioned nothing of school, friends, or family in Paranavaí. She did say that she was going to spend the holidays in Japan with Regina and would visit her friends in Homi. If we came to Brazil, she wrote, she would receive us with open arms. She signed the letter "Noriko," in Chinese characters.

# Elisa Aoshima

## *"To be Brazilian is to be clever"*

### *Graduation Day*

All week the students at Homi Chū had been rehearsing the minutiae of the middle-school graduation ceremony, scheduled for the morning of Thursday, March 7, 1996. I arrived at school early. With time to kill, I walked down past the playground toward Homi town. Spring was approaching, but the sunlight was still wintry. A Mahler symphony issued from the school's loudspeakers and rode the cold air erratically across the barren fields, which were plowed but not yet planted.

I circled back up to the school gym. Heels and women's sandals littered the entranceway. Most fathers were at work, and in most Japanese families, education is women's business. Mr. Fujita, one of the Kokusai teachers, showed me to the parents' seating area. The cavernous building exuded a faint, permanent smell of sweat, strangely appropriate to the occasion. It was crowded; I sat in the last row.

Parents and teachers had dressed formally, in dark suits, dresses, and kimonos. The girls had exchanged their usual white sailor collars for special black ones. The boys wore their black winter military-style uniforms, fully buttoned.

A red-and-white striped banner, six feet wide, ringed the interior of the unheated gym. I imagined snow drifting down from the rafters. A thin green carpet provided no insulation from the frigid wooden floor. The first- and second-year students sat behind me, segregated by sex. Boys were on the right facing the stage, girls on the left. I turned around and nodded to Edival and Jefferson, whom I knew from the Kokusai. A small band had assembled in the rear. Sandwiched between teachers and parents were the chairs of the graduating sannensei.

A white strip marked the approach route to the stage, where the students would receive their diplomas beneath flags of Japan, Toyota City, and Homi Chū. The podium, flanked by a bonsai pine tree, stood before a golden screen. Potted flowers lined the proscenium, and elaborate floral displays bracketed the scene.

An elaborate choreography would now unfold. At 9:15 the invited dignitaries—representatives of Toyota City, the Board of Education, local schools, the PTA, and neighborhood associations—filed in and took their seats to the right of the stage. A few minutes later the band struck up a march, and everyone—parents, teachers, students—began rhythmically clapping as the sannensei paraded in, two-by-two. The boy-girl pairs peeled apart when they reached the seats, boys to the right and girls to the left. They remained standing until everyone in their homeroom had arrived, then sat down en masse. The cadenced applause continued until all the graduating students were seated.

A moment of silence followed. Everyone stood and bowed. Then the assembly sang *Kimigayo*, the unofficial, controversial Japanese national anthem.[1] Edival and Jefferson did not join in. I am sure they were indifferent to the hymn, and probably they did not know the words.

Up on the stage, a kimono-clad teacher presented a tray of diplomas to the principal, who received it with white-gloved hands. For the next half-hour, one at a time, students climbed the stage. In each homeroom, the boys went first. The presentations were crisp and stylized, each gesture refined to the last detail. I kept an eye out for the Brazilian students. Miriam, who alone among the sannensei managed never to buy a Homi Chū uniform, went to the stage in a black dress. Throughout the ceremony, a solo piano cycled through popular songs: "Bridge over Troubled Water," "My Way," and the inspirational Japanese school favorite "Tomorrow."

The first- and second-year students in the audience had been instructed how to sit—boys with hands balled up, one fist on each knee; girls with hands folded in the lap; everyone with back straight, chest out, motionless. I noticed that Edival was chewing gum, undoubtedly a violation of the rules. Jefferson fiddled with his collar; maybe it was binding. The boy beside him gave him an elbow and a dirty look. I wondered how the girls, seated across the gym from me, were doing. Barelegged, in thin skirts, they couldn't have found it easy to sit like statues in that cold. The students started to fidget, furtively shifting feet and hands.

[1]*Kimigayo*, considered by many an emblem of Japanese imperialism and right-wing patriotism, is abjured by some less traditional schools. It became the official national anthem only in 1999.

By 10:00, the last sannensei, the Brazilian Elisa Aoshima, had come down from the stage with her diploma. But the graduation ceremony continued for another hour and twenty minutes, with speeches, songs, congratulations, exhortations, thanks to the sannensei from the ninensei, thanks to the teachers from the sannensei—in short, a succession of ritualized assertions of status, solidarity, and passage. There was no hint of playfulness or merriment. Nor was there casual whispering or joking in the audience. On this March morning the Homi Chū gym had become a sacred space befitting a crucial Japanese life transition.

## Out of options

Of Homi Chū's 237 graduates, 157 were headed to public high schools, 59 to private high schools, 9 to trade schools, 6 to work, and 6 to other pursuits. Almost all the students were on track. They had survived the infamous academic and disciplinary pressures of middle school and could now move on. Intense studying and long hours of juku had paid off with admission to high school, which, given more hard work, might be the gateway to a decent university.

But the Brazilians fell mostly into the last two categories: "work" and "other." Though 95 percent of all Homi Chū graduates were going to continue their secondary education, only three of the seven graduating Brazilians would do so.[2] Yukio and Júlio had, through unusual determination and effort, and with the support of their families, made it into Japanese technical high schools. Amália, a more recent arrival, had no prayer of admission to any Japanese high school, but she was returning to a *colégio* (high school) in Brazil. In contrast, Miriam had no plans whatsoever, and Hiroyuki and Renato were headed straight for the factory.

The seventh Brazilian graduate, perhaps the most gifted of all, was Elisa Aoshima. When I began working with Elisa, she had been in Japan just five months. She impressed me from the start as an unusually bright, thoughtful, mature person. The Brazilian students rarely engaged me in a serious way about my own activities, but Elisa was curious about what I was doing, about the field of anthropology, about what kind of book I intended to write. She had extraordinary poise, a modest manner, and a quiet wit. She got along with the Brazilians, with the

[2]Many Brazilian students dropped out of middle school before graduation. They never even made it into the statistics.

Japanese, with the teachers. People said that Elisa was the only Brazilian never to be persecuted by Japanese students at Homi Chū, and I could see why. She made the best of the extraordinary personal qualities with which she had been blessed.

But despite her gifts, Elisa had not learned enough Japanese to gain admittance to a Japanese high school. No one could have done so in such a short time. She had gone so far as to ask Homi Chū whether she could repeat her third year. She was told no: in effect, she would be forced to graduate. She then toyed with the idea of entering Nanzan International High School, where the famous Marly, for several years the guardian angel of incoming Brazilian students at Homi Chū, had gone. But Nanzan, a private school that caters to the children of Japanese executives and professionals who have lived abroad, is expensive, beyond her family's means. On Elisa's behalf, unknown to her, I asked Nanzan about a scholarship. Unfortunately, I was informed, no funds were available.

Elisa, who did not want to return to Brazil alone, ran out of options. Graduation was the last day of her educational career. In the end, like most teenage Brazilians who stay in Japan, she turned from the challenge of the Japanese school to the challenge of the Japanese factory.

## Departures and arrivals

Elisa Aoshima was born in 1981 to a nikkei father and brasileira mother. She first became my student in the Kokusai in November 1995, having arrived in Japan in May of the same year. Her Japanese quickly outstripped mine. She lived with her mother Djalma in a Kōdan apartment in Homi Danchi, along with her seventeen-year-old brother, who worked at an auto-carpet factory. Djalma made car seats at Aichi Industries. Elisa's father had just gone to Brazil for a visit; he returned in early 1996. Like his son, he made auto carpets.

Elisa's parents had traveled to Japan in the spring of 1993 from the family's home in Uberaba, Minas Gerais, west of Belo Horizonte. This is where, in a conversation held on April 1, 1996, we pick up her story, preceded by a bit of Elisa's characteristically sly banter.

Daniel *(speaking to the tape recorder)*: I'm here with Elisa in our apartment in Homi Danchi, on April 1, 1996—
Elisa: *(laughing)* It just so happens it's April Fool's Day [*Dia da Mentira*, "Lying Day"].

Daniel: Oh, yes, well—

Elisa: It is in Japan too, did you know that?

Daniel: Also in the United States.

Elisa: Ah, there too?

Daniel: Right. Uh, let's start like this. ... Before coming here, Elisa, what was your life like in Brazil?

Elisa: In Brazil I was just studying. My parents came [to Japan] two years earlier, so I was staying with my aunt, in Uberaba.

Daniel: Who was living there?

Elisa: Me, my brother, my aunt, and three cousins.

Daniel: [You were living in] your family's house?

Elisa: Uh-huh, but it was like, there was my house, and on one side was my grandmother's house, and on the other was my other aunt's house, so there was family all around. I think it gave more support to me and my brother, having family members nearby.

Daniel: Did your parents make a trip back to Brazil during that period?

Elisa: No.

Daniel: So it was two years in a row—

Elisa: Two years straight, in a row.

Daniel: How did you communicate with each other?

Elisa: Telephone, letters, every weekend they called. They sent a lot of photos, they wrote about what work was like, in detail, because you can't talk a lot on the telephone. I was always writing too, [saying] what I was doing in Brazil, how things were going at school.

Daniel: And how were things at school?

Elisa: School was going well, nossa.

Daniel: Describe the school you were going to.

Elisa: I know that school from top to bottom *(small laugh)*, because I began studying there when I was three and that's the only place I ever went. The school had two floors, it wasn't very big, it must have what, about ten classrooms. A snack bar, a patio, really different from the schools here.

[It was] a nice school. I liked the teachers too. A private school, Colégio Progresso. My brother went there too.

Daniel: Do you remember when your parents left Brazil?

Elisa: I remember *(small laugh)*.

Daniel: Describe it for me.

Elisa: ... Nossa. ... When I heard they were going ... it was like ... I didn't feel too much emotion, thinking it was a lie, but when the time came, when they were packing their bags, when they were getting ready to leave, nossa . . . I got very emotional, I cried a lot, because I saw they were going to be really far away.

Daniel: Did you really understand how far away they were going?

Elisa: I understood.

Daniel: Did you know other people who had made the same journey?

Elisa: Yes, in my family . . . my father's younger brother, and one of his sisters, and my grandparents had gone too. And there were more distant relatives who had gone too.

Daniel: Did you know then, when your parents left, how long it would be?

Elisa: I didn't know *(small laugh)*, they [left] in April, and [my brother and I] were supposed to come in December of the same year [1993], those were the plans *(laughs)*, except there was a problem with our papers. My grandmother [was born in Brazil but] has dual nationality, [so she could be considered either an issei or a nissei]. [If she were considered an issei], my brother and I are sansei, but [if she were considered a nissei, as her papers then showed] we would be yonsei, fourth generation, and that's where the problem was, [fourth-generation people] can't get a [long-term] visa. So we had to change all the papers beginning with hers, then my parents', then mine and my brother's. It took a long time.

Daniel: It took almost a year and a half, right.

Elisa: We thought we wouldn't be able to come, we almost gave up. But it all worked out.

Daniel: Do you remember the trip to Japan? How did you feel at that moment?

Elisa: Happy, I had such a feeling of happiness, I was going to see my parents and everything, I was feeling nervous. When we got to the airport there were relatives there, who lived in São Paulo, waiting to say good-bye to us. I'd never seen an airplane up close. . . . I was so . . . excited and everything, really excited *(laughs)*. The flight was really different from what I'd imagined. . . . Everyone says it's scary when it takes off, but I thought it was just a normal thing. We stopped in Los Angeles, then went to Korea, and from Korea we came back to Japan *(her tone throughout is animated, happy)*.[3]

When we arrived my mother came to pick us up, with the man

[3]Dekasseguis often travel by Korean Airlines, which offers inexpensive tickets between Japan and Brazil. The flight makes a stop in Seoul.

from the empreiteira. . . . When I saw my mother I couldn't believe it, that she was there *(laughs)*, that I was also there, that we were together, I couldn't believe it, and then we came here [to Homi]. My father couldn't come [to the airport] because he was working the night shift.

## Acceptance at school

Daniel: Did you go to school right away?

Elisa: No, I spent two months [at home]. I thought I'd go to work as soon as I arrived. But my age, I'd just turned fourteen, so I was . . . too young, though if I'd wanted to it would've been possible to find work, I have friends who were thirteen and arranged a job. Except everyone thought it would be better if I had some foundation in Japanese, because I didn't know anything at all. The man from the empreiteira said that if I studied at least a little bit, it would be easier for me to get accustomed to the factory. So they decided I should study.

Daniel: What were you doing during those [first] two months?

Elisa: Nothing *(laughs)*. I was staying at home, my grandmother was with me, we'd go into Nagoya and walk around, or to Toyota. [Mainly] I stayed at home.

Daniel: Then you decided to go to school. Did you know anyone who was going there?

Elisa: Nobody. When I went to the school to enroll, I asked for the telephone number of some Brazilian of Japanese descent so I could find out how it was. They gave me Marly's number, so I called Marly, I went to her house, we talked a little, she showed me the shoes I had to buy, the other things.

Daniel: Do you remember your first day of school?

Elisa: I remember *(laughs)*.

Daniel: Tell me about it *(more laughter from both)*.

Elisa: Well . . . I didn't really want to go to school, because the way people were talking, I thought it would be really bad. My mother has a friend who went to school in Japan. I think she exaggerated a little, she said that *(laughs)* the school was like a barracks, I'd have to do everything the teacher ordered me to, the food would be horrible, impossible to eat. . . . No way did I want to go to school, but then . . . I talked with Marly, so [the first day] we went to school together. To begin with I thought it was really far, that hill going up there, right from the start I thought it was the worst *(laughs)*.[4] Then when I got to the school, I didn't know where to put my sneakers, so Marly showed me everything.

Then I went to the teachers' room. My teacher was waiting for me there. He said, *Ohayō gozaimasu* ["Good morning," polite], and I just said "Ohayō" [familiar speech]. Marly told me, "Say 'Ohayō gozaimasu' to him," so then I said it right. When we got [to the classroom], he introduced me. Nossa, I was so embarrassed. He was asking me, but I couldn't understand *(laughs)*, to say my name. Then he said in English, "*Name.*" So then I said my name *(laughs)*.

There was a girl, I'll never forget, a girl sitting in front, who didn't stop laughing, laughing like crazy, it seemed she was more embarrassed than I was *(laughs and continues laughing)*. I thought it was strange *(more laughter)*, she couldn't stop laughing, so I looked at her and I laughed too. Then the girl who would be sitting beside me raised her hand and called me over, so I went and sat beside her. Everyone kept looking at me, turning around all the time and looking. But then they got used to me, and by the second day, they started to treat me normally.

Daniel: Was it hard, or not, to become a student at Homi Chūgakkō?

Elisa: I didn't find it hard. The first day, the first and second periods were PE. In PE class the Japanese girls were already coming up to talk with me. Even though I couldn't understand, they tried to communicate with me.

Daniel: Some of the [Brazilian] students suffer a type of, I won't say exactly discrimination, but at least they feel . . . strange in school—

Elisa: Mm-hmm.

Daniel:—mainly at the beginning, [they feel] that the others are talking about them, or saying things. Did this happen to you?

Elisa: Most of the Brazilians have gone through this. In my case it was different, I never felt like I was being discriminated against, never, from the first day till the day I left I never felt like that.

Daniel: How come [you were accepted]? Did you ever think about that?

Elisa: Yes, I thought about it, I think they liked the way I look *(laughs)*, something, because they never treated me differently . . . coldly, never. I don't know if it's because . . . I didn't just sit quietly in a corner feeling strange, I tried to approach them to communicate with

[4]The last stretch of the approved route to school is a steep climb.

them too, I tried to treat them normally, maybe that's why, I don't know.

Daniel: And the food?

Elisa: Well, that *(laughs)*, what bad luck I had. The first day, nattō [fermented beans, a dish widely detested by Brazilians] came with lunch, I thought ... ai, it's nattō *(laughs)*. It was a lot of food: there was rice, nattō, *nori* [dried seaweed], soup, an egg, potatoes, some meat, but I thought it was all terrible, everything. I saw that thing *(laughs)*, a carton, I didn't know it was milk, I drank some, I don't know if the taste of the milk got mixed up with the taste of the food but I even thought the milk was awful, I didn't know what I was drinking *(both laugh)*, what strange stuff.

I threw almost all of it away, but that caused a problem. I had to talk to the teacher, with a Brazilian interpreting, because I didn't want to eat the school lunch anymore, I wanted to bring a *bentō* [box lunch]. The teacher said the food that day had been pretty bad *(laughs)* but that usually it wasn't that awful, so I said, "OK, I'll try to eat it." By the second or third day I'd gotten used to it and was eating everything.

Daniel: A couple weeks ago I was over at the [primary] school. It was lunch time, I was with the teachers there, [and they said], "Ah, today we're having something really good." It was curry-rice [a Japanese dish, a sweetish meat gravy on rice], except that it arrived really lukewarm. You look at that stuff and there isn't even a little bit of steam coming off it *(both laugh)*. Well, you could eat it, but it wasn't very appetizing.

Elisa: Ah, curry, usually ... it's good when it's hot *(laughs)*.

Daniel: They all cleaned their plates, so I did too.

Elisa: You choked it down.

Daniel: So you got used to school life, even to the food. Did you run into anything at school that bothered you?

Elisa: ... I think just the language problem. I really wanted to understand what the teacher was saying. When you really want to understand, but you can't understand a single word, nossa, that left me frustrated.

Daniel: Looking at the school now, is there anything you'd change?

Elisa: ... *(clears throat)* ... Let me think. ... In the winter I'd change the uniform *(laughs)*. I suffered a lot with that. There's got to be some kind of uniform for the winter. Warmer clothes, I found that really uncomfortable.

Daniel: Yes, mainly for the girls.

Elisa: That's right.

Daniel: And could the school do something more for the foreigners? ... I don't know if you've ever thought about this, but ...

Elisa: ... Hmm. ... One of the Japanese teachers went to Australia, she said that in the school there, because there are a lot of Japanese students the Australians study Japanese, there's a Japanese class. I think that here the Japanese students could have a class in Portuguese, so they could learn something.

Daniel: That would be interesting. Do the Japanese students know anything about Brazil?

Elisa: They might know something or other but ... I think the majority don't know anything.

Daniel: Do they ask you things?

Elisa: Some people ask. I have a friend, she wants to do an exchange, she wants to go to Brazil, she sort of likes Brazilians. She asks me what it's like there, the houses, the shops, the food. Now, the others, usually they don't ask much, mostly they ask about words, how you say such-and-such.

Daniel: But about life in Brazil?

Elisa: They ask almost nothing.

Daniel: Do you think the same thing would happen in Brazil with foreigners?

Elisa: I think it would be different *(laughs)*, everyone would want to know a lot, well, at least I would ask a lot of questions. It was a surprise [here], because I think that ... It's an opportunity for them to learn what another country is like, since there are foreigners right here to ask. I think they're not very interested.

Daniel: At school do they teach anything about Brazil?

Elisa: No.

Daniel: And do the teachers know anything about Brazil?

Elisa: ... My homeroom teacher ... Well, as far as I know, he doesn't know anything, he never even asked me anything. But the teachers in the Kokusai have, Takenaka once visited Brazil. The others know something, but not much.

### Blocked

Daniel: Are you satisfied to be leaving school, or did you want to stay?

Elisa: Well, the truth is, I wanted to stay in school. I wanted to learn a little more, but . . . it wasn't possible. I asked the teacher if I could do the third year over again, but you can't do that. I wanted to study one more year, but since it's impossible *(voice trails off)* . . .

Daniel: And then go to high school?

Elisa: . . . I think that might be a little difficult too.

Daniel: Because . . .

Elisa: I-I don't know, you've got to . . . I don't know how to speak, how to write. . . . You've got to know how to write kanji, you've got to know how to speak a little more than I can, I know very little, I think it would be pretty hard for me to get in.

Daniel: So the result is . . .

Elisa: Well, I'm going to go to work, I came here in order to work, right? . . .

Daniel: A lot of people [face this problem].

Elisa: It's true, they want to stay in school but there's this problem and they can't.

Daniel: Elisa, I know you're a very intelligent person. Do you plan to continue your education in the future?

Elisa: Yes, when I go back to Brazil. Since I left school in seventh grade, I'm going to take an accelerated course to finish *ginásio* [middle school]. I want to do high school right, not in an accelerated course, because if I do it right it's easier to pass the *vestibular* [the Brazilian university entrance exam].

Daniel: Then you're not thinking about studying anymore in Japan?

Elisa: There's a [Brazilian] correspondence course here, I thought about taking it but I'm not sure if it's any good. I think you don't learn much, so I'd rather do it right in Brazil, so it would be easier to get into college.

Daniel: And study what, do you know?

Elisa: I want to study psychology.

Daniel: How do you know about psychology?

Elisa: I don't really know anything about it *(laughs)*, but I like to talk to people. When a friend has a problem, they always come to me, to ask for advice. I think I have a knack for that *(laughs)*. I like it. If psychology doesn't work out, I'd like to study . . . what's it called, astrology. Astrology also interests me a lot.

### Full of little wires

Daniel: You were telling me on the phone that you're taking a course [in preparation for work]. What's that about?

Elisa: The piece I'm going to make, it's part of the car motor, and it's got a lot of little pieces. [The job] is *kensa* [inspection, quality control].

Daniel: Ah, you're going to check the pieces that come off the line to see if—

Elisa: That's it, to see if everything's OK, if there are furyō [defects] or not. So every day I've got to go to Shizuoka prefecture [for training].

Daniel: You go [all the way] down there?

Elisa: Every day. An hour and a half each way. The firm has a bus, because it's not just me. It's me and ten other women, who are also entering this company. You've got to do a course first, so they give classes in theory and practice. There's an engineer there who teaches theory. There are a lot of parts, you have to know kanji, the names of the parts, you've got to know . . . a lot of stuff. I thought I wouldn't be able to take it all in, but when you actually do it, it's not so hard.

Daniel: And all [the trainees in your group] are Brazilians?

Elisa: No, they're Japanese. There's just one other Brazilian, but she understands a lot of nihongo, and you have to know a lot.

Daniel: So you're the only person who doesn't really—

Elisa: Who doesn't know Japanese, I'm the only one *(laughs)*.

Daniel: How long does the course last?

Elisa: Three weeks in all.

Daniel: And you have to know a lot of parts?

Elisa: Yes. The work is done by a group of three. A sample part is on the table, with everything perfect. [The first person] picks up the piece you have to check, puts it on top of the [sample], and bit by bit you compare the pieces. The part is this big, right, full of little wires, full of little things like that, you have to look at everything.

Daniel: Compare every aspect of it, right . . .

Elisa: You have to compare everything. Then the second person takes the piece and puts crepe paper in certain places, you have to put tape on it.

Daniel: What for?

Elisa: . . . I don't know why, I think it's because . . . it's full of wires, it's full of things, I think it's *(laughs)* so that everything won't be all loose.

Daniel: This is after the kensa, right.

Elisa: After the kensa. So then it goes to a third person. This third person has to look at what the first person did and what the second person did, if everything is done right, and then applies seals and puts it in a box.

Daniel: Do you have to learn all three jobs?

Elisa: All three.

Daniel: And what do you call this piece?

Elisa: *Uaia*, nossa, how I forget things, *uaiahānisu*. Something like that. It isn't a Japanese word. It's written in katakana [the script used for loan words, usually from English].

Daniel: Uaiahānisu. *Wire harness* [spoken in English].

Elisa: It must be.

Daniel: Millions of wires *(Elisa laughs)*, and you have to check them all.

Elisa: *(laughs)* Yes. It's *taihen* [terrible], it's really taihen *(both laugh)*. You have to really use your head.

Daniel: So for three weeks—

Elisa: For three weeks we'll have to do [the training]. You need [three weeks], because you have to really know it. When we go into the factory, we'll have to teach ten new people.

[The factory where I'm being trained is in Shizuoka, but the one I'll be working in] is really close, I think it's about fifteen or twenty minutes from Homi.

Daniel: And how much will you get paid?

Elisa: Per hour?—750 [yen]. It's not much in relation to what [Brazilian women usually] earn, in the range of 900, but I think it's because of my age, and because of the work too, which isn't heavy, which isn't really dirty, it isn't dangerous to your hands. I think it's fairly reasonable.

Daniel: Of the ten who are entering [with you], are they all young women?

Elisa: No *(laughs)*, I'm the only one *(laughs)*, the majority are all *obasan* [middle-aged women]. Just the Brazilian [is young]. She's twenty-seven.

Daniel: Do you think you'll like [this job]?

Elisa: I think I will. I thought I wouldn't, that I wouldn't even be able to do it, but today I did it, not the teacher just talking, but I did it myself. In Japan every job is disagreeable, you do the same thing day after day all day, but I think this job isn't quite so disagreeable. It's because you do three types of inspection, every day you do inspection, but doing three things like that it isn't quite so disagreeable.

Daniel: There's more variety, and also, inspecting, comparing, there's a certain activity—

Elisa: Yes.

Daniel: —and it's not so repetitive, maybe.

Elisa: Yes, it's true.

Daniel: Are you going to eat lunch in the factory?

Elisa: You can't bring a bentō, you have to eat in the factory.

Daniel: So let's see if there's—

Elisa: Another problem.

Daniel: Maybe the first day it will be nattō.

Elisa: I hope it's not nattō, I hope it's not that *(both laugh)*.

## That Brazilian thing

Daniel: In Brazil did they call you japonesa?

Elisa: Some people did *(laughs)*, like, japonesinha, but the majority didn't. A lot of them tease other people *(laughs)*, but in my case, no.

Daniel: Did you feel Japanese in Brazil?

Elisa: ... Mmm, I did.

Daniel: How so?

Elisa: You mean, like a descendente?

Daniel: Yes.

Elisa: Because it's different *(laughs)*, the eyes, I felt ... different from everybody, and because I hardly had any descendente friends, most of them were real brasileiros, I was the only one who was different.

Daniel: And what do you think is the difference between a descendente in Brazil and a brasileiro?

Elisa: ... Well, the difference I felt was just physical, the eyes a little more slanted, because with respect to culture ... right?

Daniel: So you didn't feel any cultural difference?

Elisa: No.

Daniel: Does your father speak Japanese?

Elisa: He speaks a little.

Daniel: Did he speak it in Brazil too, or ...

Elisa: In Brazil, I could understand a little, because we lived with my great-grandmother, who was Japanese, she spoke only nihongo. My father, when he was little, could speak a lot, but then as he grew up he didn't use his Japanese anymore. . . . When I was little I knew a fair amount because I talked a lot with her, but then I grew up, she died, and we didn't use nihongo anymore, so there was no way to learn *(laughs)*.

Daniel: And here, in Japan, do you feel Japanese?

Elisa: Brazilian *(laughs)*.

Daniel: Brazilian? How so?

Elisa: Funny, isn't it *(more laughter)*? Here I feel different not from my appearance but from my culture.

Daniel: So in Brazil, because of your appearance you felt Japanese.

Elisa: Right.

Daniel: Here, because of the culture—

Elisa: Because of the culture I feel Brazilian.

Daniel: In what sense, because of the culture, do you feel Brazilian?

Elisa: Hmm . . . well . . . The way of life is completely different, the way you act at home. . . . I think everything is different from the Japanese [way]. I was over at a Japanese friend's house, I slept there too, it's completely different from how it is at my house, the way of cooking, the way of dressing, everything.

Daniel: In the house of your Japanese friend, do you think the people relate to each other differently? . . . Or what? I'm just trying to understand more concretely how you see the difference.

Elisa: Yes, it's a little different the way they relate . . . like this, there isn't much conversation between them, I don't know if it's because I was there. . . . It's a family but it seems they're not all that intimate, mainly her [my friend] with her father, it's really . . . There isn't that real intimacy, it's more, a lot of *respect*, a lot of, fear of saying something, it seems there isn't that . . . warmth in the family, that intimacy between people.

Daniel: Could you live in Japan for good?

Elisa: . . . I think so, if I could make trips back to Brazil, if it was like that I think I could live here for good.

Daniel: Would that be easy for you or hard?

Elisa: . . . Well, the way things are now [in Brazil] I think it really wouldn't be hard.

Daniel: Do you think you'll do that?

Elisa: I don't think so. I'd rather live in Brazil.

Daniel: How come?

Elisa: . . . Because . . . *(laughs)* It's because it's better than Japan, I could live in Japan for good, but I'd rather live in Brazil, I think Brazil has ... I'm a *Brazilian*, right, I know ... Ah, it's something, there's some kind of tie *(laughs)*.

Daniel: And to be Brazilian is ...

Elisa: To be Brazilian *(laughs)*?

Daniel: Uh-huh, what does it mean to be Brazilian?

Elisa: ... Hmm ... To be Brazilian is to be roguish [*malandro*] *(laughs)*, to be clever [*esperto*] *(laughs)*.

Daniel: Uh-huh, and the Japanese aren't?

Elisa: Ah, they don't have it *(clicks tongue)*, that Brazilian thing, they don't have it *(laughs)*. . . .

### Identity measured

Elisa's combination of confidence and resilience serves her well. She has a sense of balance; she lands on her feet. Most Brazilian teenagers expressed intense frustration—frustration with parents, guardians, colleagues, the demands of the school, the food, Japanese life in general. They made me painfully aware of their fears and their insecurity. Miriam, for example, struggled unsuccessfully for self-recognition and seemed rudderless. She found her Brazilian past publicly negated and could not discern a clearly marked path to the future. Catarina, in contrast, wanted desperately to escape her empty, hurtful past and enter a new world, only to find herself condemned to a dispiriting return.

These girls saw and felt their Brazilianness and their Japaneseness in relation to the personal trials they were undergoing. Thus Miriam found Brazilianness in the Guarujá beach, in the "human warmth" of family and friends. For Catarina, such nostalgia and homely human warmth did not exist. Brazilianness, which for her signified the taunting boys of the street, her absent father, and the joyless life in Paranavaí, was something to flee. Japaneseness was preferable, for it offered her a welcome sense of security, organization, learning, and, possibly, companionship.

Elisa's perspective is something else again. There is just one point in this interview where Elisa shows deep frustration—when she speaks of the limitations in her Japanese that hampered her learning and ultimately, perhaps in concert with family pressures, sank her hopes for continuing her education in Japan. She is momentarily defeated by circumstances beyond her control. But her entire history is one of bouncing back, of not yielding to adversity. Separated from her parents for two years, she does well in school and waits out the uncertainties surrounding her journey to Japan. Entering Homi Chū, unable to speak Japanese, she gets along famously, making Japanese friends, excelling at her work, and gaining the support of her teachers. She steers clear of cliques and makes no enemies. To the contrary, she has the gift of enlisting those who know her in her behalf.

In February 1996, I attended a meeting of the Kokusai staff, including the Japanese teachers, the Japanese volunteers, and the two bilingual Brazilian teachers who regularly visited Homi Chū. At that meeting we reviewed the curriculum, talked about the upcoming school year, and discussed each of the foreign students. Several of those present lamented that Elisa was leaving school. The consensus was that this was a most unfortunate situation, but *shikata ga arimasen*—nothing could be done about it. It would be good, people said, if she were somehow able to continue studying Japanese. No one had a useful suggestion as to how she might do that, given the fact that she would be spending eight hours a day in the factory.

Surely, the situation Elisa faced in April 1996 would be enough to discourage anyone, and there is sadness and tension in her voice when she talks about her interrupted education. All the same, by the time of this interview she has leapt into the world of work, with a degree of enthusiasm if not real gusto. I am sure she will make the most of the job she is assigned and that she will be an excellent employee. I think that eventually she will go back to high school and on to university—if, that is, her return to Brazil is not delayed too long. For there is always a chance that her parents, and perhaps Elisa herself, will fall victim to the honey trap of the Japanese factory. Barring personal catastrophes, I doubt that would defeat her—as she says, she could, if necessary, live in Japan for good—but many of her considerable talents would go to waste in the drone of days filled with monotonous, exhausting labor.

Elisa's view of her own ethnicity is keenly analytical. Because of her innate equilibrium, she has the luxury of making a somewhat clinical assessment of herself. Elisa sees herself as "Brazilian" by culture, and "Japanese" by appearance. It is difference, she notes, that accounts for her ethnic sensibilities. So in Brazil, her different appearance brings to the fore her sense of Japaneseness, with her cultural sameness receding into the background. In Japan, her different culture is featured, with appearance a nonissue.

In the end, though, culture trumps appearance—she is *Brazilian*, she insists, even if she's not quite sure why. Brazilianness, as best she can formulate it, is a matter of a way of life (cooking, dress), a manner of relating ("warmth" rather than "respect"), a personal quality (being clever, roguish). She draws on her experiences in a Japanese household, in the school, in the factory training group. As always, Elisa considers her judgments, mutes her criticism, maintains a certain ironic distance from her conclusions and even—perhaps most of all—from herself.

The Elisa who is Japanese then, Brazilian now, is an object to the doubly clever Elisa who understands that context generates her feelings of difference and that culture matters more than blood. Doubly clever Elisa has learned what it is for her to be Brazilian, and in so doing has, like Bernardo Kinjoh and many others, become simultaneously other-than-Brazilian. This is ethnic identity measured, cut to size, valued but not fetishized. Held in the eye of a critical self, it is not an identity likely to consume its bearer or to bring forth the strange fruit of ethnic hatred.

CHAPTER 12

# Rosa Kitagawa

## *"Send me a blond wig!"*

### *Visitors from Anjo, January 1996*

When I walk into the Kokusai class today, something is in the air. Girls are writing on the chalkboard: *ANJO NISHI CHŪGAKKŌ, Sejam Bem-Vindos* ("Welcome, West Anjo Middle School").[1] Colorful designs and pink tulips frame the greeting. The students tell me that two Brazilians, a boy and a girl, are coming from Anjo, a nearby town. We push the tables aside and arrange the chairs in a circle. The visitors arrive, accompanied by their Japanese teacher. They sit at the front of the class, side by side. Rosa Kitagawa serves as facilitator.

The Kokusai students self-segregate by sex. The seven boys sit in an arc facing the six girls. The boys seem especially uncomfortable, joking and fooling around during the introductions, most of which are practically inaudible. Some of the Homi students laugh so much when asked to present themselves that they can barely speak. We go around the circle and get to the guests. Jackson, in a black uniform, is a sannensei. Vânia, wearing a navy sailor suit, is in her second year. Both are from São Paulo, and both have been in Japan a long time. Their teacher apologizes for speaking in Japanese, but Mr. Takenaka introduces himself briefly, to everyone's gleeful amazement, in heavily accented Portuguese.

Rosa appeals for questions. Trying hard to keep the ball rolling, she asks the guests what they plan to do after finishing middle school. Jackson will work, perhaps at McDonald's, and then return to Brazil. Vânia wants to enter a Japanese high school. We learn that Jackson and Vânia are the only Brazilians at Anjo Nishi. Jackson misses his friends back home: "There isn't that human warmth like in Brazil." Someone asks if the teachers at their school hit the students. Jackson describes such an incident. The Anjo teacher leaves the room briefly and there's joking.

---

[1]This section is edited from my January 30, 1996, field notes.

Edival says maybe she's the whacker because she fled when the question was asked, but Rosa counters, "She can't understand Portuguese."

The period ends; there is a break. More Brazilians join us. The conversation staggers on. According to the guests, students at Anjo Nishi usually wear sweat suits to school; only on important occasions (as today's) do they dress in the more formal uniforms. Jackson wants to know where the big Grampus soccer banner came from. The boys answer that Jorginho, a Brazilian player with Nagoya's Grampus team, once came to Homi Chū and gave it to the Kokusai. Jackson and Vânia lament that no Brazilian celebrity has ever visited their school. Rosa asks whom students would invite if they could. Jackson volunteers Ayrton Senna, the Formula One idol. "But it's impossible": he's dead. Fernando opts for Xuxa, the coquettish Brazilian TV star. Rosa says to Fernando, "You want to be a soccer player. Do you want to play here or in Brazil?" Fernando: "Both places" (*laughter*). Sebastião dryly observes, "In Japan, the money is better."

After this the conversation languishes and cannot be resuscitated. The visitors sit quietly. The Homi kids banter and clown among themselves. Finally, someone proposes that we play a game. Mr. Takenaka suggests *furūtsu basuketto* ("fruit basket"), a Japanese version of musical chairs. Relieved of the obligation to converse, the students run around laughing until the chimes sound. Jackson and Vânia thank us. Sebastião intones: "We would like you to come back soon." The Anjo teacher and Takenaka utter a few parting words, and the group breaks up.

This was an awkward meeting. The Homi students were not rude exactly; their alternating silence and buffoonery seemed products of embarrassment rather than discourtesy. They could not figure out whether this was school or play and did not know what attitude to take. I was struck by the contrasting demeanor of the guests, who were sober throughout. The Anjo girl and boy, who had no Kokusai, no large peer group of Brazilians, seemed nonplused. Who were these students, what was this class? Despite Rosa's valiant efforts, a spontaneous exchange never developed. Sebastião's final invitation, rather formal and issued in Japanese, acknowledged the failed connection.

### Into the breach

By 1995, Aichi prefecture, anxious over the burgeoning population of foreigners in its classrooms, had hired four bilingual Brazilian teachers to rove among its primary and middle schools. Technically known as assistant teachers for language instruction, they were charged with easing the Brazilians' transition to Japanese, but in practice they engaged the students as they saw fit, acting as instructors, counselors, and troubleshooters.

Rosa Kitagawa, a nissei with dual nationality, became one of Aichi's bilingual teachers in the fall of 1994. Following her graduation from a Brazilian college, Rosa came to Aichi in 1991 as a *bolsista*, a foreign scholarship student, at Nagoya City University. A year later she took a job with a prefectural agency, the Advising and Information Service for Nikkeis (*Serviço de Assessoria e Informação para os Nikkeis*), located in central Nagoya. Brazilians approached her with problems related to work, visas, education, and medical care. In 1993, Rosa returned to São Paulo. But the following year a colleague from her 1991 group contacted her. Now a bilingual assistant teacher for Aichi prefecture, the former bolsista asked whether Rosa might be interested in taking over her job. During her time with the counseling service, says Rosa, "I had begun to understand that the ones who suffered most were the children. So when this opportunity came up, I said, 'I'm on my way.' "

In the new job, Rosa found herself traveling all over the prefecture to primary and middle schools, usually two per day. When I met her in September 1995, she was coming to Homi Chū weekly. But as the numbers of Brazilians in the prefecture continued to grow, she had to cut the frequency to every other week, despite Homi Chū's enrollment of thirty to forty Brazilian students. Anjo Nishi, with two, was more typical of the schools Rosa visited. Many Aichi schools had a single Brazilian child.

By 1996, Rosa felt stretched thin. Every day she was on the move. She once told me she had been to forty-two different schools in the previous four months. Moreover, she had to deal with intractable problems. Many parents wanted the schools to provide substantive instruction in Portuguese, but the Japanese educational system was neither disposed toward nor able to handle such a task. In one or two visits a month, Rosa herself could do very little. She urged mothers and fathers to take more responsibility for their children's education. But the parents worked long hours: they could hardly find the time or energy to have a conversation with their children, much less teach them anything. For their part, the children, hitting the wall of Japanese-language instruction, often became discouraged and quit school. They usually did poorly in their classes and sometimes got into trouble.

Because Eli was friendly with many of the Brazilian boys, I knew something of their (and, occasionally, his) exploits. I knew less of the girls' doings outside home and school, in part because we had no daughter and in part because most girls did less. Brazilian parents demanded more domestic work from girls and reigned them in more tightly. Also, rebelliousness had somewhat less cachet among the girls than among the boys (though there were exceptions). The girls enjoyed talking with one another and going on shopping expeditions in groups or with a parent. The boys joked and teased, gathered to play soccer, hung out with older adolescents, went to the video arcade, or engaged in petty delinquencies.

The boys often violated school rules, traversing the Forbidden Path, carrying money to class, or dying their hair red. They considered the Japanese students *coitados*, pathetic victims of a system that most Brazilian boys saw as an alien adversary. In and around the danchi, the boys engaged in daredevil stunts, such as climbing high on scaffolding or scaling the fence to sneak into one of the local grade school's swimming pools. They would dodge the conductor on the train, slip candy into their sleeves at convenience stores, and filch pears and apples, crawling under the electrified wires surrounding the groves. Someone discovered that the worthless tokens discharged at a department-store pachinko game could be forced into the coin slots at a local batting cage, activating the pitching machine. On a memorable Saturday afternoon, the manager caught Eli banging one down. Opening the box, he found the tokens; the boys fled, their batting days over.

These struck me as fairly innocuous boundary-challenging escapades. But other activities of the boys, though not unusual by Brazilian or American standards, rudely transgressed Japanese norms, and the boys certainly knew it. Some of the Brazilian boys carried brass knuckles, on occasion bringing them to school. Many had air guns that shot plastic BBs. Some would tuck the guns into the front of their pants, gangster style, and take potshots at the fluorescent lights inside the danchi's apartment buildings.

And there were two sensational incidents during the time I worked in the Kokusai. Over the winter break in 1995–96, a number of Brazilian boys, including some regarded as "well-behaved," broke into a local grade school, engaging in minor vandalism and theft. Homigate, as I thought of it, caused alarm at Homi Chū, spurring consultations with parents, warnings, and punishments. Then, in the spring of 1996, there was a "drive-by shooting." A Brazilian boy, who had studied in the Kokusai but was now working as a dishwasher, cruised past the school on a motorcycle and shot plastic pellets at some students. No one was hurt in the airgun attack, though it set the Kokusai buzzing. Such events always drew the Brazilian assistant teachers into rounds of meetings with students, faculty, and parents. At issue was whether the boys were behaving as moleques, adolescent Brazilian cutups, or were on the road to becoming furyō, damaged goods, Japanese-style delinquent dropouts.

Rosa found herself wedged between Japanese and Brazilians, always explaining one group to the other and trying to reconcile disparate visions. Though her sympathies lay mostly with the Brazilians and she saw her task primarily as one of easing their lives, her designated role was that of a cultural broker. She had vastly different audiences, and was herself an audience to vastly different dramas. She was an adept performer, aware of her multiple selves: the selves she was assigned, the selves she displayed, and the self, or selves, she felt and lived. For all the Brazilians I knew in Japan, identity questions were salient, but for the cultural brokers like Rosa, the level of salience was ratcheted up. For such brokers it was not just identity—who one was—but also identity processes, the formation, negotiation, and making of identity, that drew sustained attention and prompted careful consideration.

I spoke with Rosa at my apartment on an afternoon in late January 1996, over green tea. The excerpts begin with reflections on her family and her experiences in Japan, and then move on to observations on the Brazilian children with whom she works. In our conversation, questions of identity are never far from the surface.

### That typical square Japanese

Rosa: My parents are real [that is, native-born] Japanese, so I had a lot of information through them, or through my aunts and uncles, all my relatives live here in Japan. I often ask my students, "What did you think Japan was like before you came here?" And some always say, "I thought that the Japanese wore kimonos, that they wore their hair pulled up, that they used those swords," but I didn't have that image, because I already knew what it was like here. I was more up-to-date, and also in São Paulo I had seen a lot of magazines with news of Japan.

My father came to Brazil first, right after he graduated [from college]. Why Brazil? Maybe you were going to ask me. Over there in Mie-ken [as a naval museum] there's a ship named *Brazil-Maru*, and my grandfather was the first captain of that [immigrant] ship.[2] Because he used to come to Brazil, my father's family had this idea of Brazil, so I think my father wanted to go to Brazil as an adventure. I've never really asked my father why he wanted to go, but he did, returned to marry my mother, and they went back [together].

Daniel: What year was that?

Rosa: *Iiiih* [sighing interjection], I think it was some, thirty ... thirty-three, thirty-four years ago. It wasn't during the period when there was that mass of migrants, it was a little later.[3]

Daniel: When he or your mother talk about Japan, what do they say?

Rosa: My father was here in Japan [on business] last year. I ... noticed that he had missed it a lot, because his whole family is here, his friends are here. But ... my mother, she [once] came as a tourist, she told me that *(laughs)* it's hard for her, life here in Japan. My mother is used to going around in jeans and sneakers. When she came here, she had to change. Her friends [from high school and college days] are not about to go to tea [like that], so she had to dress up more, she had to use more makeup, just to meet with her friends. She thinks that life here really has a lot of rules, and my mother finds this too narrow for her, she prefers the Brazilian way, more casual. Sometimes I think to myself, Nossa, my mother got so Brazilianized.

But I [understood what she meant] when I came as a bolsista. ... I had my circle of friends in Brazil, including some nikkeis, I knew their parents, who had practically the same attitudes as my father. But when I came here, I met my uncles, my father's brothers. For me my father was that typical square Japanese [*japonês quadrado*], doing everything just so, but when I came here and met my uncles, I saw that my father had changed to the Brazilian system. My uncles were really that image that I had of the square Japanese. My father might still be a little bit like that, because it's something that stays inside you, you can't change 100 percent, but my father had changed a lot, compared with my uncles.

[2]It did not strike me until I got back to the United States that this *Brazil-Maru* might be the same boat that I had taken to Japan in 1973. Indeed it was. See the preface.

[3]The Folha de São Paulo (1995:Especial 8) divides immigration to Brazil into three phases. During the initial phase (1908–23), 31,414 Japanese entered Brazil; 157,572 entered in the period of mass immigration (1924–42); and 53,489 entered after the war. Rosa's parents migrated during the postwar period.

So maybe my father would be somewhere in the middle. My father isn't that Brazilian Brazilian, who has a very open life. Maybe because my parents lived in Japan till university they're quite ... Japanese. In my house in Brazil there are still a lot of [Japanese] customs. For example, my house has two floors, we change our shoes to go upstairs. So—

Daniel: But do you take off your shoes when you come in the house or only when you go upstairs?

Rosa: When we come in we change shoes, [and then] we change again. I used to think, How come we have to change so many times *(amused)*. But when I came here, I saw that the bathroom, when you go in you have to change shoes [to special bathroom slippers]. That's when I realized my mother had adapted [to Brazil], because at home we don't change shoes in the bathroom, so my mother adapted [these Japanese customs] in her own way to Brazil.[4]

Daniel: So it's a special way of changing shoes *(Rosa laughs)*. You kept the custom of changing shoes, except that it's an invented way of doing it *(Daniel laughs)*.

## A problem of visibility

Daniel: So let's say, your father is somewhere between Japan and Brazil, and your mother maybe leans more to the Brazilian side ... And you.

Rosa: Me. Iiiih, that's the question *(laughs)*. I think you've already heard this, that when I was in Brazil they used to call me japonesinha, and when I came here they call me burajirujin. Now I'm starting to realize that however much they called me japonesinha in Brazil, I've got much more to do with Brazil than with Japan.

It's hard to explain why, but here ... For example, I've had a lot of not-very-agreeable experiences here in Japan, at the beginning, when I came as a bolsista. One of them was that ... because I have a Japanese face, eh, the Japanese really have the idea that a foreigner has light-colored eyes, white skin, light hair too. So *(laughs)*, for example in the dormitory where I was living, there were only Asians, Thais, Indonesians, Chinese, Koreans, and Brazilians who were usually nikkeis, like me. From time to time we were invited to some

---

[4]That is, in Japan people normally change shoes when entering a bathroom but do not change shoes to go upstairs.

event, an encounter with Japanese. But once we got there, the Japanese would say, "Where are the scholarship students?" Because they were expecting [us] to fit their image of gaijin. So we'd tell them, "But it's not quite like that, there are all kinds of people in the world, people with all kinds of appearances, including, it so happens, people who look exactly like you."

Even now, when I go to schools, when I give talks [to teachers], I say that Japanese people have the really wrong idea that all the people who live outside their island have the same appearance, different from theirs. I tell them there are all kinds of people in the world. Just as there are people with your appearance, Daniel, who aren't English[-speakers].

Daniel: Obviously. And how do they react when you say these things?

Rosa: They say, "Oh yes, sure," right *(laughs)*, there's no way they can argue *(laughs)*, they just say, "It's true, we have to change," but I don't know if [they] will, because it's something so ancient with them.

But I'm not at all embarrassed to say this. I [also] take the part of the Chinese, because in a certain way they also discriminate against the Chinese. I say, "You can't do that, it's wrong." They sometimes want to climb on top of [other] Asians. I've felt this a lot, because I have a lot of friends who are Chinese, Koreans.

And there are times when I . . . I feel this a lot when I go into the chūgakkōs, they have English teachers [from English-speaking countries, usually Caucasians], and they, eh . . . It might be just my impression, but I feel a big difference in receptivity. Since I understand it now, it doesn't bother me anymore, but in the beginning I was very annoyed. They were small things, for example, in one school, where an English teacher used to come, OK, fine, my visits were more regular, so they didn't have to stand there all the time saying "Thank you very much" and accompanying me to the door when I left. They didn't do any of that for me anymore. But with the English teachers, they did. So I think that they, the Japanese, have a certain, uh . . . complex. How come they do this for the [English] teachers and not for me. Because we're all equal, they ought to treat everyone equal. But because they feel a little inferior, they stand there making all that ceremony. At first I was very annoyed with this.

Daniel: I wonder if they saw you, I don't know, as some kind of Japanese?

Rosa: Yes. That's it. Sometimes I don't speak much Japanese [on purpose]. I just say really easy words, so they might at least look at me like a foreigner. Once I went so far as to ask my sister, in a letter to Brazil, "Send me a blond wig!" *(laughs heartily)*, because *(both laugh)* I have to put on something, they have to understand visually, it doesn't help for me to say I'm a Brazilian, because I speak Japanese, I've got a Japanese face.

A lot of people ask me, "Who in your family is Japanese?" So I say, "My mother and my father, they were born here in Japan." "Ah, so you're Japanese." I say, "My parents are Japanese, both of them, and so by blood I am too. But I was born and grew up in another country, with other customs, and that makes me not Japanese. I have a part of me that's Japanese, but maybe even a big part of that is Brazilian." But for them to understand *(laughs)*, for a Japanese person, it's really difficult. It's hard to convince them *(amused)*.

### Small things that add up

Daniel: Why don't you just let yourself become Japanese?

Rosa: Ah, but Daniel—

Daniel: It would be easy, right? They look at you as a Japanese, you speak Japanese, you look like a Japanese, so you could just let yourself become one, right?

Rosa: But Daniel, in day-to-day life, there are a lot of things that the people here, uh ... accept without much question. People say, "Do this." A lot of them, mainly those in charge, people up high, simply give orders. But the person who has to do the task doesn't question why they have to do it. It's just that I have the habit of asking questions. I remember when I was a bolsista, I had a Japanese friend who told me, "You're always asking why." I said, "But I need to ask why I have to do such-and-such." She just said, "Ah, but you ask why a lot." *(Laughs.)*

So ... look, for example, to get up, eat breakfast, go shopping, that kind of basic life, would be easy for me. But you don't just do that twenty-four hours a day, you have contact with other people, you have to talk with them, and that's what's hard, certain things don't mesh.

Daniel: Something you said that was very interesting, that seems like it bothers you, is when they [Japanese people] see you as a japonesa.

You even said that sometimes you lower the level of your own Japanese—

Rosa: Mm-hmm.

Daniel:—so they'll see you as a foreigner instead of a Japanese, and I find that interesting. . . . Why do you think you don't want them simply to look at you as a japonesa, and be done with it?

Rosa: It's not that I have an aversion to them calling me a japonesa. I'm pleased when someone says to me, "Wow, your Japanese is so fluent that I wouldn't have realized [you're a Brazilian] if you hadn't told me." That in particular makes me proud, because that's something I've fought [to achieve].

But there are lots of things in daily life that I see that . . . I can't accept about Japanese society. Because I can't accept these things, I don't want them to see me as the same as them. Certain attitudes of Japanese people. There's something that really annoyed me when I was a bolsista. It's that business inside the train, inside any public vehicle. They say, "Let's reserve a place for older people," those "silver seats" [seats designated for senior citizens], but [in fact] everyone is asleep, everyone is like this *(miming postures of sleeping passengers on the train)*, right? In Brazil, no matter how humble a person is, even if he's almost a beggar, if he's on the bus, and an older lady gets on, automatically he'll give up his seat. I grew up observing this, and for me, it's an obligation, I'm young, I'm healthy, I should give my seat to a handicapped person. Here in Japan, obviously I've seen people offering their seat, but it's *very* rare. So these are small things I don't accept.

And the school is another thing. In the hallway they have that weekly slogan, "Let's greet each other this week." So in a certain way they force you, "Let's all say, 'Good morning.'" But why? For example, now I'm living in an apartment, it's a studio apartment, only single people live [in the building]. When I moved there, I thought, Well, since I'm living here alone, I hope I can strike up a friendship with someone in the building. But when I run into someone and say "Good morning," the person walks right past. The other day my next-door neighbor, it was the first time I met him, he was going into his apartment, and I said, "Good morning." He heard me, looked at me, and ran inside. I thought, Nossa Senhora, do you think there's something about my face *(laughs)* that terrified him?

So there are these small things, Daniel, that make me sad. Maybe these are small ways in which I don't want to be compared with them, but they're things I don't do. If I see a person who's pregnant or an old person, I give them my seat. So ... these are really tiny things, but they keep adding up.

Rosa: Japanese people have an idea of Brazilians, that we walk around half-naked, that we spend the whole year dancing the samba *(laughs)*, and that the men play soccer. Maybe in a certain way I'm [also] reluctant to have them put a [Japanese] stereotype on me. I might like it if [it were the old image] of a Japanese, a long time ago there was the kind Japanese, the humble Japanese. ... They say a lot that the nikkei bolsistas have the characteristics of old Japan, because I was brought up by my Japanese parents, who had an old-time education. In Brazil they often say, "Japonesinhas are tenderhearted [*meiga*]," and I'm proud of that. But when I came here I saw the other side of it.... This reinforced my sense that I'm not really Japanese. I might be a nikkei Brazilian. I'll admit I'm that, but I'm not *Japanese*. I don't know *(laughs)*, it's hard to explain.

Daniel: It's hard to explain but you're explaining it very well. Recently I've been a little annoyed because people are always asking me, "How do you do such-and-such in the United States?" Now I just say, "Well, how does *who* do it?" *(Rosa laughs.)* Because there are so many people with different customs, different ways of being, that you can't simply ask, "How do the Americans do such-and-such," because the thing is more complicated than you can imagine.

Rosa: *(laughing)* For sure. For example, they're always asking me to describe "the Brazilian school." I say, "OK, I can describe it, but it's the school *I* went to, [the school] of the circle of friends *I* have." You can't go to one place, and say that Brazil is like that everywhere. A person who studied in the north of the country won't have gone through the same things I went through in the south.

Daniel: I'm sure of that.

Rosa: Because Brazil is a big country that provides a home for people from many other countries, it's big. Everyone has a little bit of the customs of their grandparents, of their country of origin, and even within Brazil itself, it depends on the neighborhood *(laughs)*, the city, it's all different.

Daniel: Or even having a certain descent, like your mother, they use the descent to invent something completely unique. The shoe custom in your house comes from Japan *(murmurs of assent from Rosa)* but it's—

Rosa: It's been adapted *(both laugh)*.

Daniel: I think it's hard to explain all this here. I don't know exactly why, because here too you can find a variety of customs, if you travel around Japan, you see this, right—

Rosa: Yes, yes.

Daniel:—but it seems that [the variety] is almost invisible, people don't see it very clearly, I don't know why.[5]

## His grandmother's face

Rosa: The other day I was talking with the mother of one of my students, this student is a mestiço. The school where this woman's son had gone, it was the first time they'd had a foreign student. So what did his little colleagues do? He was something completely new to them, they had to touch him, to see if he was the same as them, if he had the same kind of skin.

Or there are cases for example [like this]. Brazilians are very eager to hug others. When we meet our friends we've got the custom of kissing them. This small child doesn't know that we're in Japan now and we shouldn't do those things, so he'd go over [to his colleagues] and [hug] them. Sometimes the Japanese children would get the idea they were being attacked, or that they were being hit. So [this mother] said that at the beginning [her son] had a lot of problems.

Rosa: Another thing I've noticed about the children, mainly the little ones ... A [young] child spends a lot of time with her parents [and plays] a lot of games [typical of] the country. Those children who come when they're little, that part they didn't have. As much as everyone gets along well with those children, there are things they don't know, they can't quite participate actively with their friends.

---

[5]For example, Japan's indigenous people, the Ainu, have long been both visible and politically active. Nevertheless, "at the level of commonsense understanding," writes Richard Siddle, "a master narrative of seamless national homogeneity denies the existence of the Ainu as an ethnic minority group; the Ainu are regarded as either totally assimilated or biologically extinct" (1997:17). More generally, Japan's significant ethnic and regional differences are underplayed, indeed often denied, in both official rhetoric and common discourse. The literature on ethnic difference in Japan is vast. For two recent treatments, see Maher and Macdonald (1995) and Weiner (1997). Both volumes emphasize Japan's ethnic diversity, the homogenizing thrust of official rhetoric, and the obstacles placed before those who would openly assert ethnic difference.

Daniel: For example.

Rosa: A game, or a little story that your mother reads at your bedside before you fall asleep. It's funny, sometimes the [Japanese] teachers ask the children to describe some Brazilian game. "Since you don't know [the Japanese game], tell me something about Brazil." But the child doesn't know that either, so he feels bad because he doesn't know one or the other. He left Brazil when he was tiny, he doesn't remember it anymore. At the most he remembers his grandmother's face, but he doesn't remember where he lived, what he used to do, what Brazil is like, so I think, *Puxa* [interjection], what's going to happen when this child returns?

Daniel: You're stuck not remembering anything of Brazil and without much knowledge of Japan, so you're in between.

Rosa: Right, you're sitting on the fence *(laughs)*. It breaks my heart, that's why sometimes I say, "Well then, let's play a Brazilian game, come on, in Brazil this is how we play, in Brazil there's a place called such-and-such." Some [Japanese] teachers even ask me, "Help get the children to remember something of their country of origin."

Daniel: Can you talk a little bit about what you've seen at Homi Chū?

Rosa: At Homi Chū *(laughs softly)*. Eh ... Comparing them with students from other chūgakkōs, where for example there's only one Brazilian in the whole school, well, sure, Homi also has students who try hard, but the great majority, I think in the end they *(choosing words carefully)* ... in the end they give up, "It's too hard, I can't do it, it doesn't do any good to try, because I won't make it."

The teachers [at Homi] have so many students they can't keep track of them. For example, a lot of students have psychological problems, they don't have anyone to talk to. [Their] parents come home late, there's no time to communicate. In Brazil, we've got the custom of the whole family eating dinner together. But they're losing these things, the parents are giving them up. They want to do more zangyō, to have a better life in Brazil, and I know they're doing this for the sake of the children, but the parents have to pay attention to the children in day-to-day life too. I feel they're very needy children. They don't have their parents' love, so they rely on their colleagues. So you've got children of the same age with the same [problems], and they end up doing stupid things *(laughs)* together.

In Brazil it's easier, because when you finish middle school you automatically go to high school, but here they don't have the option of going [even though] they want to. I think they've got no prospects whatsoever. If I ask them, "What do you want to be [in the future]," they say, "I want to be a soccer player." You know, things that . . . wouldn't have much [connection to them] if they were in Brazil. We [nikkeis?] choose more solid professions, such as, "I'd like to be a teacher," or "[I'd like] to study computing." [Here] all [the boys] want to be a soccer player. Here in Japan a soccer player is a big success. And he doesn't have to study.

Daniel: Have you seen any of the boys or girls go on to the kōkō?
Rosa: The only one who went on since I've been working in this job is Yukiko. Last year [March 1995] she graduated from Homi Chū. What's happening to her now is that she has lost interest in school.
Daniel: Has she already quit?
Rosa: Not yet.
Daniel: What happened to the others?
Rosa: They go to work. To the factory. I think that last year five [Brazilian] students graduated [from all the schools I visit in Aichi prefecture]. All of them [except Yukiko], every one went to work.

Daniel: What's going to happen to these boys and girls [when they go back to Brazil]?
Rosa: I feel a certain . . . sense of sorrow, because there are students who'd like to return to Brazil to study, except that this doesn't depend just on them. It depends a lot on the parents, whether the parents do or don't want to go back to Brazil.

I had a student last year at Homi Chūgakkō. He [and his family] had lived three or four years here in Japan. He was more into the Japanese system than the Brazilian one. He went back to Brazil, and a year later his mother wrote me, because I always like the mothers to write me about what's happening with their children. She wrote that it was difficult in the beginning to adapt, her son didn't want to live in Brazil anymore, he wanted to return immediately to Japan. He had to go back to sixth grade there, and this upset him a lot. He [would say], "Mom, I'm already a young man." His whole adolescence was here in Japan, and it's different, the interior of a person here.

Sometimes I ask myself, Daniel, what's it going to be like from now on. A lot of them are going to go back to Brazil, finish their studies, and then I think the great majority will end up returning to Japan. But I wonder if Japan will still offer [them] that opportunity.

## The big country

Nikkeis often experience shock and disillusionment during their first months in Japan. But the specific shocks and people's reactions to them vary. Rosa's family and upbringing were far more "Japanese" than the norm. Her parents were native-born Japanese who had grown to adulthood in Japan; she heard Japanese at home; her family preserved Japanese customs; her relatives lived in Japan. Her information about Japan was extensive, current, and accurate. She herself is a Japanese citizen; she carries a red, as well as a green, passport.[6] Rosa knew what to expect when she first traveled to Japan, and she was well equipped by background, temperament, and abilities to enter into Japanese middle-class daily life.

And then came the rain of small surprises that recast her view of her parents, her household, Japan, Brazil, and herself. Living in Nagoya as a *bolsista*, she came into direct contact with Japanese students, the Japanese public, and her Japanese relatives. She discovered that her "Japanese" parents had changed during their years in Brazil. The formal correctness she hitherto associated with her father, she found in an unadulterated form in his uncles. Her father might be square by Brazilian standards, but Brazil had rounded his Japanese edges. She began to understand her "Brazilianized" mother's unease with her Japanese college friends, to perceive how far her mother had ventured from her Japanese upbringing. The "Japanese" customs of her parents' home in São Paulo turned out to be not so Japanese after all, but rather idiosyncratic adaptations and innovations. Brazil, where Rosa had passed her entire life, including her formative childhood years, was, it seemed, powerful medicine. And if even her square father had turned Brazilian, or at least had ventured into the twilight zone between Japanese and Brazilian, what did that make Rosa?

Her interactions with Japanese contemporaries soon provided an answer. Rosa was jarred by the inability of Japanese acquaintances to see her, for she did not fit their idea of the blue-eyed, white-skinned *gaijin*. Rosa had grown up in multiracial, multicultural São Paulo. For her, nationality was not a matter of racial homogeneity; quite the reverse. Brazil was a big country that housed all kinds of people. To grow up in Brazil, as a Brazilian, was to grow up in the presence of others, ethnically and racially different, who also claimed to be—and were—Bra-

[6]Conventional ways of referring to Japanese and Brazilian passports, respectively.

zilian. Somehow the Japanese college students had got it into their heads that Brazilians could not look like themselves. The breathtaking naiveté of that assumption, and the lack of imagination and narrow view of sameness that it entailed, revealed to Rosa an enormous gap in life experience.

In theory, one could react to the Japanese students' ingenuous presupposition in at least two ways. One could, as did Miriam and Tamara, respond indignantly to this denial of one's prior experience, reasserting and cultivating a Brazilian identity. Or one could move in the direction of a Japanese identity, accepting the race/language/culture package as personal destiny. Not all Brazilians have this option, for most are fatally branded as different (and, usually, inferior) by virtue of their appearance, bodily carriage, inability to speak fluent Japanese, or cultural clumsiness. But Rosa, a Japanese citizen with Japanese parents, well-schooled in standard Japanese language and culture, could have won acceptance as a Japanese, for her looks, manner, and linguistic ability invited others to view her as such.

She could not, would not submit to such a reclassification, nor did she opt for a generalized Brazilianness. Although flattered by praise for her fluency in Japanese, which had cost her much hard work, she felt unable and unwilling to appropriate the label of japonesa, to *become* Japanese. Her refusal had several bases. Most important was her reluctance to accede to, and identify with, practices and ways of thinking that she found questionable or repugnant. I think there is evidence in her comments of two strongly held values that she finds wanting among Japanese. I will characterize these as empathetic engagement with others, and equal treatment for all. For her to "become" Japanese would, in her view, mean betrayal of these values—hence betrayal of her self.

Rosa is offended that an able-bodied person on the train will not give a seat to a pregnant woman or an old person. This is something she noticed when she first arrived in Japan, and it has stuck with her. The train scenario epitomizes an abhorrent quality. To be sure, she sees the refusal to offer a seat as a lack of civility, but I think it has a deeper, more negative resonance. For Rosa, refusing to yield one's seat reflects a determination not to engage another empathetically. The passengers feign sleep, as if they do not even notice the grandmother standing before them. In closing their eyes, they refuse to recognize the other. More than an act of incivility, it is an act of bad faith. Her neighbors' refusals to respond to her greetings exemplify the same quality. People pass by without acknowledging her; the man next door flees into his own apartment. The neighbors spurn Rosa's efforts to forge human links. Although Rosa never uses the phrase, which I believe she would find too crude and censorious, other Brazilians cited similar events to me as examples of a Japanese lack of calor humano, "human warmth."

Rosa also finds Japanese attitudes toward foreigners disturbing. On the one hand, the English teachers get treated with deference bordering on obsequiousness, a sign of "a certain complex" toward, presumably, Caucasians. As she says, "Because we're all equal, they ought to treat everyone equal." On the other hand, non-Japanese Asians, such as the Chinese and Koreans she has met and befriended, are objects of discrimination. In her characterization, Japanese tend to see one another as a racially, culturally, and linguistically unique group governed by a special social code.

Rosa's belief in equal treatment renders this racially hierarchized view of the world anathema. Efforts to conscript her into the restricted national club antagonize her. She would rather stand outside, as a strange anomaly. In playfully asking her sister to send her a blond wig, I do not think she wishes to claim the privilege enjoyed by Caucasian foreigners. Rather, she wants recognition as simultaneously a *Japanese* and a *foreigner*. She seeks to personify a categorical challenge, forcing her Japanese friends to come to terms with who she is increasingly sure she is—a nikkei Brazilian.

She makes this point directly in two passages of the interview. Trying to explain herself to her Japanese interlocutors, she reasons: "My parents are Japanese, both of them, and so by blood I am, too. But I was born and grew up in another country . . . and that makes me not Japanese." Later she speaks of how proud she is to be identified with what she sees as the traditional Japanese image of the humble, tenderhearted japonesinha. "But when I came here," she says, "I saw the other side of [Japaneseness]. . . . This reinforced my sense that I'm not really Japanese. I might be, a nikkei Brazilian. I'll admit I'm that, but I'm not *Japanese*."

Rosa, then, is most comfortable with herself as an ethnic inhabitant of the big country, Brazil. I meet her, as I meet many nikkeis, on this terrain, for I see myself as an ethnic inhabitant of another big country. I sometimes described myself to them as an American sansei, a third-generation Jewish-American. Brazil and the United States are different in obvious respects, but for those of us in both countries who reject monoethnic, monocultural, monolingual, monoracial models of community and nation, there is much common ground. Rosa and I both resent demands by others to reduce our national diversity in lifeways to stereotyped beliefs and customs, not just because such generalization is untrue but because we both believe it *should not* be true—that there is a better way. We both endorse empathetic engagement, in recognition of the concreteness of others. We both seek human connections that transcend national and ethnic categories. We both value the components of our selves that likewise move outside such social classifications.

When Maria and I were preparing to leave São Luís in 1986, after two years' residence in that city, Brazilian friends sometimes asked us, in jest, why we did not just stay. They knew we would not: why would Americans, entitled to live in a privileged country where they had grown up amidst friends and family, resettle in a faraway foreign place? But the question was a way of saying, You are plausibly one of us. We will miss you. Phrased in terms of nation, it was a gesture of friendship, conditioned on personal affinity and appreciation rather than race, language, or cultural expertise.

I think my plausibility as one of them, or rather our mutual plausibility as members of the same human group, enabled me to do the research I did among Brazilians at Homi. I was not liked or accepted by everyone, but many did open to me. It would have surprised me, I think, had I not lived in Brazil before.

Rosa's core self—her identity as a nikkei Brazilian, and as a human being—is tightly wound around her core values of empathetic engagement and equal treatment. Her job as an assistant teacher puts her at the transnational frontier, not as a straddler or negotiator but as a militant. It might be that she would reject this characterization, for militancy is not, I think, a quality Rosa would embrace. But she might be willing to accept, more modestly, that she is an advocate and a gadfly. She is a vigorous defender of the Brazilian children, whom she sees as deserving equal treatment from the Japanese school system and empathetic consideration from their parents, teachers, and colleagues. And through her interactions with Japanese coworkers and administrators, indeed through her very self-presentation to them, she seeks to provoke in them a Copernican reorientation, a new vision of a Big Japan—a more inclusive social universe filled with strange, hitherto invisible, astonishing human galaxies.

# CHAPTER 13

# Eriko Miyagi

## *"Even I don't know how I feel"*

### *The interpreter*

As he and I were driving to an appointment one spring day in 1996, Mr. Takao Kishi[1] of the Toyota International Association pointed out the office of a local empreiteira, the Kankei Company. We agreed to pay it an impromptu visit after our scheduled meeting at the offices of a Toyota City auto-glass manufacturer. The glass company had forbidden me to enter the factory proper, and the nervous manager began by asking me not to use the firm's name in any publication. These preliminaries augured poorly for our conversation, which indeed yielded little exciting information about the firm's Brazilian employees and hiring practices.

Perhaps the empreiteira would prove more interesting. We entered the spare, white-walled office unannounced. It was a far cry from the comfortable corporate meeting room we had just left, with its etched partitions and upholstered chairs. Mr. Kishi introduced himself as a TIA representative, and an effusive middle-aged man, Mr. Ishihara, ushered us to the single table, in the center of the tiled floor. A young woman brought green tea, the sine qua non of such conversations. Then the firm's interpreter, Eriko Miyagi, joined us at the table, seating herself in one of the straight-backed chairs. Eriko described herself to me as a *quebra-galho*, a troubleshooter, and said she had been working at Kankei for over five years. At first I was wary of communicating through a member of the firm. But Eriko told me, in sympathetic tones, that she had read something about me in one of the Brazilian papers. She seemed happy to cooperate, and despite the formality of the conversation, from time to time she cautiously amplified the answers given by Mr. Ishihara.

[1] His real name.

Unlike the large empreiteiras with branches throughout Japan and connections overseas, Kankei has just this single office and hires workers only for local suppliers of Toyota Motors. Founded in 1987, Kankei has been contracting nikkeis for the past seven years. It employs 140 Brazilians and 60 Japanese, eschewing Chinese, Iranians, and Pakistanis "because of visa problems." Although Kankei currently has a half-dozen Peruvians on its payroll, the company hires them with reluctance. According to Ishihara, some Peruvians have questionable papers, and putting Peruvians together with Brazilians in apartments doesn't work well, because their customs clash.

Kankei does not advertise, depending instead on word-of-mouth and telephone inquiries. The prospective employee fills out forms, submits to an interview, and visits the factory. In the past, Kankei had employees sign a written contract. But workers broke those contracts so readily, said Ishihara, that the company decided they weren't worth the trouble. Now Kankei relies exclusively on verbal agreements.

The company houses employees in either a ryō or in the Homi Danchi Kōdan, where they share apartments. Kankei uses a specialized agency to help with visa renewals. If someone is hurt on the job, Kankei provides transportation to the doctor or the hospital. The company does not, however, offer health insurance; employees can enroll instead in *kokumin kenkō hoken*, the national insurance plan.[2]

The interview was informative, though hardly thrilling. More intriguing was Eriko. I had heard a lot about interpreters, mostly complaints and criticisms, but I had never met one. We conversed briefly after everyone had risen from the table. Born in Okinawa, a Japanese citizen, Eriko had grown up in Santo André, in the state of São Paulo. Her husband, a nissei of Kyushu descent, had owned a photographic business in Brazil. Also a Kankei employee, he worked in a nearby factory. They were living at Homi Danchi with their daughter Midori, a fourth-grader at East Homi Grade School. I took a flier. I asked Eriko if she might

[2]The Toyota City municipality customarily provides kokumin kenkō hoken to foreigners. But in some areas of Japan, Brazilians requesting national insurance have been refused coverage. These municipalities insist that employers should provide shakai hoken, social insurance. Because employers of Brazilians often do not offer shakai hoken, and because some Brazilians balk at any optional salary deductions, many Brazilian workers have no health insurance. A worker must pay the full cost of kokumin kenkō hoken premiums, whereas under shakai hoken, the company pays half and the employee half.

agree to talk in a more private setting. The following Monday, late in the afternoon, she called me to say she was home and we could meet if I so desired.

## At Eriko's

Entering a building at Homi was like boarding a ship. Stairways wound from deck to deck. The apartments reminded me of my cabin on the *Brazil-Maru*: efficiently designed and lacking in storage space, with all facilities miniaturized. You could see the pipes that carried water, painted in beige enamel. The tight, dim interior hallways seemed like passages somewhere below the water line.

Eriko welcomed me at the door of her Ken-ei apartment, apologizing for the mess. Like most Homi apartments I had visited, hers was cluttered but not disarrayed. An entranceway, heaped with shoes, led into a hall, narrowed further with piles of stuff and a mini-refrigerator. A larger refrigerator stood in the kitchen. The apartment had six small rooms—two bedrooms, a kitchen, living room, toilet, and bath. The toilet and bath were little more than closets. The sliding doors and woodwork showed gashes, nicks, and scratches, but the general condition of the apartment was shipshape, if not luxurious.

We sat at a small table, covered with white plastic, set up between the living room and kitchen. Eriko offered me mineral water. Her husband was at work. Their daughter Midori watched girls' cartoons—tales of starry-eyed teenage heroines in trouble and in love—in the living room. Once or twice Eriko spoke to her, in a creole, the Japanese sprinkled with Portuguese words. When we finished, Midori showed me her pet hamster.

The interview was interrupted several times by phone calls from employees of the empreiteira. Eriko lamented that even at home she is at work. Once, she said, a Brazilian man, extremely agitated, came to the door. He had just had a fight. He showed Eriko a knife, and said if his brother-in-law came at him again, he would stab him. Eriko tried to calm him down. Luckily, the man did not carry out his threat.

As usual, I started by asking about life in Brazil. We then moved on to the early years in Japan, Eriko's Okinawan descent, the trials and tribulations of an interpreter, and questions of identity.

## *Japanese and Okinawans*

Daniel: At home [in Brazil], did you speak Japanese?

Eriko: In my childhood, we used the Okinawan dialect. But I didn't speak actual nihongo, I [just] knew a word here and there, I could say "Good morning."

Daniel: Were there schools that taught Okinawan dialect?

Eriko: No, but there was a school that taught Japanese. I went to it for a short time, I learned hiragana, just that. But because it was far from the house, it was hard for me to keep going. I think [I went there] two or three months.

Daniel: So before coming here you didn't speak much Japanese.

Eriko: Not much *(laughs)*. I was curious: the Japanese colônia had a program on radio, on television, so I listened to music, I copied writing. I'd ask my father, and he'd explain, but I was never fluent in the language *(laughs)*.

The Okinawa colônia, they're very ... closed. People in the old days used the dialect. My grandparents spoke only that [Okinawa] dialect, not [Japanese]. . . .

Daniel: Was there an Okinawan club where you lived?

Eriko: There was one nearby, my parents were members. After a while the young people started going there too, except that I already *(laughs)* had a boyfriend. I met my husband in another club. . . . It's called a *kaikan* in Brazil, a club of the Japanese colônia.

Daniel: So you two used to go to this club of . . .

Eriko: Of Japanese. Of nikkeis.

Daniel: Were there Japanese also in the Okinawans' club?

Eriko: No, only Okinawans.

Daniel: But in the Japanese club . . .

Eriko: Okinawans went there, were admitted there.

Daniel: Can I ask a delicate question?

Eriko: Mmm *(assent)*.

Daniel: Was there discrimination against Okinawans in Brazil?

Eriko: *(Laughs.)* In the old days, the families from Okinawa didn't allow marriages with nikkeis [from areas outside Okinawa]. They did everything possible so that ... *(laughs)* people didn't form ties. Just like there's this discrimination against marriages between nikkeis and Brazilians, native Brazilians, without [Japanese] descent.

Daniel: So did the efforts to impede this kind of thing come from the Okinawan or the Japanese side?

Eriko: Well, I can answer from my side, the side of Okinawa, because really they [the Okinawans] were more closed, they thought that the customs are different, even the religion, so . . . the oldest ones really tried to stop it. But all this was in the generation before mine, because in mine *(laughs)* there isn't this kind of problem.

Daniel: So you never felt any distrust of you, as an Okinawan, from the Japanese side.

Eriko: No, there wasn't any.

Daniel: And here in [Japan]?

Eriko: Here . . . No, they just see us as Brazilians *(laughs)*.

Daniel: When [Japanese people] find out, for example, that you're of Okinawan descent, does this create . . .

Eriko: There are people who ask if I'm Japanese or Brazilian. I say I'm Japanese, and then I add that I'm from Okinawa. Maybe it's my impression, they imagine that it's another country, another culture. There are people who, maybe they're joking around, but they say, "Ah, so you're not a nihonjin, you're an Okinawan" *(laughs)*. At least my birthplace is, my nationality is, Japanese *(laughs)*.

Daniel: Did your parents teach you something of the history of Okinawa?

Eriko: I know something about the war. My mother, they went through that, they lived through that time, there in Okinawa. They don't have *(laughs)* very good memories.

Daniel: [When I was in Okinawa] I went to the nurses' museum,[3] have you heard about that?

Eriko: I know. I've heard about it.

Daniel: That museum impressed me because there I saw for the first time a type of . . . resentment might be the right word, against the Emperor system, because around here you never hear that kind of thing—

Eriko: Right.

Daniel:—but there the perception is very different.

Eriko: For sure, here they don't talk much about it, here they look at the Emperor as if he were a God, a sacrosanct sovereign. I've heard [critical] comments [from Okinawans] because they suffered for it in the flesh.

[3]See p. 148.

## *As if returning to Japan*

Eriko: [In Santo André] I helped my husband. He was working in a photographic studio and I took care of the business when he'd do his [other] job, selling electrical materials. He'd take orders from factories and sell wholesale to businesses too. Mostly [he sold] wiring, electrical cables, sockets, that type of [stuff]. . . .

Daniel: He [also] took photos of people—

Eriko: Yes, for documents, weddings, reports. On weekends he'd do weddings, baptisms. . . .

Daniel: Do you also know how to do that?

Eriko: No, I'd just stay at the counter. I took photos for documents, but I didn't take wedding photos and things like that.

Daniel: And at that time did you have a child yet?

Eriko: I was already working with him when we were engaged. When we decided to come here, my daughter was about to turn three. Because I was born in Okinawa, I especially wanted to visit [it], never mind that I still haven't gone there *(both laugh)*, but I always wanted to visit my homeland, I was always curious about it. It was the beginning of the dekassegui boom.[4] At first I thought I couldn't come [to Japan] because I had my daughter, I thought it would be hard, but . . . because my aunt agreed to come with us, together with my cousins, who were in the same situation with a child, we decided to come. [My aunt] would take care of the children and we'd work.

My husband wanted to improve his business. It was fine, it wasn't terrible for us, but he wanted to open a bigger business. And . . . there was this curiosity too, so we came, and we liked it *(laughs)*. We intended just to stay two years, but the way things went, we stayed, and it's already our sixth year.

Daniel: You entered with a Japanese passport?

Eriko: Right, it's as if I were returning *(laughs)*. We went first to Hamamatsu. We weren't with an empreiteira, we worked directly for the factory, where our [cousins] already were working. We worked there almost six months. One relative got [a job] through the other. It was a wheel factory, aluminum wheels for cars.

Daniel: And the job?

Eriko: It was kind of heavy, and they paid very little. For a woman, it was 600 and something per hour, and for a man 1,000 and some-

[4]Usually dated from the time of the change in the immigration law (June 1990).

thing. And [my husband often] worked the night shift, but didn't get anything extra *(laughs)*.

For him, sleeping was also hard because ... you just get used to the day shift and then it changes to night.[5] This was really exhausting for him.

Daniel: There are a lot of people who can't adapt to that system.

Eriko: He lost a lot of weight, and psychologically too it isn't good, he got very nervous *(laughs)*.

### The most common thing in the world

In 1990, Eriko and her family moved to Homi, where they have been ever since. They moved into an apartment with friends from Santo André, who introduced them to the empreiteira Kankei. The living arrangement, which dragged out for a month, was uncomfortably cramped and tense. Finally an apartment opened up and, relieved, the Miyagis moved out.

Daniel: At that time in Homi, were there a lot of Brazilians?

Eriko: There were [Brazilians], but not so many. If we bumped into each other in the supermarket we'd end up shooting the breeze and getting to know each other, because there were only a few of us. Today we meet Brazilians *(laughs)* ...

Daniel: The supermarket is full of them.

Eriko: Yes, they're the most common thing in the world.

Daniel: After living in Homi quite a while, I don't see much of a relationship between the Brazilians here and the Japanese—

Eriko: Right.

Daniel: You go into a Brazilian's house and it's really rare to meet—

Eriko: A Japanese, it's true.

Daniel:—and I was wondering if in the beginning it was better or worse, for example in '90?

Eriko: In the beginning, I really think it was a little better, well, I don't know if my [Japanese] neighbor was an exception *(laughs)*, she treated me very well. But today I think they're more closed. Maybe it's our fault too, [the fault] of the Brazilians themselves.

[5]Eriko's husband was working kōtai.

## Becoming a translator

Daniel: In Toyota, you were working for Kankei, in what kind of job?

Eriko: I started working in the same factory as my husband, auto parts. I worked with a press. I liked it, except that it demanded a little skill. A press is a pretty dangerous thing, but there were all kinds of safety procedures.

Daniel: What kind of press?

Eriko: I don't know how to describe it exactly. You'd take an iron plate, iron, aluminum, I don't know, I think it was aluminum. You'd put it in the press, you'd press two buttons and the press would mold it, and then you'd take out the piece.

Daniel: And the piece was, what kind of piece?

Eriko: It was very slender, it was . . . there's the car, there's the windows of the car, and that piece encases the side of the glass to secure it. The piece is very delicate, it isn't big.

Daniel: And the salary?

Eriko: It was 850 per hour. [For my husband] it was 1,300.

Daniel: So it was much better than Hamamatsu.

Eriko: Much better *(laughs)*. I worked there six months.

Daniel: And after that?

Eriko: There was a young guy in the empreiteira working as an interpreter. At that time there were a lot of requests from women to be taken to the hospital. But since the guy was uncomfortable about accompanying women to the hospital, sometimes to the gynecologist *(laughs)*, they decided to hire a woman to help out. So they called on me, maybe because there were few people who had their [Japanese] driver's licenses. [I had mine] and I understood some [Japanese], so . . . They called on me to go [to the hospital], and with a lot of apprehension I went *(laughs)*.

Daniel: With a lot of apprehension?

Eriko: Because I still couldn't really speak. I carried a dictionary around. And accompanying people to doctors, the words are more . . . different, the specific words used in hospitals. I didn't know anything, so it was thanks to the dictionaries [that I could do it] *(laughs)*.

In the beginning [it was just] the hospital. Then I started to drive people to and from the factory. Also, a lot of couples with children were coming and putting them in child care. There were no interpreters yet in the crèches or schools, so I would go with them and give them some help.

Daniel: So you stopped working in the factory?

Eriko: Yes. We call it the office but I still do a lot of work outside, [going to] the bank, meetings in factories.

Daniel: Maybe you could describe this job of interpreter for me.

Eriko: I answer phone calls from people looking for work. ... There's the company's answering machine, people who can't work that day on account of sickness or some appointment leave a message, and we have to send it on to the factories, to give them some satisfaction. There are the meetings we hold in the factories, where the factory wants to send a message to the Brazilians and they know the majority won't understand *(laughs)*.

Daniel: What kind of meeting, for example?

Eriko: Like safety on the job, tardiness and unannounced absences. They let you miss time off work, so long as you communicate with them, but if you're absent without communicating, they get a little bit ... *(laughs)*.

Daniel: They don't like it.

Eriko: Right, they don't like it.

Daniel: Do you go alone, or with—

Eriko: Always with someone from the empreiteira. I feel more secure, and maybe they want to make their presence felt.

Daniel: Is there anyone else [in the office] who speaks Portuguese?

Eriko: No, at present it's just me there.

Daniel: They can't speak anything?

Eriko: They're not even interested *(laughs)*.

Daniel: Anything else you do?

Eriko: I help people out at the bank. A lot of people send money to Brazil, or they pay bills and can't leave work to do it, so they ask us and we do it. I go to the factory, get the information, get [the money], type it all up, and send it off, everything on trust, because if I'm mugged somewhere *(laughs)*, it's a risk that I run. [Sometimes] they ask us to buy dollars.

Daniel: What else? Doctors, you go with the person?

Eriko: No, I don't do that anymore. There's a hospital in Toyota where there's an interpreter, she's a nurse, so the person goes there and asks for her and it's easier, because I'd waste nearly half a day in the hospital. So they decided to cut out that kind of assistance. Now it's only in cases of accidents at work, then I go with them. When an accident happens, the factory lets the empreiteira know. A Japanese and I go over there, check the condition [of the person], and get them to the hospital. [Sometimes] long-term treatment is necessary, like today, I'm following two cases, every day I take them to the hospital, and leave them there. They're taking therapy. When they finish, they phone the office, so then we bring them back to Homi Danchi.

Daniel: And visas for example?

Eriko: Some time ago we did all the documents, but nowadays [the company] decided to do things through a credentialed agent, because he can represent the person at the immigration office and the person doesn't have to miss work. What interests the empreiteira *(laughs)* is more days worked. I get the documents from the workers, check them over, and pass it all on to the agent.

Daniel: And there must also occur unexpected situations, rare situations, let's say.

Eriko: Sometimes there's a problem between a Japanese and a Brazilian. I try to calm them down, hear both sides, but it doesn't help, the Japanese has priority *(laughs)*, so the Brazilian either lowers his head or he's fired. These things happen, I don't know if it's because of the way Brazilians are and the way Japanese are, they each have their own way of looking at things. The Japanese thinks that whoever has more seniority is ... let's say, he's more experienced, so they're used to bossing people around. But the Brazilian doesn't accept this, he thinks, He's a worker just like me, why should I accept his orders, he's not my superior, he's nobody. And in the end the Brazilian doesn't accept it, but he knows it's going to continue the same way, so he looks for something else, where he can work more calmly.

Once some Brazilians tried to control a section. About four or five people were working on presses, and some days there wasn't any overtime. In those days, when there wasn't overtime, for them it was the end of the world, they were obsessed. So they made defective parts on purpose *(laughs)*. They had a way, where you were supposed to put one piece in the press, they put two and this stopped the press and messed up the whole programming of the factory. I thought it was really a dirty business [*sujeira*], it doesn't help to do this kind of thing. ... It ended up with them getting fired, because [the factory] found out *(laughs)*.

Daniel: I don't quite understand the reason for making those defective pieces. What were they thinking?

Eriko: They thought that by making defective pieces they wouldn't meet their daily quota. They wanted overtime, so they made the defective pieces, and then they would have to work longer. This was before my time.

Daniel: Do you remember a case you were in the middle of?

Eriko: Something like that is really rare now. But there's still, like . . . one worker trying to cause trouble for another. But we can't observe this, we can't judge who's right and who's wrong, we can only listen to both parties and try to reconcile them.

Daniel: People are always saying, "That section is hell," because everyone is trying to make trouble for the others—

Eriko: Yes, yes.

Daniel:—to get more overtime [for themselves].

Eriko: Exactly, exactly, it still goes on.

### In between

Daniel: Do you think, Eriko, that the life of a translator is difficult?

Eriko: *(laughs)* There are times it's difficult. It's happened that I've had to mediate in an argument between my superior and a [Brazilian] worker. The worker said that the superior had promised such-and-such a salary and he didn't get what he was promised. But nobody could prove this because it was between the two of them, and the Brazilian . . . Everything pointed to him being right, but it was a really ugly argument right inside the office. The Brazilian was getting worked up, yelling, and the Japanese also was worked up and I had to be there in the middle of it *(laughs)*. It's really a . . . delicate situation.

Daniel: How do you deal with this type of situation?

Eriko: Knowing that the Brazilian is beside himself, saying words that you can't possibly translate *(both laugh)*, I try to calm him down, but . . . the time sometimes comes when neither one listens anymore, their gestures speak for themselves.

Daniel: How do you translate [the profanities]?

Eriko: *(laughs)* I tell [the Brazilian] he's saying some pretty heavy stuff, I just can't translate it. Even in Portuguese I can't bring myself to say swear words.

Daniel: So then, you translate, softening it . . .

Eriko: Right, because a Brazilian, depending on the person, they have a manner that's kind of . . . I hate to say it, grotesque. I think it depends on the level of the person. If you translate [exactly what they're saying] to Japanese people, they'll look at it as a provocation. . . . It's not the right way to have a dialogue, they won't understand the way the Brazilian is trying to express himself, so you've got to try to soften it a little.

Daniel: What's the reaction [of the Japanese]?

Eriko: Japanese people are all or nothing, so if he thinks he's being disrespected, he'll fire you right there. So I try to calm things down, as long as it's possible *(laughs)*.

Daniel: In the case you described, with the two shouting at each other, did you simply remove yourself from it or what?

Eriko: I'm trying to calm down the Brazilian, because I know, he's heading toward physical aggression. I tried to explain to him that in Japan, the first one to raise his hand is the loser, however good his reasons. . . . Maybe because I'm a woman *(laughs)*, I think he heard me, it worked a little bit, and he calmed down.

Daniel: And the resolution . . .

Eriko: The resolution was that the Japanese was really in the wrong, and [the Brazilian] was paid what had been agreed upon. Maybe so the empreiteira wouldn't have any more complications because the Brazilian said that it was like this, this, and this, and that he would pursue it [through other avenues].

Daniel: Any other kind of problem, being a translator?

Eriko: Ah, yes. It involves the family. My husband works for the same empreiteira, I have a brother who works [for them], and there's a kind of discrimination among the Brazilians against my family members. For example, my brother has lately been facing difficulties in the factory because they think that he . . . eh, just because I'm his sister, they look at him as if he's a spy *(laughs)*, do you understand? Brazilians, wherever they go, have a mania for talking about work, it's "the empreiteira is this, the empreiteira is that," so they think that whatever he may have heard he tells me and I automatically tell it to the empreiteira. So they distrust [him].

He doesn't get any frills at all, because his job is heavy, he works with the polishing machine, but the guys say, "Hey, your sister works over there in the office, you've got it made, so how come you're killing yourself in a heavy job like this, why don't you ask for a better job?" Except that if it was the reverse, if he had a good job, then they'd also talk. It's something that's hard for [my family] to put up with.

Daniel: It makes their relations with their colleagues difficult.

Eriko: It's discrimination. My sister used to work for the same empre-iteira. She also says there was this talk, that the salary was low, that it used to be higher, that they wanted to complain to the empreiteira and so on, and then when she'd come up to them they'd change the topic *(laughs)*, creating a really uncomfortable atmosphere, saying that . . . she might finger them. So because of that she quit that job and doesn't ever want to go back there.

Daniel: But then . . . you, being between the firm and the Brazilian work-ers, isn't it sort of uncomfortable?

Eriko: It is *(laughs)*, it sure is. I don't have any friends, I don't even have anyone to relax and talk freely with. Because it's the Brazilians' hobby to talk about work. . . . I have another way of looking at things, so . . . they always think I'm different from them. There's no way. It's a problem.

Daniel: Here, almost everybody has a group of persons they work with, and usually people do other things with that group, sometimes on their days off—

Eriko: Sure.

Daniel:—and always, as you said, talking about work, but you're there alone in the office—

Eriko: Right.

Daniel:—I mean, do you have a close relation with the Japanese? Is it possible—

Eriko: No, not that either. No, because they . . . they're closed, and I also don't try to mix with them.

Daniel: Do they also think you're a suspect person? *(Both laugh.)*

Eriko: Yes, they also think I'm different, but . . . I also don't feel com-fortable in a place where . . . Sometimes there's a *bōnenkai*, a social lunch at the end of the year.[6] I feel out of place there too, because their talk is different from mine; it doesn't coincide. So my circle of friends is just my relatives, I have a sister-in-law, cousins, that's it. Aside from this, it's just passing people in the street and saying hello.

Daniel: Yes, I understand. I think it's the situation of every translator throughout all of history.

Eriko: Yes *(laughs)*, it's true, isn't it.

Daniel: It's structural, it's got nothing to do with the person.

Eriko: Right, they create an image, there's no way, nothing helps.

---

[6]Bōnenkai are year-end gatherings for work groups, intended as relaxed settings in which one can blow off steam.

### *Eighty percent Brazilian*

Daniel: Do [Japanese] think you're Japanese or Brazilian?

Eriko: *(laughs)* Well, it's somewhere in the middle. They don't accept me as a Japanese, nor do I feel Japanese, I'm really more Brazilian.

Daniel: Yes, but you're a Japanese citizen. . . .

Eriko: Ah, a Japanese [citizen]. Well, I . . . It's good enough to deceive them *(laughs)*, I go shopping, I go to the bank, and . . . I pass as a Japanese, at least so long as I don't have to write much. When I say I don't know how to read, that I don't know how to write, that I'm not understanding something, then they look at me, and I explain I'm a Brazilian. That's when they understand *(laughs)*.

Daniel: You were born in Japan, you came to Brazil at age . . .

Eriko: One year and a few months.

Daniel: One year and a few months, and living in Brazil with Japanese parents, as a Japanese citizen, and coming back to Japan . . . Eriko, do you . . . feel . . . Japanese, Brazilian, Okinawan, how do you feel?

Eriko: Even I don't know how I feel *(laughs)*. I think I'm really more Brazilian, there's nothing to be done about it, I spent most of my life in Brazil. I like Japanese culture, but there are also parts of it that I'm against. Brazilians are warmer people, I think Occidentals in general, Japanese people are very cold . . . I don't know if you're aware of it, they treat you a certain way in your presence, but in the back [of their minds] they're imagining something else, you never know what's inside them. So . . . I think Occidentals are more . . . explicit, more clear, they're more sincere.

Daniel: And you?

Eriko: I'm part of that [that is, the Occidental way] *(laughs)*. [But] there are things that I don't agree with that Brazilians do, and in that part I think I'm a little bit Japanese.

Daniel: Such as?

Eriko: . . . Our customs, of Brazilians, are different: [let me give you] an example from Homi. Brazilians like to turn up the volume, without worrying about what the next person might think, whether they're bothering their neighbors or not. I don't know if you could define this as egoism, but I . . . I don't want to get involved in problems with the Japanese, so I try . . . to respect them. I know that if I do [turn up the volume] they're not going to like it. I think it's easier for me to understand that part, because I'm half-and-half *(laughs)*, but for a native Brazilian it's really pretty hard. . . .

Daniel: And with respect to the Japanese? You said there are also things you don't agree with, that they do.

Eriko: Sure.

Daniel: For example . . .

Eriko: An example from the office. They always say, "It had to be a Brazilian" *(laughs)*, then they look at me and say, "Ah, but you're not a Brazilian, you're Japanese." It's so I won't worry about what they're saying, as if the discrimination was not directed at me. But I feel like it is, I'm a Brazilian too, so . . . this type of comment really hurts. They say, "It's a Brazilian thing, he's got to be a Brazilian to do something like that."

To cite [another] example, Brazilians don't usually give notice, when they want to leave the empreiteira, they say, "Tomorrow I won't be working here," and that's it. And [the Japanese] don't accept this, they get really mad. Except . . . there are Japanese [workers] who do this too, I've witnessed it, but [the bosses] don't say anything then, or sometimes they say, "They're just like nikkeijin." So either way *(laughs)*, it's blamed on the Brazilians. The discrimination is very big.

Daniel: When they say to you, "But you're not a Brazilian, you're a Japanese"—

Eriko: But I am—

Daniel:—how do you feel at that moment?

Eriko: I feel as if they're . . . just making an excuse, it's something that just escapes, "Ah, it's a Brazilian," so then they realize that I'm there. . . . It's like a plea for me to forgive them, but . . . it doesn't resolve anything, because . . . the damage has been done *(laughs)*.

Daniel: Do you ever respond, "But I'm a Brazilian"?

Eriko: *(Much laughter.)* Yes. I say, "I'm one too." So then they say, "No you're not, you were born here." It's going to be a while before Japanese people get used to foreigners. With Americans I think the reception must be better, isn't it?

Daniel: Well, I'm a gaijin, right—

Eriko: You are *(laughs)*.

Daniel:—except that . . . it might be that they . . . don't look at all gaijin the same way.

Eriko: Yes, because if you're American I think you have another status.

Brazil is a Third World, they ... know almost nothing about Brazil. A lot of Japanese don't even know there are buildings in Brazil *(laughs)*, they think it's still completely a jungle. . . . They know more about the United States than about Brazil, so they accept it more.

Daniel: For sure.

Eriko: Europe [too] ... It's going to be a long time before South America is accepted here.

Daniel: Sometimes Brazilians say bad things about Japanese. When they do this in front of you, do you also feel uneasy?

Eriko: No, not as much as the reverse.

Daniel: How come?

Eriko: Maybe because I feel myself to be more Brazilian, yes, that's it.

Daniel: Do you also have Brazilian citizenship?

Eriko: No, it isn't dual, I used to have a permanent visa, but a permanent visa has to be renewed every two years. I used to go [to Brazil] every two years, returning to renew the visa, but ... this last time *(laughs)* I didn't go. So for me to return I need to get a visa from here. From the Brazilian consulate.

Daniel: It's really interesting, because by law, you're Japanese.

Eriko: Yes.

Daniel: By feelings, you're—

Eriko: I'm Brazilian.

Daniel: You, a Brazilian, don't have a permanent visa for Brazil.

Eriko: I don't have one *(both laugh)*.

Daniel: So where does that leave us.

Eriko: Well ... eh ... there's my Japanese side, but I think I'm 80 percent Brazilian.

Daniel: You see the Japanese side mainly in this business of respect, that you were saying—

Eriko: Right, respect.

Daniel: Is there anything else?

Eriko: Customs ... I think it's really that, I really admire the respect they have for other people. . . .

Eriko: After more than thirty years in Brazil, [my father] came back last year on vacation, he was here at the house, but he said he didn't like it *(laughs)*.

Daniel: He didn't like it?

Eriko: No, he said it was very different from the image of Japan he had from thirty-some years ago, so ... he said he preferred Brazil.

Daniel: He didn't feel at home here?

Eriko: He felt like a fish out of water. The majority of people who have returned, those originally from Japan, feel that way. It's that Japanese people, it's their custom, but there are a lot of demands. In Brazil, people live with more freedom, there's a lot of space. . . . We don't have to explain ourselves to our neighbors. Here, I don't know if it's because it's an apartment complex, but I think it's general, even in their houses one neighbor knows what the other is doing, about the other's life. . . . You have to explain yourself. So I think that for those of us accustomed to the freedom of Brazil, I think it's better there.

Daniel: Do you have plans to return to Brazil some day?

Eriko: We plan to, yes, maybe in two years. The two years keep dragging out *(laughs)*. When we came we intended to stay just two years, and we're already here six. But we have plans.

Daniel: You're not thinking of staying in Japan for good?

Eriko: Ah no, it's not possible.

Daniel: Not possible?

Eriko: It's not possible, to stay here forever, no way.

Daniel: Why not?

Eriko: ... I think we manage to put up with it thinking that it's temporary. This workload is very tough on my husband. At least my job is varied, [time] passes more quickly, but my husband finds it very tough, working in the factory. And ... there's our age too, we're already over forty, and the day will come when the job will be too hard. So it's really not possible, forever, we wouldn't be able to have our own house, it would be just living in this cubicle. We need freedom and space too.

Daniel: Could she *(indicating Midori)* make a life in Japan?

Eriko: She sometimes has difficulty in school. . . . She likes it a lot, keeps up with her little schoolmates, but ... there's a little discrimination among children too.

Daniel: What do they do?

Eriko: Well, in her case ... even though she's been in school since the crèche and understands [Japanese] well, just like the Japanese kids, she says there are some children who ... discriminate. They say things, so there are times when she comes home out of sorts, she says she wants to go back [to Brazil].

## A question of sincerity

Why did Eriko, whom I had never met before, so readily agree to this conversation? I have often puzzled over that. Even though I am by now accustomed to people's eagerness to confide in strangers, I expected more caution from an interpreter, someone whose occupation, like my own, demands circumspection. But I think I have a clue. The answer is, paradoxically, bound up with that very occupation, and I believe it reveals much about Eriko's deepest sense of self.

Eriko, like Rosa Kitagawa, works at the ethnic frontier, but in a more ambiguous, tense zone of contact. A representative of the empreiteira, herself a former worker with husband and siblings currently in the factory, she sees both sides of workplace (and hence ethnic) conflicts but cannot fully endorse either. A reluctant, insecure recruit to the position of interpreter, the target of Brazilian suspicion and, indirectly, Japanese derision, she is increasingly forced to stand apart from others. Uncomfortable in the Japanese office, uncomfortable in Brazilian social encounters, she finds her circle of companionship reduced to her family, themselves under a cloud because of their association with her.

Foregrounded in Eriko's current situation, and in the interview itself, are questions of representation, of truth and appearance. Eriko's job is to represent others—to represent the empreiteira to Brazilians, and Brazilians to the empreiteira. That is what an interpreter does. Because the job offers possibilities for misunderstanding, deception, and secret agendas, it puts the interpreter in a most delicate position, rendering her the object of suspicion and distrust. She works in the office, among the Japanese bosses. Is she a spy? Does she use influence, favoring her relatives? Whose side is she on? Is she loyal only to herself, or to her family, or to her compatriots? Who *are* her compatriots? Is she, when all is said and done, "Japanese" or "Brazilian"? Or what?

Thus Eriko's occupation brings her face-to-face with persistent questions about her complexly interrelated identities. Her identity fragmentation extends beyond the split between Japanese citizenship and Brazilian upbringing, for she is ethnic Brazilian (Japanese-Brazilian), ethnic Japanese (Okinawan-Japanese), and even ethnic nikkei (Okinawan-nikkei). Eriko is not fully at ease in any of these ascribed positions. By forcing her constantly to shift perspectives, her job reinforces in her a certain ironic subjectivity, a self partially detached from categorical labels. Her history of migrations also involves identity ambiguities. Eriko becomes adept at analyzing the strength and conditions of her own identifications. But she does not, in the end, surrender to the interpreter's position, the mediator's lack of self-commitment.

Eriko's ironic distance from her ethnic identity emerges frequently in her talk about herself. She travels to Japan "as if returning"; she "still look[s] like a Japanese"; she can "pass" for one if not pressed too hard. Brazilians are sometimes "we"; elsewhere they are eyed with clinical detachment. One can occupy an ironic self, becoming a manipulator, for good or ill, of identities and allegiances. But Eriko, who faces daily challenges to her sincerity, rejects that option. Perhaps *because* of such challenges, Eriko refuses to break fully with herself. That self holds the value of sincerity at or near its core. By "sincerity" I mean, as she puts it, explicitness, clarity, a correspondence between feeling and expression. The value she places on sincerity leads her, inevitably and despite equivocations, to Brazilianness.

For Eriko, sincerity is what distinguishes Brazilians (and "Occidentals," including, in her taxonomy, nikkeis) from Japanese. Thus Japanese "treat you a certain way in your presence, but in the back [of their minds] they're imagining something else, you never know what's inside them." When her Japanese bosses tell her, "You're not a Brazilian, you're Japanese," they are dissimulating. In contrast, Brazilians, even at their most "grotesque," speak their minds. When the incensed worker hurls profanities at the boss, or when colleagues accuse Eriko's sister of being a spy, they are behaving outrageously, but you know where you stand with them.

In Eriko's formulation, sincerity and Brazilianness go together; Brazilians (but not Japanese) are sincere. I believe that talking with me offered Eriko the opportunity to proclaim her sincerity and its identity correlate, her Brazilianness. I offered her a chance not just to *assert* these facts—the true Eriko is sincere; the true Eriko is Brazilian—but to *demonstrate* and *reinforce* them, to me and to herself, in a personal interaction.

At one point Eriko announces, perhaps ruefully, "I think I'm really more Brazilian, *there's nothing to be done about it* [emphasis mine], I spent most of my life in Brazil." Taken one way, the statement is a simple affirmation. Despite her red passport, if she must put a label on the mass of experiences, orientations, and values she has accumulated in the course of her life, "Brazilian" fits better than "Japanese." But her statement is also, pragmatically, a demonstration of sincerity. She cannot feign to be other than what she feels she is. And what is more Brazilian, in her terms, than that? Because she views the personal quality of sincerity as emblematic of Brazilianness, the speech act proves the ethnic claim.

To be Japanese, in contrast, is to be insincere. We see this in her account of discrimination at the office. The comments of her Japanese co-workers—"It had to be a Brazilian"—are hurtful and alienating to Eriko for several reasons. They make Eriko uncomfortable, not just because her bosses criticize Brazilians unfairly, but because by granting her an honorary superior Japanese status—"After all, you're Japanese"—they show bad faith by verbally including her in a group she feels they in practice undoubtedly exclude her from, and they implicate her against her will in the act of criticizing those with whom she feels an affinity. Acceding to this manipulation would, in her terms, be a manifestation of her own insincerity, of her own bad faith. Although assuming a Japanese identity would be to value "respect," a quality she (like many others) admires, it would also mean practicing insincerity. She cannot do this.

It is not that she wholeheartedly embraces Brazilianness. She criticizes and distances herself from certain Brazilian practices: playing loud music, without considering one's neighbors; the dirty business of subverting the quota, in order to work more overtime; the tendency of Brazilians to blow up in confrontations; the crass fixation on work.[7] This last quality, in combination with implied tendencies toward distrust and spitefulness, has produced the discrimination against her and her relatives. But I would suggest that her description of such persecution is more analytical than censorious: the suspicions of spying, though unjustified and hurtful, seem more a product of a built-in conflict than outright malevolence. And the Brazilians, unlike the Japanese, do not conceal their wariness and rejection.

Though Eriko does not spare Brazilians in her narrative, when all is said and done she comes down on their side, on the side of the devil she knows and, in a manner of speaking, trusts. She commits herself to sincerity, to saying what she means and acting transparently. If she cannot convince Brazilians or Japanese of this fact, she can at least try to convince me, an anthropologist outsider, whose sincerity is also, as a matter of professional risk, in question. I might be expected to understand. And I am convinced: I think Eriko is, as she claims, according to her own lights, overwhelmingly Brazilian.

[7]Note that she modulates some of these criticisms: not considering neighbors is also a kind of "freedom"; the trickery and sabotage seem, in her presentation, a bit clever and perhaps amusing; the Brazilian worker was right in his claims, and, unusually, won a victory.

CHAPTER 14

# Naomi Mizutake

## *"The eighth wonder of the world"*

### *The school trip*

The final chimes had sounded. As I was leaving Homi Chū I witnessed an uncomfortable scene in the hallway. Carlos and his homeroom teacher Mr. Nomura were discussing the June 1996 trip for third-year students, a highlight of the last year of middle school. Nomura wanted a reason why Carlos was not going. Naomi Mizutake, Toyota City's roving bilingual teacher, was called upon to translate. The confrontation—for it had that air—was designed to pressure Carlos and, indirectly his family, into assenting to the trip. Nomura was direct in his questioning, and Carlos, casting his eyes toward the floor and shifting his body weight from one foot to the other, mumbled his responses.

Nomura wanted to know if Carlos did or did not want to go to Tokyo. Carlos was equivocal. He said it was all right with his mother but not with his father. Nomura wanted to know exactly why his father had a problem. It was an educational trip, the teacher explained; Carlos would learn new things in Tokyo, and if he stayed home he would have to attend school anyway. If Carlos could not go, Nomura wanted a letter from his parents explaining the precise reason. But first Carlos should have another talk with his father.

The conversation went on for a long time, covering the same ground over and over. Naomi patiently mediated but seemed as ill at ease as Carlos. I guessed that the problem was the considerable expense of the trip. I also suspected that all was not well in Carlos's family. Each of the several times I had run into Carlos's father, he was drunk. On one occasion, an evening at a local Brazilian restaurant, his wife and children seemed tense and abashed, visibly upset by his uncontrolled behavior.

The parents ultimately provided a letter stating that the excursion was beyond their means. I later learned that Carlos had wanted to go.

During Golden Week, a string of national holidays in early May, Carlos's older sister had arranged to take him and his little brother on a day trip to Tokyo Disneyland. Two hours out of Nagoya the radiator blew. The car was towed and everyone returned to Toyota by train. The trip was scrapped, a big disappointment for the children.

In July, I ran into Nereci, Carlos's mother, who looked unhappy. She and the boys had just moved in with Carlos's sister, occupying one of the two bedrooms in her tiny Ken-ei apartment. At home Nereci and her husband had been fighting over the little money they had saved during their years in Japan. And her husband's drinking had led to rows and sometimes violent attacks. Nereci told me she was embarrassed by her separation and reluctant to talk about it for fear she would become an object of gossip.

Carlos, a quiet, likable, but mildly rebellious and sometimes melancholy boy, quit Homi Chū to take a part-time job delivering videos in the danchi. He would not graduate with his class. I guessed that Nereci needed the money, and in any case Carlos's schooling would soon end.

### Naomi's mini-autobiography

Naomi Mizutake, the bilingual teacher summoned by Mr. Nomura, visited Homi Chū twice a week to assist students in the Kokusai class. A dynamic presence, Naomi often encouraged them to talk about themselves, to value their unusual perspectives as Brazilians residing in Japan, and to formulate aspirations for the future. Like her colleague Rosa Kitagawa, she was a key fixture in the students' often chaotic lives.

The conversation I had with Naomi in July 1996 was unusual. She needed little prompting other than the setting, a free afternoon in our Homi Danchi apartment, to launch into a narrative reaching back to the times of her grandparents and extending to the present. I will therefore depart from my usual format. Most of the "interview" was really a spoken mini-autobiography, a fascinating, coherent monologue. I will present it as such, omitting my often redundant or irrelevant interjections. Toward the end of the nearly three hours I spent with her, however, we began talking explicitly about matters of identity. That discussion more closely resembled a conversation.

Here is Naomi's story.

## *"Do you think my father went off to hell?"*

My mother was born in Brazil, but her parents are Japanese [from] Yamagata-ken, up north. My father was born in Kobe. He went to Brazil after graduating from high school, at age eighteen or nineteen, alone. It was a poor family. His two older brothers went to college. But when my father was in high school, he saw that the financial situation at home wasn't good, so he thought it was better for him to follow his own path in life. He didn't mention his plan to emigrate, he did all the paperwork himself and one week before boarding the ship he told his parents. He needed his father's and mother's signatures. He asked their forgiveness, and . . . [in 1959] he went to Brazil.

And he stayed there. He was an immigrant, but he didn't work in the fields, because he had some education. It was hard at the beginning. I've heard that from my mother and from my grandmother's letters, because my father doesn't talk about how he went through hell. But he came out of it OK.

His dream was someday to send his three children to Japan. We grew up with this idea. As he says, "Japan is my native land, I grew up there. I was raised Japanese, and however much I'd like to change myself there are things I can't ever change. But I love Brazil, and I'd never want to live again in Japan." But . . . from time to time he misses it and he wants to hop over here.

Kobe is a port, and historically it's one of the [Japanese] cities that has most warmly welcomed foreigners. The idea of going overseas was almost normal for the people of Kobe. One of his high-school teachers had gone to Brazil. The [other] teachers would announce, "If you'd like to go to Brazil, get in touch with Mr. So-and-So, because he can give you some help," "Brazil is a country," that old idea, "of riches, you can get anything you want" *(laughs)*.

In Japan, in the old days, if you weren't first in your class you couldn't get into a public university. My father was second or third. And my grandparents couldn't possibly have afforded to send him to a private university. So when [people here] say, "It was a shame he had to go to Brazil," I say, "It's not a shame, do you think my father went off to hell? Brazil is a terrific country, he did well there, he's got a business, he lives in a huge house. He'd never have been able to live in a house like that if he'd stayed in Japan."

That teacher [from his high school] had a little shop [in Brazil] that made small things, like bicycle chains, so [my father] began as a sales-man. At that time a salesman had to pound the pavement, there wasn't any telephone. He traveled around the state [of São Paulo], to all the cities with lots of Asians.

My father isn't a naturalized Brazilian. He's got a resident visa. He says, "I have two homelands. If I take out Brazilian nationality, what will it get me? OK, I'm not getting anything extra having Japanese nationality, but what am I going to gain trading my nationality for a Brazilian one? Since it won't change anything, let it be."

### *"American spy!"*

My mother went to a Brazilian school, but at home she only talked in Japanese. She grew up in São Paulo. My grandparents from Yamagata were immigrants. It was their dream to enrich themselves in Brazil and return to Japan. The minute they managed to get a lot of money to-gether, and send it all to Japan, the Second World War began. They wouldn't let anyone board a ship, and the money, *prruu (gesture of money flying away)*. No one knows where it ended up. They say my grandmother tried to kill herself, because she'd worked fifteen years, and the minute they said, "Finally we're in good shape, let's go back" the war broke out.

They'd sold all their land and packed their bags. So my grandparents had to start all over again. At that time, in '41, my mother hadn't yet been born. My grandparents had four children. The oldest died of ma-laria, up in the Amazon, when my mother was a child. My mother was born in '44. This was a difficult time, my grandparents had even consid-ered an abortion. But they thought if four can eat so can five.

[My grandparents] went straight to the Amazon to plant black pep-per. Then they went to São Paulo to plant cotton. They started as share-croppers [*meeiros*]. The land isn't yours: you plant the crop, you do eve-rything, and whatever you harvest, half goes to the landlord. They man-aged to buy a small piece of land, and so it went. . . . Farming is subject to storms and droughts. One day it rains, [the next] it hails, it wrecks everything and you lose the whole year's crop. So [they] started to sell canned and packaged goods, rice and beans, in the market in São Paulo.

My mother's father died at age thirty-something, or forty, he died in '45, when my mother was eleven months old. My grandfather now, in reality he's my mother's stepfather, and he's also my mother's uncle.

He's my grandfather's [younger] brother. [He] married his sister-in-law because it was his idea for his three older brothers and his sister-in-law to go to Brazil. At that time he was sixteen or seventeen and his older brothers were already married. The oldest one was my grandfather. [The younger brother] told him, "Brazil is a good place, there's land there," and he convinced everyone to go. Then they lost their money during the war, and afterwards my grandfather died, and he felt responsible for it all.

So he wanted to raise his four nieces and nephews, to provide for them. And Japanese people, on this point they're kind of square, to live in the same house without being married or anything, a man and a woman, well, you can't. So they got married, but [he] and my grandmother don't have any children, because he said, "I'm just going to get married on paper, so no one can speak badly of us. I'm just getting married so I can raise my four nieces and nephews who lost their father on account of me."

And he really meant it. They got married, it was a normal family, they slept in the same room, but nothing more. No relations, no children, nothing. And today the four nieces and nephews consider [him] to be their father, because of everything he did for them. There's really no other word to call him except "father." He's an angel, he doesn't see evil in anything.

When my mother was six, they again managed to get some money together, and [all of them] went back to Japan. My mother went to school here, first, second, and third grades. As they say, the language you learn as a child, that's the one that sticks. You can't even tell that she's Brazilian. Her Japanese is super-perfect, she loves to read books in Japanese.

They lived here three years, in Tokyo. They came in '51, when Japan was trying to get back on its feet. There was a lot of hunger, a lot of poverty.

But not in Brazil. My mother says, "I had leather shoes, a little dress, a pretty little hat." But at school, everyone would taunt her, saying, "You've got things, we have nothing." They called her an American spy, because she came from overseas, and even worse, she came all pretty. If you think about it, my mother really was a foreigner. Even though she spoke Japanese she'd been born on Brazilian territory, she's a Brazilian, right? That was a tough time for her, she had to put up with many insults, many offenses, and keep quiet.

Sometimes my grandmother would dress her up pretty, but she'd say, "Mom, I don't want to go out like this." She wasn't able to explain it, she'd just say, "I don't want to go out in these clothes, give me those," "But those are old, they're dirty," "But if I go all pretty they'll say that I'm . . . " And my grandfather didn't have straight hair like Japanese people, he had really wavy hair. So they'd say he had a permanent wave, American-style. My mother would say, "But why American, we came from Brazil, why do they keep saying American?"

But for the Japanese kids it was really hard. Anyone who came to the door asking for a loan, [my grandfather] would give it to them. He saw people going hungry, and he couldn't stand it. All the money they'd got together during those six years in Brazil, they ended up losing, loaning it out. Nobody, of course, was going to repay it, and in the end they decided to go back to Brazil again. Everyone.

[In Tokyo] there wasn't much rice, but they had rice at home because they were planting it. The kids all had to carry a bentō to school. Everybody was taking cooked sweet potatoes, or cooked turnip, but not my mother. My mother brought *onigiri* [rice balls wrapped in seaweed], white rice. She felt sick eating onigiri, every swallow she took she felt everyone looking at her.

[The return to Japan] had been really bitter. A lot of people around them were going hungry and suffering, so anyone who had a little more in the way of luxury, people tormented. The worst was that they weren't "Japanese," in quotes—that's what made the reception so bad. For the Japanese, Brazil and the United States must have been the same thing, because it's all America, it's all way over there. I think that distinguishing between them wasn't something they cared about. "You're well off, at our cost because you won the war, we got hammered and you're so pretty," so . . . it was really tough. The only worthwhile thing was that [my mother] learned Japanese. She loved comic books. . . . They fascinated her and that's really the only good memory she has.

My grandmother keeps [my mother's] report card. It says she's a quiet girl, very shy, who doesn't talk much. My mother doesn't talk much? Sometimes I tell her, "Mom, that's enough, stop talking, OK?" She gets on a bus, and two minutes later she's talking with the person next to her. So I was looking at that report card, and I said, "Nossa, 'doesn't talk much,' " and she said, "I couldn't speak." Because whatever she said [the Japanese children would say], "Ah, you're talking that way because you're an American," and if she agreed with [them] it would be, "You're just agreeing because you want something," and if she disagreed, there would be a fight. So she said, "I couldn't say anything."

### *"Who's that idiot doing handstands?"*

[Three years later the family] came back to São Paulo. There they struggled all over again, and as my grandfather had done before, he started selling prepared foods, canned goods, grains. He had a stall [in the market]. He got orders from tiny quitandas, and made deliveries.

When my mother returned [to Brazil], she had lost her Portuguese. A lot of children are in this situation [in the schools here], and I really feel for them, because of my mother. ... My mother keeps saying, "Help these children, because in my time I didn't have anyone to help me." She had to start first grade all over again. A girl of ten with everyone else six, she always walked around hunched over so she wouldn't seem so big. She finished high school and then studied design, sewing, she did a course in fashion. In the end, she says that she—in quotes—had an "easy life" in Brazil, once they got back. Her brothers were a lot older, some just finished middle school and had to [work], but not my mother. She says, "I didn't have to, but I'll never forget that I saw everyone doing the heavy work."

When my father met my mother, he was still working as a traveling salesman. In the Japanese community in São Paulo, everyone knows everyone else. There was a man who was a good friend of my grandparents and also of my father. He was like a second father for my father. That teacher from the [high] school gave [my father] a job, but for the rest, he didn't do anything at all. But this other Japanese man helped out: when he needed [a place to sleep] he invited him to sleep at his house, he gave him food.

[My parents] met at the beach. My grandparents and my mother had gone there, to a hotel, and my father was on holiday at the same hotel. They say my father liked my mother at first sight *(laughs)*. The way my mother tells it, my father was doing handstands on the beach to get her attention. My mother said, "Who's that idiot doing handstands?" *(laughs)*. This man who knew both of them [said], "No, he's a serious guy, that's Mizutake." So they introduced themselves, and when they went back to São Paulo, they started going out together.

At the time my mother was working at the Bank of Tokyo. Most clients were Japanese, and she spoke Japanese well. Since my father's firm had an account there, he'd often go there to do paperwork. He'd say, "What a coincidence *(laughs)*, meeting you here," and it went on like that.

They got married in January 1968. But my [mother's mother] was terminally against it. She'd say, "A roving Japanese, he doesn't have anything, just imagine me letting my daughter marry a guy like that. You'll see he's got women scattered all over the place, in every town. No, no, no!" They went together three years, with my grandmother constantly running him down. [One day] my grandfather said, "Can't you see he's a good guy? If your daughter chose him, be quiet. Trust her." My grandmother had a pile of photos of *miais* [that is, potential husbands for an arranged marriage], nikkeis who had graduated in law, engineering, and so on. "Look, there are so many good matches, why do you like that Japanese peddler? Marry this nikkei who's doing well, he graduated from the university." But in the end, my grandmother stopped talking and they got married.

### "How is Santa Claus going to get
### through there with a bicycle?"

In '69 I was born in São Paulo. My father was still on the road. My mother said, "This is no good," because sometimes she saw my father only twice a month. So she decided to move to the interior [of the state of São Paulo] with me, so that my father could at least come home every week. I lived there four or five years, and then we moved back to São Paulo. My sister was born [during that period]. She's two years younger than me.

My father got a job with another firm, a branch of Mitsubishi, in São Paulo. I started pre-school, and we bought a house. It was a neighborhood sort of like the countryside. But today it's all built up. We lived there ten years. There were lots of kids, and so my childhood was playing in the street all day *(laughs)*, riding my bicycle, skating, playing dodgeball. . . . Even though it was a simple childhood, I didn't feel it was simple, but after we grew up our parents would say, "Back then we didn't have enough to buy things, so your father would invent a bunch of excuses."

Once I wanted a bicycle from Santa Claus. There was a tiny chimney in the bathroom of the house. I wrote letters to Santa Claus saying I wanted a bicycle. But there wasn't any money. So [my mother] pulled me over and said, "Naomi, look up there. You see that little hole? How is Santa Claus going to get through there with a bicycle?" *(Laughs.)* So I thought a little and said, "It's true, Mom. It's better to ask for a smaller present." Then I rewrote the letter asking for a doll.

By then they were selling Yakult [a yogurt drink] in Brazil, a woman passed by the house every day with a refrigerated cart. Yakult was expensive back then, but all the neighbors, the mothers bought a Yakult for the kids. But my mother couldn't spend money like that every day. So she'd say, "Look, that Yakult is really great, but if you drink too much, it'll give you diarrhea" *(laughs)*. So Mom would buy it two or three times a week, except [my sister and I] divided it up. We made a line with a pen. Some days I'd draw the line on the container, drink half, and give the rest to her, and other days she'd draw the line. I had a really great childhood, but . . . for my parents I know it was really hard.

## *"I thought he was the eighth wonder of the world"*

My father adapted well to Brazil. He knows Brazilian customs well and he's open, there's none of this fixating on small things. But there's another side of his personality that seems more Japanese. My mother is a nikkei, a brasileira. She's not one of those submissive Japanese women, quiet as a mouse, who lowers her head to her husband and does everything he wants. That's why there are often big brouhahas at home, because my father says something and my mother says, "But I don't think so, don't you think—" "But why do you argue right away?" "I'm not arguing, I'm stating my opinion" *(laughs)*. So my father would say, "What kind of Japanese woman are you?" "I'm not a Japanese woman." Back then, Japanese women, the husband said "Drink" and the wife drank. Not my mother, I mean the pattern was, on this point, more Occidental.

My father really likes Brazilian food, rice, beans, beefsteaks, he doesn't like misoshiru, he detests *tsukemono* [pickles] and nattō. [But] he always taught us to eat everything that's on the table. Because he went hungry during the war, to throw out food is a holy sacrilege. When my mother makes misoshiru, he eats it. During the war, the only thing there was to eat was what was buried in the ground, especially in Kobe, where bombs fell. Nothing was left of what was on top. And they didn't have seasonings, at most they had salt and soy sauce. My father had to eat a lot of cooked *nabo* [turnip]. Whenever we have cooked nabo, you can see the sad look in his eyes.

Since my mother never went hungry, there's nothing she doesn't like and she makes everything. Whenever she makes turnips, she also makes something else, because she knows that my father won't want to eat only turnips. When I was a child I didn't know about all this. He'd look at that turnip, and he'd avoid it until the end of the meal. My sister and I, we didn't know, "Ah, Dad, you have to eat turnip," because he made us eat everything, "at least a mouthful." "OK, OK," he'd grab a little piece and eat it. Later my mother told us, and afterwards when she'd cook turnips we wouldn't say anything. Or we'd say, "Oh, Dad, you don't have to eat it if you don't like it, leave it," but in the end, so as not to contradict himself, he ate it. We'd see that he swallowed that mouthful of turnip with sorrow and hurt.

But if you think about it, my father had a more open way of thinking than a normal Japanese. And my mother seemed more Japanese in certain respects than my father. Because my father decided to go to Brazil, he struggled all alone, but not my mother. My mother was raised by Japanese, in a totally Japanese culture. OK, she speaks Portuguese well, she went to school in Brazil. But in terms of her children marrying people who are not descendentes, she doesn't say anything now, but when I was young, no way would she accept that.

One day my mother was talking so much that my father said, "You want your daughters to marry descendentes? Then go to Japan. In Brazil, you can't demand something like that, you're in a country that has white people, black people, yellow people, blue people, green, there's everything. If one day your daughter shows up with a blond, with a black man, you can't say anything. But if you want so badly for her to marry a descendente, then leave Brazil, for Japan. You go and I'll stay," he said. When I heard my father say this, I thought he was the eighth wonder of the world *(laughs)*. My friends' Japanese fathers were really square. I thought, My father is a wonder, and after that I came to respect him like crazy.

We were sixteen, seventeen, there were dances, there were parties, we'd go to the movies. I had friends whose fathers were nikkeis, they had to be home at nine. After nine, the father would be waiting at the door and would yell at her loud enough to bring the house down. Not my father and my mother. At first, they slept with their bedroom door open. [My sister and I] would come home at one in the morning, so I think they were worried. But afterwards they saw that we came straight home, so they started sleeping with the door closed. My father never said, "You can't go out," he just said, "Take care of yourself, who are you going with," with So-and-So, "Where are you going," such-and-such a place, "OK." My friends would say, "Your father who's Japanese, he lets you go, but my father won't let me." So I went to dances more with Brazilians than with my nikkei friends. My father's got a hard head just like a Japanese, but he's got another side, he's got a mind that's really open. He's very radical.

## *"Even the elevator girl treats you well"*

His dream was for us to come to Japan. But I thought, I don't know if I'm going to Japan, because I'm so used to Brazil, I don't know how to speak Japanese. My father spoke Japanese sometimes, I understood but I always responded in Portuguese. My mother can't say a whole sentence only in Japanese or only in Portuguese. All her sentences are one word in Japanese and the next in Portuguese, all messed up.

I studied nutrition at the USP [University of São Paulo]. My sister also started university, but during her first year she said she wanted to go to Japan. She knew less Japanese than I did, because before I went to school, I only spoke Japanese at home. At school, I started to speak Portuguese. So when my sister started to talk, "Mommy, Daddy," I taught her Portuguese.

My father was very pleased. She said she wanted to stay here a year. But my father said, "I'm not rich enough to support you for a year in Japan." She said, "Well, then, I'll work." And she came to work here as a dekassegui, at age seventeen. Seven years ago, they treated dekasseguis really well, because most of them were university students. She got a contract for six months, and the round-trip ticket was free. Afterwards she spent three months traveling all over Japan.

After I graduated, my boyfriend [Darcy] decided to come here. A *shachō-san* [company president] of a firm here was always going to Brazil, and [Darcy] always took the shachō-san around. He said he needed a trainee here. I'd passed the public exam for the HC [Hospital das Clínicas, in São Paulo], the Children's Institute, in February [1992]. [Darcy] decided to come here in April, so he said, "Let's go." I said to myself, Look, I studied for four years, I killed myself at the university, I managed to get into one of the best hospitals in Brazil, am I supposed to give all this up and go to Japan to do who knows what? So I said, "I'm not going. You go. I'll work a year, and during my vacation I'll visit you in Japan."

I stayed there, in the hospital. But it's a public institution, you want to do a lot of things, there's no money, you want to help a lot of people, the boss won't let you, you want to learn a bunch of new things, there's another boss who's afraid you'll start to know more than he does. So they hold you back. My ideal bit the dust. I did stay a year, but then I resigned. In December of '92 I told my father, "Dad, I'm thinking of trying to get a scholarship," bang, the next day he brought me information about a thousand scholarships in Japan.

There are scholarships from the ken [province]. My father was from Kobe, Hyōgo-ken, and my mother was from Yamagata-ken. The year before, on holiday with my mother, I'd gone to both places. I thought, It's better to go to the countryside, because the people will treat me better there. So I chose Yamagata, and the next year, in '93, I came [to Japan].

My sister had already returned [to Brazil]. Her impressions of Japan were much different from mine. She'd say, "Japanese people are a drag, they're really irritating." She came as a dekassegui, but I came [the first time] as a tourist. If you come here as a dekassegui, you're treated one way, if you come as a tourist, even the elevator girl in the department store treats you well.

So it was a really good image that I had. OK, it's a really agitated lifestyle, the first week I was already sick of seeing only Japanese people, because wherever you go, there are just Japanese, Japanese, Japanese. Sometimes I would close my eyes to try to imagine [a] Brazilian. But people treated me really well.

My scholarship was from Yamagata-ken. The first day we had a meeting with the governor of the province. There were ten foreigners altogether, Indonesians, people from Ghana, Tanzania, Samoa. There were Chinese, and there were three more Brazilian nikkeis. One of the girls was from Belém [near the mouth of the Amazon]. She got to São Paulo early the day of the flight. That afternoon she went all around São Paulo, and was amazed by the subway. I said, "The subway?" "In Belém, we don't have a subway" *(laughs)*. "You don't have a subway?" I didn't even know Brazil very well.

Any store I went into, the first thing I'd say was *Watashi wa gaiko-kujin desu, sumimasen* ["I'm a foreigner, excuse me," spoken in simple Japanese]. They'd explain very slowly, they were super-nice, any store, any place, any person. A taxi driver would say, "Have you been to such-and-such a place, here in Yamagata?" "No." "Well, then, I'll take you there." "No, no." "But it's for free," and they'd take me to some touristic place. People in the provinces have more human warmth [calor humano], there aren't many foreigners there and so they don't treat foreigners badly.

It was a training period of ten months. It was there that I learned Japanese. I also wanted to learn more in my field of study. I came to do a traineeship in nutrition, in a country that is, in quotes, "developed." I was able to learn a lot [in my field] but things that aren't viable in Brazil. Nutrition in a hospital depends on a bunch of services, not just on you. And in Brazil, things just don't move along. There are things you can apply, but only halfway. But it was worthwhile.

I asked to work in a hospital. They sent me to the biggest hospital in the province. It was the first time the nutritionists there had received a foreigner. They said a fax came with a xerox of my photo. In that photo I looked like a black person. The people there were beside themselves, "Look at her face, do you think she speaks English, what are we going to do with her." They couldn't imagine I was a nikkei. They said, "Her name is nikkei, but look at [her] face, my God." When they saw me for the first time, you could see smiles opening up in their faces, "It's nothing like we imagined, what a relief."

My boss was a warm-hearted person, a wonder. Her idea was for me to write a diary of everything I did during the day, of everything I thought, of everything I didn't understand, in Japanese of course. With the dictionary, I tried to write one or two pages. Then she'd correct it, comma by comma, word by word. She'd ask, "What were you trying to say here? Ah, in that case it's better to write it this way," and that's how I learned Japanese.

### *"You're going back to Japan right away, aren't you"*

At that time my boyfriend was in Toyota. When the traineeship ended, I had to go back to Brazil. The governor gives you a round-trip ticket. He puts you on the plane, because if you stay here in Japan you're his responsibility. My boyfriend was saying that he wanted to stay here longer. So I sat there thinking, "Well, what now." I couldn't just arrive in Brazil and tell [my parents], "I'm going right back to Japan."

I returned to Brazil in April of '94. . . . When I arrived at the airport, my father, my mother, and my sister met me. As we were heading for the car my mother said, "You're going back to Japan right away, aren't you." There in the airport. I said, "Mom, calm down, I just got here" *(laughs)*. She had a mother's intuition. I said, "Let's go home and we can speak more calmly." When I said, "Darcy is going to stay in Japan," my father told me, "If you really want to be together, it's better for you to go." I said, "Well, I'm really thinking about going. I don't know what kind of job I'll get." So my father said, and this really put me at ease, "You don't have to worry, the way you are, I'm sure you'll arrange something." I said, "I think I'm going to have to work in a factory, as a laborer." He said, "Everything will work out."

So everything was fine within ten minutes, my father and mother agreed. My father said, "Look, you don't have to get married if you don't want to, but tell Japanese people that you're married, because you're living together and no Japanese is going to approve of that." My father's brothers were in Japan, they're Japanese. "I'm going to send them a letter, I'll say that you're married."

And in the end we decided to get married, right when I got back, right there in Toyota, in the city hall. We didn't have a party. There were no relatives, not even friends. I didn't rent a chapel, or wear a bridal dress, financially we weren't prepared to do that.

### *"Take it, eat this"*

In the hospital kitchen, there were cooks who were fifty, the same age as my father. Some were stubborn just like my father, but had that other really kind side. There were a lot of things that I'd never accepted, that I couldn't understand, about him, that I began to admire and respect, thanks to that traineeship.

Japanese don't have that . . . human warmth of Brazilians, right? For example, my father never kissed me. My father never had that side, that affection of the flesh. He showed his love for his children in other ways, trying to send us to the best schools, or if on Sunday I'd say, "Let's go to the circus," he'd take us. Or if a chair broke, and I couldn't study, he'd fix it right away. He loves to do things with electricity, or plumbing. He didn't have an older son, because my brother was still very small, he'd call me over, he'd teach me everything, so this was the way he showed his fatherly affection. For me, sometimes it was shocking, I'd hand over the pen-knife, or whatever, all wrong, and he'd give a holler, and I'd cry. Every time he called me to help him fix the plumbing, I'd think, Ai, my God, I'm going to get yelled at again *(laughs)*, the pliers, ai, which one is the pliers, so I'd give him something, "This is a hand-saw." But in the end I learned, thanks to him, I could do some small installations by myself.

This way of showing affection is typically Japanese. When I came here, those cooks, those old guys of fifty or sixty, wouldn't even say good morning. I'd wonder if I did something wrong, I'd think they're really mad at me, but then they'd go to the kitchen, prepare a sweet, and then come up to me, "Take it, eat this." I'd think, He seemed angry, but no, it's his way of showing affection. There was one who every morning stopped at the vending machine to buy coffee, he brought me a can of *café com leite*, he thought I'd never had it before *(laughs)*. One morning I said, "Ohayō" and he didn't reply, he just went into his room. When he came out, [he said], "Here, try this" *(laughs)*.

I started to realize: it's just like my father. The side of him that some-times scared me, that I didn't understand, I realized were ways he showed affection to his children.

I gave a speech about my father [in a contest], and I won, and ap-peared on television. The next day there were five or six videotapes on my table. I thought, What's all this *(laughs)*, everyone who knows me recorded it for me. So I sent a tape to my father. [I heard that] some-times he'd go off, in secret, and sit there watching the tape alone *(laughs)*. When I returned after the traineeship, he saw that I understood him better, and he understood me better too. Because we never had any kind of dialogue, and I said in my speech that there were such and such parts of my father that I really couldn't understand. . . . So he thought, "I didn't know that my daughter thought that about me. I didn't know that I was so . . . *like that*, that way." Just as I came to understand him, he came to understand me.

### "Why is the child here?"

On the 17th of July [1994] I came back [to Japan, after] three months in Brazil. The next day my husband's shachō-san took me to the TIA, where I met Mr. Kishi.[1] If it weren't for Kishi-san I wouldn't have this job now. I brought all my diplomas. Kishi-san called hospitals, but it was impossible for me to work as a nutritionist. Then I said I liked chil-dren, and he asked if I could teach, and I said I could. So he called the Board of Education, and I got lucky. They said, "We were desperately looking for someone who spoke Portuguese and Japanese. *At that exact moment* you called."

I'm doing a thousand more things than the city thinks I'm doing. The

[1]See p. 227.

contract is very vague, it says *gogaku sōdan-in*, [someone who] gives an orientation in language. But there are endless translations, if I collected one yen for each translation I do I'd be a billionaire by now. There are family problems we have to resolve, teachers who can't communicate with the children's parents. It doesn't matter if it's Saturday or Sunday, if the teacher asks us to come, we have to come, to translate, to try to resolve a situation. I like what I'm doing, but I'm really overworked.

I started in September '94, [part-time]. From Monday to Friday I went to two schools every morning. Each school wanted something different. One has a child who can't speak any Portuguese because she's totally adapted to Japan, so they want me to speak Portuguese. Then there's another school that's the opposite, the child just got here, and doesn't speak any Japanese, so they ask me to teach Japanese. And they want me to help out in the day-to-day activities of the school, so there's a bunch of notices [to parents], there's going to be a meeting at such-and-such a time, the child will have to bring such-and-such materials. The parents can't read [Japanese], so it's got to be translated.

At the end of September, I became a [full-time] employee. Then they raised the number to three schools per day, two in the morning and one in the afternoon. My job includes *everything* that has to do with foreign students, not just Brazilians. Sometimes there's a Filipino, who speaks Tagalog. And I never even knew Tagalog existed. Now I know how to say good morning and thank you in Tagalog. When there's a Peruvian child, they don't understand Portuguese. The adults understand, but the children don't, so I have to mess around with my Portuguese to see if I can manage to teach them Japanese. So I'm teaching Portuguese, teaching Japanese, translating notices, resolving family problems, talking to the father, talking to the mother, counseling the student who doesn't want to go to school.

[I go to] primary and middle schools. In East Homi [Grade School] there are now ninety foreign students, Homi Chū has around forty. In West [Homi Grade School] there are around thirty-five or forty also. In the other schools I go to, there are fewer.

Most of the [Japanese] teachers are happy to accept a foreign student. That's the good side [of the Japanese school], that they're welcoming [foreigners], they're trying to find a way to deal with the situation.

But there are teachers who think, Why should I kill myself trying to learn to say "Bom dia"? I'm going to say "Ohayō gozaimasu," and if the child doesn't understand, too bad. *They're* the ones who are in Japan, let *them* try to adapt to Japan. I say to [those teachers], "But why is the child here? Because Japanese don't want to do heavy work in the factory. They don't want to get their hands dirty, they just want to sit there quietly, neat and clean, writing away with their little pen. So who does the dirty work? It's the father of that child over there. She didn't come here just to make work for you. Her father, she herself, is suffering to relieve some of the suffering of Japanese people." That's the bad side [of the Japanese school]. [Some] people are only helping because they want the child to adapt, to become a Japanese, they keep trying to force the child to the Japanese side.

If I think about my own situation, I graduated from a Brazilian university, I learned to speak Japanese, today I'm here in Japan and this work I'm doing now is a cut above factory work. I got it because I had some education in Brazil. And if I think the opposite way, that since the child is here, and the parents aren't returning to Brazil anytime soon, if she really manages to get an education, even in a Japanese school, one day she can go back to Brazil, learn Portuguese, and be somebody in life.

Except that's not quite the reality of it. The parents say they're going to stay here maybe two more years, maybe three years, maybe five years. The child lives in that instability, so she doesn't try hard, not in Japanese and not in Portuguese. If she asks the parents for a definite answer they don't know ... "Ah, maybe we'll be leaving next year." "When?" "Ah, between March and August." When August of next year comes, "Ah, we postponed it. Maybe next year."

When there's a parents' meeting, I ask the mother, "How long are you going to stay here?" "Ai, I don't know." "But look here, the child isn't studying this, and isn't studying that." "Ah, I'm thinking of sending her to Brazil." "But who's she going to live with there?" "Ah, I think with my mother-in-law." "OK, maybe so. If you're able to send the child back, if she can stay with her grandmother, and if she'll be able to go to school, fine, but don't keep everything up in the air." But it doesn't help. Of course they know what's best. But they don't take one single step in that direction.

### *"Seeing a way out is hard"*

It's not long until a vicious circle will start. The parents came to Japan. The children are going to be semiliterate because they can't speak either language well. They'll get some money together in five years, and go back to Brazil. And then the child, if he's already an adolescent he's not going to want to go to school anymore. . . . He won't be educated, as he grows up he'll see there's no place for him in Brazil, and then he'll return here again. And he'll get married and have a child, thinking all the time about one day going back to Brazil. And now this grandchild of the first [migrant] will also be in this going-not-going, going-not-going.

Seeing a way out is hard.

In Brazil, [if a student's attendance is bad], the student repeats the year. [Here] there's no repetition. When they want to go [to class], they go, when they don't, they don't. "Ah, today there's art class, I like art, so I'll go," "Today there's just mathematics, and Japanese, I don't understand any of it." [Take] math, it's useful, it's the same everywhere, but a child doesn't think this way. They just think, "You don't have to repeat the year, right?" They don't even try, "I'm not going to understand." So it's really easy for them to skip school.

Japanese think that in Brazil nobody goes to school. I tell them, "In Brazil people know it's important to go to school, but the educational system is completely different." [Here] the parents are suffering a ton of pressure at work. They don't speak Japanese well. So if a child grabs them and says, "Ai, Dad, today I'm tired, the teacher talks and I don't understand," [the father] feels sorry for him. "Well, then, stay home today, son."

When a student gets [bad] grades, he says, "So what, this grade doesn't mean anything, there's no repetition, and anyway I don't know Japanese, it's obvious I was going to get this grade, so fine." He's not shocked, so for him, grades are useless.

I know a lot of technical terms in the area of nutrition. But [one day] the teacher asked me to translate a bunch of mathematical terms. I said to him, "I don't know a single thing here, please come over here." They're like that, they throw the translation on your table. "I'm busy and I can't do this now." "Then when can you?" "During the free period." The free period comes, and I ask, "This here, what is it?" So he writes it in mathematical terms. "Ah, this is called a second-degree equation." The minute he shows it to me, I can associate it with the Portuguese name I learned, except that for the student . . . it's the first time he's ever seen that. So I say to the teacher, "It doesn't help to translate, to write 'second-degree equation' in place of the Japanese. . . . The student has no idea what a second-degree equation is." "But there's the Portuguese in case he wants to go and get a book." I say, "What book?" "A mathematics book from Brazil." "But from where? Not everyone has a mathematics book at home." Imagine the rest, *rika* [science]. No way. To ask me to translate a whole book—well, just wait a minute. Then go ahead and hire a teacher who teaches [everything] in Portuguese, it would be easier than me translating whole books.

Writing is a terror, but even when [the students] speak, they don't have that analytical part of the language. However much I write "photosynthesis," it's a word [the student] never used, or even if he knows what it is more or less, he explains it, "Ah, some business enters the leaf and then some dust goes out, some air things go out." If you think about it, OK, it's photosynthesis, "some business goes in there and sunlight hits it and then some little things come out that are good for your body."

The way things are, you'd have to set up a *Brazilian* school, but a decent school, similar to an American school or a Japanese school in Brazil. The tons of students that there are, one or two people, Rosa and I, to do it all, there's no way.

There's not a single day I go [to Homi Chū] that I don't have some problem to resolve. Like the other day. "Tamara didn't come." "Huh? What do you mean, Tamara isn't coming anymore?" *(Laughs.)* So the teacher says, "You didn't know?" "I just got here, I just set foot in the school, I've got no way to know." One day I went there, "Socrates is going to quit" *(laughs)*. Another day, "Carlos has left school," another day, "Sebastião left the country all of a sudden." Every time I go there it's something or other. It's exhausting.

In the beginning, every day *(laughs)* it was a shock: "Oh no, oh my God." I would get home with my nerves frazzled. Then I saw that if I was going to get nervous with everything that happened, I would drop dead. So I don't get worked up anymore, I go prepared to resolve [problems], to give advice, I walk along breathing slowly, thinking about my guardian angel, I say to myself, "My God in heaven, help me now *(laughs)*, give me strength," but ... it doesn't work, I'm just one person, I have defects like everyone else.

The other day, they were marking tests. Eiko wrote her name perfectly, but of course, [the test] was all in Japanese, she didn't understand anything. The teacher was saying, "Wow, she's trying so hard, I think if it was me I couldn't do it." And how was the test? "Oh, the test was a zero *(laughs)*, but she wrote her name perfectly, if we could just give her a point for her name *(laughs)*, because just look, the writing is so beautiful."

## *Green or red?*

Daniel: Well, Naomi, let's go to the last matter. You're there with a green passport and a red passport, and with dual nationality. So are you a Japanese, or are you a Brazilian? . . . Are you a Japanese?

Naomi: No.

Daniel: Are you a Brazilian?

Naomi: Yes, well, I look at this in a practical manner. I'm Brazilian, right? Except I'm Brazilian and I had the luck to get myself a Japanese passport. Right? And this red passport opens many doors, right?

Daniel: And how come you don't see yourself as, let's say, Japanese with the bad luck to have a—

Naomi: Brazilian passport? Because it's that matter of a *furusato*. *Terra natal* [native land]. Now that I'm going back [to Brazil for a visit] this July, people are saying, "This month you're radiant." I tell them, "I'm radiant because I'm going back to my native land." "But you're so Japanese, you get along so well . . . " "I *am* Japanese, I *like* Japan, but furusato is furusato, my furusato is there, it's Brazil.[2] I was born, I grew up, my friends are [there]." A lot of things about Japan I understand but I don't accept. But I'd never think of saying that I was a Japanese with the bad luck to have [a green passport], no, I'm a Brazilian with the good luck to have a red passport.

Daniel: So, here's a question that's a little complicated, for me, as an anthropologist, something I'm always trying to understand, it goes more or less like this. . . . You're a Brazilian because you have a furusato . . .

Naomi: Over there in Brazil.

Daniel: In Brazil, and how is it that a furusato gets inside someone to make the person, in your case, Brazilian. Because by blood you're Japanese—

Naomi: *(echoing)* Yes, Japanese, exactly, but I think you must have heard this a million times, that you only really get to know your country after you leave it, when you're outside it. Anyone who never left Brazil just speaks badly of Brazil. Yes, it's your country, but "Brazil will never get ahead." So you can only really discern your country after you've left it. And I think this happened to me too.

[2] In Japan people often travel to their hometowns during summer months, a time of year when furusato is heavily romanticized.

When I came to Japan, the first time, I really saw Brazil from outside. I also saw what people outside think about my Brazil ... and seeing it that way, I began to value a bunch of things that were normal for me. To be able to speak in Portuguese, to be able to communicate, to be able to go out whenever I wanted to, to have friends with more human warmth, and not have these Japanese-style relationships that were really cold or really full of ceremony. So things that for me were normal ... I thought, Puxa, that stuff isn't so normal, it's something *super good*. But I was only able to discern all this after I left there.

I was born and lived in that place, I really like all that, that's really not a normal thing, it's a terrific thing, so I incorporated all that as really being my native land, my homeland [pátria] ... my place, my place where I really feel good.

The same as my father, my father is the opposite. He loves Brazil, he never wants to live in Japan again, but his native land is Japan, so from time to time he misses Japan. With his business now he can come fairly often, but the first time he returned he'd been living in Brazil almost thirty years. But when he can return he feels super good, it's as if he pulled in energy from his native land. ... And even having lived in Brazil I don't know how many decades, and having a Brazilianized manner ... his native land is Japan.

Daniel: How does blood enter into all of this?

Naomi: My blood is Japanese. If you see it only in terms of blood. My ancestors are all Japanese, so my "blood" in quotes is Japanese. Except that I think a person isn't only formed by blood, they have their life experience, so I'm half and half, because my blood is Japanese but my life experience, everything I know, everything I like, everything, right ... it's Brazil. But because I also have my Japanese side, and I have the chance to live here in Japan, the good things about Japan, I incorporated into myself. ... And there are good things from Brazil that I will never stop being. So I have both. ... There's no way to separate them.

Daniel: Do Japanese people sometimes think you're Japanese?

Naomi: It's like this, I speak Japanese, but I don't speak it that well, so the first time they see me, of course they think I'm Japanese because my blood is Japanese, my face is Japanese. But when I talk, they realize my Japanese is kind of different. And by my way of acting they know I'm not Japanese. I'm more expansive, there are things I don't know about Japanese habits and that I go around doing my own way.

But when I have to be ceremonious with the [school] principals, I'm super-ceremonious, on this point they say I'm more Japanese than the young people of today. Because my father is old-fashioned, I learned all that with him. So when I have to be polite, really ceremonious, with an old person of Japan, I know how to do it.

Daniel: When they say admiringly that you're very Japanese, how do you receive it?

Naomi: I receive it well because my blood is Japanese, there's a tradition, that's the tradition of my family, of my ancestors. But if someone grabs me and says, "When you do that you seem more Japanese than the Japanese," I say right away, "But I'm a burajirujin." A lot of times I don't say *gaikokujin* ["foreign country person"], I say, "I'm a *gaijin* [foreigner]. ..." It's a pretty pejorative word, but it's so that the person will never forget that I said that.

OK, I accept that type of Japanese ceremony, I respect it, I do it, I like it, and I'm happy to be praised, but never forget *(strikes table softly)* that I'm a Brazilian. ... Don't ever think I'm going to do everything the way you want, the way you think I'm going to do it. Because there are things I don't accept. So when someone says that, I say, *Ah, demo burajirujin desu, watashi wa gaijin desu yō* ["but I'm a Brazilian, I'm a foreigner," emphatic] *(laughs)*. ... You can ask around, there are a lot of principals who have praised me. But after they praised me they heard this: "I'm a burajirujin *(strikes table again)*, I'm a gaijin."

## Furusato and terra natal

Naomi Mizutake has incorporated both Japan and Brazil into her sense of self. Unlike some Brazilians, she speaks of both countries, and both aspects of herself, with generosity, and her evaluations are judicious.

She appropriates her ethnicities in the context of her autobiography, a reflective, intricately narrated personal history. She has honed that narrative not just as a presentation to others, but, I believe, as a self-presentation. It is a story that enables her to think about and elaborate her own past and to set a course for the future. It is a story that constitutes a generative self.

Every one of the interviewees actively engages the world. But agency comes in different forms and intensities. One can, for example, act in the world without awareness of oneself as the source of action.

We might call this nonconscious agency. Alternatively, one may experience an action as the product of reflection and volition, of conscious agency. Or, generalizing, one may experience *oneself* as a product of conscious agency, of self-fashioning. The generative self occupies that level or mode of consciousness in which one's self, taken as an identity, is an object of agency.[3] Reflective consciousness, awareness of the contingency of identity, is a precondition for the emergence of a generative self. The move from Brazil to Japan thrust every one of the interviewees into new situations that shifted experienced identities. Those shifts awakened reflective consciousness: identity feelings, now experienced as mobile, became objects of reflection. To varying degrees, the interviewees sought to seize upon, formulate, and intervene in those feelings, rethinking and reshaping their identity-selves. That is, a generative self emerged as an agent whose domain was identity.

Thus Naomi is not unique in constituting a generative self, but that self has a particularly strong presence in her account. She warns that she may defy appearances and expectations—"Don't ever think I'm going to do everything the way you want, the way you think I'm going to do it." The warning is directed at those who insist on her quintessential Japaneseness, but she could as easily be talking to her mother, her father, her fiancé. She has created a defense against ascriptions and predictions, a region of self-autonomy. Although she is by no means a reflexive nay-sayer, her own self-conception grants her the ability to determine whether she conforms or dissents, approves or disapproves, acts this way or that. This self learns and applies its lessons in its own refinement: Naomi's narrative is studded with realizations that she then uses as levers in becoming other than what she was.

Naomi's self-concept should not be confused with that of a willful loner or stereotypical "Western" individualist.[4] To the contrary, she fashions herself in dialogue with others. That is, she sees herself as a participant in exchanges through which she reformulates her own sense of who she is. What stands out most vividly for me in her narrative is the

[3]Varied senses of agency affect people's engagements in the world, which in turn affect senses of agency. The circuits are surely complex, diverse, and hard to specify, but it seems likely that such self-perceptions produce significantly different modes of experience and action.

[4]The contrast between "Western" individualist selves and "non-Western" relational selves is, as many have demonstrated, vastly overdrawn. Geertz (1984 [1974]) sketches a vivid portrait of the "Western" self; for critiques, see McHugh (1989), Hollan (1992), Spiro (1993), and Parish (1996), among others.

set of links and oppositions she sets up between herself and her parents. Their histories, as she understands them, become resources for her in imagining herself, and her interactions with them lead to discoveries about who she feels she is and who she feels she is not. Naomi acknowledges a continuity with her parents as she affirms her ability to learn from them. She builds a self-in-relationships that she can nevertheless claim as her own, using materials contributed by and scavenged from others.

Although Naomi's mother is an energetic and sympathetic presence in her narrative, I think Naomi identifies more closely with her father. Her self-journey bears a striking mirrorlike resemblance to his: she takes his transnational experience as a precursor of and inspiration for her own. Hence she sees herself as replaying, with adjustments, transformations, and innovations, her father's geographic and interior migrations, under different, often obverse circumstances. Despite some ambivalence, Naomi regards her father with respect, admiration, and affection—as "the eighth wonder of the world." His career is a model for her own negotiation of a multiple, yet coherent, identity.

In Naomi's narrative, her father left Kobe, his furusato, as a young man to make a life in Brazil, a country to which he readily acclimated. Over time he came to value Brazil's multiracial, multiethnic mix, more so than many nikkei men. His receptiveness to Brazil showed a liberal turn of mind, reflected in his openness to his daughters' potential romantic friendships with non-nikkeis and his personal indifference to the formalities of marriage. At the same time, he could be hard-headed, taciturn, irritable. Unlike most non-nikkei Brazilians, he was reluctant to demonstrate his affection in direct, tactile ways. This seemingly distant side of his personality remained a puzzle to Naomi until she went to live in Japan. She then began to reinterpret her father's behavior in light of her treatment by the hospital cooks. Naomi now saw her father's behavior not as remote or gruff but as a culturally Japanese way of demonstrating love. It was other, but it was also good.

The reinterpretation also revealed to her a general truth: that certain aspects of oneself are so deeply grounded in ethnic culture that they never disappear. Such groundedness is less a constraint than a source of vitality. Her father's periodic longings for his homeland evidence the strength of a rejuvenating primordial tie. Naomi found here a blueprint for her own transnational experience. What furusato is for her father, terra natal is for her: she describes her radiance on the eve of a trip back to Brazil.

Note that her claim to Brazilianness at times becomes, paradoxically, a defense of her supra-ethnic generative self. Once more we see the boomerang effect of the attempt by well-meaning Japanese to reclassify a Brazilian. Naomi can outdo Japanese at punctilious ceremonial behavior, but she rejects their attempts to interpret her virtuosity as a sign of Japaneseness. She counters the inference with a proclamation of her Brazilianness. In announcing herself as other, she affirms that her self is ultimately her own, not theirs.

This Naomi-self is a customized hybrid: part Brazilian, part Japanese, and part other; modeled on a template she has inferred from her father's biography; informed by her knowledge of a historical past of migration, war, reconstruction, and an accepting new land in the tropics; and colored by her own unique experiences and temperament. The self Naomi has built, and continues to rebuild, is both flexible and solid. It seems unusually well suited to the life she is currently leading.

To understand better the complex link between Naomi's self and profession, we need to take a closer look at her engagement with her mother. Naomi is, like her mother, a nikkei rather than a Japanese; her mother too crossed from Brazil to Japan; and both are, obviously, female. Without question Naomi's mother provides a crucial starting point in Naomi's elaboration of her female nikkei identity. But I think Naomi aspires to be a different sort of nikkei, and a different sort of woman, from her mother. Naomi views her mother, raised in a narrowly ethnic social universe, as a product of the Japanese colônia, with a more cramped vision of people and the world than Naomi's Japanese father. In contrast, Naomi sees herself as a nikkei of the big country, not the colônia.

Similarly, although she admires and finds inspiration in her mother's kindness, outspokenness, and pursuit of an occupation, Naomi projects herself more assertively into the professional world outside the home. She finishes a demanding course at one of Brazil's outstanding universities; secures a job at one of Brazil's premier hospitals; wins a trainee scholarship for practical study in Japan; throws herself into that traineeship, to great advantage; finds the teaching job in Toyota, which she pursues with tremendous energy. Like Elena Takeda, Rosa Kitagawa, and Eriko Miyagi, she moves assertively and effectively into a challenging world dominated by men. She has made herself into a cosmopolitan thinker, a culturally adaptable person, and a professionally dynamic woman.

Yet in practicing her current profession, Naomi has seized on her mother's life in important ways. In her narrative of her mother's past, the arresting event is the family's return to Japan after the war. If her father's transoceanic journey opens onto an expansive new world, her mother's sojourn in Japan yields isolation and alienation. Her mother, harassed and marginalized, is treated badly, as a privileged "American." For Naomi, the situation of the Brazilian schoolchildren echoes that of her mother's harsh, lonely postwar stay in Tokyo. Encouraged by her mother, she seeks to offer them what her mother never had: help, sympathy, recognition, and advocacy. Thinking of her mother, she recognizes the pain of stigmatization and misrecognition. When she insists to a school principal, "I'm a burajirujin, I'm a gaijin," she is speaking for her voiceless mother, an inscrutable and resented "American" in a 1950s Japanese grade school, and for the struggling Brazilian children whose problems she deals with on a daily basis.

For all its frustrations and exhausting demands, in her work as a bilingual teacher in the Toyota City schools, Naomi Mizutake mobilizes who she is in the service of meaningful engagement with others. She brings a personal ethnic history into harmony with a consuming current pursuit. If anything deserves to be called the practice of self, this is it.

# PART FOUR

# The Nation in the Mind

# CHAPTER 15

# National Banners

### The polymorphous nation

What and where is the nation? The evidence presented here raises anew, in an acute form, this perplexing question. To begin: nations are profoundly unnatural objects. Long ago Max Weber noted that "empirical qualities"—shared language, religion, customs, or descent—have no intrinsic link to nationhood (1946 [1921]:172). Nations are conspiracies: like gods, money, and the Queen, a nation exists because people agree, and feel, it does. A nation is a "community of sentiment" fostered through "cultivation of the peculiarity of the group" by cultural specialists (ibid.:176).

Weber's incisive but fragmentary analysis anticipated Benedict Anderson's famous description of nations as "imagined communities" (1991 [1983]). Nations, Anderson observes, are historical and cultural creations. They emerge when people who have never met, and who may share few objective characteristics, are persuaded to regard one another as compatriots. Anderson's treatise, together with an important volume on the "invention of tradition" (Hobsbawm and Ranger 1983), occasioned a flood of case studies of national discourses. Such discourses, politically motivated narratives that tend to emphasize a population's putatively common origins, history, and customs, project the national collectivity through time and across space.

But the catch phrase "imagined community" is deeply ambiguous, and the ambiguities are theoretically hazardous. Is the community "imagined" in public narratives or in the minds of those who encounter them? To what degree do narratives intended to foster sentiments of identification, distinctiveness, and empathy actually do so? In this book, nine persons have discussed their attachment to, alienation from, and ambivalence toward national representations. How are we to understand the gap between the representations and what the interviewees have made of them?

Weber recognized, at least implicitly, this slippage between representations and imaginings. He stressed that people's attitudes toward the nation vary widely: "The scale extends from emphatic affirmation to emphatic negation and finally complete indifference" (1946 [1921]:174). This is a crucial point, for it challenges us to characterize the entity that mediates between representations and imaginings. It moves us, I would argue, to insert the reflective self into accounts of identity.

We have heard a lot in the academy recently, mostly in the postmodern or poststructuralist vein, about how discourses "construct subjectivities" or "create positions for subjects"—as if living were a matter of absorbing narratives or choosing among pre-established mental niches. There is much to this talk, which encourages a focus on the forceful propositions about reality that confront all of us from birth onward. But the view of persons implicit in such academic discourse is impoverished. I find the overly literary, antihumanist turn discouragingly mechanistic and, what is more to the point, unrealistic.

In Japan I chose to look as directly as I could at Brazilians' experiences of nationality. The interviews suggest that national narratives do tend to socialize thought—but also that people simultaneously personalize the narratives. They *respond* to those narratives, interpreting, using, reformulating, and recirculating them as they live their particular lives.

The polymorphous nation proclaims itself in banners and rattles around in minds. The nation-in-the-mind draws upon national banners, but biography and consciousness intervene between representation and imagination. That intervention is not trivial, a matter of copying representations into experience or choosing among discursive alternatives. People's responses are adaptive, reflective, creative, transformative, unpredictable. This book's central claim is that a robust account of identity must therefore attend seriously to persons.

This chapter looks at Japanese and Brazilian banners: the narratives that propose grounds for national membership. Chapters 16 and 17 explore how Japanese-Brazilians in Japan personalize nationalities, turning public representations into idiosyncratic identities.

### Japan's blood narrative

"The idea of the 'nation,'" wrote Weber, "is apt to include the notions of common descent and of an essential, though frequently indefinite, homogeneity" (1946 [1921]:173). National narratives, including those state-sanctioned narratives we call law, often emphasize shared substance, "blood" or a bloodlike essence. Japanese nationality, for example, is governed legally by *jus sanguinis*, the principle that citizenship is conferred through blood. The children of Japanese nationals are Japanese.[1] Jus sanguinis aligns nationality with kinship; the nation is, by virtue of its shared blood, an enormous family. Following this logic, the law classifies those lacking "Japanese blood"—even culturally and linguistically assimilated Koreans or Chinese, born in Japan and phenotypically indistinguishable from Japanese—as foreigners.[2]

Jus sanguinis articulates closely with the indigenous theories of Japanese distinction commonly gathered under the rubric *Nihonjinron* (Befu 1993; Yoshino 1992). This eclectic literature specializes in celebratory studies of Japanese uniqueness. "Its drumbeat," writes William Kelly (1988:365), "is the coherence, continuity, and above all, the uniqueness of an entity variously hypostatized as Japanese society, or the Japanese personality, or the Japanese brain, or the Japanese language, or Japanese sensibility." Nihonjinron's core claims, as outlined by Harumi Befu (1993), are remarkably simplistic: A genetically superior Japanese race, arising primordially in the islands of Japan, speaking the Japanese language (which encodes singular and singularly advantageous elements of Japanese culture and the Japanese spirit), has developed a uniquely efficient, harmonious, unified, successful nation.

In proposing that Japanese blood, culture, and language come in a package—a superior package—Nihonjinron strikes me as a retreat to pre-Boasian scientific racism.[3] Despite Nihonjinron's anachronism, Befu counts over a thousand works in the genre published since World War II (ibid.:109). Many have been reprinted dozens of times. Because

[1]More precisely, they are entitled to Japanese nationality if they comply with certain registration procedures (Yamanaka 1996:74). Children of Japanese parents born in Japan routinely file the proper documents. However, many isseis, owing to procedural burdens or indifference, do not. Most Brazilian nisseis do not therefore have Japanese citizenship.

[2]Japanese naturalization is possible, but it is neither easy nor necessarily attractive. Although the formal requirements do not seem onerous at first glance (Wetherall 1988), in fact the Ministry of Justice, which carefully scrutinizes each application, employs confidential criteria that make approval difficult and the reasons for it opaque.

[3]Yoshino argues (1992:28) that Western racism proposes genetically determined cultural superiority; theories of Japanese uniqueness propose, more neutrally, cultural difference associated with genetic difference. I find Yoshino's distinction unconvincing. In both cases the link between culture and genes is presumed to be strong, and, although it may be that many Japanese are inclined to see differences between Japanese and others in fairly neutral terms, many others regard Japanese race, culture, and language as, on balance, superior to that of the West or other regions of the world.

of their ethnocentric appeal, their pretensions to scientific validity, and the high status of their academic champions, Nihonjinron theories have proved plausible and attractive to many, within and without Japanese intellectual circles.[4] Moreover, the Japanese state has aggressively promoted Nihonjinron through its sponsorship of policy forums, research centers, scholarly foundations, and cultural initiatives (ibid.: 116–21). In short, Nihonjinron's central tenets constitute a powerful, widely disseminated state ideology.

Nihonjinron ideology implicitly underpinned the 1990 immigration reform granting exceptional privileges to nikkeis. According to Keiko Yamanaka (1996:76–77), "Admission of nikkeijin was envisioned by the incumbent conservative politicians as a means to kill two birds with one stone—to maintain racial purity while responding to the labor shortage." That is, the law aimed to replace workers of alien blood (for example, Pakistanis and Iranians) with workers of Japanese blood who were supposedly familiar with, or at least innately attuned to, Japanese customs and the Japanese language. Any post-Boasian anthropologist could have predicted that in practice this scheme would produce unwelcome surprises. Those who came to Japan were not Japanese reared in Latin America but Latin Americans who looked Japanese.[5] The Japanese government, and many Japanese, may have expected Japanese blood to bring with it Japanese culture and Japanese spirit—but most of the Two Crows I interviewed denied this.

The Brazilians had grown up with narratives that did not equate national continuity with the perpetuation of uncontaminated bloodlines. For them, the ideology of common blood, despite its grain of truth, was at best a partial account of relatedness.

[4]According to Befu, Nihonjinron "seems to have effectively silenced contradictory views" (Befu 1993:117). Maher and Macdonald, terming Nihonjinron a "deadly rose," argue that it has "dominated the descriptive landscape of Japan over the last hundred years, forcing all commentary into its furrow" (1995:5). These claims seem overstated. For critiques of Nihonjinron and related ideologies, including criticisms by Japanese, see Dale (1986), Maher and Macdonald (1995), Mouer and Sugimoto (1986), and Weiner (1997).

[5]Nikkeis' generally poor command of the Japanese language and indifference to Japanese ways have proved confusing and unsettling to many Japanese. Befu notes the incredulity with which many Japanese regard a nikkei's inability to speak Japanese (1993:116). Conceivably, the challenge nikkeis present to commonsense theories of Japanese racial uniqueness could provoke a Boasian rethinking of Japanese national identity, especially as Brazilian nikkeis become an ever-more-visible presence as a minority group: Japanese in blood and ethnic Brazilian in culture.

## Brazil's fusion narrative

Narratives of shared blood and/or *Geist*, such as those codified in jus sanguinis, promoted in Imperial Rescripts, and given a scholarly imprimatur by Nihonjinron, are prevalent in the world, and they can be emotionally potent (see, for example, Delaney 1995; Handler 1988; Schneider 1969). But we should not assume that all national narratives rest on a foundation of shared substance, or that narratives of substance are necessarily more effective than other discourses of community.

Consider, for example, the remarkably varied U.S. narratives and practices of citizenship. To be sure, blood has its advocates in the United States. American nativists, such as white-power devotees, define Americanism in terms of deep roots, race, and patriotic spirit, and their arguments sometimes persuade others to back harsh anti-immigrant laws and other discriminatory legislation. And it is true that the children born to Americans overseas have the right to American citizenship—an application of jus sanguinis in U.S. law. But American nationality rests most fundamentally not on jus sanguinis but on *jus soli*, the principle, unrecognized in Japan and many other countries, that birth on a nation's soil confers citizenship.[6] Moreover, the United States is currently naturalizing enormous numbers of immigrants each year.[7]

Hence Americanism cannot be easily or convincingly located in the flesh. To the contrary, pluralist American narratives, symbolically condensed at national landmarks such as Ellis Island and the Statue of Liberty, emphasize the benefits of diversity, the mutability of citizenship, the

---

[6]On jus soli and jus sanguinis, see São Paulo-Shinbun (1991:36) and Yamanaka (1996:74).

[7]Numbers of naturalizations in Japan are far lower than in the United States. One reason is that the largest group of permanent foreign residents, Japan's 700,000 ethnic Koreans, have tended to view naturalization as a form of betrayal, of surrender to Korea's former colonial rulers (Johnstone 1996). A Korean who refuses to adopt a Japanese name, for example, has little chance of becoming naturalized (Maher and Kawanishi 1995:170). In 1995, just 14,104 people received Japanese citizenship, compared with 445,852 American naturalizations that fiscal year and over 1,000,000 in fiscal 1996. Indeed, between April 28, 1952, and December 31, 1995, a period of more than forty-two years, Japanese naturalizations totaled 257,160, a fraction of the number performed in the United States *in a single year*. (Japanese figures come from the Ministry of Justice. The U.S. figure for fiscal 1995 is cited in Migration News [1996]; the 1996 figure is from the U.S. Immigration and Naturalization Service.)

establishment of a multiethnic national space, and the equation of American with human rights. Despite the circulation of nativist versions of Americanism, I do not believe that shared substance, be it blood or metaphoric blood (an "American spirit"), is the hegemonic representation of American national membership. That is, a common American "blood" or "spirit" is, undeniably, one idiom of national relatedness. But many American narratives downplay communion in favor of commotion, the engagement of diverse persons and groups in self-determined pursuits and self-interested interaction governed by a loose social and economic compact.

In certain respects, Brazilian national discourse approximates that of the United States. In Brazil, as in the United States, blood, naturalization, and birthplace offer alternative routes to citizenship. Blood confers citizenship on babies born to Brazilian parents overseas, such as Elena Takeda's son. Naomi Mizutake's Japanese father could easily have naturalized himself Brazilian, though he saw no compelling reason to do so. By virtue of jus soli, his children would in any case have Brazilian citizenship.

Furthermore, Brazil's legal flexibility is, like that of the United States, matched by narrative multiplicity. But there are significant differences in the stories told here and there. With respect to blood, for example, contemporary public representations of the American nation emphasize a mix rather than an amalgam. Extreme nativist versions aside, such narratives tend to celebrate the country's multiethnic, multiracial composition; waffle on the question of cultural unity; differentially evaluate the components; and skirt the charged issue of interracial sexuality. Given enough time, strangers or their children may become (hyphenated) Americans, preserving certain ethnic diacritics. But the blending of blood is unnecessary and by inference, in a stance reflecting prejudices and fears of contamination, possibly undesirable. Hence substance enters American narratives not as blood, a social glue, but as bloodlines: threads of racial and ethnic difference woven awkwardly and unevenly into an unfinished national fabric.

In contrast, Brazil has a putatively nonracist, blood-based narrative of identity, the myth of racial and cultural fusion, propagated in a host of popular and official representations (Linger 1992:4–5). Its best known intellectual statement, Gilberto Freyre's classic, controversial historical ethnography *The Masters and the Slaves* (1956 [1933]), locates Brazil's origins in the sixteenth-century sugar estates of Pernambuco, where Portuguese, native Brazilian, and African, fatally conjoined in a patriarchal, exploitative plantation regime, meld genes and customs to conceive a novel, rich, harmonious Brazilian civilization.[8]

*The Masters and the Slaves* is no innocent history of northeastern colonial Brazil. In his choice of epoch and place, Freyre made a polemical decision. The book was strategic mythmaking, meant simultaneously to stand on its own and to stand against adversaries. *The Masters and the Slaves* most obviously countered a scientific racism that painted Brazil as a degenerate, mongrel nation with a gloomy future. But the book had another, less visible target. *The Masters and the Slaves* also obliquely attacked a Brazil-in-formation, the new pluralist society that was taking shape in the South. For Freyre, the real Brazil, the distinctive Brazil worth cultivating, was the three-race amalgam forged in the hothouse of the patriarchal, colonial, rural Northeast. As Alistair Hennessy observes, if scientific racism was the present enemy, São Paulo modernism was the specter haunting the future:

[Freyre] continued to believe that the North-East was the repository of traditional national virtues against the corrupting virus of foreign ways introduced by European immigrants. The regional revival of the 1920s and 1930s in the North-East, of which he was a leader, was a response to the vertiginous growth of São Paulo, with its assertion of modernity in the Week of Modern Art held there in 1924. Sharpening tensions in the 1920s . . . gave an added urgency to his argument that the Brazilian genius lay in that spirit of accommodation exemplified by the interlocking social and racial networks of the Big House. This, rather than imported foreign ideas, was the model for the social democracy towards which Freyre saw Brazil progressing. (1989:764)

In Freyre's view, massive immigration threatened to destroy the great experiment, Brazil's "new world in the tropics" (1963 [1945]), by re-Europeanizing it. This was, of course, exactly the aim of those Brazilian devotees of scientific racism who welcomed European immigration as a way to "whiten" and Aryanize Brazil (Skidmore 1974). But their efforts to restrict admission to approved groups (such as Germans

---

[8]Many have argued that notwithstanding its antiracist pretensions, Freyre's narrative fails to free itself from racist premises. His work has been debunked on both factual and ideological grounds. See, for example, Harris's attack on "the myth of the friendly master" (1964) and Medeiros's analysis of Freyre's conservative leanings and racial presuppositions (1980). For further discussion of controversies surrounding the book, with useful citations of both Brazilian and foreign works, see Costa (1988 [1985]), Hanchard (1994), and Skidmore (1974). Despite a growing, well-founded recognition that racial discrimination is a serious problem in Brazil, the fusion myth has not lost its hold on the popular imagination.

and Italians) were only partially successful. Although the entry of sup-posedly inferior groups was controversial in Brazil, as in the United States, Brazil did eventually open its doors to significant contingents of Arabs, Slavs, Jews, and Japanese (Lesser 1995, 1999). In the relatively wealthy South, where most immigrants settled, ethnic neighborhoods and ethnic towns proliferated; people held ethnic festivals and ate ethnic foods; ethnic concerns animated specialized publications and works of art.

Although the time is more than ripe, the pluralist vision of Brazil has not yet found its great mythmaker, its Gilberto Freyre. But for decades influential writers have been producing a body of self-consciously eth-nic literature, propagating images of a multicultural Brazil.[9] The most compelling work of art rendered from a Japanese-Brazilian perspective, and the closest perhaps to a pluralist myth, is Tizuka Yamasaki's ac-claimed 1980 film *Gaijin—Caminhos da Liberdade* (*Gaijin—Roads to Freedom*).

### A Brazilian pluralist alternative

Yamasaki's riveting account of Japanese ethnic experience is fa-mous among nikkei Brazilians, and its major themes—the suffering and ultimate Brazilianization of the immigrants—are staples of their ethnic discourse. During my 1995–96 stay in Japan, *Gaijin*, which had never before circulated in Japanese theaters, toured cities heavily populated by Brazilians.[10] Clearly, the return of nikkeis to Japan had revitalized the film's message. These special showings were aimed at, and at-tracted, a predominantly nikkei audience. Yamasaki herself visited Ja-pan during the movie's revival, scouting sites for a prospective sequel set in the world of the dekasseguis.

A sentimental, occasionally overdrawn but well-wrought and often affecting piece of ethnic mythmaking, *Gaijin* deserves extended com-mentary. The title of Yamasaki's film has shifting referents. Who is a gaijin? From the vantage point of the Japanese villagers we meet at the

---

[9]See, for example, Pozenato (1985), Rawet (1956), and Scliar (1986 [1978]; 1987 [1976]). Fiction about Japanese-Brazilians includes Suzuki (1986) and Honda-Hasegawa (1991). For other fascinating works set in Japanese Brazil, see the novels of the American writer Karen Tei Yamashita (1990, 1992).

[10]According to Yamasaki, Japanese distributors "were not interested in showing the Japanese people that period of history, when the country was penniless" (Audi Magazine 1996).

film's beginning, those who live overseas are gaijin. For the Japanese immigrants arriving at the port of Santos, in the state of São Paulo, the Brazilians are gaijin. For the paulistas, the Japanese are *estrangeiros* (foreigners), as are the Italians, Spaniards, and even the Northeastern-ers who labor in the coffee fields. For the Brazilian-born children of the Japanese immigrants, Japan is impossibly far away, and their parents' origins unimaginable. For the parents, their children seem products of an alien environment. Who then is *not* a gaijin? Brazil seems a country teeming with gaijin; in the end, the motley strangers make it their home together, inventing ties across barriers of language, culture, ethnicity, gender, and generation.

The story, set in the early decades of the twentieth century, brims with ironies, unintended consequences, and forced accommodations. It unfolds on a plantation, patriarchal and authoritarian—shades of Gil-berto Freyre. A polyglot labor force is working the São Paulo coffee fields. The atmosphere is heavy with misunderstanding, and often out-right incomprehension. Much of the film is subtitled in Portuguese, and much of the rest is spoken in a mishmash—more or less intelligible to a Portuguese speaker but heavily Italianized or rendered in thick Japanese accents. Brazil itself seems as big as the world. "There's everything in Brazil," comments the worker Enrico to a group of mystified Japanese: "Portuguese, Russians, Arabs, Negroes, Indians, Germans, even Bra-zilians!"

Outsiders play major roles in the drama. Enrico is an Italian immi-grant who heads an informal labor movement and befriends the cau-tious Japanese. Ceará, a field-worker who speaks with the distinctive sonority of the Brazilian Northeast, seems almost as foreign as the mi-grants, with whom he feels a kinship. As they are felling trees in the for-est, in a moment of sad, fragile connection Ceará tells Yamada, husband of the heroine, Titoe, "Your country is far away—mine, too." His single prayer is to die in his drought-ravaged homeland. Another character, an English investor and coffee broker, lectures his partner, the plantation-owner, on the necessity of cutting costs, suppressing agitation, and eventually mechanizing production. The plantation is a node in a worldwide labor and commodity web, drawing workers from Europe, Asia, and the extremities of Brazil; attracting investment from the im-perial centers; and sending its crop to every corner of the globe. The times are precociously postmodern.

A series of striking vignettes brings us into the workers' new lives. On a Sunday afternoon, as an accordion plays and gaijin dance, Titoe daydreams of a Japanese festival. A suicidal Japanese woman hallucinates a black man among cherry blossoms. Ceará bandages a Japanese worker's injured arm, and later teaches Japanese children the Portuguese word for "rain." A Brazilian foreman shows Titoe how to wash clothes by beating them on the rocks beside the river. Japanese men buy beef jerky and manioc flour at the company store. Such flashes demonstrate the permeability of the moment to past and future, and the vulnerability of the present self to poignant memories and unexpected changes. Rupture and reintegration are themes that echo throughout the film.

The story can be simply told. Titoe comes from a traditional Kyushu village, viewed in the opening sequence through the haze of her memory as old woman. It is 1908: the war with Russia has ended, and the country is in economic trouble. A Japanese bamboo flute traces a sinuous melody as children play. The villagers, clad in kimonos, gather round a notice that reads: "Brazil wants immigrants!" Because Brazil accepts only family groups, Titoe's brother, who is eager to go, marries her off to his friend Yamada. In tears, Titoe, a girl of sixteen, leaves her home village for the port, together with her brother, her unwanted husband, and her cousin.

When the Japanese, now dressed in neat Western clothes, finally disembark, they are dispatched by rail to Santa Rosa, an immense coffee plantation ("It's bigger than our province of Fukuoka!"). Unknowingly they have been imported as substitutes for the troublesome European workers who replaced the slaves freed in 1888. A Japanese child dies on the train from bad food, the newcomers' housing is appalling, and the work is backbreaking. Japanese and Brazilians can communicate only through gestures.

In an early scene, Tonho, a Brazilian bookkeeper and foreman, brings the new workers food: carne-seca and coffee. "It's rotten!" says one. "That's the meat that killed my son!" cries another. Yamada pleads for rice, using the Japanese word—*kome*—and motioning toward his mouth. *Come* ["Eat"], repeats Tonho, in Portuguese. Words fail, but sentiments leak through. As the film progresses, it becomes clear that Tonho feels a special warmth for Titoe, and she for him.

Tonho shares management duties with the evil-tempered Chico Santos, a crude, harsh overseer anxious to get rid of the European troublemakers. The chief "agitator," the genial Enrico, befriends the Japanese, offering wine and regaling them in his effusive Italo-Portuguese patois with stories they enjoy but cannot understand. He tries, unsuccessfully, to cajole the leery Japanese into joining the other workers to petition for higher wages. Yamada, the savviest of the newcomers, senses that Enrico understands something he doesn't, but cannot quite bring himself to join the labor movement.

In the evenings, dead tired, the Japanese dream of foods unavailable in Brazil. They consider harvesting shoots from the plantation's stands of bamboo, or tending gardens on Sundays and holidays, maybe even introducing Brazilians to vegetables and making a fortune. The men build a bathhouse. In one relaxed scene, they are washing and conversing.

"I should have brought a woman from Japan."

"There are women here, too."

"Japanese women are better."

"I want a woman—it could even be a gaijin."

Later that evening, Yamada watches Titoe bathe. Afterward, he grabs her roughly; she struggles, then yields. For the first time they have sex together. He strokes her hair. A relationship marked by indifference and hostility begins to soften into one of respect and, increasingly, affection.

The landowner's English partner urges him to stop the labor unrest "before it takes root." Late one night, armed men invade Enrico's house, seize him, and beat him. Charged with agitation, he is to be expelled from Brazil, along with his family. The deportation order is read to the assembled workers. Before leaving the *fazenda*, Enrico approaches Yamada, doffs his cap, and touches his hand to his heart.

One day in the fields Titoe passes out. Yamada, learning that she is pregnant, is ecstatic: "It'll be a boy! A man to continue my blood!" But the baby is a girl. Stricken, Yamada gets drunk, muttering, "A girl isn't good for anything." In the next scene Shinobu, now about one, sits on a blanket in the field, as the Japanese workers break to drink a *cafezinho*, a demitasse of coffee. They are on the eve of their third harvest and have nothing to show for their labor: the fazenda has cheated them of their earnings. They should leave, Yamada urges, and start anew.

But Yamada's chronic headaches and nausea have been worsening, and one day he collapses. Titoe runs for Tonho, tearfully beating on his door. Tonho joins the family, in a gesture of solidarity and sympathy. Delirious and dying, Yamada tells Titoe: "Go back to Japan, and find a father there for our daughter."

Titoe lights incense before her husband's photo, and resolves to flee the fazenda. She leads a party of Japanese away, under cover of darkness. Armed men track them on horses. Tonho discovers the group, and confronts Titoe. She tells him firmly, in careful, accented Portuguese:

"Our homeland is Japan. Santa Rosa is no good for us. We'd rather die than stay at Santa Rosa." Tonho touches her cheek, holds her tenderly, kisses her hair. "Enough," he says, "enough." He whirls his torch through the greenery, starting a fire and allowing the Japanese to escape.

We next see Titoe some years later, walking solemnly down a São Paulo street among Brazilians. She enters a factory. The siren sounds; she takes her place at a loom. After work, Titoe picks up her daughter, who has been playing with Brazilian children. At home that night, they converse. Titoe speaks in Japanese, Shinobu in Portuguese. Shinobu says, "Mom, I want a little brother." Titoe begins to tell her about the beautiful boat that brought her to Brazil, but Shinobu cuts her off.

"No, talk about Dad."

"He always said he'd take you to Japan. So I'll take you to Japan."

"Mom, can I bring my friends?" Titoe hesitates. Shinobu continues: "You go, I'll stay here. Then come back."

Titoe sings Shinobu to sleep with a Japanese lullaby. To the photo of her deceased husband she murmurs, *Gomen nasai*. There is no subtitle for the Brazilian audience: addressed to Yamada, the words—"Please forgive me"—sound in a vanished world.

In the movie's penultimate scene, Titoe and Shinobu pass a street demonstration: Brazilian workers are confronting police. At their head, urging the workers on, is Tonho. He spots Titoe, falls silent, and respectfully removes his cap, echoing Enrico's earlier gesture. A series of flashbacks recapitulate Titoe's memories of kindnesses received from Tonho. We are, perhaps, to infer that Tonho will be the father of Shinobu's little brother.

The film closes with an extended shot of crowds surging down a 1980 São Paulo sidewalk. The soundtrack is a cacophony of city noise and Brazilian percussion. People of every color pass before the camera. The scene ironically recalls the film's opening moments in Titoe's home village, placing a final bracket on her incredible metamorphosis.

### A personal thing

*Gaijin* can be read as a symbolic displacement of *The Masters and the Slaves*. The Portuguese title of Freyre's classic is *Casa-grande e senzala*: "Big House and Slave Quarters." Freyre focused on the domestic world of plantation slavery in Northeast Brazil: bedrooms and kitchens were the cauldrons of racial and cultural fusion. At Santa Rosa, there is still a Big House, occupied by the master and his wife, and there are, if not slave quarters, workers' hovels. But the relation between bosses and laborers has become more attenuated and abstract, mediated not by floggings, wet-nursing, sensual food, and sexual heat but by numbers: wages and prices, tons harvested, advances, purchases, repayments, account balances. Santa Rosa is a dirty business, but it is, above all, a business. Its exploitative practices—disenchanted, efficiently brutal, rationalized—belong to the Electro-Steel, rather than the Big-House, variant of plantation capitalism.

In *Gaijin*, we again meet Brazil on an isolated patriarchal domain embedded in a transnational economic regime. Once sugar was king; now coffee reigns. Wage servitude has replaced slavery. The world system has replaced colonialism. Europeans and Asians have replaced Africans; Northeastern migrants have replaced Indians. The labor net spreads more widely; the product travels farther. At Santa Rosa, mechanization, the final displacement of the worker, is on the horizon. The rhythms of procurement, production, and distribution have accelerated; money, the "frightful leveler," has "hollow[ed] out the core of things" (Simmel 1964 [1902–3]:414); the globe has shrunk; the changes come in dizzying succession.

Yamasaki, like Freyre, has taken a galvanizing moment in Brazilian history and made of it a national myth. *Gaijin* portrays a delicate, but fertile, instant of ethnic encounter within a crude class society. Brazilians, Italians, and Japanese meet unexpectedly in the coffee fields. Slowly, tentatively, and erratically, the veterans reach out to the Japanese newcomers through the fog of difference. They offer food and drink, medical treatment, talk and music, practical instruction, compassion and comfort. And in the end, Tonho turns principled traitor to his employers, opening roads to freedom for himself and for the Japanese woman who has, despite enormous obstacles of culture, language, and class, profoundly touched and changed him.

*Gaijin* offers a pluralist alternative to the fusion myth, but like Freyre, Yamasaki celebrates the transformative power of Brazil, a product of the Brazilian affinity for the concrete. Freyre may have been writing against pluralism, but the pluralism of *Gaijin* is, like his fusion, a personal thing. It is not the hands-off, identity-obsessed pluralism of billiard-ball ethnic groups so often extolled in the United States, an individualist multiethnicity. The people in *Gaijin* breach abstract barriers of nationality, color, and class with acts of humanity and kindness. If the touching in this film is mostly figurative, a reaching out in words, gifts, and deeds, it also, as the

movie progresses, becomes increasingly literal. Tonho's stroking of Titoe's cheek at the movie's climax, his kiss to her hair, are harbingers of
things to come, a neo-Freyrian future in which these immigrant races too
will dissolve into a universal Brazilian metarace.

## The promise of a touch

Something happened to Rosa Kitagawa, Eriko Miyagi, and Naomi
Mizutake. All are Japanese nationals, the children of Japanese parents.
All trace their Japanese ancestry as far back as anyone can know. Yet
all, like Titoe, have come to *feel* Brazilian. In them, national sentiment
has run off the rails of Japanese discourse, diverging from official reck-
onings of affiliation. For them, Japanese blood matters, but not all that
much.

One reason is that while growing up in Brazil they were exposed to
Brazilian national narratives. But exposure alone cannot produce con-
viction. People reject or remain indifferent to narratives as often as they
embrace them. To be compelling, a narrative must resonate with memories, feelings, hopes, and dreams. It must have emotional depth. That is
why Yamasaki presents a national myth through the eyes of Titoe. The
big country comes to life in Titoe's changed relationship with Yamada,
in her love for her alien daughter Shinobu, in the sincere friendship
shown her by Tonho. To the degree we can empathize with Titoe, vi-
cariously experiencing her sufferings, yearnings, and discoveries, we
simultaneously engage the national narrative.

Like *Bye Bye Brasil*, another important film of that era, *Gaijin* bade
farewell to Brazilian Brazil, painting a new, more uproarious watercolor. It pointed to a break with the past. But for many dekasseguis, I
imagine that the film is more a foreshadowing than a memoir.[11] Viewing
Titoe laboring in the coffee fields, can Brazilian workers fail to see
themselves laboring in the auto-parts factory? Santa Rosa is like a place
in a dream, familiar and transmogrified at the same time.

And like a dream, *Gaijin* expresses a profound wish. As nikkeis repeatedly insisted to me, with great passion, they crave above all "human warmth." In Japan, many felt they could not break out of their
categorical prisons, as Titoe broke out in Brazil. Eduardo Mori, seven

---

[11]I regret that I did not interview people about this film, which many had seen.
Its significance became fully apparent to me only after I returned to the United
States.

years in Japan, is still beating against "the great barrier"; Miriam and Tamara Moreira's photos, chunks of their lives, are dismissed as frauds; Rosa Kitagawa fantasizes that a blond wig might make her visible; Naomi Mizutake's mother is misrecognized and despised as an "American"; Eriko Miyagi is condescendingly "reassured" that she is Japanese. Their frustration is palpable; they themselves are not.

If you do not register on the senses, do you still exist? If you are treated as a categorical abstraction, are you an Invisible Person (Ellison 1952)? *Gaijin*'s version of the pluralist myth recapitulates the suffering of one's Japanese grandparents and foreshadows the auto-parts factory. But its most powerful message may be its promise of a Brazilian touch.

CHAPTER 16

# Human Warmth

### Quotidian nationality

For Chaplin's bewildered worker, capitalism is not the labor market, the profit motive, or mass production, but the repetitive motion and shouted commands of the Electro-Steel assembly line. Similarly, nationality up close is not the flag or history but distinctive sensory and interactional patterns.

National myths are most compelling when their explicit message rests on quotidian nationality. *Gaijin* figures Brazil as a grand multicultural, multilingual, multiethnic encounter. It does so by portraying intimate engagements between persons of different ethnicities. The film thereby mobilizes implicit Brazilianness—the promise of a touch—in the service of its pluralist national vision. Hence *Gaijin*'s mythmaking draws on ubiquitous and deeply felt, but usually nonconscious and nonnationalized, Brazilian relational practices. In this chapter I argue that such practices, thrown into relief by their Japanese counterparts, are what nikkeis have in mind when they speak of "human warmth" (*calor humano*).

"Brazilians are warm; Japanese are cold": that was a message people conveyed to me repeatedly and insistently. Though Brazilians' talk of human warmth is ethnocentric and ingenuous, we should not dismiss it as nonsense. Their reflections contain a core of insight, born of uncomfortable experiences in Japanese factories and schools. Like anthropologists, Brazilians in Japan convert a sense of strangeness into a cultural account. They become lay ethnographers, with themselves the prime objects of analysis.

Their conclusions, though rendered in nontechnical and morally charged language, recall midcentury studies of national character. National-character theory currently has a bad name, though it was invented by some of the most brilliant anthropologists of the time.[1]

[1]Including Ruth Benedict, Margaret Mead, Gregory Bateson, Rhoda Métraux, Geoffrey Gorer, and Martha Wolfenstein, among others.

Branded overly psychological and stereotypical, the literature has faded into semioblivion.[2] Judiciously treated, however, it offers a trove of insights into quotidian nationality.

Ruth Benedict's *The Chrysanthemum and the Sword* (1946), the most accomplished work in the genre, reveals subtle forms of the Japanese nation customarily overlooked in recent discussions of national narratives. In tandem with Gilberto Freyre's *Masters and the Slaves*, an unacknowledged forerunner, Benedict's book helps us understand why human warmth emerges as a key index of Brazilianness among dekasseguis in the 1990s. For Brazilians' references to human warmth recognize, in a compressed form, a clash in interaction styles implied in those earlier scholarly explorations of Japanese and Brazilian character.

### Relational common sense

*The Chrysanthemum and the Sword* is a dazzling work of the anthropological imagination. Its shortcomings and excesses—static analysis, overgeneralization, and overemphasis on the motivational force of duty and shame—are well known, but one should not be too quick to condemn a book for such faults. The task of an ethnography is, after all, to simplify—to present a condensed, incisive account of human life, precisely because human life is too expansive and disorderly to be grasped whole. *The Chrysanthemum and the Sword* seizes hold of cardinal issues in Japanese lives. It has the acuity of great ethnography, forwarding provocative claims that have fired countless debates in the years since.

Benedict seeks the order underlying apparently disparate, bizarre, or contradictory Japanese practices. In spite of her reputation as an aesthete, the patterns she identifies are neither fanciful nor merely stylistic. The book offers a powerful theory of human behavior, privileging face-to-face interaction as the primary locus of cognitive, emotional, and motivational learning. That learning, argues Benedict, was harnessed by a determined, ruthless state to terrifying and disastrous national adventures. The insight, which links imagined community and quotidian

---

[2] As Roy D'Andrade (1995:3–6) points out, changes in the practice of social science are not always Kuhnian paradigm shifts. Sometimes social scientists just turn to new questions when their research gets stale or unwieldy and begins to generate diminishing returns. D'Andrade calls this "agenda-hopping." When agendas are abandoned, outstanding work often falls by the wayside, stigmatized as passé or misconceived.

nationality, makes *The Chrysanthemum and the Sword* a more profound, consequential book than its famous predecessor, *Patterns of Culture* (1934).

Benedict stresses that the force of the state's appeals rested on their articulation with a form of everyday nationality that I will call *relational common sense*. Japanese domestic wartime propaganda worked because it drew upon emotion-laden understandings of familial relationships. It highlighted ties of blood or the sharing of a unique "spirit"; at the same time, it emphasized hierarchical relations. Nationalist rhetoric took as its metaphoric source the coresident family, a face-to-face realm governed by moral obligations that reconciled blood and hierarchy. One could and should acknowledge, through offerings of respect and obedience, the immeasurable, unrepayable debt that one owed to parents—and therefore, by extension, to the Emperor.

In short, wartime leaders mobilized deeply felt moral obligations by presenting the nation as a transformation of the family with the Emperor at its apex. Japan's distinctive hierarchical solidarity was legitimized, and could most convincingly be legitimized, through appeals to ideas of virtue, indebtedness, honor, respect, and "proper place" learned and invested with strong emotions as one grew up within the family circle.

Where is Japan in Benedict's account? Benedict proposes that the discourses of Tokugawa shoguns, Meiji reformers, and twentieth-century militarists alike are instances of national *parole* built upon a national *langue* of relational common sense.[3] Japanese politics and policies are multifarious; the quotidian nationality that lends them credibility, Japan's deep structure, quietly reproduces itself in the intimacy of the home.

## A categorical interaction style

An aspect of relational common sense with crucial implications for this study is *interaction style*. Interaction style belongs to a class of anthropological terms applied to subtle, nonverbal, thematic, often un-

[3]Benedict did not, as is sometimes charged, ignore history. Rather, she used it to demonstrate cultural stasis—the more the nation changed, the more it stayed the same. In her account, both Tokugawa feudalism and Meiji reform evidenced Japanese "character," as did the decisive and apparently radical turn from one to the other. No surrender in the Pacific islands and total surrender after Hiroshima and Nagasaki were, again, surface manifestations of underlying coherence. Time and again the nation's leaders persuaded, cajoled, and inspired citizens to make incredible sacrifices and stunning reversals in attitudes and behavior.

conscious aspects of human behavior. Well-known examples are Geertz's "ethos" (1973 [1957]) and Bourdieu's "habitus" (1977 [1972]). All are products of what Gregory Bateson (1972 [1942]) dubs "deutero-learning," the apprehension of a durable disposition, often unconscious, through repeated engagement in learning experiences with the same general structure.

Narrower in scope than either ethos or habitus, interaction style refers to a characteristic demeanor adopted in interpersonal encounters. According to Benedict, Japanese seek to operate in a known world where encounters unfold smoothly. Uncertainties are reduced through a tacit agreement that one treats others as occupants of statuses relative to one's own rather than as unique or unpredictable persons. Having learned to do so first in the family circle, and then in other spheres, people habitually calibrate face-to-face behavior by reference to gender, age, hierarchical position, and so on. Circumspection, calculation, and "a strong sense that other people are sitting in judgment" (1946:222) are the subjective correlates of these practices.[4]

Let us call this interaction style "categorical."[5] I want to underline a strong concern with defining the situation, especially in terms of relative status, as essential for conducting appropriate interpersonal transactions.

### Japanese selves-in-interaction

Contemporary ethnographers of Japanese selves-in-interaction have refined Benedict's observations. They have demonstrated the importance of relative status in language use and interaction rituals. At the same time, they have refused to reduce Japanese selves to anxious, punctilious calculators of status who lack individuality or integrity. Instead, they propose that Japanese selves are typically multidimensional.

[4]This is the basis for Benedict's classification of Japan—with reservations usually ignored by commentators (1946:222)—as predominantly a "shame culture."

[5]In characterizing this interaction style as "categorical," I am not arguing that Japanese people are just status constellations—statuses do not swallow up people in Japan or anywhere else, even in caste systems (Bailey 1960; Parish 1996) and total institutions (Goffman 1961). Indeed, the *personal* difficulty of meeting the demands of *social* roles is a central motif of Japanese philosophy and moral practice, and a focus of Japanese bodily and spiritual disciplines (Benedict 1946:chapter 11; Plath 1980; Smith 1983:98–103). Nor am I saying that Japanese lack individuality—an absurd claim that would grossly contradict my own experience in Japan and has been amply rebutted in the literature.

In a discussion of the Japanese "interactionist self," Robert J. Smith (1983) identifies two important features of the Japanese language: *keigo* (see also Benedict 1946:47–49), and the absence of personal pronouns. Keigo, or respect language, "has the effect of establishing at the outset the relative social standing and degree of intimacy of the speaker, the listener, and any third-party referent" (1983:74). "It is impossible," he adds, "to speak or write Japanese without employing *keigo*" (ibid.:77). Relative status is thus inevitably encoded in the very language one uses to address another.

People likewise signal relative status in their choice of personal referents—names, kin designations, terms of deference, and so on. Unlike personal pronouns such as "I" or "you," Japanese personal referents "indicate categories and degrees of communicative distance." Hence "the selection of one from among the great array of such referents will reflect the human and social relationships that obtain between the two parties" (ibid.:77). Learning how to employ personal referents begins early in life, and the skill continues to be refined as the child enters increasingly complex social worlds (ibid.:79).

The uses of keigo and personal referents reflect a tendency to treat others as, within the context of a given interaction, occupants of statuses relative to one's own. Yet another manifestation of that tendency is the well-known ritual of exchanging *meishi*, or business cards. The "primary purpose," writes Smith, "is to reveal at once the social status of each party through the titles or affiliations printed on them. The recipient of a card has been given an invaluable clue to the level of speech it is appropriate . . . to adopt" (ibid.:82).

But note that the self is more than the self-in-interaction. The complex biographical person is off-stage, not erased. As Smith puts it: "The autonomy of the individual is protected and assured not in society, but away from it, where one may legitimately indulge in self-reflection and introspection" (ibid.:102).

Smith's distinction between the (public) status navigator and the (private) autonomous self is echoed and amplified by Takie Sugiyama Lebra (1992). Lebra develops a sophisticated model of a three-dimensional Japanese self: the "interactional self," the "inner self," and the "boundless self." The inner self "provides a fixed core for self-identity and subjectivity, and forms a potential basis for autonomy from the social world" (p. 112). It is not, therefore, the self usually experienced or exposed in interaction. Nor is the boundless self, associated with Buddhist concepts of disengagement and transcendence, which is "absolutely passive and receptive" (ibid.:115).

Lebra's interactional self, our main concern here, has two orientations, the "presentational" and the "empathetic." The presentational self

involves the surface layer of self, metaphorically localized on the person's face, visible or exposed to others either in actuality or imagination. The person's self-awareness is sharpened as the object of attention, inspection, and appraisal by others around. (ibid.:106)

For the presentational self, saving face is of the utmost importance. As Lebra notes, Japanese terms for self-awareness (*kao, mentsu, taimen, menboku, teisai, sekentei*) "might be translated as honor, self-esteem, dignity, reputation, and the like, but such translations do not fully convey the self's sensitivity to interactional immediacy and vulnerability entailed in the Japanese terms" (ibid.:106). And preserving one's own face is, in turn, partly a matter of preserving others': "An organizer of ceremonies like weddings and funerals pays great attention to the proper rank-ordering of attendants in seat arrangements, order of speakers, order of incense burning, etc., so that every face may be sustained or at least no face smeared" (ibid.:107–8). In short, the presentational self is acutely sensitive to failure to maintain its own status or to appropriately acknowledge the statuses of others.

The empathetic self, on the other hand, "feels attached or bonded to the other. . . . The ultimate state of this orientation is a feeling of fusion, synergy, or interchangeability of self and other" (ibid.:109). But sentiments of "fusion" do not obliterate status distinctions; to the contrary, they enhance them. Lebra details relations that mobilize the empathetic self: "intimate friends, fellow members of a group, parent and child, leader and follower, master and disciple, patron and client, *senpai* (senior) and *kōhai* (junior)" (ibid.:107). These are (with the possible and important exception of the category "intimate friends") egalitarian ("fellow members") or hierarchical (senpai/kōhai, etc.) relations within a socially demarcated group. One would not want to overstate the case, but empathy seems to flow largely within delimited, culturally recognized status circles.

For both Smith and Lebra, there is a split between the self-in-interaction and the inner, or autonomous, self. The interactional self is sensitive to relative status, tries to preserve face, and seeks predictability in interpersonal transactions. The inner self is singular, autonomous, reflective, spontaneous. But the inner self is hidden to all but intimates.

Brazilians who come in contact with Japanese inevitably meet interactional selves, skewing their perceptions of Japanese "character" and its differences from their own. Of course, Japanese also meet Brazilian interactional selves—but that is another matter, as we shall see.

It is easy to be misunderstood. I am not suggesting that only Japanese attend to status relations, loss of face, and minute relational cues, or that only Japanese channel empathy in accord with group membership. Nor am I arguing that Japanese interactions can always be reduced to status rituals or virtuoso displays of etiquette, which would be a caricature, and certainly intimate relationships in Japan permit considerable exposure of inner selves.[6]

As Lebra takes pains to emphasize, what is at stake here are variations on general human themes. I am pointing to differently weighted, not mutually exclusive, orientations. The evidence suggests that in interactions many Japanese are unusually sensitive to questions of status, face, and context. Those aspects of Japanese interaction style are, in Robert Levy's terminology, hypercognized (1984:219): they are foci of attention, self-investment, and cultural elaboration. There is no a priori reason to suppose—indeed, I think it is demonstrably not the case—that they necessarily assume such centrality in interpersonal experience elsewhere.

In Brazil, one learns a quite different interaction style. Again it will be useful to begin with an outstanding study of national character.

## Masters, slaves, and everyday Brazilianness

The search for Brazil in the realm of the face-to-face has a distinguished intellectual lineage, beginning sensationally with Gilberto Freyre's *histoire intime* (1956[1933]:lxx) of family, slavery, and patriarchy in northeast Brazil. Freyre's *The Masters and the Slaves*, briefly introduced in the last chapter, bears comparison with Benedict's better-known classic. Though it antedated those works (such as Benedict's) that

---

[6]Japanese also tend to assign a high value to the quality *kejime*. Kejime is "the ability to make distinctions . . . between *omote* and *ura* (front and rear), *tatemae* and *honne* (appearance and real feelings), and *uchi* and *soto* (home and outside)" (Tobin 1992:23, citing Lebra 1976 and Hendry 1986). Such distinctions, taken together, contrast realms of formality/distance (omote, tatemae, soto) with those of spontaneity/intimacy (ura, honne, uchi) (Bachnik 1992). That is, kejime is the ability to know when a given interaction demands "outside" behavior and when it demands "inside" behavior. Kejime is such a vital skill that it is "the most important lesson to be learned in the Japanese preschool" (ibid.:24).

came to be known as national-character studies, *The Masters and the Slaves* falls within the genre, and, like *The Chrysanthemum and the Sword*, Freyre's masterful, daring historical ethnography has become a controversial yet indispensable standard reference on a national society.

There is urgency to both *The Chrysanthemum and the Sword* and *The Masters and the Slaves*. Benedict's study was a product of its apocalyptic times, written under the gun. Freyre's was a product of a different era, a different national context, and different, though no less heated or momentous, controversies.

Gilberto Freyre was, like Benedict, a student of Franz Boas at Columbia University. Boas remains best known for his insistence that "race" and "culture" vary independently—that culture is not in the genes. His target was race-based orthogenetic evolutionism, the speciously scientific claim of white Christian Europeans to a preordained monopoly on "civilization."[7] But Freyre engaged Boas's ideas as a Brazilian, for whom the evolutionist doctrine had a national sting. If the exponents of scientific racism were right, then miscegenation condemned Brazil to a perpetual state of national degeneracy (Graham 1990; Skidmore 1974). In the preface to the second English-language edition of *The Masters and the Slaves*, Freyre writes:

I do not believe that any Russian student among the romantics of the nineteenth century was more intensely preoccupied with the destiny of Russia than I was with that of Brazil at the time I knew Boas. It was as if everything was dependent upon me and those of my generation, upon the manner in which we succeeded in solving the age-old questions. And of all the problems confronting Brazil there was none that gave me so much anxiety as that of miscegenation. . . .

It was my studies in anthropology under the direction of Professor Boas that first revealed to me the Negro and the mulatto for what they are—with the effects of environment or cultural experience separated from racial characteristics (Freyre 1956 [1933]:xxvi–xxvii).

Freyre's tour-de-force redeemed Brazil from a dismal fate decreed by biology. He was the revolutionary alchemist whose celebration of racial mixture recast his own country as a promising tropical hybrid.[8]

---

[7]Boas had left Germany in 1886. He was a Jew, a member of a minority that the spurious science racialized and dehumanized.

[8]Freyre's celebration of miscegenation comes close, in its acceptance of racial categories and its parallel accounts of racial and cultural mixing, to reproducing certain aspects of scientific racism. However, his appreciation of the cultural contributions of nonwhites breaks importantly with the scientific racists' evolutionary scheme.

Freyre's chronicle of the sugar estates is written in a vivid, effusive, at times flamboyant style well suited to his thesis that history is made in bedrooms and kitchens. In contrast to Benedict's spare, penetrating, painstakingly organized ethnography-at-a-distance (Mead and Métraux 1953), *The Masters and the Slaves* offers a cascade of rich descriptions and telling scenes. "Nothing seemed to escape [Freyre's] curiosity," notes Alistair Hennessy (1989:764), "as he incorporated into his work the analysis of child-rearing patterns, intra-family relations, women's roles, nutrition, disease, the study of culinary evidence, medicinal cures, the intricacies of decoration, architectural symbolism, toys, religious expression, dress, defecating customs and the influences of foreign cultures." The book overflows with evocations of the sights, smells, and sensations of colonial Brazil. In the end, the intimate violence and power-laden eroticism of conquest and slavery yield a beneficial miscegenation, an adaptive Luso-tropical synthesis.

Brazil's so-called "racial democracy" has long been a ballyhooed centerpiece of national pride. It has also been dismissed as a national fantasy. The matter is complex. Measured by any objective indicator—income, say, or the occupation of high and influential statuses—the evidence against racial democracy is incontrovertible (Hasenbalg 1979; Levine 1997). At the same time, face-to-face interactions across racial lines in Brazil differ from such contacts in the United States or Europe. There is a peculiarly Brazilian paradox here: though highly visible and discriminatory in the public realms of income and power, color distinctions do not strongly deter warm personal relations, including those of friendship and sexual intimacy.[9]

As a herald of racial democracy, *The Masters and the Slaves* misses the mark, and Freyre has often been taken to task for painting an overly benign, skewed picture of the racial situation in Brazil. But I think it would be a mistake to dismiss the book for this failing. For like *The Chrysanthemum and the Sword*, *The Masters and the Slaves* explores relational common sense. It captures an elusive, but enduring and important, feature of national life, a characteristic style of face-to-face interaction evident in transactions across many kinds of status lines. That "personal" style features direct engagement, sensuality, and above all concreteness, a sense of the singular physical presence of the other.

[9]Sexual orientation in Brazil has a similar double valence. Though discrimination and even incidents of violence against gays are widespread, close personal relations between gays and heterosexuals are common (Levine 1997:73–74, 194).

## A personal interaction style

To adapt a distinction made by Roberto DaMatta (1991 [1979]), we might contrast "personalism" with "individualism." If "individualism" entails the assumption that others are fundamentally alike, deserve equal treatment, and should be granted a sphere of autonomy, "personalism," by contrast, rests on the assumption that others are unique, deserve special treatment, and should be engaged. Both styles have a democratic flavor, but otherwise differ radically. In a personal world everyone is sui generis, with a characteristic physical presence, biography, and personality. Unlike Geertz's archetypal Westerners (1984 [1974]), such people are irregular, spiky, and sticky rather than round, smooth, and hard. One adopts a hands-on rather than hands-off attitude toward others; interactions and relationships must be improvised, tailored to those who enter into them.

The tailoring depends in part, of course, on social attributes, but importantly on personal factors. An interaction, even a relatively anonymous public interaction, in which the participants do not recognize one another as physical, biographical persons *apart from their social attributes* is a failure. To be treated anonymously in Brazil is to be dismissed.[10]

In Brazil, as in Japan, people attend to audience, status relations, and interactional context (Linger 1992). But in Brazil, there is such a thing as *too much attention* to such matters. Outside unusually ritualized, formal, or dangerous situations, spontaneity in interaction is of the utmost importance. The moment should come alive; it is better, within limits, to err on the side of carelessness than on the side of cautiousness. Hence dexterity at interpersonal improvisation, featuring flexibility, playfulness, demonstrations of personal interest, and particularistic forms of engagement, is a highly cultivated skill among Brazilians. Above all, one should demonstrate appreciation of another's presence and value as a unique (rather than categorical) human being. Interactional selves should be more than status constellations; inner selves should show through.

Although almost all the ethnographic literature on Japan takes the United States (or the "West") as its foil, in an important respect Japanese and American interaction styles resemble each other. The categorical style, like the individual style associated with the United States,

[10] For an unforgettable novelistic treatment of a quintessential Brazilian "nobody," see Lispector (1987 [1977]).

tends to treat others as abstractions rather than as concrete singularities. Except among intimates, one should not "see" others too distinctly, or try to discern or reveal the "inner self" that lies beneath their presentation. Hence the personal mode of interaction sketched by Freyre contrasts strongly with both the American individual style and the Japanese categorical style.

In sum, Benedict's and Freyre's books differ greatly in historical sensibility, in content, and in presentation. Benedict's Japan seems eternal, the origins of its replicating psychocultural formation lost in the past. Freyre excavates the historical roots of a new "Brazilian civilization." In precise language, Benedict emphasizes the timeless importance in hierarchical Japan of taking one's proper station, fulfilling one's obligations, and adopting behavior in accordance with a precisely drawn social map. In evocative language, Freyre plunges us into the maelstrom of the intimate transactions of those caught up in a historically transient regime of colonial plantation slavery.

But the books converge in their insistence that the nation is lived in quotidian interactions and in associated inner landscapes. Quotidian nationality is usually invisible to those who practice it. Going about one's business, meeting others, eating dinner, having a conversation, getting angry—for most of us, most of the time, such practices are just living. They become discernible as *national* practices only when they come under the eye of certain formal theories or when one's own displacement to a foreign environment renders them suddenly distinctive.

For Brazilians in Japan, navigating unfamiliar scenes and subjected to unfamiliar demands, life in Brazil becomes an object of heightened reflection, as people seek to understand and come to terms with sensations of discomfort and alienation. Set against memories of home, Japanese life too becomes a focus of conscious thought. The migrant's objectifying gaze resembles that of the anthropologist, though the migrant is far more a participant than an observer. The products of that gaze are, for example, the reflections collected in this volume, in which autobiography and lay ethnography inform each other.

### "*Human warmth*" vs. "*respect*"

Friction in interaction styles pushed Brazilians in Japan toward national-character analyses. Brazilians often talked of Japan in terms of exotic customs: cherry-blossom excursions, tea ceremonies, communal bathing. They admired the speedy, punctual trains and disparaged what they saw as poor taste in clothing. Material Japan drew their attention. But what struck them most was the strangeness of their everyday encounters with Japanese.

Rarely did I speak to a Brazilian in Toyota City who did not lament the absence of "human warmth" (*calor humano*) from interpersonal relations involving Japanese.[11] At the same time, many Brazilians emphasized the "respect" (*respeito*) they detected in its place. By "human warmth" Brazilians meant personalist interaction that penetrated categorical ascriptions. Human warmth was epitomized in touching and kissing, the tactility so characteristic of Brazilian greetings, even among those who may not know each other well, and so markedly absent among Japanese, even among intimates. By "respect" Brazilians meant formality, distance, correctness, dutiful treatment, careful calculation, expectations fulfilled. I sometimes felt as if their comments had been channeled from Benedict and Freyre, emerging in simplified, slightly garbled, morally charged, but recognizable terms.

"Human warmth" and "respect" were for Brazilians contrary modes of human interaction, emblematic of Brazil and Japan, respectively. Just as Benedict and Freyre drew portraits against an individualist (Protestant Anglo-Saxon) other, Brazilians in Japan elaborated their national character analyses within a bipolar universe. Brazil and Japan, human warmth and respect, were coconstituted. The perception of one enabled and entailed the perception of the other.

Most Brazilians, though not all, viewed both "human warmth" and "respect" with ambivalence. The problem with human warmth was that direct engagement could be troublesome, generating inefficiencies, psychological wounds, and conflicts. In Brazil, where human warmth reigned, one could not count on things working right, on the fulfillment of promises or the orderly operation of a public office or enterprise. Particular concerns, ambitions, proclivities, and contingencies would always intervene to upset plans and force spontaneous adjustments. And human warmth was even dangerous, for the direct expression of human passions could be frightening. São Paulo, the home of many Brazilians in Japan, is, after all, one of the most violent cities in the world, and I was often regaled with stories of robberies, muggings, and murders.

But admiration for respect was tempered with distaste for presumed insincerity. Brazilians approved of respect when it took the form of consideration and proper treatment, but they often interpreted it as defer-

[11]See also Tsuda (1999b).

ence to status, as the suppression of true feelings in the interest of preserving harmony, buttressing order, or increasing efficiency. At times respect even assumed, in Brazilian eyes, the profile of hypocrisy, of two-facedness.

In the end, most Brazilians I knew felt more comfortable with human warmth than with respect. They were willing to pay the price in terms of potential conflict for the chance to touch and be touched, and wanted to be persons who engaged others forthrightly. Their desire for engagement undoubtedly stemmed in part from alienation, from the frustration of second-class status in a foreign land. Stigmatized foreigners often find the natives cold and untrustworthy, and many Brazilians spent most of their waking hours on factory assembly lines, where industrial status relations were paramount. School life, too, was, as I have indicated, shot through with status distinctions and minutely regularized interactions.

But I think it is also true that over the better part of a lifetime in Brazil most, including nikkeis, had without realizing it learned to approach others in a particular way. Faced with rules meant to be broken and illegitimate hierarchies, they had learned to use *jeito*, to creatively mobilize personal and relational resources to deal with bureaucratic regulations and procedures. They had learned to beware of *safadeza* and *sacanagem*, self-serving and manipulative treatment by others. They had come to value hospitality, generosity, informality, fluidity. As members of an identifiable ethnic minority in Brazil, and therefore liable to discrimination, many nikkeis had embraced an extended version of the Brazilian ideal of racial democracy, celebrating ethnic pluralism and racial equality. They were acutely conscious of wildly different ways of being and had become adept at transactions across ethnic boundaries. They were steeped in personalism: concrete presence overshadowed abstract category. They had, in short, learned the general lessons, sometimes codified in stated values, of interpersonal dealings in Brazil, lessons that, attaining the status of an emotionally freighted interaction style, could not easily be unlearned.

The irony, of course, is that in Brazil many (though far from all) nikkeis had regarded themselves as "square," somewhat aloof, unspontaneous, and solidly responsible. They took these perceived characteristics, lessons learned mainly in family and community settings, as symptoms of Japaneseness to be both celebrated and lamented. But in Japan figure and ground reversed. Brazilian relational common sense was profiled. In their national character analyses, they glossed these Brazilian deutero-lessons, now dimly visible in the unfamiliar light cast by life in Japan, as "human warmth."

The world of human warmth, of Brazil, was for them imperfect; it was good to inhabit the safe, predictable world of Japan. But to trade their own human warmth for an attitude of respect—for restraint, distance, correctness, and formality—would be, for many of them, to become alien to themselves. To give up human warmth was, in a word, unthinkable. Or, more to the point, *unfeelable*. That is why Eriko Miyagi acknowledges, with a hint of plaintiveness, that when all is said and done, despite her blood, despite her citizenship, she is Brazilian— "there's nothing to be done about it."

CHAPTER 17

# Discontinuities

### *Small can be bigger than big*

The transnational scenes lived by nikkeis in Japan lead many to find meaning in Brazilian national narratives. But that is the beginning, rather than the end, of the story, for people always appropriate narratives in their own ways. They scramble, sift, and, most of all, elaborate narratives into subtle and fabulous experiential patterns woven into the distinctive fabrics of their lives.

Imaginings are not congruent with narratives, for two related reasons. First, people appropriate and transform narratives according to their own lights, as I have suggested above. Second, imaginings are "bigger" than narratives. This point requires clarification.

In a book on "moral knowing" in Nepal, Steven Parish observes that Newars personalize moral discourse. People's understandings go far beyond what their culture "tells" them; the concepts, as lived, become panoplies of idiosyncratic meanings. Of *dharma*, the Hindu concept of fundamental moral order, Parish writes:

The notion of worlds within culture may seem paradoxical, as if what is "inside" culture is bigger than culture itself. In a sense, I think this is true: the ... experience[1] of actors is richer and more complex than the cultural ideas that make that experience possible. Dharma is an abstract idea, a concept that frames Newar moral thought, experience, and action. It can be treated as a value that people learn—internalize—and enact. Yet look at how Newars represent what dharma means to them. They *formulate a world* to constitute the meaning of dharma. The meaning of the concept of dharma is in the world *formulated around the lives they live*. Different Newar actors *project different worlds* around the base concept of dharma. In doing so, they generate radically different meanings for this key moral and religious concept (1994:98–99, emphasis in original).

[1]Parish writes "the cultural experience of actors." I find the modifier confusing, but agree with the statement in all other respects.

The paradox of dharma—that personal moral knowing is "bigger" than the sociocultural moral world that seems at first glance to enclose it—is analogous to the paradox of identity discussed in this book. Both cases point to a serious misperception in human theory.

Most "social theory"—and the fact that we generally call it "social" theory is itself revealing—situates persons within collectivities. Without thinking, we speak of people as living "in the United States"; we say, "in my culture we do it like that." Society is big; a person is small. This container model, founded on social-scientific common sense, makes it reasonable to assume that the important questions deal with collective phenomena. "History," "social relations," "culture," "society," and so on set the conditions and constraints; once we manage to historicize things, or identify symbolic formations, persons become almost incidental, for they are assumed to be under the sway of the mighty collective forces. Persons skitter this way and that within collective boundaries, mostly as rational actors (or, as the economists say, "utility maximizers") whose mechanical calculations are based on the sociocultural givens of the moment. The more precisely we can define the constraints the more precisely we have explained those who live within them, for their autonomy, seen as their ability to move in the zone described by the constraints, becomes progressively reduced. Social accounts colonize the personal: where society advances, the person retreats. In short, the "better" our social theory, the more dispensable are persons.[2]

The container model of society makes use of a conduit model of language and, more generally, representations (Langacker 1987, 1991; Linger 1994; Reddy 1979). According to that model, language carries or (in discursive variants) "constructs" meanings. Language colonizes subjectivity. That is why an archaeology of knowledge, the excavation of symbols from the past, strikes some as a reasonable way to uncover the subjectivities of the dead. As society contains persons, representations contain meanings.

The conduit model of language, in tandem with the container model of society, yields a powerfully socialized vision of human beings. In particular, the joint model suggests that subjectivity is an overwhelmingly social phenomenon that can be analyzed without reference to persons or

[2]Mainstream economics and political science are probably the chief practitioners of such theorizing, but it strongly characterizes all the human sciences, including anthropology.

minds. In recent years, some authors have seen fit to reduce persons to effects of discourse. This has the advantage of unifying human theory within the social, but the fatal flaw of turning away from, or disfiguring, complicated and significant human phenomena such as learning, consciousness, and agency. But listening closely to others reveals that human thoughts, feelings, and experience move away from, transform, and expand upon public representations. Subjectivity occupies a different realm from the social, and requires different modes of investigation, description, and analysis.

The model of subjectivity I prefer highlights personal engagement rather than social containment or construction. Persons engage others, as they engage representations, continually remaking lives and subjective worlds. Just as a life cannot be reduced to "social relations," a subjectivity cannot be reduced to "discourse," "language," or "culture." Such abstractions manifest themselves to persons in discrete interactions with others and discrete experiences of the world. Under appropriate conditions, the personal subjectivities thereby precipitated become themselves objects of reflection and subjective refashioning. That is why collective theories of representation that pay no heed to biography and consciousness cannot address subjectivity, except in crude, shorthand terms, and it is why, in a manner of speaking, a person is bigger than society.

### Effects of consciousness

This book's central claim is that in continuously engaging the circumstances of their lives, and especially in engaging others, persons make big worlds and big selves. Minds intervene between encounters and experience, and further subjectify experience itself, spinning tears, resentment, and laughter into constellations of meaning, and turning that meaning back into feeling. A tear is an intellectual thing, as Blake observed; conversely, an idea is an emotional thing. Catarina Iemura transforms the tears of her loneliness into a yearning vision of herself as Japanese, evoking a nostalgia for a self that will never be. Our current understandings of how minds work are just good enough for us to understand that their complexities far outstrip our current understandings.

I have focused on conscious self-making.[3] Consciousness is one of the

---

[3]Let me emphasize that nonconscious mental processes are extremely important. I have discussed some of these (e.g., the learning of an interaction style) in earlier chap-

most vexing and widely debated issues in philosophy, psychology, cognitive science, artificial intelligence, neurophysiology, and anthropology. But this much seems clear, and important to recognize: consciousness throws a monkey wrench into determinist accounts of subjectivities, and, especially, determinist accounts of selves.

Because persons are sentient beings, they are enmeshed in their environment but not wholly of it. They inhabit what A. Irving Hallowell called a "behavioral environment" (1988 [1954]). A construed environment—that is perhaps a better term—cannot be easily inferred by an observer or dictated by others. Often anthropologists take culture as the lens that brings surroundings into focus. This approach, as I have emphasized, severely understates personal subjective diversity growing out of different life experiences, sensitivities, and inclinations among those who "belong to the same culture." Persons "of the same culture" do not necessarily apprehend given circumstances—say, a transnational scene—in the same way. Elena and Horácio Takeda both work and live at the Chubu Iron Company, but they certainly do not inhabit, in experiential terms, the same place. Nor do Elisa Aoshima and Catarina Iemura occupy anything like the same Kokusai classroom. The particular twists and turns of different life courses dramatically shape perceptions of any new situation or event.

That elementary fact is extremely important, but consciousness has stranger, more dramatic effects. One of the most significant aspects of human learning and human perception is, as Gregory Bateson noted, that it is subject to "hierarchic discontinuities" (1972 [1960]:252.) Consider this hypothetical interaction in a mental hospital:

The schizophrenic is what is called a patient, vis-à-vis a member of a superior and unloved organization, the hospital staff. If the patient were a good pragmatic Newtonian, he would be able to say to himself: "The cigarettes I can get by doing what this fellow expects me to do are after all only cigarettes, and as an applied scientist I will do what he wants me to do. I will solve the experimental problem and obtain the cigarettes." But human beings, and especially schizophrenics, do not always see the matter this way. They are affected by the circumstance that the experiment is being conducted by somebody whom they would rather not please.

---

ters. But a comprehensive, detailed examination of implicit and unconscious aspects of identity would require another book, or other books. An outstanding recent study of unconscious aspects of self-making, highlighting personalizations of gender, is Chodorow (1999). See also Kumekawa (1993), who discusses unconscious dimensions of Japanese-American ethnicity.

They may even feel there would be a certain shamelessness about seeking to please one whom they dislike. It thus comes about that the *sign* of the signal which the experimenter emits, giving or withholding cigarettes, is reversed. What the experimenter thought was a reward turns out to be a message of partial indignity, and what the experimenter thought was a punishment becomes in part a source of satisfaction. (ibid.:246, emphasis in original)

Hence even the setting as construed by our hypothetical patient is grossly unstable. If he perceives the context as transactional ("Newtonian"), an occasion for instrumental exchange, he accepts the cigarette and subjects himself to the experiment. But once he apprehends the situation in terms of relations rather than transactions, the "sign of the signal" reverses, and he reverses his behavior accordingly. In so doing, he reconstitutes both himself and his relation with the experimenter.

Of course, one can also engage in the Newtonian transaction while recognizing its relativistic aspects, or one can oscillate between disjunctive perceptions. The by-product of the disjunction, for Brazilians in Japan, is a sharp awareness of difference, possibly colored with feelings of rejection, sullenness, or resentment.

Japanese factories pay Brazilian workers a salary in return for conformity with the requirements of the Japanese workplace; Brazilian children receive signs of approval for good performance in Japanese schools. Though some rebel outwardly, refusing to play the role assigned by superiors, most Brazilians subject themselves to the "experiment." Yet their integration into these institutions does not, in general, mold their subjectivities in conformity with the values, norms, and expectations of those superiors. Rather, the social encounters elicit compliance while confirming Brazilians' perceptions that however much they may have thought themselves Japanese in Brazil, in Japan they are certainly not so. Consciousness reverses the sign of the signal, throwing selves into relief, with unpredictable consequences.

### Identities and selves

The self, or rather the constellation of ego-perspectives that constitutes a self, seems especially prone to hierarchic discontinuities. Hence Naomi Mizutake, called on to behave as a Japanese in ritualized encounters with school principals, does so, beautifully. But her performance, which momentarily absorbs the dancer into the dance, is a matter of choice: she warns her admirers not to count on her responses. Her Japaneseness is an identity she can occupy but from which she can exit. Its conscious display communicates to Naomi herself (and perhaps to perceptive others) that Naomi Mizutake has both a Japanese and, discontinuous with it, a supra-Japanese self.

Thus the phenomenological self, the "I" that is the immediate locus of perception and sensation, can shift levels as well as horizontal locations. One reason why it is often misleading to speak of the "identity" of an interviewee, or anyone else for that matter, is that the phenomenological self makes dizzying moves, disrupting tendencies toward a convergent perspective. Indeed, many of the interviewees have, during their sojourn in Brazil, become virtuosos in perspectival dislocations. One minute Eduardo Mori is "Brazilian," the next "Japanese," and then—making the jump—"someone who is sometimes Brazilian and sometimes Japanese." The perspectives are jumbled but coherent, bound together by a discernible intrapersonal logic. But they do not necessarily converge on a particular national identification, a national identification with a particular content, or even on the *meaning of having a national identification*.

Transnational scenes are, as I have emphasized throughout, situations conducive to hierarchical discontinuities in the experience of self. But the realization, for example, that one's identity is contextual is ultimately a feat of reflective consciousness, what I take to be an innate, variably actualized human capacity. The consequences of the leap in perception may be irreversible. Thereafter one cannot, perhaps, "be Brazilian" again in quite the same way. Brazilianness may come to seem contingent or artificial, or carry a scent of play-acting. Alternatively, the reflective self—that is, the self-observing-self, the phenomenological self in the mode of reflective consciousness—may develop a theory of the conditions that embed identities in persons. Many of the interviewees—Miriam and Tamara Moreira, Eriko Miyagi, Elisa Aoshima, and others—argue that growing up in Brazil conferred an ineradicable Brazilian identity upon them. This analysis permits a more substantial appropriation of "Brazilianness," which comes to seem fated, a product of biographical accident. But now given an explanatory ground, demystified, it is an identity displaced from its formerly unreflective status. And the door swings open to a future change of identity through alternative identity processes that one might later grasp.

Yet another leap is possible. Critical perceptions of a plastic identity may engender the notion that the self can intervene in its own identity construction. Thus is born a generative self—a self-constructing self, visible in many, if not all, the interviews. Eduardo Mori tries on different identities, seeking a comfortable self-definition; Bernardo Kinjoh and Elena Takeda assimilate alien experiences into rooted, but cosmopolitan, selves; Catarina Iemura tries to make herself Japanese; Naomi Mizutake explores her ethnic possibilities through an imaginary reconnaissance of her family's past. ... I do not wish to overtheorize or unduly reify a state of mind; a notion such as "generative self" simply draws attention to conscious identity experimentation, chronic or fleeting, which can take myriad forms, as evidenced by the interviewees' explorations, self-questioning, and dialogic play during our conversations.

"The individual is certainly creative within (and possibly outwith) the current and received terms of the collectivity to which she or he belongs," write Anthony Cohen and Nigel Rapport (1995:4). "Rather than talking glibly of collective consciousness," they continue, "we would now advocate the more cautious, 'consciousnesses within collectivity'" (ibid.:13). Basically I agree with this statement, and endorse the authors' commitment to what Cohen has called "an alternative anthropology of identity" (1994) focused on conscious appropriations rather than collective representations. But I think their parenthetical hedge "and possibly outwith" deserves a better fate. There is no consciousness, and no experience, "within" a collectivity. To speak that way is to play mix-and-match with levels of analysis, for consciousness and experience are not the collectivity's but *someone's*. Through a creative, complex, contingent transformative process people's consciousnesses render representations into rich, "bigger," idiosyncratic subjectivities—the only kind there are.

## Gardens of self

Presented the choice, as we have seen, the interviewees overwhelmingly felt themselves to be Brazilian, not Japanese, regardless of their descent or legal citizenship. They felt to some degree estranged from Japan, and even many isseis, such as Naomi Mizutake's father, found that their commitment to the Japanese blood narrative had attenuated over the years they spent in Brazil. Everyone understood the blood narrative: people did not question that group membership could be based on descent, nor did they question that they, therefore, were in some sense "Japanese."

But few felt that was the end of the story. For their contacts with Japanese in Japan convinced them that if they were "Japanese," then Japaneseness came in different flavors, and their flavor was unmistakably, and strongly, Brazilian. The clash they felt between Brazilian "warmth" and Japanese "respect," apprehended through the compelling medium of face-to-face experience, signaled that there was much more to them than blood. If Japaneseness came through the blood, well and good, they were "Japanese"; but their Brazilianness, a quality disconnected from blood, ran deeper.

Brazilianness, though also a type of national identity, was a different sort of identity from Japaneseness. For Brazilianness was not a categorical essence; rather, it was a flight, or liberation, from categorical essence. It was, perhaps, in Tizuka Yamasaki's words, a "road to freedom," a shared identity that, paradoxically, enabled one to be taken for what one was, apart from the categorical abstractions, and to treat others the same way.

Grounded equally in a personalist common sense, the fusion and pluralist narratives of Brazil both appealed to my friends in Toyota. Miriam Moreira, for example, seems to subscribe to an updated version of the fusion narrative. Like her sister Tamara, she describes herself not as a nikkei, not as Japanese, but as a Brazilian mestiça. Miriam is the child of a nikkei mother and a father of European descent. For her, an extension of fused-race Brazilianness, one that would add "Japanese" to the Brazilian racial mixture, is easy to imagine and accept. Naomi Mizutake, among others, leans more to a pluralist narrative, according to which nikkeis comprise an ethnic strand in a multicultural, multiracial community. Naomi considers herself an ethnic Japanese in a pluralist Brazil. For her, ethnicity and nation are differently based; ethnicity is a matter of blood, nation a matter of open relations with others, who are usually different, in terms of descent, from oneself.

But we should be wary of trying to characterize people as adherents of this or that narrative. Those narratives belong to a representational universe; they are symbolic, not subjective, phenomena. Particular life paths and particular selves are "bigger" than narratives. Narratives, be they legal specifications, cultural histories, or fictional films, are better regarded as skeletal propositions than subjective stuff. They enter lives as postulates about reality that a person may learn, believe, reject, transform, embellish, experiment with, ignore . . . The possibilities, save one, are endless. Narratives are never "faxed" into consciousness (Strauss 1992:9–10). Meaning, in the thick, subjective sense, emerges only in living a life, and the efficacy of a narrative depends on how it engages those who encounter it.

How, for example, can we reduce Eduardo Mori, who has moved

through several identities and may move through many more, to the product of a narrative? What about Catarina Iemura's idiosyncratic "Japaneseness": which narrative is that? And what of Eriko Miyagi: is she Japanese-Brazilian or Brazilian-Japanese, or something else altogether?

Upon closer examination, Naomi Mizutake, whom I cavalierly described as having a pluralist identity, is in fact infinitely more complicated. In good Boasian fashion, and with considerable satisfaction, she separates race, language, and culture, in contrast to what she sees as the provincial, determinist blood perspective of many of her Japanese acquaintances. Naomi rises above her own identity in embracing its components in her self-analysis. Who, then, is she? Her perspective *enables* her to be, much of the time, a nikkei Brazilian, but that perspective itself, *which is also (and perhaps more fundamentally) "Naomi,"* is neither nikkei nor Brazilian.

Bernardo Kinjoh is similarly complex. An Okinawan-Japanese-Brazilian who has worked in Guinea-Bissau and in Japan, who accepts both his Brazilianness and his Japaneseness and is willing to embrace other perspectives as well, Bernardo escapes narrated categories. He has turned those categories themselves into objects of reflection, working out a self-conscious stance with respect to them. Bernardo becomes a variety of cosmopolitan, but that term too is suspect, for it smoothes over the specific texture of his worldliness. Bernardo's "nationality," his "ethnicity," and his "cosmopolitanism" are unmistakably *his*.

Much the same could be said, I believe, for all the interviewees. They escape the narrative categories, because they have engaged those categories in their own ways as they have gone about their own pursuits and struggled with their own circumstances. From history and culture they have made, and continue to make, lives, each bringing a reflective, often generative consciousness to bear on ready-made narratives. The results are the wild, intricate, dazzling, ever-changing gardens of self glimpsed through the window of our conversations.

## From Santa Rosa to Toyota City—and beyond

Works of art emerge at a particular moment, accruing new meanings as the years pass. *Gaijin* is not the same movie it was in 1980: the Toyota City factory now casts its shadow upon Santa Rosa. Today, in retrospect, even the multicultural São Paulo of the film's end seems a point of transfer rather than a final destination. The immigrants have remigrated elsewhere. They are wandering the far margins of the blue hemisphere: the sun is stuck high in the sky, and the road, its signs marked in several languages, stretches, shimmers, evanesces. Home is an idea at the end of a satellite beam, but it is nowhere in sight.

In some respects, just as Santa Rosa echoed the sugar plantation, history seems to be mimicking itself in Toyota City. Again, competition in the global economy and difficult local conditions pressure producers into adjustments. Cheap, reliable labor is imported; a necessary luxury is exported. In place of the São Paulo fields, we have the factories of Aichi prefecture. In place of coffee beans, auto parts. A public-housing complex and the company dormitory substitute for the quarters of the plantation. Once again, workers enter a world where they are illiterate, ignorant of local customs, and only dimly aware of their place in the overall scheme. There are deceptions; there is exploitation. Expectations are not met, and plans for return are postponed. People make massive adjustments. Adults feel lost; there are suicides, accidents, and deaths. The children begin to speak a foreign tongue and to act in foreign ways.

But I am not confident that history will repeat itself by turning the immigrants into ethnic citizens, nikkei- or Brazilian-Japanese. For Japan is not Brazil, and is not likely to become Brazil. It is a different sort of place, where the dominant narrative of pure blood obstructs narratives of racial inclusion and ethnic pluralism. Nikkei Brazilianness rests precisely, I have argued, on the rejection of a pure-blood narrative of nationality. In Japan, nikkeis are making themselves into New Brazilians, or something else perhaps, and their Japanese bosses, hosts, and colleagues are struggling to discern them, and (by reflection) themselves, in the oblique transnational light.

It seems doubtful that Japan will, anytime soon, open itself to Brazilian difference, or that Brazilians can find a secure, comfortable home in Japan. But then again ... if anything is sure, it is that the future will surprise us, as has the past. My conclusions are at best informed guesses. I do not think the Brazilians, most of them, will "turn Japanese"—but they might. I do not think Japan will embrace multiethnicity—but it might. Stranger things have happened, and will: lives and histories do not move in either circles or straight lines.

"Don't ever think I'm going to do everything the way you think I'm going to do it," Naomi Mizutake cautions her Japanese friends. Is she also addressing herself?

REFERENCE MATTER

# Glossary of Foreign Terms
# and Phrases

Below I provide brief glosses of Japanese (J) and Portuguese (P) expressions used in this book. Only relevant meanings are given. In romanizing Japanese words, I have generally followed the standard Hepburn system. Exceptions in the text include familiar place names: "Tokyo" rather than "Tōkyō," and so on. (I have not included place names in the list.)

Many Japanese words have entered the everyday Portuguese of Brazilians living in Japan. The usual Portuguese renditions of such words, though inconsistent, occasionally differ in spelling and inflection from the Hepburn romanizations. The word *issei*, for example, like most Japanese nouns, does not change in the plural. But Brazilians generally say *isseis*, pluralizing the word in the Portuguese manner. In the Hepburn romanization, *nisei* denotes the child of an immigrant Japanese; in the Portuguese romanization, for phonetic reasons the word is written *nissei*.

ai (P): interjection indicating distress or surprise

"Alô" (P): "Hello"

bāchan (J): "granny"

bairro (P): neighborhood

baka (J): stupid

bem (P): darling

bentō (J): box lunch

bolsista (P): scholarship student

"Bom dia!" (P): "Good morning!"

bōnenkai (J): year-end party

bōsōzoku (J): motorcycle gang

brasileira, -o (P): Brazilian person

buchō (J): department or division manager

bukatsu (J): school club or athletic activity

burajirujin (J): Brazilian person

cachaça (P): Brazilian sugar-cane liquor

café com leite (P): coffee with milk

cafezinho (P): demitasse of coffee

caipirinha (P): drink made with cachaça, sugar, and lime

calor humano (P): human warmth

carne-seca (P): beef jerky

chacoalho (P): shaker

chūgakkō (J): Japanese middle school (grades 7–9)

churrascaria (P): barbecue pit

coitada, -o (P): poor soul

colégio (P): Brazilian public school, especially high school (grades 9–11)

colônia (P): immigrant community; rural ethnic settlement

"Come!" (P): "Eat!"

consulta (P): consultation
cortiço (P): slum tenement
coxinha (P): chicken-flavored snack
daikon (J): white radish
daiku (J): carpenter
danchi (J): public housing complex
dekasegi (J): migrant laborer
dekassegui (P): migrant laborer (usually referring to workers from overseas)
descendente (P): descendant
-dōri (J): street; avenue
eigo (J): English language
empreiteira (P): firm that supplies workers
estrangeiro (P): foreigner
farinha (P): flour, often made from manioc, sprinkled on Brazilian food
favela (P): slum; poor community
favelada, -o (P): inhabitant of a favela
fazenda (P): plantation
feijoada (P): stew made from black beans and various meats
festa (P): party; celebration
Fujinkai (J): women's association
furo (J): Japanese-style bath, designed for soaking
furusato (J): hometown; homeland
furūtsu basuketto (J): "fruit basket," a children's game resembling musical chairs
furyō (J): damaged; delinquent
furyōhin (J): damaged goods; defective parts
gaijin (J): foreigner (sometimes with connotations of disrespect)
gaikokujin (J): foreigner ("foreign-country person")
"Ganbatte!" (J): "Keep trying!"
geshuku (J): rooming house
ginásio (P): Brazilian middle school, grades 5–8
gogaku sōdan-in (J): language consultant; assistant teacher for language instruction
"Gomen nasai" (J): "Please forgive me"; "Excuse me"

gomi (J): garbage
guaraná (P): soft drink made from the seeds of an Amazonian fruit
hakengaisha (J): firm that supplies workers
hanabi (J): fireworks
hanbaiki (J): vending machine
hanchō (J): group leader
hentai (J): weirdo
hiragana (J): syllabary used in writing native Japanese words
hirukin (J): day shift
Hondo (J): Japanese mainland; home islands
honne (J): true feelings
hontō (J): really
ichigatsu (J): January
ichinen (J): first year (of middle school)
ichinensei (J): first-year student (seventh-grader)
ih (P): sighing interjection
ijime (J): hazing; bullying
ikebana (J): art of flower arranging
"Irasshaimase!" (J): "Welcome!"
issei (J, P): first-generation overseas Japanese; immigrant from Japan
japonês (P): Japanese language
japonês, japonesa (P): Japanese person
japonesinha (P): Japanese girl or woman (diminutive)
jeitinho (P): jeito (diminutive)
jeito (P): an improvised way of getting something done
jūdōkan (J): martial-arts building
juku (J): cram school
kachō (J): section chief
kaikan (J): hall; club
kanji (J): Chinese characters used in Japanese writing
katakana (J): Japanese syllabary used for writing foreign words
keigo (J): respect language
kejime (J): ability to make distinctions between "inside" and "outside" behavior
ken (J): prefecture

kendō (J): the art of fencing

Ken-ei Jūtaku (J): prefectural housing

kensa (J): inspection; quality control

kiken (J): dangerous

Kimigayo (J): Japanese national anthem

kitanai (J): dirty

kitsui (J): difficult; demanding

Kōdan (J): Housing and Urban Development Corporation

kōgyō (J): industry

kōhai (J): junior in rank or age

kōkō (J): Japanese high school (grades 10–12)

kokumin kenkō hoken (J): national health insurance

Kokusai Kyōshitsu (J): international classroom

kome (J): rice

kōtai (J): alternating day and night shifts

-kun (J): suffix of address or reference, sometimes used for young males

kusai (J): stinking

kutsubako (J): shoe compartments

kyūshoku (J): school lunch

lanchonete (P): snack bar

mãe (P): mother; Mom

mãe de santo (P): leader of a Spiritist or Afro-Brazilian religious congregation ("mother of the saints")

malandra, -o (P): scoundrel

manshon (J): apartment building

maranhense (P): native of the state of Maranhão

meishi (J): business card

mestiça, -o (P): person of mixed descent (here, usually part Japanese)

mestiçagem (P): racial mixing

miai (J): arranged meeting, with an eye to possible marriage

misoshiru (J): soup made from fermented bean paste

mochi (J): dumplings made from pounded rice

moleque (P): punk; delinquent

"Muito prazer" (P): "Pleased to meet you"

mulata, -o (P): person of mixed (especially African and European) descent

nabo (P): turnip

Naichi (J): Japanese mainland; home islands

nattō (J): fermented soybeans

nigatsu (J): February

nihongo (J): Japanese language

nihonjin (J): Japanese person

nikkei (J, P): person of Japanese descent born or living overseas

nikkeijin (J): person of Japanese descent born or living overseas

ninensei (J): second-year student (eighth-grader)

nisei (J): second-generation overseas Japanese (child of Japanese immigrants)

nissei (P): second-generation overseas Japanese (child of Japanese immigrants)

nordestina, -o (P): native of Brazilian Northeast

nori (J): dried seaweed

Nossa (Senhora) (P): Our (Lady), exclamation indicating emphasis or surprise

novela (P): soap opera

obasan (J): middle-aged woman

"Ohayō" (J): "Good morning" (informal)

"Ohayō gozaimasu" (J): "Good morning" (formal)

omote (J): front

onigiri (J): rice ball wrapped in seaweed

onsen (J): hot spring

oshibori (J): wet towel, usually hot

pachinko (J): Japanese pinball, played on upright machines

paranaense (P): native of the state of Paraná

pátria (P): home country

paulista (P): native of the state of São Paulo

praça (P): plaza

preta, -o (P): dark-skinned person

puxa (P): exclamation indicating emphasis or surprise

quebra-galho (P): trouble-shooter; problem-solver

quitanda (P): corner shop; mom-and-pop store

rāmen (J): Chinese-style noodle soup

real (P): unit of Brazilian currency, worth about $1 in 1995–96

respeito (P): respect

rika (J): science

rocambole de chocolate (P): filled, rolled chocolate pastry

rōmaji (J): roman letters used in writing Japanese

ryō (J): company dormitory

sacanagem (P): self-serving dirty business

safadeza (P): shameless, cynical behavior

-san (J): polite suffix of address or reference

sannensei (J): third-year student (ninth-grader)

sansei (J, P): third-generation overseas Japanese (grandchild of Japanese immigrants)

são-luisense (P): native of the city of São Luís

sashimi (J): sliced raw fish

saudade (P): melancholy longing; nostalgia

semai (J): cramped; narrow

senhora (P): older woman (respectful term)

senpai (J): senior in rank or age

senpai-kōhai (J): senior-junior relationship

sensei (J): teacher

sentō (J): public bath

sertão (P): arid backlands of Northeast Brazil

shachō (J): company president

shakai hoken (J): social insurance

"Shikata ga arimasen" (J): "There's no way"; "It can't be helped"

shinyū (J): best friend

shitamachi (J): downtown; popular urban quarters

shōgakkō (J): grade school

síndrome de regresso (P): returnee's syndrome

sōji (J): cleaning

soto (J): outside

sugoi (J): wonderful; awesome; cool

sukebe (J): lecher

"Sumimasen" (J): "Sorry"; "Excuse me"

sumō (J): Japanese wrestling

sunakku (J): intimate night club

surdo (P): deep drum

taihen (J): terrible; awful

takoyaki (J): dumplings made of octopus bits, steamed in an iron mold

tannin-no-sensei (J): home-room teacher

tatemae (J): appearances

"Tchau!" (P): "Bye!"

terra natal (P): homeland; land of birth

tsukemono (J): pickled vegetables

turma (P): group; gang

uchi (J): house

ura (J): back; rear

vestibular (P): university entrance exam

yakin (J): night shift

yakiniku (J): grilled meat

yakisoba (J): fried noodles

yonsei (J, P): fourth-generation overseas Japanese (great-grandchild of Japanese immigrants)

zangyō (J): overtime

zōkin (J): cleaning cloth

# References

## Statistical Sources

Aichi Prefecture
Centro de Estudos Nipo-Brasileiros
Foreign Ministry, Brazil
Homi Chūgakkō
Immigration and Naturalization Service, U.S.
Japanese Consulate General in São Paulo
Kōdan (Housing and Urban Development Corporation)
Ministry of Communications, Japan
Ministry of Education, Japan
Ministry of Justice, Japan
Toyota City Government
Toyota International Association

## Films and Television Shows

*Bye Bye Brasil* (Carlos Diegues, 1979)
*Gaijin—Caminhos da Liberdade* (Tizuka Yamasaki, 1980)
*Modern Times* (Charlie Chaplin, 1936)
*Sannen B Gumi, Kinpachi-Sensei* (episode aired March 28, 1996)

## Books and Articles

Allinson, Gary D.
    1997    Japan's Postwar History. Ithaca: Cornell University Press.
Anderson, Benedict
    1991 (1983)  Imagined Communities: Reflections on the Origin and Spread of
            Nationalism. London: Verso.
Appadurai, Arjun
    1990    Disjuncture and difference in the global cultural economy. Theory,
            Culture, and Society 7:295–310.
Audi Magazine (Brazil)
    1996    [Interview with Tizuka Yamasaki.] (Internet document http:// www.
            audi.com.br/audi_magazine/ ed9/ htmls/ e9017aud.html)
Bachnik, Jane
    1992    *Kejime*: Defining a shifting self in multiple organizational modes. *In*
            Japanese Sense of Self. Nancy R. Rosenberger, ed. Pp. 152–72. Cam-
            bridge: Cambridge University Press.

Baert, Patrick
  1998    Social Theory in the Twentieth Century. New York: New York University Press.
Bailey, F. G.
  1960    Tribe, Caste, and Nation. Manchester: Manchester University Press.
Baldwin, James
  1990 (1955)  Notes of a Native Son. Boston: Beacon.
Barth, Fredrik
  1969    Introduction. *In* Ethnic Groups and Boundaries. Pp. 9–38. Boston: Little, Brown.
Basch, Linda, Nina Glick Schiller, and Cristina Szanton Blanc
  1994    Nations Unbound: Transnational Projects, Postcolonial Predicaments, and Deterritorialized Nation-States. Amsterdam: Gordon and Breach.
Bascom, William
  1955    Urbanization among the Yoruba. American Journal of Sociology 60:446–54.
Bateson, Gregory
  1972 (1942)  Social planning and the concept of deutero-learning. *In* Steps to an Ecology of Mind. Pp. 159–76. New York: Ballantine.
  1972 (1955)  A theory of play and fantasy. *In* Steps to an Ecology of Mind. Pp. 177–93. New York: Ballantine.
  1972 (1960)  Minimal requirements for a theory of schizophrenia. *In* Steps to an Ecology of Mind. Pp. 244–70. New York: Ballantine.
  1972 (1968)  Conscious purpose vs. nature. *In* Steps to an Ecology of Mind. Pp. 426–39. New York: Ballantine.
  1972 (1970)  Form, substance, and difference. *In* Steps to an Ecology of Mind. Pp. 448–66. New York: Ballantine.
Befu, Harumi
  1993    Nationalism and *Nihonjinron*. *In* Cultural Nationalism in East Asia. Harumi Befu, ed. Pp. 107–35. Berkeley: Institute of East Asian Studies, University of California Press.
Benedict, Ruth
  1934    Patterns of Culture. Boston: Houghton Mifflin.
  1946    The Chrysanthemum and the Sword: Patterns of Japanese Culture. New York: New American Library.
Bernardes, Betina
  1995a   Brasil já possui quinta geração. Folha de São Paulo (19 October):Especial 2.
  1995b   Comunidade de japoneses formam elite em São Paulo. Folha de São Paulo (19 October):Especial 10.
Bestor, Theodore
  1989    Neighborhood Tokyo. Stanford: Stanford University Press.
Block, Ned, Owen Flanagan, and Güven Güzeldere (eds.)
  1997    The Nature of Consciousness: Philosophical Debates. Cambridge: MIT Press.

Bourdieu, Pierre
  1977 (1972)  Outline of a Theory of Practice. Cambridge: Cambridge University Press.
Brown, Jacqueline Nassy
  1998  Black Liverpool, black America, and the gendering of diasporic space. Cultural Anthropology 13(3):291–325.
CCEYH (Committee for Compiling Eighty-Year History of Japanese Immigration to Brazil)
  1991  Burajiru nihon imin hachijūnenshi. [Eighty years of Japanese immigrants to Brazil.] São Paulo: Burajiru Nihon Bunka Kyōkai.
Chodorow, Nancy J.
  1999  The Power of Feelings: Personal Meaning in Psychoanalysis, Gender, and Culture. New Haven: Yale University Press.
Clifford, James
  1994  Diasporas: Cultural Anthropology 9(3):302–38.
Cohen, Anthony P.
  1994  Self Consciousness: An Alternative Anthropology of Identity. London: Routledge.
Cohen, Anthony P., and Nigel Rapport (eds.)
  1995  Questions of Consciousness. London: Routledge.
  1995  Introduction. In Questions of Consciousness. Anthony P. Cohen and Nigel Rapport, eds. Pp. 1–18. London: Routledge.
Cole, Robert E.
  1971  Japanese Blue Collar: The Changing Tradition. Berkeley: University of California Press.
Collins, Peter
  1998  Negotiating selves: Reflections on "unstructured" interviewing. Sociological Research Online 3(3). (Internet document http://www.socresonline.org.uk/socresonline/3/3/2.html)
Comissão de Elaboração da História dos 80 Anos da Imigração Japonesa no Brasil
  1992  Uma epopéia moderna: 80 anos da imigração japonesa no Brasil. São Paulo: Editora HUCITEC and Sociedade Brasileira de Cultura Japonesa.
Cornelius, Wayne A.
  1998  The role of immigrant labor in the U.S. and Japanese economies: A comparative study of San Diego and Hamamatsu, Japan. With the assistance of Yasuo Kuwahara. San Diego: Center for U.S.-Mexican Studies, University of California, San Diego.
Costa, Emília Viotti da
  1988 (1985)  The Brazilian Empire: Myths and Heroes. Chicago: Dorsey.
Cultural Anthropology
  1992  [Theme Issue: Space, Identity, and the Politics of Difference. James Ferguson and Akhil Gupta, eds.] Vol. 7, No. 1.
Dale, Peter N.
  1986  The Myth of Japanese Uniqueness. New York: St. Martin's.

DaMatta, Roberto

    1991 (1979) "Do you know who you're talking to?!" The distinction between individual and person in Brazil. *In* Carnivals, Rogues, and Heroes: An Interpretation of the Brazilian Dilemma. John Drury, trans. Pp. 137–97. Notre Dame: University of Notre Dame Press.

D'Andrade, Roy

    1995 The Development of Cognitive Anthropology. Cambridge: Cambridge University Press.

Delaney, Carol

    1995 Father state, motherland, and the birth of modern Turkey. *In* Naturalizing Power: Essays in Feminist Cultural Criticism. Carol Delaney and Sylvia Yanagisako, eds. Pp. 177–99. Routledge.

Dore, Ronald

    1973 British Factory—Japanese Factory: The Origins of National Diversity in Industrial Relations. Berkeley: University of California Press.

Dorsey, J. Owen

    1884 Omaha sociology. *In* J. W. Powell, director. Third Annual Report of the Bureau of Ethnology to the Secretary of the Smithsonian Institution, 1881–82. Pp. 211–370. Washington: Government Printing Office.

Eck, Diana L.

    1985 Banaras: Cosmos and paradise in the Hindu imagination. Contributions to Indian Sociology 19(1):41–55.

Ellison, Ralph

    1952 Invisible Man. New York: New American Library.

Eriksen, Thomas Hylland

    1993 Ethnicity and Nationalism: Anthropological Perspectives. London: Pluto.

Field, Norma

    1993 In the Realm of a Dying Emperor: Japan at Century's End. New York: Vintage.

Finnegan, Ruth

    1998 Tales of the City: A Study of Narrative and Urban Life. Cambridge: Cambridge University Press.

Folha de São Paulo

    1995 Brasil Japão 100 anos (caderno especial), 19 October, 12 pp.

Fox, Jason M.

    1998 Employment and Ethnicity among Brazilian Immigrants in Japan. M.A. thesis, University of Florida (Gainesville).

Freyre, Gilberto

    1956 (1933) The Masters and the Slaves: A Study in the Development of Brazilian Civilization. 2d English-language ed. New York: Knopf.

    1963 (1945) New World in the Tropics: The Culture of Modern Brazil. New York: Vintage.

Geertz, Clifford

    1973 (1957) Ethos, world view, and the analysis of sacred symbols. *In* The Interpretation of Cultures. Pp. 126–41. New York: Basic Books.

1984    Distinguished lecture: Anti-anti relativism. American Anthropologist 86:263–78.

1984 (1974)    "From the native's point of view": On the nature of anthropological understanding. *In* Culture Theory: Essays on Mind, Self, and Emotion. Richard A. Shweder and Robert A. LeVine, eds. Pp. 123–36. Cambridge: Cambridge University Press.

Gilroy, Paul
1993    The Black Atlantic: Double Consciousness and Modernity. Cambridge: Harvard University Press.

Goffman, Erving
1961    Asylums. Garden City, N.Y.: Anchor.

Graham, Richard (ed.)
1990    The Idea of Race in Latin America, 1870–1940. Austin: University of Texas Press.

Gramsci, Antonio
1971    Selections from the Prison Notebooks of Antonio Gramsci. Ed. and trans. Quintin Hoare and Geoffrey Nowell Smith. New York: International.

Gupta, Akhil
1992    The song of the nonaligned world: Transnational identities and the reinscription of space in late capitalism. Cultural Anthropology 7(1):63–79.

Gupta, Akhil, and James Ferguson
1992    Beyond "culture": Space, identity, and the politics of difference. Cultural Anthropology 7(1):6–23.

Güzeldere, Güven
1997    The many faces of consciousness: A field guide. *In* The Nature of Consciousness: Philosophical Debates. Ned Block, Owen Flanagan, and Güven Güzeldere, eds. Pp. 1–67. Cambridge: MIT Press.

Hallowell, A. Irving
1988 (1954)    The self and its behavioral environment. *In* Culture and Experience. Pp. 75–110. Prospect Heights, Ill.: Waveland.

Hanchard, Michael George
1994    Orpheus and Power: The Movimento Negro of Rio de Janeiro and São Paulo, Brazil, 1945–1988. Princeton: Princeton University Press.

Handler, Richard
1988    Nationalism and the Politics of Culture in Quebec. Madison: University of Wisconsin Press.

Hannerz, Ulf
1992    Cultural Complexity. New York: Columbia University Press.
1996    Transnational Connections. New York: Routledge.

Harris, Marvin
1964    Patterns of Race in the Americas. New York: Walker.

Harvey, David
1989    The Condition of Postmodernity. Oxford: Blackwell.

Hasenbalg, Carlos
    1979    Discriminação e desigualdades raciais no Brasil. Rio de Janeiro: Graal.
Hendry, Joy
    1986    Becoming Japanese. Honolulu: University of Hawaii Press.
Hennessy, Alistair
    1989    Reshaping the Brazilian past. Times Literary Supplement 4502:763–64.
Hobsbawm, Eric, and Terence Ranger (eds.)
    1983    The Invention of Tradition. Cambridge: Cambridge University Press.
Hollan, Douglas
    1992    Cross-cultural differences in the self. Journal of Anthropological Research 48(4):283–300.
    1997    The relevance of person-centered ethnography to cross-cultural psychiatry. Transcultural Psychiatry 34(2):219–34.
Holland, Dorothy, and Jean Lave (eds.)
    (in press)    History in Person. Santa Fe: School of American Research Press.
Homi Chūgakkō
    1995    Manual Escolar de Homi. Toyota: Homi Chūgakkō.
Honda-Hasegawa, Laura
    1991    Sonhos bloqueados. São Paulo: Estação Liberdade.
Huizinga, Johan
    1950    Homo Ludens: A Study of the Play Element in Culture. Boston: Beacon.
Inagaki, Tadahiko
    1986    School education: Its history and contemporary status. In Child Development and Education in Japan. Harold Stevenson, Hiroshi Azuma, and Kenji Hakuta, eds. Pp. 75–92. New York: W. H. Freeman.
International Press
    1995    Falece estudante golpeada pelo professor. July 30:3-A.
    1995    Brasileiros enviam US$2 bilhões por ano. July 30:4-A.
    1995    Estudo indica que dinheiro é mal aplicado. September 17:5-A.
    1995    "Butajirujin." November 19:7-A.
    1995    Brasileiros formam terceira comunidade estrangeira no Japão. December 17:1-C.
    1996    Ligações internacionais a partir do Japão em 94. January 28:7-B.
Jameson, Fredric
    1991    Postmodernism, or, the Cultural Logic of Late Capitalism. Durham, N.C.: Duke University Press.
Johnstone, Christopher B.
    1996    Japan's foreign residents and the quest for expanded political rights. Japan Economic Institute Report, July 19. (Internet document http://www.gw.japan.com.ftp/ pub/ policy/ jei/ 1996/ a-series/ 0719–96a.txt)
Jornal Tudo Bem
    1995    Sakamoto prejudica família Sakamoto. August 26:5.
Joyce, James
    1990 (1934) Ulysses. New York: Vintage.

Kawamura, Lili
   1999   Para onde vão os brasileiros? Imigrantes brasileiros no Japão. Campinas: Editora da Unicamp.
Kearney, Michael
   1995   The local and the global: The anthropology of globalization and transnationalism. Annual Review of Anthropology 24:547–65.
Kelly, William
   1988   Japanology bashing. American Ethnologist 15:365–68.
Kitagawa, Toyoie
   1993   Hamamatsu-shi ni okeru gaikokujin no seikatsu jittai/ishiki chōsa: Nikkei burajiru/perujin o chūshin ni. (Survey of Living Conditions and Consciousness of Foreigners in Hamamatsu City, Focusing on Nikkei Brazilians and Peruvians.) Hamamatsu: Hamamatsu Planning Section/International Exchange Office.
Klintowitz, Jaime
   1996   Nossa gente lá fora. Veja (April 3):26–29.
Koyama, Chieko
   1998   Return Migration of Japanese-Brazilians: The Transformation of Ethnic Identity in the Country of Their Ancestors. M.A. thesis, University of Florida (Gainesville).
Kumekawa, Eugene
   1993   Sansei ethnic identity and the consequences of perceived unshared suffering for third generation Japanese Americans. *In* American Mosaic: Selected Readings on America's Multicultural Heritage. Young I. Song and Eugene Kim, eds. Pp. 204–14. Englewood Cliffs, N.J.: Prentice-Hall.
Langacker, Ronald W.
   1987   Foundations of Cognitive Grammar. Volume I: Theoretical Perspectives. Stanford: Stanford University Press.
   1991   Foundations of Cognitive Grammar. Volume II: Descriptive Application. Stanford: Stanford University Press.
Leach, Edmund R.
   1977 (1954)   Political Systems of Highland Burma. London: Athlone.
Lebra, Takie Sugiyama
   1976   Japanese Patterns of Behavior. Honolulu: University of Hawaii Press.
   1992   Self in Japanese culture. *In* Japanese Sense of Self. Nancy R. Rosenberger, ed. Pp. 105–20. Cambridge: Cambridge University Press.
Lesser, Jeffrey
   1995   Welcoming the Undesirables: Brazil and the Jewish Question. Berkeley: University of California Press.
   1999   Negotiating National Identity: Immigrants and the Struggle for Ethnicity in Brazil. Durham: Duke University Press.
LeVine, Robert A.
   1982   Culture, Behavior, and Personality: An Introduction to the Comparative Study of Psychosocial Adaptation. New York: Aldine.

Levine, Robert M.
  1997    Brazilian Legacies. Armonk, N.Y.: M. E. Sharpe.
Levy Robert I.
  1973    Tahitians. Chicago: University of Chicago Press.
  1984    Emotion, knowing, and culture. *In* Culture Theory: Essays on Mind,
          Self, and Emotion. Richard A. Shweder and Robert A. LeVine, eds. Pp.
          214–37. Cambridge: Cambridge University Press.
  1990    Mesocosm: Hinduism and the Organization of a Traditional Newar
          City in Nepal. Berkeley: University of California Press.
  1994    Person-centered anthropology. *In* Assessing Cultural Anthropology.
          Robert Borofsky, ed. Pp. 180–89. New York: McGraw-Hill.
Linger, Daniel T.
  1992    Dangerous Encounters: Meanings of Violence in a Brazilian City.
          Stanford: Stanford University Press.
  1994    Has culture theory lost its minds? Ethos 22(3):284–315.
  1996    Brazilians in Toyota City: An Ethnographic Field Report. Toyota City,
          Japan: Toyota International Association.
  1997    Brazil displaced: Restaurante 51 in Nagoya, Japan. *Horizontes Antro-
          pológicos* (Porto Alegre, Brazil) 5:181–203.
  (in press) The identity path of Eduardo Mori. *In* History in Person. Dorothy
          Holland and Jean Lave, eds. Santa Fe: School of American Research
          Press.
Lispector, Clarice
  1987 (1977)  The Hour of the Star. Trans. Giovanni Pontiero. New York: Car-
          canet.
Maher, John C., and Yumiko Kawanishi
  1995    Maintaining culture and language: Koreans in Okinawa. *In* Diversity
          in Japanese Culture and Language. John C. Maher and Gaynor Mac-
          donald, eds. Pp. 160–77. London: Kegan Paul.
Maher, John C., and Gaynor Macdonald (eds.)
  1995    Diversity in Japanese Culture and Language. London: Kegan Paul.
Malkki, Liisa
  1995    Purity and Exile: Violence, Memory, and National Cosmology among
          Hutu Refugees in Tanzania. Chicago: University of Chicago Press.
Margolis, Maxine L.
  1994    Little Brazil: An Ethnography of Brazilian Immigrants in New York
          City. Princeton: Princeton University Press.
Marx, Karl, and Friedrich Engels
  1972 [1848]  Manifesto of the Communist Party. *In* The Marx-Engels Reader.
          Robert C. Tucker, ed. Pp. 331–62. New York: W. W. Norton.
McHugh, Ernestine L.
  1989    Concepts of the person among the Gurungs of Nepal. American Eth-
          nologist 16(1):75–86.
Mead, Margaret, and Rhoda Métraux (eds.)
  1953    The Study of Culture at a Distance. Chicago: University of Chicago
          Press.

Medeiros, Maria Alice de Aguiar
    1980    Casa-grande e senzala: Uma interpretação. Dados 23(2):215–36.
Migration News
    1996    Naturalization controversy. Vol. 3, no. 10. Davis: University of California. (Internet document http:// www.undp.org/ popin/ popis/ journals/ migratn/ mig9610.html)
Mitchell, J. Clyde
    1956    The Kalela Dance: Aspects of Social Relationships among Urban Africans in Northern Rhodesia. Rhodes-Livingstone Papers No. 27. Manchester: Manchester University Press.
Mitsugui, Janete
    1995    Depressão pode estar ligada à emoção negativa. Folha Mundial (July 30):12.
Mouer, Ross, and Yoshio Sugimoto
    1986    Images of Japanese Society. London: Routledge and Kegan Paul.
Nagel, Thomas
    1974    What is it like to be a bat? Philosophical Review 83(4):435–50.
Nakane, Chie
    1970    Japanese Society. Berkeley: University of California Press.
Nojima, Toshihiko
    1989    Susumetai nikkeijin no tokubetsu ukeire. [Toward the special admission of the nikkeijin.] Gekkan Jiyū Minshū (November):92–99.
Oka, Takashi
    1994    Prying Open the Door: Foreign Workers in Japan. Washington, D.C.: Carnegie Endowment for International Peace.
Oliven, Ruben George
    1992    A parte e o todo: A diversidade cultural no Brasil-nação. Petrópolis: Vozes.
Ong, Aihwa
    1992    Limits to cultural accumulation: Chinese capitalists on the American Pacific Rim. *In* Toward a Transnational Perspective on Migration: Race, Class, Ethnicity, and Nationalism Reconsidered. Nina Glick Schiller, Linda Basch, and Cristina Blanc-Szanton, eds. Pp. 125–43. New York: New York Academy of Sciences.
    1993    On the edge of empires: Flexible citizenship among Chinese in diaspora. Positions 1(3):745–78.
Otake, Tomoko
    1998    Parents cope with slaying of Japanese-Brazilian son. *Japan Times*, March 2. (Internet document http:// www.japantimes.co.jp/ news/ news3–98/ news3–2.html)
Ozaki, Fábio
    1995    Da linha de montagem para a Universidade de Kyoto. Jornal Tudo Bem (December 2):2.
    1996    Brasileiro é encontrado morto em Yamanashi. Jornal Tudo Bem (April 27):3.

Parish, Steven M.
  1994    Moral Knowing in a Hindu Sacred City. New York: Columbia University Press.
  1996    Hierarchy and Its Discontents: Culture and the Politics of Consciousness in Caste Society. Philadelphia: University of Pennsylvania Press.
Park, Robert E.
  1969 (1916)  The city: Suggestions for investigation of human behavior in an urban environment. *In* Classic Essays on the Culture of Cities. Richard Sennett, ed. Pp. 91–130. Englewood Cliffs, N.J.: Prentice-Hall.
Parlato, Juliana
  1996    Origem é a síndrome de regresso. International Press (May 5):7-A.
Plath, David W.
  1980    Long Engagements: Maturity in Modern Japan. Stanford: Stanford University Press.
Pozenato, José Clemente
  1985    O quatrilho. Porto Alegre: Mercado Aberto.
Rapport, Nigel
  1997    Transcendent Individual: Towards a Literary and Liberal Anthropology. London: Routledge.
Rawet, Samuel
  1956    Contos do imigrante. Rio de Janeiro: J. Olympio.
Reddy, Michael J.
  1979    The conduit metaphor—A case of frame conflict in our language about language. *In* Metaphor and Thought. Andrew Ortony, ed. Pp. 284–324. Cambridge: Cambridge University Press.
Rohlen, Thomas P.
  1974    For Harmony and Strength: Japanese White Collar Organization in Anthropological Perspective. Berkeley: University of California Press.
  1983    Japan's High Schools. Berkeley: University of California Press.
Rosenberger, Nancy R.
  1992    Tree in summer, tree in winter: Movement of self in Japan. *In* Japanese Sense of Self. Nancy R. Rosenberger, ed. Pp. 67–92. Cambridge: Cambridge University Press.
Rosenberger, Nancy R. (ed.)
  1992    Japanese Sense of Self. Cambridge: Cambridge University Press.
Roth, Joshua
  1999    Defining Communities: The Nation, the Firm, the Neighborhood, and Japanese Brazilian Migrants in Japan. Ph.D. dissertation, Cornell University.
Rouse, Roger
  1991    Mexican migration and the social space of postmodernism. Diaspora 1(1):8–23.
  1992    Making sense of settlement: Class transformation, cultural struggle, and transnationalism among Mexican migrants in the United States. *In* Toward a Transnational Perspective on Migration: Race, Class, Ethnicity, and Nationalism Reconsidered. Nina Glick Schiller, Linda

Basch, and Cristina Blanc-Szanton, eds. Pp. 25–52. New York: New York Academy of Sciences.

Saito, Hiroshi (ed.)
1980 A presença japonesa no Brasil. São Paulo: T. A. Queiroz, Editora da Universidade de São Paulo.

Saito, Hiroshi, and Takashi Maeyama (eds.)
1973 Assimilação e integração dos japoneses no Brasil. Petrópolis: Vozes; São Paulo: Editora da Universidade de São Paulo.

Sakae, Yaemi H.
1996 Nikkei se enforca em árvore de parque municipal. International Press (May 5):7-A.

São Paulo-Shinbun
1991 200 dicas de sobrevivência no Japão. São Paulo: São Paulo-Shinbun.

Sapir, Edward
1917 Do we need a "superorganic"? American Anthropologist 19:441–47.
1949 (1938) Why cultural anthropology needs the psychiatrist. *In* Selected Writings in Language, Culture, and Personality. Pp. 569–77. Berkeley: University of California Press.
1949 (1939) Psychiatric and cultural pitfalls in the business of getting a living. *In* Selected Writings in Language, Culture, and Personality. Pp. 578–89. Berkeley: University of California Press.

Schiller, Nina Glick, Linda Basch, and Cristina Blanc-Szanton (eds.)
1992 Towards a Transnational Perspective on Migration: Race, Class, Ethnicity, and Nationalism Reconsidered. New York: New York Academy of Sciences.

Schneider, David M.
1969 Kinship, nationality, and religion in American culture: Toward a definition of kinship. *In* Forms of Symbolic Action. Robert F. Spencer, ed. Pp. 116–25. Seattle: University of Washington Press.

Schwartz, Theodore
1978 Where is the culture? Personality as the distributive locus of culture. *In* The Making of Psychological Anthropology. George D. Spindler, ed. Pp. 419–41. Berkeley: University of California Press.

Scliar, Moacyr
1986 (1978) The Gods of Raquel. Trans. Eloah F. Giacomelli. New York: Ballantine.
1987 (1976) The Ballad of the False Messiah. Trans. Eloah F. Giacomelli. New York: Ballantine.

Sellek, Yoko
1997 *Nikkeijin*: The phenomenon of return migration. *In* Japan's Minorities: The Illusion of Homogeneity. Michael Weiner, ed. Pp. 178–210. London: Routledge.

Shintaku, Juvenal, and Helenice Nakamura
1996 Brasileira passa em duas faculdades japonesas. International Press (January 28):6-A.

Siddle, Richard

    1997    Ainu: Japan's indigenous people. *In* Japan's Minorities: The Illusion of Homogeneity. Michael Weiner, ed. Pp. 17–49. London: Routledge.

Simmel, Georg

    1950 (1902–3)    The metropolis and mental life. *In* The Sociology of Georg Simmel. Kurt H. Wolff, trans. and ed. Pp. 409–24. New York: Free Press.

Sjoberg, Gideon

    1955    The preindustrial city. American Journal of Sociology 60:438–45.

Skidmore, Thomas E.

    1974    Black into White: Race and Nationality in Brazilian Thought. New York: Oxford University Press.

Smith, Robert J.

    1960    Pre-industrial urbanism in Japan: A consideration of multiple traditions in a feudal society. Economic Development and Cultural Change 9(1, part 2):241–57.

    1983    Japanese Society: Tradition, Self, and the Social Order. Cambridge: Cambridge University Press.

Sökefeld, Martin

    1999    Debating self, identity, and culture in anthropology. Current Anthropology 40(4):417–47.

Sperber, Dan

    1996    Explaining Culture: A Naturalistic Approach. Oxford: Blackwell.

Spiro, Melford E.

    1993    Is the Western conception of the self "peculiar" within the context of world cultures? Ethos 21(2):107–54.

Strauss, Claudia

    1992    Models and motives. *In* Human Motives and Cultural Models. Roy D'Andrade and Claudia Strauss, eds. Pp. 1–20. Cambridge: Cambridge University Press.

    1997    Partly fragmented, partly integrated: An anthropological examination of "postmodern fragmented subjects." Cultural Anthropology 12(3):362–404.

Strauss, Claudia, and Naomi Quinn

    1997    A Cognitive Theory of Cultural Meaning. Cambridge: Cambridge University Press.

Suzuki, Ana

    1986    O jardim japonês. Rio de Janeiro: Record.

Taira, Koji

    1997    Troubled national identity: The Ryukyuans/Okinawans. *In* Japan's Minorities: The Illusion of Homogeneity. Michael Weiner, ed. Pp. 140–77. London: Routledge.

Tobin, Joseph

    1992    Japanese preschools and the pedagogy of selfhood. *In* Japanese Sense of Self. Nancy J. Rosenberger, ed. Pp. 21–39. Cambridge: Cambridge University Press.

Tokairin, Mário
 1995   Adeus, dona Lúcia! Jornal Tudo Bem (September 23:5).
Tsuda, Takeyuki
 1998   The stigma of ethnic difference: The structure of prejudice and "discrimination" toward Japan's new immigrant minority. Journal of Japanese Studies 24(2):317–59.
 1999a  The permanence of "temporary" migration: The "structural embeddedness" of Japanese-Brazilian immigrant workers in Japan. Journal of Asian Studies 58(3):687–722.
 1999b  Transnational migration and the nationalization of ethnic identity among Japanese-Brazilian return migrants. Ethos 27(2):145–79.
Turner, Victor
 1987   Carnival, ritual, and play in Rio de Janeiro. *In* Time out of Time: Essays on the Festival. Alessandro Falassi, ed. Pp. 76–90. Albuquerque: University of New Mexico Press.
Wallace, Anthony F. C.
 1961   Culture and Personality. New York: Random House.
Waters, Malcolm
 1995   Globalization. London: Routledge.
Weber, Max
 1946 (1921) The nation. *In* From Max Weber: Essays in Sociology. H. H. Gerth and C. Wright Mills, eds. and trans. Pp. 171–79. New York: Oxford University Press.
Weiner, Michael
 1997   Japan's Minorities: The Illusion of Homogeneity. London: Routledge.
Wetherall, William
 1988   How to become a Japanese citizen. *Japan Times*, October 13:14.
White, Merry
 1994   The Material Child: Coming of Age in Japan and America. Berkeley: University of California Press.
Wikan, Unni
 1995   The self in a world of urgency and necessity. Ethos 23(3):259–85.
Wirth, Louis
 1938   Urbanism as a way of life. American Journal of Sociology 44:1–24.
Yamanaka, Keiko
 1996   Return migration of Japanese-Brazilians to Japan: The *Nikkeijin* as ethnic minority and political construct. Diaspora 5(1):65–97.
 1997   Return migration of Japanese-Brazilian women: Household strategies and the search for the "homeland." Pp. 11–34. *In* Beyond Boundaries. Diane Baxter and Ruth Krulfeld, eds. Arlington, Va.: American Anthropological Association.
Yamashita, Karen Tei
 1990   Through the Arc of the Rain Forest. Minneapolis: Coffee House.
 1992   Brazil-Maru. Minneapolis: Coffee House.
Yoshino, Kosaku
 1992   Cultural Nationalism in Contemporary Japan. London: Routledge.

# Index

In this index an "f" after a number indicates a separate reference on the next page, and an "ff" indicates separate references on the next two pages. A continuous discussion over two or more pages is indicated by a span of page numbers, e.g., "57–59." *Passim* is used for a cluster of references in close but not consecutive sequence.

abstractions, analytical and sociological, 11f, 47f, 112, 306
accidents, *see* work, accidents at
admission exam, *see* entrance exam
adolescents, 60, 65f, 134, 154, 189, 206; working in factory, 132–35 *passim*, 171, 183, 193f, 201–7 *passim*, 222
Africans, in Brazil, 22, 280, 287. *See also* slaves and slavery
agency, 112, 268–69, 306
agenda-hopping, 291n
Aichi Industries, 51–56 *passim*, 101f
Aichi Loop Railway (Aikan), 29ff
Aichi prefecture, 29ff, 54, 68; Brazilians in, 6, 26, 37, 75, 169, 210f, 222, 313
Ainu, 220n
alienation, feelings of, 68, 78, 212, 272, 300, 302, 310
alienness, feelings of, 107–10 *passim*, 128, 134, 155f, 283
Amazonia, 4, 79, 90, 115, 117, 128, 130, 161f; *nikkeis* in, 3, 21, 250, 258
Americanism, 279f
Americans, 108f, 113, 116, 140, 148, 158, 177, 187, 189, 226; Japanese perceptions of, 28, 88–89, 241, 250ff, 272, 289
Anderson, Benedict, 275
Anjo Nishi Middle School, 209ff
Aoshima, Elisa, 14, 72, 95, 191–208, 307, 309
appearance, physical, 83, 101, 109, 156, 163–66 *passim*, 204–7 *passim*, 215ff, 267
*Aquarela do Brasil* (song), 4
*Aqui Agora*, 83, 162, 166
Arabs, in Brazil, 282f
Assembly of God Church, 153

Australia, 100, 133, 152, 200
auto and auto-parts manufacturing, 6, 30, 45, 50–56 *passim*, 227, 288f, 313

Baldwin, James, 95–96, 112
barrier, between Japanese and Brazilians, 100–104 *passim*, 109, 289
Barroso, Ary, 4
baseball, 59, 64–65
Bateson, Gregory, 16, 75, 290n, 293, 307
Battle of Okinawa, 148–51 *passim*, 231
Befu, Harumi, 277, 278n
behavioral environment, 307
Belém do Pará, xxi, 5, 90, 258
Benedict, Ruth, 12, 62, 290n, 291–301 *passim*
Berry, Chuck, 59
Bespalhok, Flávia, 76n, 80–86 *passim*
"big country" (Brazil), 219, 223, 225, 271, 283, 288
Big House, 281, 286f
bikers, 40, 178
bilingual teachers, 207–11 *passim*, 226, 247, 261–65, 271f. *See also* Kitagawa, Rosa; Mizutake, Naomi
biocentrism, 154
biography, 18, 112, 189, 271, 276, 294, 299, 306, 309
Bisa (Zambian ethnic group), 76, 91
Blake, William, 306
blood, 128, 279f; as idiom of Japaneseness, 18, 23, 144, 146, 208, 217, 225, 266ff, 288, 303; in Japanese national narratives, 25, 276–79 *passim*, 292, 310–13 *passim*
Boas, Franz, 12, 272, 278, 297, 312
Bolivians, 120–23 *passim*, 148

*bolsistas*, 211–19 *passim*, 223
*bōnenkai*, 239
*bōsōzoku, see* bikers
bossa nova, 20, 115
Bourdieu, Pierre, 293
*brasileiras, nikkei* perceptions of, 122–28 *passim*
Brasília, xxi, 51, 97
Brazil: Japanese perceptions of, 20, 28, 88f, 101, 161–63, 200; immigration policy, 20, 21n; economic conditions, 22ff, 135, 137
Brazilianization, 214f, 223, 267, 282
Brazilianness, 18, 78, 91f, 290f, 296, 313; personal appropriation of, 166f, 189, 206f, 224, 245f, 271, 309–12 *passim*
Brazilian newspapers, 4, 27f, 80–85 *passim*, 90, 227
Brazilian products, 37, 78, 80, 90, 157
Brazilian restaurants, 9, 14, 17, 49, 74–92, 99, 247
Brazilians, Japanese perceptions of, 107, 219–24 *passim*, 241f, 264
*Brazil-Maru*, xiii–xiv, 213f, 229
Brown, Jacqueline, 26n
Buarque, Chico, 3f
Buddhism, 32, 79, 112f, 294f
Buddhist temples, 32, 79, 112
Building 141, 33–36 *passim*, 40, 153
Building 142, 33–38 *passim*, 178
*bukatsu, see* clubs, school
Buraku settlements, 30
*Bye Bye Brasil*: song, 3–4; film, 3n, 288

*cachaça*, 51, 79–83 *passim*, 90
*calor humano, see* "human warmth"
capitalism, 46f, 74, 287, 290
Carlitos, *see* Chaplin, Charlie
Carlos (Homi student), 247f, 265
Carnival, 40, 75, 86, 92, 115, 161f
Carpenters (pop singers), 88
Chaplin, Charlie, 45–47, 74, 108, 290
Chiba prefecture, 170, 176, 187
Chinese (people), 113, 258; in Japan, 177, 215f, 225, 228, 277
*Chrysanthemum and the Sword*, 62, 291–92, 297f
Chubu Iron Company, 116–19 *passim*, 307
*chūgakkō, see* middle school
Circle K, 27, 60, 74
cleverness, 191, 206, 208, 246n
Clifford, James, 26n

Clube Nova Urbana, 85f
clubs, school, 60, 64f
coffee shops, 32, 89
Cohen, Anthony, 310
"coldness," of Japanese, 72, 88, 109, 159, 166, 240, 267, 290, 302
Collor de Melo, Fernando, 23f, 138
*colônias*, 21, 105, 230, 271
*Communist Manifesto*, 11
conduit model of language, 305
consciousness, 12, 48, 165, 269, 276, 300, 306–12 *passim. See also* reflective consciousness
consulate, Brazilian, 84f, 242
container model of society, 305
Copperbelt (Zambia), 76, 91
creolizations, 9
cultural relativism, 147, 151
culture theory, *see* theory
Curitiba, xxi, 170, 172

Dachau, 149
Daiichi Kōgyō (*empreiteira*), 97, 118–23 *passim*
DaMatta, Roberto, 299
D'Andrade, Roy, 291n
Dean, James, 88
*dekassegui* "boom," 232
*dekasseguis (dekasegi)*, 26ff, 55, 80, 89f, 110, 129n, 196n, 257f, 282, 288, 291
Denny's, 169f
depression (mental), 47n, 83. *See also* stress
deutero-learning, 293, 303
*dharma*, 304f
diaspora, 24ff
Diegues, Carlos, 3n
disappearances, 47n
discrimination: in Japan, against South Americans, 103f, 132f, 155, 159, 166, 198, 243, 272, 302; in Japan, against other Asians and Okinawans, 149f, 216, 225; in Brazil, 149, 230f, 281, 297f
discursive theory, *see* theory
Disneyland (Tokyo), 27, 129, 248
documents, *see* visas
Dona Lica's restaurant, 76–79 *passim*, 91
Dorsey, J. O., 11
dual nationality, 23, 27n, 144, 146, 211, 223, 242, 266

East Homi Grade School, 34ff, 228, 262
Edival (Homi student), 191f, 210

educational system, Japanese, 61f, 69
Electro Steel factory, 45f, 74f, 287, 290
Ellis Island, 279
emigration, *see* migration
emigration policy, Japanese, 20
Emperor, 231, 292
*empreiteiras*, 50–55 *passim*, 85, 97, 103,
    107, 118–26 *passim*, 141, 143, 197, 227–
    44 *passim*
Engels, Friedrich, 12
England, 133, 162
entrance exam, high-school, 60f, 68, 171
ethnicities, multiple, *see* identities, multiple
ethnicity, xiii, 76, 91f, 279f, 287, 313; in
    Brazil, 151, 164ff, 223–26 *passim*, 244,
    281–88, 290, 297f, 302. *See also* race
ethnocentrism, 154, 166, 278, 290
ethnography, person-centered, *see* person-
    centered ethnography
ethnography at a distance, 298
ethos, 293
Europe and Europeans, 19f, 25, 28, 74, 88,
    133, 167, 242, 281–87 *passim*, 297f
exchange rates, 37, 37n
experience, 12, 17, 38, 47f, 267, 276, 304–
    11 *passim*

*Fantástico*, 83, 90
farewell party, *see* sayonara party
*favelas*, 161f
First World, 25, 28, 46, 140, 145, 156, 158
Forbidden Path, 57, 60, 69
foreigners, Japanese perceptions of, 216–17,
    223ff, 241, 259. *See also* Americans,
    Japanese perceptions of; Brazilians, Japa-
    nese perceptions of; *gaijin*
France and French people, 137, 139f, 145,
    162, 165
"freedom," in Brazil, 146f, 243, 246n, 282,
    287, 311
Freud, Sigmund, 16
Freyre, Gilberto, 280–91 *passim*, 296–301
    *passim*
*Fujinkai*, 124, 128
Fukuoka, xx, 284
*furusato*, *see* native land
*furyō*, 30, 178, 213
fusion myth (or narrative), Brazilian, 279–
    82, 286f, 311. *See also* pluralist myth, Bra-
    zilian

*gaijin*: in Japan, 81, 88f, 107–11, 163–66

*passim*, 216, 241f, 258, 268; in Brazil, 22,
    122, 163. *See also* Americans, Japanese
    perceptions of; Brazilians, Japanese per-
    ceptions of; foreigners, Japanese percep-
    tions of
*Gaijin—Caminhos da Liberdade* (film),
    282–90, 312
Geertz, Clifford, 269, 293, 299
Gentlemen's Agreement, 21n
Germans, in Brazil, 113, 170, 172, 281, 283
Ghana, 258
Gifu prefecture, 4, 29, 36f, 82
globalization, 7f, 48f, 287, 313. *See also*
    transnationalism
Goiás, 51
Golden Week, 248
*gomi*, 38
goodbye party, *see* sayonara party
Gorer, Geoffrey, 290n
grade schools, 58n, 60f, 199, 211, 262. *See
    also* East Homi Grade School; West Homi
    Grade School
graduation, middle-school, 58, 60, 68, 131,
    154, 167, 191–93
Grampus (soccer team), 210
Gramsci, Antonio, 12n
*guaraná*, 79–82 *passim*, 86, 90
Guarujá, 58, 153, 161, 206
Guinea-Bissau, 136–40 *passim*, 146, 312
Gunma prefecture, 27

*habitus*, 293
*hakengaisha*, *see empreiteiras*
Hallowell, A. Irving, 307
Hamamatsu, 4, 5n, 26, 82, 232, 234
*hanbaiki*, 38ff
Hannerz, Ulf, 9
health care, 21n, 24n, 29, 46n, 47n, 211,
    228, 234ff
Hennessy, Alistair, 281, 298
hierarchic discontinuities, 307–9. *See also*
    consciousness
hierarchy: in factory, 74, 100–104, 109; in
    middle school, 64f, 193; in Japan, 292f,
    300
Higashi Homi Grade School, *see* East Homi
    Grade School
high school, 153, 253; in Japan, 58–62 *pas-
    sim*, 131ff, 167, 171, 183, 193, 201, 209,
    222, 249
Himeyuri Peace Museum, 148, 231
Hirabari (Nagoya neighborhood), 123f

*hiragana*, 27n, 69, 177, 181, 230
Hiroyuki (Homi student), 180, 193
*hirukin*, 51
Hokkaido, 51, 149f
Homi Chū, *see* Homi Middle School
Homi Danchi, 34f, 46n, 70, 87, 131, 151ff,
    170, 189f, 194, 203, 236, 248; Brazilian
    life at, 6, 9, 17, 30–41, 75, 97ff, 212, 226–
    29 *passim*; arrival at, 107, 123, 141, 177f,
    197, 233. *See also Ken-ei Jūtaku; Kōdan
    Jūtaku*
"Homigate," 212
Homi Middle School, 10, 17, 34ff, 57–73;
    students' viewpoints, 131–34 *passim*,
    152ff, 167–70 *passim*, 177–83 *passim*,
    188–201 *passim*, 207; teachers' view-
    points, 209–13 *passim*, 218–22 *passim*,
    247f, 262–65 *passim*
Homi Praça, 17, 35, 38–41, 75, 153
Homi Station, 30–35 *passim*, 169
Homi town, 34, 191
*Homo Ludens*, 74
*Hondo*, 147ff. *See also Naichi*
Honshu, xx, 21n, 29
Hospital das Clínicas, 257
hot springs, 89, 183
Huizinga, Johan, 74
human theory, *see* theory
"human warmth," 18, 88, 166, 188, 225,
    258, 288, 290–303; cited by interviewees
    as index of Brazilianness, 110f, 114, 156,
    163f, 205–9 *passim*, 240, 260, 267, 311
Hyōgo prefecture, 258
hypercognized concepts, 296

*ichinensei*, 64f, 132, 174, 191f
identity and identities, 166, 245, 248, 269,
    271, 311; importance of, xiii, 189, 208;
    making of, 41, 75, 96, 104, 111–13, 146f,
    213, 224, 276; in-place and displaced, 75–
    79 *passim*, 91f; multiple, 76, 136, 147n,
    208, 240, 244, 268ff, 308–12 *passim*;
    path, 104–14, 165. *See also* self; selves
Iemura, Catarina, 10, 71, 169–90, 206,
    306–12 *passim*
Iemura, Regina, 170–79 *passim*, 184–90
    *passim*
*ijime*, 98
*ikebana*, 99
imagined communities, 275f, 291
immigration law (June 1990), 23, 51, 55,
    109, 232n, 278

Indaiatuba, 153, 156, 165
Indians (native Brazilians), 101, 161f, 283,
    287
individualism and individuality, 269, 293,
    299, 301
Indonesians, 177, 215, 258
Inka Kola, 37, 81
insincerity, 246, 301. *See also* sincerity
interaction, 28, 90, 290–96 *passim*, 311
interaction style, 88f, 291–302 *passim*, 306n
interactional self, 294–99 *passim*
international classroom, *see Kokusai Kyō-
    shitsu*
interpreters, 10, 159, 227, 229, 234–39 *pas-
    sim*, 244f. *See also* Miyagi, Eriko
invention of tradition, 275
Iranians, in Japan, 22, 228, 278
*isseis*, 21, 26, 116, 150, 196, 223, 249, 277n,
    310
Italians, 98, 108; in Brazil, 113, 282–87 *pas-
    sim*

"*japonesinha*" ("*japonesa*"), 163–66 *pas-
    sim*, 181, 185, 204, 215, 219, 225
J League, 20
Jameson, Fredric, 8
Japan: economic conditions, 22, 135; immi-
    gration policy, 23, 46, 278; Brazilian per-
    ceptions of, 25, 28, 105f, 119f, 144f, 155f,
    175, 213–19 *passim*, 249
Japanese-Americans, 28
Japanese-Brazilians, *see nikkeis*
Japanese-Canadians, 28
Japaneseness, 17, 25, 28, 189, 206, 225,
    271, 302, 308–12 *passim*
Japanese people, Brazilian perceptions of,
    89n, 100, 113, 162, 258. *See also* "cold-
    ness," of Japanese
*jeitinho* (*jeito*), 161, 302
Jews, in Brazil, 282
jobs, for Brazilians in Japan, 50
*juku*, 37, 193
*jus sanguinis*, 277, 279
*jus soli*, 279f

Kagasawa, Yasuaki, 59
*kalela* dance, 91
Kamiōsako, Hiroshi, 112
*kanji*, 27n, 132, 177, 181, 201f
Kankei Company (*empreiteira*), 227f, 233f
karaoke, 120, 122
Kariya, 5, 54

*Kasato-Maru*, 20, 21n
*katakana*, 27n, 69, 177, 181, 203
KDD, 70, 80
*keigo*, 294
*kejime*, 296n
Kelly, William, 277
*Ken-ei Jūtaku*, 33, 35, 178, 229, 248
*kensa*, 202ff
KFC, 30, 129
*Kimigayo*, 192
Kinjoh, Bernardo, 10, 24, 51, 131–52, 208, 309, 312
Kinjoh, Júlio, 131–37 *passim*, 151–52, 154n, 193
Kinjoh, Selene, 131–42 *passim*, 147, 152
Kinpachi-sensei, 60f
Kishi, Takao, 227, 261
Kitagawa, Rosa, 70, 169, 209–26, 244, 248, 271, 288f
Kobe, xx, 162, 249, 255, 258, 270
*Kōdan Jūtaku*, 33, 35, 98f, 153, 194, 228
Koga, Eunice, 27
*kōkō, see* high school, in Japan
*kokumin kenkō hoken*, 227f, 233f. *See also* health care
*Kokusai Kyōshitsu*, 65–73, 131, 191, 194, 200, 207–13 *passim*, 248, 307
Korea, xx, 196
Koreans, in Japan, 177, 187, 189, 215f, 225, 277, 279
*kōtai*, 51, 98, 233
Kyoto, xiv, xv, xvi, xx, 59n, 112
Kyushu, xx, 21n, 55, 149f, 228, 284

language, difficulties of Brazilian students with Portuguese, 167–68, 211, 253, 262f, 265
language barriers, 27f, 67, 79, 89f, 141, 234, 278; in Japanese schools, 61, 67–72 *passim*, 132, 159ff, 179, 194–211 *passim*, 224, 262f. *See also* bilingual teachers; interpreters
Lebra, Takie Sugiyama, 294ff
leisure, 38–41, 74–92. *See also* Brazilian restaurants
Levy, Robert, 296
Liberdade (São Paulo neighborhood), 21, 90
Linger, Eli, 6, 38, 57ff, 65n, 67f, 71, 151, 153, 190, 211f
Lisbon, 153
Londrina, 21, 80

loneliness, 83–92 *passim*, 154, 165, 221, 272
love hotel, 50, 81
Luanshya (Zambia), 76, 91

*mãe de santa*, 173
Maher, John C., 278n
Manaus, 115, 129f
Manchuria, 20
Mandela, Nelson, 124
Maranhão, 77f
Márcia (*nikkei* entertainment figure), 162, 166
Maria, *see* Simons, Lynn
Maringá, 5, 21, 90
Marly, 179, 194, 197f
Marx, Karl, 12
*Masters and the Slaves*, 280–82, 286, 291, 296–98
McDonald, Gaynor, 278n
McDonald's restaurant, 30, 209
Mead, Margaret, 12, 290n
Meiji regime, 21n, 292
*meishi*, 294
Meitetsu supermarket, 33–40 *passim*, 153, 171, 233
Melbourne, 152
Menescal, Roberto, 3n
*mestiçagem*, 22n
*mestiças, mestiços*, 20, 163, 220, 311
Métraux, Rhoda, 290n
*miai*, 254
middle school, 58n, 189, 211, 216, 221, 253, 262. *See also* Anjo Nishi Middle School; Homi Middle School
Mie prefecture, xiv, 29, 170, 177, 213
migration, 22, 103n; Japan to Brazil, 20–25 *passim*, 51, 105, 135, 145, 213f, 249ff, 282–88; Brazil to Japan, 20–28 *passim*, 105f, 163, 282, 313; Europe to Brazil, 20, 281–87 *passim*; return or reverse, 25, 106, 282; yo-yo (circular), 27, 251–53, 264
Mikawa region, 30–31, 39
Minas Gerais, 5, 81, 194
miscegenation, 297f. *See also Masters and the Slaves*
Mitchell, Clyde, 76, 91
Miyagi, Eriko, 10, 227–46, 271, 288f, 303, 309–12 *passim*
Mizutake, Naomi, 14, 70, 163, 247–72, 280, 288f, 308–13 *passim*
*Modern Times*, 45–47

Moji das Cruzes, 5, 21
Moreira, Miriam, 10, 58, 71, 153–68, 192f,
206, 224, 289, 309, 311
Moreira, Tamara, 58, 71, 153–66 passim,
224, 265, 289, 309, 311
Mori, Eduardo, xiii, 14, 23, 51–56, 95–114,
165f, 288, 309, 311
mulatos, 4
myths, see national narratives

Nagano prefecture, 29, 123
Nagoya, 75–85 passim, 115–20 passim,
126, 148, 197, 210f, 223; location and description, xx, 28–31, 34; Brazilian workers in, 5f, 26f, 36, 99, 107, 121, 123;
schools in, 58, 71, 131, 152, 159, 165
Naichi, 147. See also Hondo
Nakajima, Amália, 72f, 193
national character analyses, 290f, 296, 300ff
national imaginings, 275f, 304
national narratives (myths), 18, 275–89,
290ff, 304, 311ff
national sentiments, 275, 288
native land, 249, 266–70 passim
nattō, 199, 204, 255
naturalization, 111, 250, 277–80 passim
Nepal, 304
Newars, 304
newspapers, see Brazilian newspapers
Nihonjinron, 277–79
nikkeis, 6, 16–28 passim, 105f, 131f, 145–
51 passim, 230f; Japanese perceptions of,
23, 100ff, 252, 267f, 278; brasileiros' perceptions of, 25, 156, 164, 166
ninensei, 58, 64, 191ff, 209
Nishi Homi Grade School, see West Homi
Grade School
nisseis, 21, 23n, 36, 83, 121, 125, 147, 196,
277n
Nisshin (suburb of Nagoya), 115ff, 129
non-nikkeis, 16n, 22, 37, 97, 103, 117, 122,
125, 153, 194, 270
nordestinos, 149f, 283, 287
Northeast Brazil, 77f, 86, 149, 281, 286, 296
Northeasterners, see nordestinos
novelas, 28, 37, 83. See also videos

Occupation, U.S., 148
Okazaki, 30–31
Okinawa, xx, 5n, 147–51, 228–32 passim
Okinawan identity, 136, 147n, 240, 244,
312

Osaka, xx, 81
Osu Kannon temple, 79, 92, 117, 129
Ota-Oizumi, 4, 5n, 27
overtime, see zangyō

pachinko, 27, 30, 79, 83, 89, 116, 123, 212
Pacific Rim, 19f
Pakistan and Pakistanis, 22, 228, 278
Paraná, 21, 80, 170, 172
Paranavaí, 172f, 184f, 189f, 206
Parish, Steven, 304
Park, Robert, 9
passport, retention of, 51, 85, 121
Patterns of Culture, 292
paulistas, 149, 151, 283. See also São Paulo
Pernambuco, 280
personalism, 299, 301f, 311
personal referents, 294
person-centered ethnography, 14–17, 47–48,
95f, 187–88
Peruvians, 27n, 37, 81, 177; workers, 55,
102ff, 118, 228; students, 65n, 169, 179f,
182, 189, 262
physical discipline in schools, 99, 180, 209f
pinball, see pachinko
plantations: coffee, 20f, 51n, 283–87, 312f;
cotton, 21, 105; sugar, 280f, 287, 298,
300
pluralism, see ethnicity
pluralist myth (narrative), Brazilian, 289f,
311. See also fusion myth, Brazilian; Gaijin
Portugal and Portuguese people, 145, 283
Portunhol, 170
postmodernity, 7ff, 14f, 45ff, 74, 104, 151,
283
primary schools, see grade schools
prostitutes, 85, 92
psychological anthropology, 12
public representations, 13, 18, 276, 306,
310. See also national narratives

Quinn, Naomi, 13n
quitanda, 40, 253
quotidian nationality, 290–92, 296, 300

race, 109, 223–26 passim, 277–88 passim,
297f, 302, 311. See also ethnicity
rāmen, 86, 170, 176
reflection, 12, 49f, 104, 268f
reflective consciousness, 10, 13–15, 269,
309, 312. See also self, reflective

relational common sense, 291–92, 298, 302
religion, 153, 155, 165, 231, 275
"respect," 88, 145ff, 205, 208, 240, 242,
   246, 292, 300–303, 311
Restaurante, 51, 75–92 *passim*, 115, 117,
   166
returnee's syndrome, 27, 47n, 135
Rh incompatibility, 117, 124–28 *passim*
Rieko (Peruvian student), 169, 179f, 182
Rio de Janeiro, xxi, 5, 28, 98
*rōmaji*, 27n
Russia and Russians, 287, 297
Russo-Japanese War, 284
*ryō*, 32, 141, 177, 228

safety, 25, 87, 156, 178
Saitama-ken, 140
Sakae, 30, 79, 85n
salaries, *see* wages
samba, 82, 86, 91, 114f, 219
Samoa, 258
*Sannen B Gumi, Kinpachi-Sensei*, 60–61
*sannensei*, 58–66 *passim*, 131, 191ff, 209,
   247. *See also* graduation, middle school
*sanseis*, 21, 23, 83, 147
Santa Rosa (plantation), 284–88 *passim*,
   312f
Santo André, 228, 232f
Santos (port), xxi, 21, 105
São Luís, xxi, 9, 77f, 97, 226
São Paulo, city of, xxi, 90, 119, 138, 161,
   257, 301; hometown of migrants, xvii, 81,
   85, 117, 132, 209, 211, 223, 250, 254;
   *nikkei* presence in, 21, 24n, 25n, 213, 253;
   point of departure and return, 28, 72,
   129f, 169, 196, 258; multiethnic aspects,
   281, 286, 312
São Paulo, state of, 149, 153, 157, 172, 228,
   254; Japanese immigrants in, 21, 51n,
   250, 283, 313. *See also* Santa Rosa
Sapir, Edward, 11f
*saudade*, 77, 92, 129, 152
Sawada, Mayumi, 115–19 *passim*
sayonara party, 108, 115, 128f, 157, 169,
   171
"School Days" (song), 59
schools, 17, 46f, 49, 99, 159; in Brazil, 165,
   173–76 *passim*, 180f, 193, 195, 201, 221.
   *See also* grade schools; high schools; middle schools
scientific racism, 277, 281, 297
Sebastião (student), 180, 210, 265

Sedona, 151
self, xiii, 165, 226, 245, 269, 272, 294–99
   *passim*, 309; sense of, 13, 17, 268f, 309;
   reflective, 50, 208, 276, 294f, 307, 309,
   312; interactional, 293–96; generative,
   268f, 271, 309f, 312
self-making, 17f, 112f, 165, 269ff, 306
selves, multiple, 213, 271, 293ff, 308
Senna Ayrton, 210
*senpai-kōhai* relationship, 64f, 72n, 103,
   295
Shimoji, Rosa, 148
Shinto shrines, 32
*shinyū*, 72n
Shizuoka prefecture, 26, 29, 37, 202f
*shōgakkō, see* grade schools
Simmel, Georg, 8f, 87
Simons, Lynn (Maria), 6, 39, 59, 68, 70n,
   97, 131, 169ff, 190, 226
sincerity, 240, 245f. *See also* insincerity
singularity (uniqueness), 10, 95, 112f, 299f
slaves and slavery, 280–87 *passim*, 296–300
   *passim*
Slavs, in Brazil, 282
Smith, Robert J., 294f
soap operas, *see novelas*
soccer, 70, 86, 161f, 210, 212, 219, 222
*sōji*, 54, 64, 125, 161
Spain and Spaniards, 145, 170, 283
Spiritism, 46, 173, 175
Statue of Liberty, 279
status, relative, 293–96 *passim*, 302
Strauss, Claudia, 8, 13n
stress, 47, 99, 171
subjectivity, 12f, 18, 48, 244, 276, 305–11
   *passim*
suicides, 47, 284, 313
*sunakku*, 101, 129
supermarket, *see* Meitetsu supermarket
Suzano, 21

Tagalog, 262
Takeda, Elena, 95, 115–30, 271, 280, 307,
   310
Takenaka, Takefumi, 69, 200, 209f
*takoyaki*, 52, 79
Tanzania, 258
teenagers, *see* adolescents
*terra natal, see* native land
theory, 9–13 *passim*, 75–76, 95f, 112, 276,
   304–7
Third World, 20, 28, 45, 242

Titoe, 283–88 *passim*
Tokugawa, Ieyasu, 29, 31
Tokugawa Shogunate, 21n, 29, 292
Tokyo, xx, 9, 27, 107, 119f, 140, 247–52 *passim*, 272
Tōsei Machine, 51–56 *passim*, 141ff
Toyohashi, 26, 29
Toyota City, described, 28–32
Toyota International Association (TIA), 31, 170, 227, 261
Toyota Motors, 6, 117f, 228
translators, *see* interpreters
transnationalism, 8f, 13, 19, 26n, 28, 74, 92, 287
transnational scenes, 10, 17, 38, 40f, 47–50, 75, 100, 304–9 *passim*
truce-seeking, 112f
Tsuda, Takeyuki, 89
turning up the volume, 178, 240, 246
TV-Globo, 90
Two Crows, 11f, 14, 278

Uberaba, 194f
Ueyama (*empreiteira*), 54f, 141
uncertainty (unpredictability), 10, 12, 95, 100, 104, 154, 188
undocumented workers, 22
uniqueness, *see* singularity
United Nations, 139
United States, 88, 139, 145–51 *passim*, 161f, 225f, 242, 252, 279f, 287, 299. *See also* Americans
University of São Paulo, 146, 257

values, 224–26, 245f, 267
Varig Airlines, 28, 81

videos, 27, 37, 80–85 *passim*
Vietnamese, in Brazil, 113
visas, 23n, 37, 84, 157, 172, 196, 211, 228, 236, 242

wages, 24, 50f, 203, 232, 234, 239; gender differential, 50n, 125, 232, 234
warmth, *see* "human warmth"
Weber, Max, 74n, 275f
Week of Modern Art, 281
West Homi Grade School, 34ff, 132, 262
White, Merry, 60, 72n
Wirth, Louis, 9
Wolfenstein, Martha, 290n
work: conditions of, 50–56, 84, 87, 99, 117ff, 125, 141f, 234; accidents at, 53, 56, 84, 235f, 313; disputes at, 121–23, 236–38, 244
World Health Organization, 56
World War II, xv, 22, 28, 148, 163, 231, 250–55 *passim*, 271f, 277, 292

Xororó, 84, 92
Xuxa, 85f, 210

*yakin*, 51
Yamagata-ken, 249f, 258
Yamasaki, Tizuka, 282, 287f, 311
Yamashita, Karen, 21n
Yokohama, xiv, 4, 19, 107
*yonseis*, 22n, 196
Yoshino, Kosaku, 277n

*zangyō*, 50, 59, 142, 221, 236f
Zen garden, 112f